DO593754

**WILLIAM E. DONOGHUE'S**

LIFETIME

FINANCIAL PLANNER

By William E. Donoghue with Thomas Tilling

*William E. Donoghue's Complete Money Market Guide*
*William E. Donoghue's No-Load Mutual Fund Guide*

By William E. Donoghue

*Donoghue's Mutual Fund Almanac*
*William E. Donoghue's Guide to Finding Money to Invest*

By William E. Donoghue with Dana Shilling

*William E. Donoghue's Lifetime Financial Planner*

William E. Donoghue's

# LIFETIME
# FINANCIAL
# PLANNER

Straight Talk About
Your Money Decisions

WILLIAM E. DONOGHUE
with DANA SHILLING

HARPER & ROW, PUBLISHERS, New York
Cambridge, Philadelphia, San Francisco, Washington
London, Mexico City, São Paulo, Singapore, Sydney

1817

FIRST EDITION

*Designer: Sidney Feinberg*

---

Library of Congress Cataloging-in-Publication Data

Donoghue, William E.
  William E. Donoghue's lifetime financial planner.

  Includes index.
  1. Finance, Personal. 2. Investments. I. Shilling,
Dana. II. Title.
HG179.D63   1987        332.024        86-45091
ISBN 0-06-015616-3

---

87 88 89 90 91 **RRD** 10 9 8 7 6 5 4 3 2 1

To
Elizabeth B. Donoghue, my mother,
and Norman E. Donoghue, II, my brother,
for their continuing support and encouragement

# Contents

# Acknowledgments

An interviewer recently asked me what I consider the greatest accomplishment of my career. I had to reply, "Assembling the wonderful group of people with whom I have the privilege of working." That includes everyone on staff at The Donoghue Organization, our freelancers and collaborators, our friends at Harper & Row—who have taught me a great deal about writing bestsellers —and my friends and acquaintances in the media—who have helped to make the public aware of our ideas, books, and newsletters.

This is a very special book for me, since it will most likely be the one that will take us over the "one million books in print" mark. It was exciting to see my *Complete Money Market Guide* become the best-selling investment guide of 1981. It was equally exciting to watch *No-Load Mutual Fund Guide* hit the best-seller lists in 1983 and then to see *Guide to Finding Money to Invest* follow suit in 1985. My *Investment Tips for Retirement Savings,* written earlier this year, and the 17th edition of our *Mutual Funds Almanac,* published by The Donoghue Organization, have also been very well received.

I am obviously proud of all these books, but, more important, I hold the deepest respect and admiration for researchers and writers who have helped me keep up the pace. I could not have done it alone.

I would like to extend special thanks to those people who worked so hard to make this book a reality: first and foremost my collaborator, Dana Shilling, a talented lawyer and crackerjack financial writer, who specializes in translating legal and financial concepts into English; Mary Driscoll, vice president of editorial at The Donoghue Organization and a seasoned financial editor, who gave this book its shape; Cynthia Andrade, CFA, our manager of research, who applied her keen analytical and editing skills to the manuscript; Peter Reilly, CPA with Joseph Cohan & Associates in Worcester, Massachusetts, fact-checker extraordinaire; and Gail Scho, our art director, whose charts and graphs enhance all our publications.

The production of a demanding book such as this requires the efforts of many; therefore, my sincere thanks also goes to the editorial staff at The Donoghue Organization: Lisa Harrison, editor of *Donoghue's MONEY-LETTER;* Connie Bugbee, editor of *Donoghue's Money Fund Report* and *Donoghue's Mutual Funds Almanac;* Leslie McDonnell, editorial assistant; and Walter Frank, contributing editor.

Special mention must be made of the efforts of Frank Harrison, president of The Donoghue Organization (his steady hand helped us maintain a sorely needed focus); Mary Ann Bonomo, vice president, whose marketing acumen keeps us in touch with our readers; and Lynda Morgan, my assistant, without whom my busy schedule would be impossible.

I would also like to thank our good friends at Harper & Row: Ed Burlingame, the publisher, and Sallie Coolidge, the insightful and extremely supportive editor of this book.

Finally, I want to thank a very special group of people. Over the years, our consultants have provided me with invaluable insights. They are: Allen Grieve and B. P. Fulmer, banking professionals; Van Sternbergh, management consultant; Conrad Grundlehner, economic consultant; Robert Charron, accounting and tax adviser; and Michael Healy, legal counsel.

**WILLIAM E. DONOGHUE'S**

LIFETIME

FINANCIAL PLANNER

# 1

# Take Charge of the Money in Your Life

One classic moment of early television featured the legendary Jack Benny squaring off with a mugger. "Your money or your life," hissed the thief. Benny, in his calculated style, replied, "Not so fast. I'm thinking!"

Benny got a lot of laughs with his miser routines. Audiences believed that money was his number-one concern—and they found that hilarious. Let's stop and think about the money in our lives. Next to family and good health, isn't money the one thing we worry about most? Although some people deny it, money is important to our self-esteem.

## Gaining Confidence

This book is about the money in your life and how you can manage your finances with confidence. As I have said repeatedly in all my books, to be a successful investor, you've got to pay attention to the financial markets. Getting caught off guard can cost you dearly. The same philosophy applies when it comes to managing your lifelong financial security. Whether it's your real estate holdings, your estate plan, or your divorce settlement, understanding your options—and therefore being able to make the right decisions at critical moments—is what counts.

How can you learn to make smart financial planning decisions? First, you must identify the obstacles in your way, one of which may be your own sense of incompetence. The sad fact is that many people pass up wealth-building opportunities because they succumb to anxiety over financial matters. They throw in the towel when they should be taking charge of their financial well-being.

In the pages that follow, we hope to instill you with the confidence you need to make clever financial moves at various times in your life. What's more, once armed with the basics of sound financial planning, you can, in turn, teach your children to develop good financial habits. You'll no doubt want them to get a head start on handling credit and investing their savings. It is unfortunate that our educational system offers little help in this regard—the school will teach little Suzie how to cook but not how to balance a checkbook or apply for a mortgage. That task falls squarely on parents' shoulders.

## Our "Friendly" Advisers

Another obstacle that may prevent you from making good financial decisions is the unwieldy financial services industry that has emerged in recent years. Industry regulators freed banks from the shackles of interest rate regulation but did not force them to sell their products in plain English. As a result, consumers are bombarded with solicitations packed with technical mumbo jumbo. No wonder consumers often feel confused and intimidated. For example, it is very difficult to compare yields on bank certificates of deposit without knowing the intricacies of interest rate compounding.

Mutual fund companies and stock brokerages are just as guilty. They confuse customers with claims of stellar returns while neglecting to point out the inherent risks of certain investment vehicles. And they do not clearly explain how sales charges eat into investors' returns. For its part, the Securities and Exchange Commission has had little success policing the presentation of mutual fund performance statistics.

The sellers of financial services do not exactly mind if you stay in the dark. In fact, many service providers prey on consumer ignorance. Whether you are buying life insurance, selecting mutual funds, hiring a financial planner, or applying for bank credit, the challenge becomes one of learning how much bang you'll get for your buck. A perspective on how financial service providers turn a profit helps. Profitability is based on charging commissions, management fees, service charges, and/or paying noncompetitive yields. A so-called adviser sells a product—he or she does not make money by telling you to go across the street and buy the right product from a competitor.

Brokers are paid for selling you securities—not for telling you when to sell and take your profits. Bankers pay noncompetitive yields and invest your money for the benefit of "the house." Insurance agents primarily sell insurance policies, despite all their talk of financial planning. Few advisers are paid solely for giving you good, objective advice or for keeping a close watch on your investments. We tackle this issue in many of the following chapters. We want you to know your options and where your money is going before you sign on the dotted line.

### The Press Could Be More Helpful

Consumers are not the only ones nervous about discussing financial subjects. The press is often just as skittish about giving investment advice. There is a long-standing tradition in the general press that keeps reporters from making judgment calls. You'll see story after story about the mechanics of, say, investing an IRA in mutual funds, but you'll never get a clear signal on which fund to choose. Sure, you'll read about the fund with the best investment track record, but how do you know which fund offers the best combination of investment performance, responsible management, customer service, ease of switching in and out, and lowest service charges? If you turn to your local newspaper for the answer, all you'll get is "Just the bare facts, folks, just the bare facts."

Another yellow light. Although the majority of editors are scrupulous, some tend to avoid information that makes advertisers uncomfortable (such as warning people about the risks of bonds at the bottom of an interest rate cycle when bond ads are paying the freight). Many people feel it is worth their while to subscribe to financial newsletters, which don't have ads and therefore offer advice that is, as we say in the trade, "pure as the driven snow."

### Whom Do You Trust?

The sad fact is that sometimes the important people in our lives are the ones who prevent us from making sound financial planning decisions. I'm referring to ex-spouses, children, bankers, stockbrokers, and financial planners. These people can do damage when they don't truly understand our financial situation. They also may play on our anxiety to "get it over with," inadvertently encouraging us to make bad decisions.

Our ex-spouses can be so anxious about protecting themselves that they pressure us to agree to arrangements that cost everyone more in taxes. Children whom we cannot trust with financial matters cost us opportunities to tax-shelter money for their education. Vendors of financial services—like sales-people of any ilk—are reluctant to suggest services that they don't profit from, even if such services are best for us. Together, all these people sap the investment power of our hard-earned savings.

## Financial Security Comes from Personal Security

Millions of people are so insecure about their finances that they make foolish, hurried financial decisions. The result is increased anxiety and a potential crisis put on the back burner. That crisis will eventually boil over—when the effects of poor decisions come home to roost. This book is written for people who want to stop making lousy financial planning decisions, people who realize they need perspective on life's most critical financial transitions. You will get the most out of this book if you are someone who believes in the old adage: "Identify the problem and you're halfway to the solution." By realizing that you need an educated perspective on the money in your life, you will be halfway to financial security.

## It's the Curves in the Road That Can Get You in Trouble

This book will help you successfully manage critical financial transitions. At certain crossroads, you may long for a confident voice of reason, someone to help you sort out your options. Perhaps it is when you first enter the working world, start housekeeping alone, get married, have and raise children, face divorce, grow older, or retire.

As you read through the chapters of this book, imagine yourself sharing a glass of fine brandy—or, if you prefer, tea—with your favorite uncle. You know, the one that the extended family of yesteryear went to for advice at those very special times when everything seemed to be happening at once or when it was time to make a happy or unhappy change.

In these pages, not only do you have the friendly security of that wonderful "uncle" who served as mentor for the traditional family, but the "uncle" speaking to you here happens to be an expert in the business and technology of today's financial services marketplace. The combination of friendly advice and assertive, informed strategies for using financial alternatives is unbeatable. No more passbook savings accounts, Christmas Clubs, and unnecessary whole life insurance. Instead, you will hear of no-load mutual funds, IRAs and 401(k)s, smart estate planning, savvy tax tips, insurance alternatives, personal credit plans, asset management, debt advice, financial market timing, and much more.

## Financial Transitions Are the Hardest to Make

When you finally begin to get your finances in order—consolidating all of those credit card balances, paying into a systematic savings plan, closing your passbook savings accounts, borrowing on the cash value of your whole life insurance, investing for safe but strong returns—you will find this book especially useful. Reread the chapters that apply to your current situation, get your problem in perspective, and you are on your way.

This book is loaded with nuggets of good advice—they will jump out and almost demand that you reorganize some part of your life or your finances. Here's a sneak preview of some of the issues we tackle:

- Despite what the politicians say, tax reform did not "simplify" our tax code. The phrase "tax simplification" is still an oxymoron, like "jumbo shrimp" and "Rapid City, South Dakota." We've analyzed the new law, and we know that it contains more twists and turns than a country road. In the chapters that follow, you'll learn how to manage your family finances in light of the new law. For instance, many folks will no longer be allowed to make tax-deductible contributions to IRAs. But—negative publicity notwithstanding—millions of people can still have tax-advantaged retirement programs involving IRAs. How, then, can you build the most powerful retirement kitty? You've got to know about, and use, the retirement plans that most successfully survived tax reform. We spotlight the new appeal of deferred annuities (perhaps the best game in town), new strategies for 401(k) investing, and the enhanced role of Keogh plans.

- The year 1987 will be a confusing one for taxpayers. We alert you to special transition rules. In 1987, to take one prominent example, there will be five tax brackets, ranging from 11 percent to 38.5 percent. After 1987, the old system of 14 brackets (15 for single taxpayers) will be replaced by a system that theoretically has only two brackets: 15 percent and 28 percent. "Theoretically," because high-income taxpayers will lose some of the benefit of the 15 percent bracket and the increased personal exemption. Moreover, most traditional tax planning devices have vanished. For instance, income averaging, preferential treatment of long-term capital gains, and Clifford Trusts have been thrown on the scrap heap. The new law's definition of passive versus active losses from real estate deserves careful consideration by anyone who owns property. We suggest new approaches to tax planning in chapter 16.

- Thanks to program trading, portfolio insurance, risky options plays, and the like, the financial markets have become very complex and danger-ously volatile. The typical individual investor shouldn't try to go it alone. How can you invest for maximum reward but avoid losing your shirt? The new Donoghue Investment Strategy identifies top-performing mutual funds (no-load and low-load) that promise consistent, strong returns. It also flags the funds heading for a nosedive. With our sound strategy for timing the market, you'll know when to invest in stock market mutual funds and when to seek shelter in money market mutual funds.

- Our investment advice sports an impressive track record: of the no-load mutual funds we recommend, the top five earned on average more than 26 percent annually over the past five years. That beats the performance of 98 percent of all mutual funds in existence, both load and no-load.
- So, you've been investing for some time and want to move beyond the beginner's rank? Perhaps you're curious about some of the more exotic vehicles available today: put and call options, futures trading, commodities, and so on. But you're still hesitant to climb into the ring with the heavy hitters. We explain the risks involved, as well as the potential rewards.
- You can save significant amounts of interest expense on your mortgage by taking two actions: refinancing your mortgage at today's lower rates and perhaps paying off your mortgage in fifteen rather than thirty years. For many, the combination of the two actions may even mean lower monthly payments plus a paid-off home fifteen years sooner.
- Knowing how to negotiate a divorce agreement can save both you and your ex-spouse thousands of dollars in unnecessary income taxes. It's much better to learn how to accomplish this before you start the negotiations.
- Because tax reform phases out the deductibility of consumer interest on personal loans and credit card purchases, you'll want to know how to use an equity access loan (a line of credit secured by the equity in your first or second home). Using an equity access loan allows you to make big-ticket purchases and still deduct the interest payments on your tax return. We spell it all out for you.
- Antenuptial or premarriage agreements between professionals with significant amounts of assets, or couples marrying at a later age, make a lot of sense. They keep money from becoming a political football between spouses.
- There are rewards and perils associated with professional counsel. There

are times when you'll want to avoid the sharks who simply want to sell you a new will, unnecessary insurance, or dubious investments.

- You must manage your debts as well as your assets. Perhaps you need to build (or rebuild) your credit rating, consolidate your credit card debt, and cut both the interest costs and monthly payments. Can't handle credit cards? We offer some money-saving tips for keeping the wolf from your door along with a few recipes for roast wolf.
- In a typical family, one spouse might save for retirement through a company-sponsored 401(k) program, while the other spouse, perhaps a nurse or a teacher, might save through a 403(b) or 403(b)7 program. Because both work weekends for the family business, each might have a Keogh account. How much money should go into each plan annually? When withdrawals begin, what are the tax consequences of withdrawing from each plan? What should the timing be for those withdrawals?
- Trust funds are not just for the rich and famous. How can you use trusts to enhance your family's tax plan?
- There is no financial service more confusing and misunderstood than insurance. Ironically, some people buy much more insurance than they need and others buy much less than they need and buy the wrong kind at that. What are the smart choices?
- Getting off on the right foot (instead of putting your foot in your mouth or having creditors put their feet elsewhere) is essential to lifetime financial planning. You don't have to be married or monied to begin taking responsibility for your financial security. How can the single person get started?
- Marriage, that most venerable of institutions, can be a wonderful experience. But the modern couple must enter marriage as they would any financial partnership—with eyes wide open. The partners should openly state their financial goals and how they intend to work toward those goals. We suggest that spouses designate one day each year as "contingency planning day"—a time for talking honestly about what happens to family finances in the event of death or divorce.
- Some things just don't work out as you planned—mature individuals sometimes agree to face the music, dissolve the band, and find a new dancing partner. A look at the divorce process and the costs of required legal assistance offers a sobering view on the financial implications of splitting up.
- Children are more than "minor" adjustments in your life. They will need to learn practical financial habits and how to contribute to the college

fund. Because of tax reform, they'll also be learning how to pay taxes on any scholarship money that is earmarked for room and board.

- The three biggest expenses you have in life are buying a home, buying a car, and, perhaps, paying for your funeral. It is a neat trick for some people to manage life's major expenses. What financial strategies make sense for you?

- Nothing is certain except death and taxes. There are, however, numerous legal ways to reduce your tax bill. What you need is a sound approach to tax planning, one designed to enhance your overall financial picture *and* pay Uncle Sam as little as possible. Where to begin? What levers to pull? What schemes should you avoid? What happens if you get audited?

- Retirement offers some unique financial planning opportunities, but there are many critical decisions to make. You'll need a solid grip on your sources of income, and a clear strategy for managing the value of all your assets. Social Security rules, pension plan payment alternatives, tax planning, health care expenses, the ins and outs of Medicare and, perhaps, Medicaid, all present dilemmas to retirees. How to cope and assure that your golden years are financially secure?

- Smart estate planning can save you and your loved ones a lot of surprises and grief. What do you need to know to do it right?

## Take Charge of Your Lifetime Finances

More than anything else, this book is designed to give you the confidence you need to ask the right questions about your lifetime finances. As we said earlier, asking the right questions gets you halfway to the right solutions. With an educated perspective on the decisions you'll face at different stages of your life, you'll be able to harness the true power of all your family's assets. You'll finally be able to make everything work in sync.

You'll need to be in the driver's seat—it is hard to get very far when you do not understand what you are doing and you rely on someone else to make the important decisions for you. "Take charge of your finances!" is a battle cry repeated in my three previous best-selling books *(William E. Donoghue's Complete Money Market Guide; William E. Donoghue's No-Load Mutual Fund Guide;* and *William E. Donoghue's Guide to Finding Money to Invest).* It's a battle cry that subscribers to *Donoghue's MONEYLETTER* hear often. Finally, it's a consistent theme in my syndicated newspaper columns and in my speaking engagements that bring me face to face with consumers across the nation.

During the past ten years, through my writing and speaking I've offered investment advice to millions of people. It is tremendously rewarding when I hear the success stories—and I do hear more than a few. People who have taken my advice and have done well with their investments are not shy about letting me know. (My mail keeps the tiny Holliston, Massachusetts, post office humming.) It is uncanny, but I hear over and over: "Bill, once you demystified the jargon for me, I was able to take it from there."

I urge you to use this book in that spirit of self-sufficiency. While there will be times in your life when you need the help of an attorney, financial planner, or accountant, you can learn how and when to do certain things on your own. My point is twofold: first, avoid wasting your hard-earned dollars on advice that is nothing more than a product sales pitch in disguise; and, second, become increasingly savvy about managing your finances as you go. Take the plunge now—learn to handle the financial transitions in your life. And let me know how you make out.

# 2

## Where Do You Stand?
## Getting Ready to Plan

The Duchess of Windsor said that you can never be too rich or too thin. But most people are chubby and short of cash—because they delude themselves that "extra" calories and purchases don't count. It's not the once-a-year glorious seven-course dinner, or the long-awaited vacation or fur coat, that causes fat bellies and skinny bank accounts. The real culprits are the handfuls of peanuts nibbled in front of the TV set, and the unnoticed expenditures—the electric bill for the lights you forgot to turn off, the restaurant dinner because nobody remembered to defrost the chops. In both cases, the remedy is the same—strict dieting and strict budgeting—and the outcome is the same—an attractive, healthy body or bank account.

Married people (and couples living together) probably fight about money at least as much as they fight about sex. Part of the problem is that it's sort of embarrassing to talk about money, so honesty is not always an option. No one likes to admit to being a poor provider, a financial failure, a lousy homemaker, or fiscally irresponsible. Some households have strict money roles divided by sex: either he or she, as chief breadwinner, is responsible for making and sticking to the family budget. That's fine, as long as they both understand and accept their roles, and as long as their expectations are based on financial reality—even the best homemaker can't keep a spouse and five children fed, clothed, and amused on $100 a week.

### Planning Helps

Changes in society can come faster than changes in psychology. For many couples, it's an emotional strain if she earns as much as, or more than, he does. Still other couples conflict when she thinks of her salary as all hers to spend, expecting him to support the family (or vice versa). Sometimes the problem is that the spouses or live-ins have radically different priorities about money —priorities that they've never communicated openly. Then, the fights start when one wants to spend today by moving to a better home, going out to dinner, going to the theater or a nightclub, decking the house with the latest electronic marvels—while the other one wants to defer consumption and put money in the bank or invest it.

Another source of trouble: couples who are unprepared for economic downturns. A fast-track couple can live up to (or past) two high incomes, then discover that one spouse has lost his or her job, or one has traded in high-tech and high salary for strained peaches and no salary by quitting her job to take care of the kid(s). Some couples have solved this problem by living on one income while the kids are still in the planning stage, and investing the second income. That way, their expectations are lower, and funds are available when child-related costs pile up. Sometimes the problem is a simple lack of communication: both partners have access to the checkbook, both have credit cards, but they don't find out what the other has spent until the end of the month, when the bills come crashing in. For couples the key is setting up a procedure for making a budget and balancing the books, and sticking to it; and making sure that each spouse has full information about the family finances.

For singles as well as couples, money problems can come from money styles. Although cash, checks, and credit cards are all forms of spending, and all come out of the family exchequer, people have wildly different reactions to them. Just as there are compulsive eaters and anorexics, there are compulsive spenders and compulsive misers. Some people spend freely as long as they have cash in their pockets, but stop short when they have to write checks or produce a credit card; for other people, cash is "real" money, the other forms are just "play money" that they can spend with a light heart and an open hand.

Be honest with yourself—do you have a psychological bias about one or more kinds of spending? If so, it may help to impose self-control. If you go wild with a credit card, keep it locked up and take it out only once a month; in extreme cases, cut up your credit cards and refuse all invitations to get more.

If you go hog-wild when you're carrying cash, pay as many bills as possible by check. Many supermarkets will accept checks—some even take credit cards. Get newspaper and magazine subscriptions instead of spending $2, $3, $5 a week at the newsstand and cut back on the amount of cash you carry—and therefore the amount you could waste. If checks are your downfall, keep your checking account lean and mean (good advice for many people, anyway), and pay bills only once a month, transferring the funds from your money market or cash management account. Stop writing those impulsive checks for a new item of clothing, record albums, or whatever is your weakness; if you can't fit it into your credit card budget, don't buy it.

Many dieters learn to reprogram their behavior by writing down everything they eat, and keeping a running calorie total. Overspenders can do the same thing to identify how and where the money melts out of their pockets.

As a last resort, forced saving is better than no saving. Although, as we'll explain in chapter 10, it's usually a bad strategy to get a tax refund, it's a good move for people who have trouble saving—provided that the tax refund goes straight to a mutual fund, money market fund, or your IRA. If your employer offers a salary reduction plan—(SARA, or 401(k) plan)—grab it. You can set up your own informal salary reduction plan (though it won't be a tax shelter): when you get a raise or a bonus, earmark the entire amount for investment.

Take some time to think about your life-style—what gives you pleasure, what you wouldn't mind giving up and what you'd really miss, what you'd like to improve. And, remember, if you had everything, what would you have to look forward to? We're not saying that you should give up champagne and caviar for tap water and no-frills tuna fish—just that you should buy your champagne by the case when you get a good price on your favorite vintage (and that you shouldn't spend a fortune to show off when you can't tell Aloxe-Corton from Coca-Cola Classic).

One woman swears by her imported skin-cleansing ritual; another is content with soap and water. One man keeps fit with $40-an-hour court time at his squash club; another does Royal Canadian Air Force Exercises at home. There's all the difference in the world between luxury and waste.

Luxury makes your life-style enjoyable. A vacation that you'll remember forever, fine-quality furniture for your living room, a wardrobe that makes you feel sensational, a racing bicycle your kid enjoys for ten years (then passes along to a younger sibling)—these are all luxuries, things to aspire to. The potato chips you can't remember you ate (but which show up on your waist-line), the $50 game your kids play with twice and then forget, the $300 you paid because you didn't shop carefully for a new appliance, are all examples of waste. They don't enrich your life-style, they only impoverish you.

## Developing a Family Budget

The reason for maintaining and sticking to a family budget is that you'll be able to cover all your bills—and pay them according to your cash-management agenda—with enough left over to invest. Once you save and invest wisely, you'll be able to take your financial future into your own hands. You'll have a cash cushion for emergencies. You'll be able to retire in style. You'll be able to quit a hateful job and start your own business, or move to a job that's better for you (even if the salary is lower). If you're an apartment-dweller, you'll be able to improve your residence and your balance sheet at the same time by buying a home. After all, which would you rather get in the mail, a statement showing your investment interest or capital gains, or a wheedling (or threatening) letter from a bill collector?

By now, we hope you're convinced of the need to track your income and expenses and trim expenses to provide investment funds. But a glance at your newspaper will show you that the budget process is no snap. Luckily, in a family you don't have to worry about party politics. Let's start by filling in the blanks in the worksheet below.

### WORKSHEET: FAMILY CASHFLOWS

1. What is your monthly income from salaries, wages, and business or professions? $_____

2. What is your monthly income from the investments you already have? $_____(To estimate, add up last year's investment income and divide by twelve; or project the return you expect this year from your investment portfolio.)

3. What is your monthly interest income? $_____

4. What is your monthly income from rental property that you own? $_____

5. What is your monthly income from other sources (e.g., alimony, child support)? $_____

    TOTAL MONTHLY INCOME: $_____

    Okay, now for the hard part.

1. Monthly rent/mortgage payment: $_____

2. Monthly food bill: $_____

3. Annual costs of clothing (divide by 12): $_____

4. Monthly car payment: $_____

5. Monthly payment for life, health, auto, homeowners insurance: $_____

6. Total monthly payments for other loans: $_____

7. Average monthly credit card bill: $_____

8. Average monthly utility bill: $_____

9. Average monthly telephone bill: $_____

10. Average monthly entertainment costs: $_____

11. Average amount spent in restaurants each month: $_____

12. Monthly costs of laundry, dry cleaning: $_____

13. Average cost of gasoline: $_____

14. Average cost of fuel oil, gas for heating, cooking, etc.: $_____

15. Alimony and/or child support per month: $_____ (Be honest—list what you pay, not what you're supposed to pay.)

16. One-twelfth of annual gifts: $_____

17. Average monthly health care costs not covered by insurance: $_____

18. One-twelfth of annual tuition paid: $_____

19. Monthly commuting, traveling costs (except gasoline): $_____

20. Taxes (might as well estimate it as one-quarter of your gross income—that's about what most people pay): $_____

21. Kids' allowances, pocket money, miscellaneous: $_____

    TOTAL AVERAGE MONTHLY EXPENSES: $_____

How do you stack up? If you're like most people, you're a little behind, or at best a little ahead of the game. If your average monthly income exceeds your average monthly expenses, you're part of the way there. Before you can invest, you'll need a cash cushion (say, a month's or two months' pretax income) to cope with the fact that not all expenses arrive in predictable monthly packages. For example, the very well organized who have plenty of storage space buy Christmas and birthday presents throughout the year, whenever they find just the perfect gift for someone at a temptingly low price. Everyone else buys Christmas presents just before Christmas, in an orgy of consumption. The start of each new school year usually signals a new wardrobe for the kids; most people take their vacations in the summer; and if you have annualized utility bills, you'll probably have a hefty bill once a year when actual usage catches up to the bills you've been getting.

### What if Expenses Outstrip Income?

If the bills are bigger than the income, here are some things you can do:

- Lock up the credit cards until you get everything paid off, or at least until you reduce your balance.
- Check loan rates. You're probably paying more than 18 percent on your credit card balances. If you can get a personal loan at 14 percent, or a loan on your life insurance policy for 9 percent, you may be better off by using the loan proceeds to pay off your credit card bills.
- Boring, old-fashioned things like saving energy and cutting back on telephone calls can save a surprising amount of money.
- Sure, you deserve a break today—but you also deserve a future of financial solvency. Those trips to the coffee cart, fast-food lunches, and take-out pizzas put a hole in any budget. A few weekend hours spent together cooking and freezing meals for the week build family solidarity —and family wealth.

If your income outpaces your expenses, and you've set aside an emergency reserve, congratulations! You're ready to start investing. Study chapter 3 to set your long-range goals, and move along to chapter 4 to pick the best investment media for your family's resources and goals.

### Financial Record Keeping

If you don't keep score, you'll never know who's winning the game. You'll need good financial records to prepare your tax returns; the records also let you fine-tune your goals and see how close you've come to achieving them.

Your check register is the bedrock of your financial record-keeping system. It's a good idea to pay as many expenses by check as possible (unless, as we've explained, you have a psychological hang-up about them). The canceled check gives you a record and proof of payment. Be sure to enter every check immediately; if two of you have access to the checkbook, make sure each knows about the checks the other has written, and set a consistent policy about when bills will be paid and who is entitled to spend how much money for what.

Reconcile your bank statement promptly—and hold the line if your bank tries to fob you off without canceled checks. They get to play with your money —so make them operate for your convenience, not their own.

As your bills pour in day after day, you'll need to develop a logical system to keep all the payment dates straight—most of us are not fortunate enough to have all our bills due on the same day. As each bill comes in, mark the payment date on your calendar. Then, in an expandable file with at least twelve pockets (one for each month) or in a series of envelopes, file your bills chronologically according to due date. As each is paid, put your receipt in the back of the pocket, along with each month's bank statement—after you balance your checkbook. At the end of the year, you'll be secure in the knowledge that all your records are in one easy-to-find place.

You'll also need a notebook or accounting pad. Keep a running record of potentially tax-deductible expenditures (for example, charitable contributions and medical bills). If you're a homeowner, keep track of repairs and improvements to your house that could affect your taxable gains when you sell the house. This record may also come in handy when you want to deduct interest on a home-equity loan, which is secured by your residence plus the value of home improvements. (See chapter 7.) If you live in part of a multifamily house and rent out the rest, keep records of the money you spend on the tenants' apartments and of the depreciation you can claim on this property. Although you will be allowed smaller depreciation deductions than under prior law, the deductions are still valuable. Records of the work you did, contractors you hired, and late-night phone calls you fielded could also be helpful in proving to the IRS that you're an active investor, entitled to large all-purpose deductions of tax losses, and not a passive investor who can use only a portion of his losses.

With this simple system, you'll have all the information you need to have your accountant prepare your tax returns (or to do it yourself). You'll know where the money goes each month. You'll be able to track your expenditures and how they change over time. As soon as your personal income statement shows a profit, you may want to add another page to your financial records: the income from your money market fund, and the profits from your equity mutual fund.

The budget gives you the information you need for day-to-day financial planning, and gives you the discipline to save the money you need to start on the road to financial independence. (It also shows you when you can ease up a little and make some enjoyable, if wasteful, expenditures.) But our whole point is that you need to look beyond the day-to-day grind, and start to look at your financial plans over the long term. Our next chapter shows you how to do just that.

## CASE HISTORY
### *Where Do You Stand?*

The commuters were packed like sardines, although no reputable sardine packer would have tolerated the variations of posture that the early-morning train riders adopted. It was too crowded for the stand-up riders to read, though Lord knows some of them tried, and long columns of folded *Wall Street Journals* encroached on the limited air space. Ken Allbeury and Martin Hoveck had long ago given up the attempt; each clutched an attaché case in one hand, the pole down the middle of the car in the other. They gazed meditatively at the ad on the wall directly in front of them; it showed a couple of cars, glistening metallic silver or bronze, tastefully accessorized with people in fox-hunting togs or full evening dress.

"Say, what do you think about that Mercedes convertible?" Ken asked.

"Looks like a damn pickup truck. I'd like a Continental, myself."

"Definitely. And what about a yacht?"

"I don't know. My brother-in-law has a Continental. He does a little better than we do but he's a long way from the Fortune Four Hundred."

"And one thing you can say about other people's things, you can't tell if they're paid for or not."

"Yeah, one thing I can tell you about mine," Martin said dourly. "I can tell you they're not paid for. I knock down a pretty good salary, Carla's working now, and at the end of the year, I don't know, it seems like there's nothing left."

"I feel a little better about it than you do," Ken said, "but then you've got a kid in college, and my oldest is fourteen, so I don't have to worry about that for a couple of years."

"If I were you," Martin said, "I'd start worrying now. I mean, if you put away ten grand a year between now and when Lucy is eighteen, you still maybe couldn't pay for it all. And—no offense—I don't think you could just reach into your pocket and find ten grand every year."

"That's why I'd rather stand here and dream about my Mercedes."

"Yeah, right, now it's your Mercedes. Why don't you stand here and dream about not having to stand here? If I were really rich, the first thing I'd do would be to ditch my job."

"Would you really? I mean, first of all, I don't think I'd really think of myself as much of a man if I didn't have a job. My father always taught me that that's what a man does—he works hard and takes care of his family. He didn't bring me up to be some playboy, you know, let's get on the Concorde and go to Monte Carlo, darling, kind of thing."

"If my family is taken care of, I don't care if it's from my job, from the lottery, from Carla's job, hell, I don't care if it's from the tooth fairy. And my family is making out okay, but I'd like to have a little more. You know, give each of the kids a car for high school graduation, even if it's an old one; be able to go on vacation without worrying, can we afford this, can we afford the other thing. What do people do, if they're not born rich?"

"Like you said, the lottery. Or they invent something, or they're real hot supersalesmen and they make a million dollars in commissions. Or, I don't know, I saw a movie once, a guy made a million dollars buying pork bellies."

"How much did he start out with? Five million?"

"It's like this joke I heard. How do you set up a Democrat in a small business? Buy him a large one, and wait a couple of years."

"I don't know," Martin said, turning more serious. "We have this program for our home computer, it's supposed to help you analyze stocks. I got really into it over the summer, you know, I'd read the stock page every day, plug in figures, play around with it. I really wasn't too bad. I pretended I had one hundred thousand dollars, and by the end of the summer I was up to one hundred twenty-nine thousand, three hundred eighty-nine."

"Why didn't you really buy some stocks?"

"I was afraid," Martin said simply. "Believe me, I don't have a hundred thousand dollars. And if I took what we have in savings, what would we do if I lost it? And, anyway, I would be embarrassed to walk into a stockbroker's office and not even know what to say, what to ask for. You know what it's like, you don't want some snot-nosed kid laughing at you."

"We have a money market fund," Ken said. "Not like we have a million bucks or anything. But we kind of looked around and said, hey, why are we sticking all our money into the Christmas Club, it hardly pays any interest. And we weren't getting any interest on the checking account at all. So we got one of those checking accounts that pays interest, and we got into a money market fund. Just about when the bottom fell out of the interest rates, but, hey, that's just the way it is. And, anyway, the extra money we're earning pays for Tina's ice skates and stuff like that."

"I was talking to one of the guys in my office," Martin said. "He's about fifty-three, fifty-four, and he's planning on taking early retirement. He says he's going to take a lump sum from the pension fund, instead of getting a pension every month, and he's going to invest it. His IRA is pretty good, he took some big chances and they really paid off, and he says he has his eyes on some investments that will get him about thirteen percent without too much risk."

"Like what?"

"I'm not sure they really exist," Martin said. "It used to be that guys would tell you about how tough they were because they drank so much or they were always getting another girl into bed, and now they tell you how tough they are because they made umphtey-umph dollars on this deal or that deal."

"Well, I'm not going to retire," Ken said. "They can carry me out. And, anyway, wouldn't I make a lot more money working than sitting on my tail?"

"Not necessarily, if you have a good pension deal, and you own property, maybe you have some rent coming in, or you have something that sends you a check every month. That's what I'd like. Not that it's going to happen, but I'd like it."

"All this investment stuff seems too risky for me," Ken said, looking out over the heads of the seated commuters to assess the progress toward the next station. "Pam and I plan to open up an IRA this year, and we've thought about it, and we're going to get a bank certificate. That's the safe way—it's insured and we can't lose our money."

"Safe, safe, safe," Martin mused. "It's kind of, well, exciting to take some risks. Maybe I will buy some of those stocks after all. I heard on the grapevine that the bonus checks will be pretty good this year."

The train ground to a halt, sending a few injudicious straphangers flying through the air (or the limited amount of air that was not occupied by beige trenchcoats and gnomelike Irish-tweed hats).

"Hey, maybe we'll get rich," Ken said. "It's not that we're poverty-stricken right now, but wouldn't it be great to get a little bit ahead?"

As Martin and Ken headed for the office, the din of the city brought an end to their chat. Each man fell silent, preoccupied with a nagging sense that there was something awry. Both longed for lifetime financial security, and each worked hard to meet his family's financial needs, but neither had a comprehensive plan for meeting realistic goals.

# 3

## What Are You Saving Your Money For? Setting Realistic Goals

Two contrasting perspectives are: the currently popular motto "Whoever has the most things when he dies, wins" and St. Paul's "We brought nothing into this world and assuredly we can take nothing out of it." No matter which view you subscribe to, the first step in life-style planning is deciding why you want money, how much you want, and what you will do with your money as you get it.

If you take a thousand families, each with the same income and the same number of children of about the same age, you'll find hundreds of different patterns of spending and hundreds of different goals. Some of those families will have solid plans, adapt the plans as necessary for changing circumstances, and will meet their goals. Other families will make unrealistic plans or be too rigid about a good plan that no longer conforms to current reality. Still others will drift along, not bothering to plan or feeling overwhelmed by the task. Some of them, by sheer dumb luck, will achieve what they want—but the majority in this group will find themselves swamped with bills and wondering why they never get the things they want.

### Assessing Your Needs

If you didn't want to locate yourself solidly in the first group, you wouldn't be reading this book. So your task, right now, is to assess your current and future financial needs from two perspectives: the psychological and the practical.

Money has psychological meanings: it can represent power, security, sexual potency, a way to buy love (or at least a pretty good imitation). Some people see money as a way to measure worth. Some people want to have a lot of money so they can associate with those whom they believe to be aristocratic, powerful, special. Others want to have enough money to keep up with the Joneses, or to make the Joneses struggle to keep up with them.

Some people find it necessary to have ample funds for a rainy day, while others are breezily sure that something will turn up if and when an emergency strikes. There are parents whose major goal is setting up their children in life; others believe that it's good for kids to have to find their own way to the top. High-rollers relish the challenge of being flush one day, busted the next; the fiscally cautious prefer a secure job with a measurable, if never expansive, return. Consumers want to buy things to enjoy now; deferrers want to save the funds for future enjoyment (and frequently reap the benefits as things like color television sets, food processors, and VCRs change from superluxury items to common, more affordable commodities).

Some people really want to be rich (however they define "rich"); others would really prefer to keep their present style of life, or perhaps exchange it for one slightly more comfortable. If you aspire to wealth, how much risk are you willing to take—and what are you going to do if your plans don't pan out?

Your ultimate objective is to have enough money to keep up the life-style you want; to have enough money for comfortable retirement; and to make any provisions for your surviving spouse and children that fit into your estate plan (see chapter 18). In addition to meeting current maintenance needs (food, the rent or mortgage payment, the phone bill, keeping the oil tank filled and the car gassed up), you'll need to budget for future consumption (vacations, home entertainment systems, nights on the town) and future family needs (medical bills, education). If you're like most people, it's a struggle to cover the bills each month; but you'll never get ahead unless you also find a way to invest for your future financial well-being.

In chapter 2, we showed you how to make a family budget for the ordinary expenditures of everyday life. Now we'll show you how to set your long-range goals, so you'll know how much you have to invest to keep your life-style at the level you choose. Every year, in addition to your basic budget, you'll need money for special goals. Depending on your priorities and the stage of your life cycle, the special goal could be the down payment on your first house, co-op, or condo; a new car; a family vacation; your kid's tuition in nursery school, private school, college, or postgraduate work; a renovated kitchen; state-of-the-art ski equipment, or a power boat.

Use this worksheet to anticipate your major expenses for the next few years, ten to twenty years, and the long-run picture over twenty years. Of course, the more remote in time, the less exact your figures can be. To estimate your financial needs, estimate the current price for the items. If it's a long-range plan, try to figure out what it will cost when you're ready to buy it—understanding that this is an inexact science at best.

## WORKSHEET: LONG-RANGE PLANS

1. House, co-op, or condo:

   ☐Don't want ☐Have—don't want a better one ☐Have—want to replace/improve ☐Don't have—want one
   ☐Now ☐In 1–5 years ☐5–10 years ☐10–20 years ☐20 years+
   Current cost. $_____Down payment: $_____
   Estimated cost when purchased: $_____
   Down payment: $_____

2. Education (for self, spouse, child or children):
   ☐Don't want ☐Have—don't want a better one ☐Have—want more
   ☐Don't have—want one
   ☐Now ☐In 1–5 years ☐5–10 years ☐10–20 years ☐20 years+
   Current cost: $_____Cost per year: $_____
   Estimated cost when spent: $_____
   Cost per year: $_____

3. Car (make/model):
   ☐Don't want ☐Have—don't want a better one ☐Have—want to replace/improve
   ☐Don't have—want one
   ☐Now ☐In 1–5 years ☐5–10 years ☐10–20 years ☐20 years+
   Current cost: $_____Down payment: $_____
   Estimated cost when purchased: $_____
   Down payment: $_____

4. Home renovations:
   ☐Don't want ☐Have—don't want more ☐Have—want to replace/improve
   ☐Don't have—want more
   ☐Now ☐In 1–5 years ☐5–10 years ☐10–20 years ☐20 years+
   Current cost: $_____
   Estimated cost when purchased: $_____

5. Furniture:
   ☐Don't want ☐Have—don't want a better one ☐Have—want to replace/improve
   ☐Don't have—want
   ☐Now ☐In 1–5 years ☐5–10 years ☐10–20 years ☐20 years+

Current cost: $_____
Estimated cost when purchased: $_____

6. Collections:
   ☐Don't want ☐Have—don't want a better one ☐Have—want to replace/improve
   ☐Don't have—want one
   ☐Now ☐In 1–5 years ☐5–10 years ☐10–20 years ☐20 years+

7. Home electronics (stereo, color TV, VCR, projection TV, home computer, etc.):
   ☐Don't want ☐Have—don't want a better one ☐Have—want to replace/improve
   ☐Don't have—want one
   ☐Now ☐In 1–5 years ☐5–10 years ☐10–20 years ☐20 years+
   Current cost: $_____
   Estimated cost when purchased: $_____

8. Vacations:
   ☐Don't want ☐Have—don't want a better one ☐Have—want to replace/improve
   ☐Don't have—want one
   ☐Now ☐In 1–5 years ☐5–10 years ☐10–20 years ☐20 years+
   Current cost: $_____
   Estimated cost when purchased: $_____

9. Boat, RV, etc.:
   ☐Don't want ☐Have—don't want a better one ☐Have—want to replace/improve
   ☐Don't have—want one
   ☐Now ☐In 1–5 years ☐5–10 years ☐10–20 years ☐20 years+

10. Kid's wedding:
    ☐Now ☐In 1–5 years ☐5–10 years ☐10–20 years ☐20 years+
    Current cost: $_____
    Estimated cost when purchased: $_____

11. Other_____
    ☐Have—want to replace/improve ☐Don't have—want one
    Current cost: $_____
    Estimated cost when purchased: $_____

12. Other_____
    ☐Have—want to replace/improve ☐Don't have—want one
    Current cost: $_____
    Estimated cost when purchased: $_____

These are your long-range financial plans. In addition to your plans for maintaining and improving your life-style, you'll also need to have a retirement reserve (see chapter 17 for tips on computing the reserve and making sure it'll be available when you need it) and insurance and/or a reserve for emergencies (check chapter 9 for insurance savvy).

Now go back to the worksheet, and add up the sums in each category. (For very large expenditures like buying a house or a car, add in the down payment —but remember that the monthly payments will have to come out of the household budget we explained in chapter 2.) For long-range plans, estimate the year. Finally, fill in this table with the amount you think you'll need each year for long-range life-style expenditures:

| | | | |
|---|---|---|---|
| 1986 $_____ | 1987 $_____ | 1988 $_____ | 1989 $_____ |
| 1990 $_____ | 1991 $_____ | 1992 $_____ | 1993 $_____ |
| 1994 $_____ | 1995 $_____ | 1996 $_____ | 1997 $_____ |
| 1998 $_____ | 1999 $_____ | 2000 $_____ | 2001 $_____ |
| 2002 $_____ | 2003 $_____ | 2004 $_____ | 2005 $_____ |

That's the challenge you have to live up to. Don't panic! As we'll show you, you can control your own financial future. Assertiveness and good planning will make it possible for you to achieve your goals—or at least most of them. What can you do if you don't think you can meet your goals?

- Cut back on today's life-style so you'll have more money to invest for the future. Keep tighter controls on your cash; borrow less, or find lower-interest alternatives for high-interest-rate obligations; cut back on vacation and entertainment spending; switch to generic paper towels— whatever you need to close the gap.
- Improve your investment results—shift funds out of low- or no-interest savings and checking accounts into money-market funds or bank money-market accounts; monitor the performance of your mutual funds; analyze your real estate investments; be ready to switch from equities to the money market, or back again, when the time is ripe.
- Fine-tune your goals. If designer clothes are important to you, maybe you can meet your goal by shopping at outlet stores that carry designer labels, learning how to sew, or accepting "knock-offs" instead of the real McCoy. If your psyche and your image require you to drive a Yupmobile, maybe a used BMW will do.
- Don't go it alone. If you're part of a one-earner married couple, maybe the other spouse can work part- or full-time. As we'll show you in chapter 13, kids can pay for part or all of their college and postcollege education; and you can teach your kids to appreciate the true value of money, so they won't spend you out of house and home (or spend themselves out of house and home once they leave the nest).
- Find legal ways to reduce your taxes—and make sure you have the discipline to save your tax refund or tax savings instead of spending it.

# 4

## The Donoghue Investment Strategy and Other Investment Basics

Once you've got your head above water—that is, once you've tamed your monthly cash flows, created a tax plan, and stashed an emergency hoard of a few months' salary in a highly liquid, income-producing parking lot such as a money market mutual fund or a NOW account—you can, and should, think about learning to swim. In other words, it's time to manage your investments. Having your head above water is just not good enough—you have to start swimming toward a goal. That means making sense of the available choices.

### "Your Money or Your Life!"

There's an almost infinite panoply of investment vehicles that can make your hard-earned dollars grow. And there's an equally diverse gang of financial service firms that would just love the chance to manage your assets. Banks, mutual funds, credit unions, thrifts, brokerages, insurance firms, and so on are all scrambling for your bucks.

A quick glance at your Sunday newspaper proves how fierce the competition has become. Giant ads scream about the benefits of one investment or another. The well-heeled financial companies jockey for ad time on network TV. It's no wonder novice investors quickly get overwhelmed—each pitch seems to offer the best of all possible worlds.

The fact is, however, that not all investment vehicles are created equal. As we'll see in this chapter and in chapters 5 and 15, there are, to varying degrees, pluses and minuses in just about any route you choose. The tough part is that financial service firms busy grabbing for your funds won't volunteer to tell you about the unattractive features of their products. Never fear! We will.

That brings us to the fundamental tenet of successful investing: know what you're getting into and what you hope to achieve. This requires a little elbow grease on your part—if you're not willing to do some homework, you're a prime target for the marketing wolves of the financial services industry.

How, then, can you get a handle on selecting the best investment? Well, you're getting off to a good start by reading this book. The score is now: Investor: 1, Wolves: 0.

But you've only just begun. You should develop the habit of reading the financial news regularly to keep abreast of economic events and market gyrations. You should also make it a point to send away for investment product literature, to study how various options work and to compare performance track records. Of course, many veteran investors subscribe to an investment newsletter—one written by *independent observers* of the financial scene—to get the honest lowdown on product, market, and investment trends. The idea is to do all you can to enhance your investment savvy and become a smart shopper.

## Invest Confidently and Competently

To develop your skills as a confident *and* competent investor, you need two things: first, perspective—the ability to sort the winners from the losers—and, second, a sound strategy for managing your investments once you get rolling. The last thing you want to do is buy an investment and then stick your head in the sand. As we'll explain later on in this chapter, it's crucial to monitor the current *and* future health of your investment portfolio. Nothing lasts forever, especially mouth-watering investment yields.

It's wise to remember two basic rules of investing: first, never invest in something you don't understand; and, second, never invest unless you know precisely under what conditions you'd sell. The first one will keep you from doing something dumb; the second will assure that you'll do something smart.

Confidence comes easily once you've seen a few of your decisions pay off. Maybe you invest a few thousand dollars in an international equity mutual fund just as economies overseas start to rebound. You watch as your money earns a nifty 20 percent return in six months. (In 1985–86, some international funds rose over 90 percent!) At this point, you're feeling pretty good—after all, you didn't follow Cousin Ralph's advice and throw your money down a high-risk rathole. But the danger is that you'll become too sure of yourself.

Investment risk, however, can be easily managed if you know how to proceed. Think about it. If you are a motorist, you know that a car can be a lethal weapon. (Bostonians, are you listening?) But if you learn how to manage that risk by driving defensively, tempering your lead foot, and following the rules, you can turn that weapon on wheels into a safe mode of comfortable transport. You can then have easy access to those new experiences that make life worthwhile: friends, movies, sightseeing, shopping for compact disks, etc. A managed risk can be rather profitable—the fear of taking that risk can paralyze you.

This is where competence comes in. Keeping your eyes wide open, and following an investment strategy that balances risk and reward in a very personal way, you'll avoid making expensive mistakes. (You'll also avoid sarcastic remarks from Cousin Ralph.) We'll give you some pointers on strategy below when we explain how you can time your investments to take advantage of market trends.

### Investments Come in All Shapes and Sizes

As we look at how investments differ, you'll realize that you must construct a portfolio that fits like a glove. (After all, that *is* the challenge here—blending the earning power of your money with the way you conduct your life.) If you are new to investing, a quick study of the basics will help; more seasoned investors may want to skip down to the section on market timing.

Investments vary in their:

- Current yield.
- Potential total return—you know how much you'll earn on an 11.5 percent certificate of deposit, but the sky's the limit (and the sea bottom's the floor) when you plunk money down for shares of a start-up company.
- Risk—some investments, like U.S. Treasury bills, are safe, at least as long as the United States government hasn't been overthrown; others, however, ask you to risk your principal in return for the mere *promise* of hefty profits. You have a unique investment personality that, among other things, determines how much risk you can assume and still sleep at night.

- Volatility—some investments have a fairly predictable return or stable value; others "whipsaw" up and down.
- Transaction costs—an important and often ignored factor. If you're a knowledgeable investor, you can avoid "hidden charges." Depending on the vehicle, fees for opening, maintaining, or closing the account, or fees for trading your holdings, can be either negligible or quite high. At first, you may not worry about investment costs (such as early withdrawal penalties on bank CDs or those sleazy fees charged by some load mutual funds to reinvest dividends), but they can be a drain on your annual return.
- Tax consequences—some forms of investment return are tax exempt; some are merely tax-favored; and others are fully taxed at ordinary income tax rates. What's more, sometimes you can use a loss to offset a taxable gain and come out ahead, in the process weeding the losers out of your portfolio.
- Liquidity—you can pull funds, at par (principal value does not fluctuate), out of a money market mutual fund any time you want it. And you can probably find a buyer for a "blue chip" stock or bond whenever you want to sell, though not necessarily at the price you'd like or even the price you paid (price *does* fluctuate when you invest in stocks and bonds). But it can be very tough to find a buyer for small company stock, or for your interest in a real estate syndication.

Worse, you may have agreed to keep your money tied up for a certain amount of time. If so, you may get hit by an *opportunity cost*—that is, you're locked into a fixed-return for a given time period (until the investment "matures") when you could be making relatively higher profits somewhere else.

There are also *degrees* of liquidity you must consider. For example, you may have $4,000 stashed in a stock fund that you went to great lengths to select. The prospectus said you could redeem your shares any time. So far, so good. But you failed to notice that the fund company does *not* offer switching, via a toll-free phone call, into a money market mutual fund with check-writing privileges. Sure enough, the proverbial you-know-what hits the fan. Your roof just caved in and you need a fast down payment for the housing contractor. You can call your stock fund and ask them to mail you a check. But you'll have to watch your mailbox, deposit your redemption check, wait for it to clear, wait some more for it to clear (thank you, banking industry)—only then can you use your own money!

Is that what you call a liquid investment? Certainly not, especially when you could have invested in an equally hot stock fund that lets you switch into a money fund with check writing. Need the dough? Make a call and write a check. The point to keep in mind is that there's liquidity, and then there is liquidity coupled with instant access—the ability to sell an investment at the drop of a hat and have instant use of your cash.

How do you know which mutual fund companies offer solid performance, no-load funds (no sales charge), and the ability to switch among funds as market conditions change (or as your house crumbles around you)? If you turn to appendix A, you'll see a list of SLYC funds. (SLYC stands for the features you should look for in mutual funds: safety, liquidity, yield, and catastrophe-proofing.) *Donoghue's MONEYLETTER* tracks the investment results of these well-respected growth equity and money market mutual funds. Of course, we chose the funds that offer you the maximum flexibility, strong historical track records, responsible management, and no-loads. Although we also track the top-performing equity funds that impose a small sales charge (so-called low-load funds), we strongly recommend the no-load route, all things considered. (More on no-load and low-load funds below.)

### Diversify Once, Diversify Again

The concept of investment diversification is often misunderstood. In short, the idea is to avoid putting all you eggs in one basket. It makes much more sense to spread your risks among investments. However, some folks go overboard, investing in a stock market mutual fund, a money fund, a bond fund, a "hot" stock, an insurance program, a savings account, and several retirement plans. As a result, they never have the time to track the performance of all their investments—and they inadvertently risk receiving only mediocre returns or, worse, finding that the rotten eggs have wiped out the returns produced by the winners. Smart diversification means identifying risks and reducing your exposure to them. For example, in the spring of 1986, we advised our newsletter readers that the U.S. stock market seemed due for a correction (a temporary decline). We told them to move some of their money earmarked for stock funds into two international stock funds. When the Dow Jones Industrial Average dropped 62 points on July 7, our readers didn't get too upset—their stock market investments were well-diversified. That's the point of good diversification strategies.

### What's a "Good" Investment?

The definition of a "good" investment depends on your life-style. For example, can you afford to gamble with, and maybe lose, some of your funds; or do you just want enough regular fixed income to maintain your current living standard? A good investment is also one that matches your investment objectives; it is also in sync with how much you know about the financial markets and the amount of time you're willing to commit to learning more. Finally, a good investment is one you make after carefully considering all the factors we mentioned above: current yield; total potential return; your ability to tolerate investment risk; transaction costs; taxes; liquidity; and need for diversification.

For example, a retiree may prefer an investment that provides steady dividend payments that can augment Social Security. On the other hand, a young rocket scientist making relatively big bucks might be wise to load up on company stock—especially if the company is headed for the new issues market.

Another example has to do with your ability to afford and/or tolerate risk. Is your peaceful nightly shut-eye contingent upon whether your investment is backed by federal deposit insurance? Many people feel strongly about putting money only in banks that are insured by the Federal Deposit Insurance Corporation—despite the fact that banks are failing in record numbers; despite the fact that there may not be enough FDIC funds to bail out all the ailing banks; and, finally, despite the fact that the alternative to bank deposits, money market mutual funds, have an impeccable safety record. But, in the final analysis, if you just can't stomach the idea of pulling your money out of your local FDIC insured bank, then at least you know something about your own investment personality—either that, or you know a whole lot about your stomach.

Then there's the matter of investment goals. For example, if you're funding an individual retirement account, and you have thirty years to go before you get the gold watch, maybe you'll want your nest egg in very aggressive stock market investments. Since your investment is going to have thirty years to gain ground, lose ground, and make it all back again, why not strive for mega-growth and frost the cake with tax deferral of investment earnings?

These few scenarios are intended to show why investing is such a personal endeavor. Everyone is different, with different needs, goals, and tax plans. (But there is only *one* IRS.) We can explain investment features and approaches, the major markets, how and why returns vary from the money market to the bond market to the stock market, and so on, but you're the only person to decide the makeup of your eventual portfolio.

### Risk Versus Return

A classic way to explain risk versus return is to say that you have to strike a balance between eating well and sleeping well. Put another way, to earn high returns, you usually have to accept some risk of performance failure, or even the risk of losing some of your investment (see figure 1). *Fortune* magazine calls it "finding the path between fear and greed."

The risk-return equation is strictly a multiple-choice: there are no right or wrong answers, only answers that fit your personal needs. Usually, though not always, the possibility of return goes up as risk does. After all, if you knew you could get an absolutely safe 10 percent return on your money, you'd have to be crazy to invest in something that would pay somewhere between absolutely nothing and 8 percent—especially if "such a deal" calls for risking some or all of your principal in the process.

Furthermore, there is more to risk than meets the eye. There are several kinds of risk you must consider, including:

- Risk of decrease in return over time. That is, if you invest in an income-oriented mutual fund, you may get a return equivalent to 9 percent annually in the month of your initial investment—but that may drop to only 7 percent six months later.
- Risk of loss of capital—if you invest in a money market mutual fund, you may be disappointed in the return (money funds just about mirror the current cost of cash in our society at any point in time), but you *can* be sure that you'll get your initial investment back. If you invest in a share of common stock, you may never get *any* dividends, and the price of the stock may go down. However, even if the company goes bankrupt, you can't be forced to pay any of the corporation's debts; the maximum loss is your entire investment. There are some investments—for example, short sales and selling "naked options" (see chapter 15)—where you can lose *more* than you invest. As you can imagine, you should stay out of such investments unless you're *sure* you know what you're doing, or if you don't really mind losing the money just for the excitement of the game. (As essayist Roy Blount, Jr., described the caveperson's learning process: "Well, now I know not to barbecue a live mammoth that close to the hut . . . sure glad I got to see it, though.")
- Risk of falling behind inflation: a particular concern for those who are

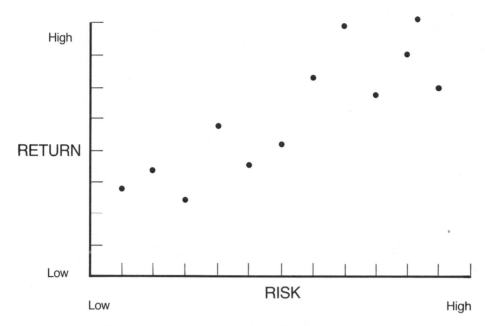

**Figure 1    Risk and return characteristics of hypothetical investments.**

heavily, or entirely, invested in fixed-income instruments (e.g., bonds that they hold to maturity). But wouldn't you rather have 100,000 devalued, inflation-ridden dollars than 50,000 devalued, inflation-ridden dollars? And whatever you do, as long as you can preserve your capital, you're better off investing (even unsuccessfully) than stuffing the money in the mattress or keeping it in a passbook savings account.

• "Woulda-coulda-shoulda" risk: you buy a stock for $19 a share and it goes up ten points. Your sister-in-law buys a stock for $19 a share and it goes up twenty-two points. So, being human, you probably think that you lost money. The money you could have earned if you'd chosen a different investment isn't a real loss. Anyway, don't believe everything people tell you about their investment successes (or their investment failures, if they're trying to borrow money). Investment boasts, like sexual boasts, should trade at a deep discount.

### Coping with Risk

There are a number of ways you can reduce risk: by buying government or government-insured securities; by sticking to blue chip stocks; by buying insured investments; by diversifying your holdings among the three major markets (the money market, equity, and bond markets) and among investments within each market; by getting hybrid investments like convertible bonds or convertible preferred stock (see chapter 15); and by investing in mutual funds, rather than investing in the markets directly. We strongly urge you to go the mutual fund route, unless you have the wherewithal to take on the bulls and bears all by yourself. The bottom line—if you'll excuse the lingo—is that there's no such thing as a free lunch, and, it follows, no such thing as free insurance against investment risk. The reassurance that you won't tumble into the basement may keep you out of the penthouse.

## Managing Your Portfolio Maturity

To be a successful investor, you have to be able to make long-range plans for your portfolio, not just make the single investment you think you can afford today. You have to distinguish between cash for immediate needs; short-term parking of funds; a small, highly liquid reserve for emergencies; and investments you can buy and hold until the optimum time for selling arrives. You should also distinguish between money you know you'll need at a given point in time—say, for your retirement, for a European vacation, or for education expenses—and money that is, as they say on Wall Street, "discretionary." Discretionary investment funds represent money you won't enjoy losing, but can do without if you had to. Put another way, don't invest your next six months' mortgage payments in a risky, high-tech stock fund.

Furthermore, the more time you have before you need a particular sum, the more risk you can take. For instance, your child's college fund can absorb more investment risk if little Sallie is only four, and not sixteen. Why? There's more time to recoup any losses.

The best of all possible worlds is a risk-free investment with a high return. As you can imagine, these fabled creatures are hard to find. For a while, money market mutual funds, yielding an absolutely safe 16 percent or 17 percent, were the answer to many investors' prayers. But interest rates have tumbled since the heady days of the money market fund rush (see figure 2).

## Why Interest Rates Are Crucial

In broad terms, there are two main reasons to invest: current income and growth. If you want current income, essentially, you become a lender. You lend someone (e.g., the issuer of a bond) some of your money. The borrower, which can be any entity from General Motors to the U.S. Treasury, pays you interest for the use of the money.

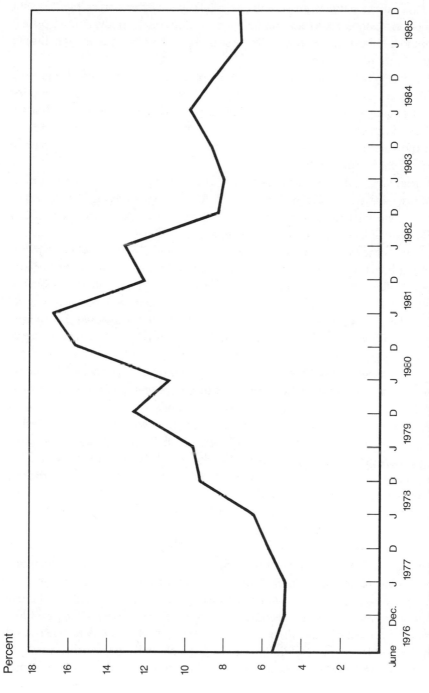

**Figure 2** Taxable money market mutual funds: historical yields, 1976–85. (*Source: Donoghue's Money Fund Report*)

In contrast, if you want growth, essentially, you become an owner. You buy shares in an enterprise (or a mutual fund owning shares in lots of enterprises), hoping that you can earn a profit later on by selling the shares after they've become more valuable.

Again in broad terms, investors favor bonds for income, stocks for growth. But it's not as simple as that. For one thing, many stocks pay income in the form of quarterly dividends—sometimes quite substantial dividends. For another thing, bond prices fluctuate, and you can make a profit by selling a bond for more than you paid for it—or, of course, lose money by dumping a bond for less than you put up.

Although there are a lot of factors determining stock and bond prices, interest rates are among the most crucial. After all, a bond issuer is a borrower, and no one will lend money at 6 percent when 10 percent returns are available elsewhere at the same level of risk—unless the 6 percent return is tax exempt or offers other tax advantages. If you own a bond already, and want to sell it, your bond will become less valuable as interest rates rise. That's because you're selling the right to receive, say, 7 percent in annual interest income. If 11 percent returns are common today, you'll have to cut the price of your bond to make it a worthwhile purchase. As interest rates go down, your bond becomes more valuable, because the right to receive 7 percent interest looks great if everyone else is only paying 6 percent.

But interest rates affect stocks, too. The corporations issuing the stocks have to borrow money to do business. If they have to spend too much money on interest, their profits will suffer, and dividends eventually may be cut or eliminated. If corporate profits slide steadily, they won't be able to invest in research, new equipment, better staff, new distribution channels, or advertising. Future growth will suffer. When the prospects for a corporation's earnings begin to look shaky, the "big boys" on Wall Street know what to do with their shares of stock: dump the stuff.

## Income Versus Growth Investments

For the investor, then, one of the fundamental choices is deciding how much to allocate to investments that are primarily income-oriented (e.g., bonds, preferred stock, and stocks with a history of paying high dividends) and those that are primarily growth-oriented (e.g., stocks that are now selling at a low price, but have the potential to become much more valuable). Wish you owned IBM in 1960? It was the darling of the growth stocks back then.

If interest rates have been rising, you'll want to favor certain income-oriented investments. However, if interest rates have been declining, you'll want to concentrate on growth-oriented investments—first, because you won't do too well buying newly issued bonds (though you may do well selling old ones), and second, because you hope that the companies you invest in will take advantage of low interest rates to expand and prosper. Of course, there are variations on these themes. We will see below, for example, that there are specially designed mutual funds, the growth-and-income funds, that seek a combination of growth and income. Unfortunately, many do only a mediocre job.

Our private investment management subsidiary, W. E. Donoghue & Co. (WEDCO), advises income-oriented clients to think in terms of how much cashflow they need, not how much income. We suggest that they arrange their finances to include a regular "check-a-month redemption program," which provides regular cashflow to pay bills and allows us more flexibility to invest their portfolios. You *can* have your cake and eat it too if you know how to cook.

### Allocating Your Money

In general, you'll need to decide where to launch your investment program, and how you want to diversify so you've got capital growth and income on the horizon. But these pleasant little mind-benders don't end there. You'll have to keep selecting investments—finding new ones or adding to what you've got already—as you generate new investment dollars. You will also have to reorganize your portfolio if you begin to draw on your investments to maintain your life-style. The idea is to allocate assets, new and old, to take advantage of market moves and keep in sync with life's notorious vagaries.

As you prepare to launch your investment program, you'll have to pick a mix of investments that is right for you. You'll need to decide which way the economy is heading; select the best-managed companies and stocks that will be most attractive to other investors; and select the safest bonds, the best government obligations, and the most convenient money market fund. Once you get rolling, you'll have to keep monitoring your portfolio for performance and suitability.

That's easy for us to say. How can you do all this and still earn a living? Some people love studying and monitoring investments; others would rather go to the dentist. Some people have a financial flair and a nose for picking the hottest new stocks; others can be counted on to be wrong. If you're in the second group in each case, or if you have a small investment kitty that won't stand up to repeated transaction costs, mutual fund investing may be for you.

### Ninotchka on Wall Street

In the film *Ninotchka,* Greta Garbo, the loveliest of commissars, invites some Bolshevik buddies to her home, where they pool their meager rations for dinner. "That's what socialism is," Garbo explains fervently. "Under capitalism, we would each be eating a boiled egg in our rooms. But together, we are having an *omelette!"*

### The Ease of Mutual Funds

However, even under capitalism, investors can pool their egg rations, so to speak—they can invest in a mutual fund. The fund, in turn, can invest in a portfolio far more diversified than the individual investors could afford. The fund can also trade actively, at commission rates lower than the individual investors could extort from their brokers.

The mutual fund also offers the benefits of professional management. In other words, there's a fund manager whose job it is to sort through annual reports, quarterly statements, industry journals, and leading indicators to decide *which* of nineteen start-up biotech companies is likely to prosper. He or she has to decide whether Poughkeepsie sewer bonds are a better bet than San Francisco revenue anticipation notes. (Nice work, if you can get it.)

### Types of Funds

Once again, exotic hybrids flourish, but these are the basic choices:

- *Money market.* A money market mutual fund invests in high-quality, short-term, debt instruments such as Treasury bills, commercial paper (corporate IOUs), large-dollar CDs issued by commercial banks, and bankers' acceptances. Some money market funds are "government only": they invest in nothing but government securities, for greater safety. But no money market fund invests in anything at all speculative. Because the maturities are so short, the funds can respond quickly if an investment seems likely to turn sour, or if interest rates are on the move. Money market funds, unlike other mutual funds, have a fixed share price of $1 a share; as your fund investment grows more valuable, you simply acquire more shares or receive a regular check. Money market funds usually give you easy access to your money through checks you write against your account. A limit on the number of checks permitted per month, and/or limits on the minimum amount of the checks you can write, are common.

- *Government securities funds.* These are easy to confuse with government-only money market funds. However, a government securities fund can invest in Ginnie Maes, Fannie Maes, and other government agency securities that are not backed by the full faith and credit of the federal government. While the government will promise to stand behind one of these issuers, there is no rock-solid guarantee that it will back every cent of agency debt. (See chapter 15 for more about Fannie and her friends.) A government securities fund, like other non-money-market mutual funds, has a fluctuating share price: you could buy shares for $3.19 each, say, and sell them for, well, $4.08 or $2.99 each, depending on conditions. The upshot? You could have a capital gain or loss in addition to income from the shares.

- *Bond funds.* These funds buy a diverse portfolio of long-term bonds issued by government, municipal, or corporate issuers. A true "managed" bond fund can buy or sell bonds in an effort to improve the return to investors and to replace bonds as they mature (i.e., are paid off). A unit investment trust, on the other hand, buys a certain number of bonds when it starts up, then holds those bonds to maturity, paying out interest to participants in the trust. But no further trades are made, as long as the trust is in force. As bonds mature, the principal is not reinvested—rather, it is returned to unitholders. Unit trusts have very low management fees (since nothing much has to be done after the initial purchases are made). They also pass up the opportunity to earn capital gains by actively trading bonds as bond prices fluctuate in response to interest rate changes. It is sometimes possible to sell your units back to the trust manager—note that the manager will probably earn more buying the units back than it earned selling them to you in the first place.

- Some funds invest in corporate bonds—some of which are safe but stodgy and low-yielding. Higher-yielding bonds are riskier; *junk bonds,* appropriately enough, are riskiest of all, but pay very high returns. A junk bond fund lets you play this high-stakes game with the benefit of professional management to sort out the likely defaulters from the corporations temporarily down on their luck.

- Investors have various reasons for buying or trading bonds, and there are various kinds of bond funds. There are *tax-exempt funds* that buy nothing but tax-exempt securities (generally, municipal bonds). If you live in a high-tax state (especially if your city also has an income tax), look for double and triple tax-exempts. The "doubles" escape state and federal taxation of income while the "triples" are free of local taxes as well.

- Tax-exempt investments in your portfolio may deserve special attention now that tax reform has arrived. After all, Congress went on a search-and-destroy mission for juicy tax shelters and just about obliterated them. The tax-exempt investments that survived—municipal securities—let you keep at least some investment returns from the clutches of the tax man, but keep in mind that the new lower tax rates essentially reduce the advantage that tax-exempts once held over fully taxable investments. You will have to carefully compare yields on tax-exempt and taxable securities. If you want shelter, our advice is to keep abreast of trends in the muni market, then invest if the numbers add up for you. Be aware that munis may deliver a few surprising twists and turns over the next few years. Experts agree that the muni market will be rather unpredictable—with securities prices and yields perhaps behaving strangely—until the full effects of tax reform are digested by market participants. This once rather staid market will take on a new degree of uncertainty, and for investors that may mean more risk and more potential returns.

The funds described above invest in income-oriented vehicles. Before adoption of the Tax Code of 1986 (TC '86), investors had to choose between investments producing dividend or interest income (taxable at ordinary income rates) and investments promising long-term capital gains (taxable at the lower long-term capital gains rate.) To qualify for long-term capital gains treatment, securities had to be held for longer than six months.

Tax reform just about eliminated the preferential tax treatment of long-term capital gains, but the distinction between ordinary income and capital gains and losses hasn't disappeared completely. For one thing, you can use losses on capital assets to offset gains on capital assets. That is, if you sell two stocks in the same year—say, 100 shares of Highflyer Enterprises at a gain of $5,000 and 100 shares of Mouldy Crypt at a loss of $2,000—you can use the loss to reduce your taxable profit to a mere $3,000.

If the luck of the draw had gone the other way, and you had lost $5,000 on Mouldy Crypt and gained $2,000 on Highflyer, you could deduct the $3,000 loss from your ordinary income. However, you can't deduct more than $3,000 a year for capital losses in any year—but you can "carry over" the leftovers and use them in later years.

Anyway, a little vestige of the capital gains preference is retained, sort of like a fossilized fly in a lump of amber. For the record, TC '86 says that the maximum tax rate on any capital gain is 28 percent in 1987. It can be as high as 33 percent in subsequent years, depending on your income level.

How does all this affect your choice of investments? In essence, because long-term capital gains will now be taxed at ordinary income rates, you may feel that there is no longer sufficient reason to take on the higher level of risk that comes with investing for capital growth. That's the conventional wisdom, anyway. The Donoghue wisdom dictates that when the outlook for the stock market is promising, you ought to get in position to profit from equity invest-ments. In other words, you don't want to be invested in the fixed-income market when all the action is in equities just because the tax picture has changed. The tax consideration is only one part of your investment decision. What you really want to aim for is maximum after-tax returns, and when conditions are right you'll want to be in the stock market, which has tradition-ally outperformed the fixed-income market. We'll talk more about the stock market in chapter 15. Here's how equity mutual funds stack up:

- Aggressive growth funds specialize in low-priced stocks that they expect to soar in the future.
- Sector funds specialize in a particular industry—say, health care, high-tech, or gold mining (so-called gold funds invest in gold-mining stocks, not in the actual metal). Sector funds can range from very conservative to very speculative in investment policy.
- Growth funds also look to future increase in value, rather than current income, in their investment policies, but take fewer risks than aggressive growth funds.
- Growth-and-income funds invest in blue chip companies that pay high, steady dividends *and* provide good—but not great—capital growth dur-ing market upturns. The steady dividends act as a cushion during stock market bummers.
- Income funds concentrate on high-yielding stocks such as utility issues and preferred stock.

As a general rule, large funds (with assets over $50 million) tend to perform better than small funds. They can afford to diversify more—if a fund has invested 3 percent of its assets in a stock that turns sour, it suffers more than if it had ½ of 1 percent of assets in that stock.

Even better for investors, many mutual funds (like many investors) are part of a fund family. So you can choose a family of funds, and start out with half your investment in a money market fund, half in a growth-and-income fund.

Once you get the hang of it, you may want to switch part of your growth-and-income investment to an aggressive growth stock fund—that's where you can shoot for the maximum returns. When you really get cooking, you may want to try fund switching (explained below) and try to move toward the best market opportunities as they evolve. Many fund families offer funds for each of the major markets, and switches are free, at least up to a certain number per year. Others charge a nominal amount to switch.

Switching between mutual funds that aren't in the same family can be difficult at times. The Schwab Mutual Fund Marketplace makes buying, selling, and trading shares much easier. With over 250 no-load and low-load mutual funds, investors can, with one phone call to Schwab (1-800-526-8600), move into any of these funds. In addition, if you don't want to be fully invested but want your cash available for immediate use, Schwab allows you to park it in Kemper money funds.

Schwab charges a flat fee plus a small percentage of the principal amount on transactions. But if you are moving your investment directly from one fund to another, Schwab will charge you a fee only on the sale; the next day it will execute your designated purchase free of charge. Be warned, however, that if the fund you're selling charges a redemption fee (or back-end load), you must pay it in addition to any Schwab charges (More on loads below.)

For those of you who are willing risk-takers, the Mutual Fund Marketplace will allow you to purchase shares of mutual funds on margin. For instance, if you wanted to buy $20,000 of fund shares but had only half that amount available, you would be required to put your money in a margin account. Schwab would loan you the remainder. Your account would have a market value of $20,000, a loan balance of $10,000, and an equity (market less loan) value of $10,000. Your margin (equity value divided by market value) is 50 percent. Should your margin fall below 30 percent (i.e., your shares decline in value) you would get a call from Schwab to increase your margin account. The danger is that you might not have the cash needed and thus be forced to sell off part of your position.

### A Load of Loads

Speaking of charges, you wouldn't expect those nice fund managers to make your investment decisions for nothing, would you? All funds charge an annual management fee (typically in the area of ½ of 1 percent to 1 percent of your investment). Many funds charge an initial fee, or "front-end load," when you open your account; others charge a "back-end load" when you close out an account. Some funds, a really strange crowd—the "12b-1 funds"—charge for management and sales expenses. Basically, you kick in for their marketing budgets—and help pay the fat salaries of fund marketing managers.

Your job as a mutual fund investor is to pick a fund family that gives you the highest yield after taxes and after all transaction costs, an appetizing menu of fund alternatives, the best customer service—this includes convenient access to your money *and* perky, well-trained phone answerers—and responsible management.

## More on Loads

"A few more days for to tote the weary load . . . no matter, 'twill never be light . . . just a few more days 'till we totter on the road . . . then, my old Kentucky home, good-night!"

Well, weep no more, my lady or gent. You can find high-performance, no-load mutual funds and their low-load cousins (sales charge equals no more than 3 percent of your assets) in, you guessed it, *Donoghue's Mutual Fund Almanac* (call 1-800-343-5413). In case you're wondering, the original distinction was between load mutual funds (sold by brokers with sales charges equaling about 8.5 percent of your assets) and no-load funds (sold directly by the funds through ads in newspapers and magazines with no sales charges). Today, however, the lines are blurred, and many fund families contain both no-load and load or low-load funds.

In addition to a "front-end" load, which is charged when you buy into a fund, you may face a "back-end load" or "contingent deferred sales charge" of up to 6 percent of assets, which is charged when you sell your fund shares, or sell before you've held them for a certain length of time.

A "12b-1" fund (named after the SEC rule permitting them) is often described as a "no-load" fund because there's no initial sales charge. However, 12b-1 funds charge about ½ to 1¼ percent of your fund assets each year to cover commissions, distribution, and marketing costs. If the prospectus mentions a "distribution fee," that's what it means. If the prospectus doesn't mention a distribution fee, it still may be a 12b-1 fund.

A clue: check the expenses-to-net-assets ratio given in the prospectus. If it's much above the industry average of 0.70, you're likely to be looking at a 12b-1 fund. Whether or not the fund is a 12b-1, check the trend in the expense ratio. What you're looking for is a decline, over time. Some expenses are fixed, and there's not much the fund management can do about them. (That's one reason to favor large funds: the fixed expenses are a relatively smaller portion of total expenses, and expenses as a whole can be decreased by economies of scale.) But you want a fund that grows progressively more efficient.

We urge you to avoid the full-tilt load funds that hit you up for 8.5 percent of your assets. After all, why on earth do you need to fund a broker's vacation kitty when there are such sound choices available among the no-load and the low-load funds on the market? Traditionally, we preferred no-load funds; however, today we cannot ignore some of the true high fliers—Fidelity Investments' Magellan Fund, for instance—that have earned stellar returns for shareholders year in, year out, and charge a low load.

If you do find a low-load fund that offers you the kind of performance you want, check to see if the sales load is imposed on switches within the fund family, and whether it's imposed on sums you later add to your initial investment. You'll want to watch out for sneaky deals like loads charged on dividend reinvestments (you take your profits in the form of additional fund shares). In any case, a "no" answer is more reassuring for you. And compare the real cost over time—if you buy mutual fund shares and hold them (instead of switching or trading actively), you may do better with a low-load fund than with a 12b-1 fund that imposes a heavy—and annual—expense charge.

### Comparing Fund Performance

After all, you don't want to invest in a fund just because they can hire a good design firm to produce ads and brochures. You're interested in investment performance that meets your objectives (safety; after-tax results; good customer service; and, perhaps, balance between current income and growth).

The yields quoted in mutual fund ads are only a first step in the analysis. For one thing, funds tend to project the performance of the best week or month as if it could be sustained for a whole year. For another thing, funds have different practices in computing yield: which expenses are included, what assumptions are made about reinvestment of dividends and profits, and the like. So your best bet is to consult the annual roundups in investment-oriented magazines like *Money, Forbes,* or *Fortune,* or check out the *Almanac.* But remember: you can't be sure who'll win this year's World Series or Kentucky Derby just by reading last year's sports pages. A fund that does well in a bull market (one where stock prices are rising) can get wiped out in a declining (bear) market.

That's one reason why wise investors tend to prefer well-established funds to new ones: they can see how the fund did in both good and bad years. (To eliminate this scrutiny, some funds simply buy shares of all the stocks in the Standard & Poor's 500, the Dow, or some other index; these "index funds" naturally do exactly as well as the index, so they can't be accused of falling behind—but can't do any better, either.)

To some investors, this track record is an important tool: they will invest in a fund that does better than the pack in down years, even if it isn't the zippiest fund in years when the market is up. This is less of a consideration for other investors, who rely on indicators and their sense of market timing to switch out of a fund in down years.

## Market Timing and the Donoghue Investment Strategy

The Donoghue Investment Strategy is a multifaceted tool for selecting top-performing mutual funds and keeping your investment portfolio in tune with the markets. That means investing in stock market mutual funds when the stock market is rising and avoiding them when stock prices are falling. No system is infallible, of course, but the Donoghue Strategy can certainly help you seize many investment opportunities—and avoid costly mistakes you'd probably incur if you flew solo.

If you had followed the investment strategy outlined in my second book, *William E. Donoghue's No-Load Mutual Fund Guide,* for the five years ended June 30, 1986, and invested in the top five funds listed in *Donoghue's MONEYLETTER,* you could have earned over 26 percent a year—and your money would have tripled. You could also have beat the performance of nearly all of the top mutual funds.

The Donoghue Strategy is a conservative approach in that it strives to safeguard your assets by avoiding losses. It was built on several strategic components to help you respond confidently to economic events, especially changes in interest rates. It helps you get in position for major stock market moves, both bullish and bearish. By telling you when to increase or decrease your holdings in carefully chosen equity funds—and where to invest when the stock market is on the blink—the Donoghue Strategy delivers more investment profits than you could possibly earn with the old buy-hold-pray approach.

"But is it risky?" you ask. Compared to other fonts of investment advice, the Donoghue Strategy is rather conservative, since it attempts to spot substantial, long-term market moves. In other words, we won't have you trading your portfolio of mutual funds on a daily basis. Keep in mind, however, that every approach to stock market investing involves a certain level of risk.

Finally, as you'll see below, the Donoghue Strategy is extremely easy to use. It's simple without being simplistic. You don't have to waste hour after frustrating hour attempting to decipher confusing statistics and investment legalese.

## What Happened to SLYC?

Loyal readers of earlier Donoghue books will recall the evolution from SLY to SLYC (safety, liquidity, yield, and catastrophe-proofing). What we now call the Donoghue Strategy is simply a much more sophisticated version of the SLYC system. The idea now is to incorporate mutual fund industry innovations and address the growing savvy of investors operating in today's highly volatile market environment.

When the first Donoghue book, *William E. Donoghue's Complete Money Market Guide,* was published in 1981, short-term interest rates were near 18 percent, exorbitant inflation and recession were terrorizing the American economy, and many folks were scared stiff by the stock market.

We all know that the economy and the financial markets have changed tremendously since then. And it was the nature of that change that led us to develop the next logical step for SLYC. We studied how the market shot to record-breaking heights and, in the process, grew so very complex and so dangerously volatile—what with program trading, portfolio insurance, risky option plays, and the like making the job of the individual investor darned near impossible.

What's more, we asked investors how they wanted to participate in the surging bull market without losing their shirts. Folks who attended our seminars, wrote letters to our office, and subscribed to *Donoghue's MONEYLET-TER* all seemed to be saying loud and clear: "The current bull market is too good to be true; direct investment in the stock market is too risky. We want to know which equity funds—low-load and no-load—will likely outperform the pack, and we want to know when it's safe to take the plunge. Moreover, we want to know when to put only a portion of our money in the stock market and when to go whole-hog."

The Donoghue Strategy meets these investor needs. To see how it works, let's walk through a step-by-step, decision-making process for choosing and investing in equity mutual funds.

## Fund Selection

First, you'll need a fund family that offers convenient telephone switches (and doesn't put too low a limit on the number of switches you can make before incurring a per-switch fee); a low minimum investment requirement and a low additional investment requirement; and preferably a choice of at least a money market fund, a bond fund, and several equity funds with different approaches to the risk/return equation. If you want to switch among equity funds sold by different fund families, you may want to use the Schwab Mutual Fund Marketplace. As we explained earlier, you can open an account with the Schwab Mutual Fund Marketplace and conveniently switch among funds from different families and have instant access to the Kemper money funds. (The Kemper money funds, by the way, have been consistent top performers over the years.) As we'll see below, being able to move into a money fund with one quick phone call comes in handy when the stock market heads south. Whether you use Schwab or a fund family that offers a full menu of equity, bond, and money funds, your goal is to invest only in funds that offer instant liquidity—the ability to move your money in a day—with a simple phone call. Obviously, a toll-free 800 number is ideal.

How do you begin to select funds? First, refer regularly to *Donoghue's Mutual Funds Almanac.* Published annually, the *Almanac* gives crucial details on more than 1,400 funds. Our twice-monthly newsletter, *Donoghue's MONEYLETTER,* reports on the performance of the funds included in our carefully selected "fund universe" and lists the ones we think are especially hot. *MONEYLETTER* has recently been redesigned to include "Donoghue's Recommendations"—a list of our current buy, hold, and sell signals. Although we now include low-load funds with stellar returns, we suggest that you go the no-load route when their returns are competitive. After all, why pay a 3 percent sales charge when a no-load fund is just as good? (We'll bet that our newsletter currently has a "sell" recommendation on a fund you now own.) *Donoghue's MONEYLETTER* also notes funds we currently do *not* recommend. (For a free sample, call 1-800-343-5413.)

Our specific advice on which equity funds look to beat the pack—and which funds are preparing for a nosedive—is based on our analysis of fund performance over three key time periods: four weeks, six months, and twelve months. (We considered longer time periods, such as five years, but tests showed they did not provide useful data on which funds are likely to outperform the competition in the near future.) To this analysis we apply a weighting factor, which identifies the consistent winners and at the same time weeds out flash-in-the-pan funds that occasionally land by fluke on our four-week, top-ten list. We assign to each fund a numerical rank, which reflects overall fund performance by taking into account the different time periods. The ranking lets you choose funds that have delivered consistent top performance.

When we developed the Donoghue Strategy, we knew that a ranking system based purely on past performance only gets you halfway there. So we designed a built-in trend confirmation system that attempts to spot funds that will likely provide consistent, strong returns in the future and, just as important, will spot funds that are losing position and will likely remain back in the pack. Here's how we confirm a fund's performance trend.

To achieve a buy signal, a fund must be on Donoghue's top-ten list—that is, ranked one through ten by our time-weighted analysis—for three consecutive weeks. We issue the buy signal on the confirmation of the trend on the third week. If a fund drops from the ten spot and into the eleven-to-fifteen range, we attach a hold signal. Of course, a hold only applies to a fund on which we have issued a buy. Then, if the fund comes back onto our top-ten list, it must go through the three-week confirmation process all over to once again achieve a buy signal. Should a fund drop below the fifteen mark for two consecutive weeks, it then becomes a sell. When necessary, we put on our qualitative hats and study a fund's particular operating environment. Once in a great while, we may need to override the signals generated by our mechanical system—for example, if a famous, top-notch portfolio manager suddenly quits or becomes seriously ill, we might want to advise you to proceed with caution until the new portfolio manager gets the situation under control. Because we are in very close touch with the fund companies, we learn about problems almost as soon as they occur.

Like any other system forecasting future relative performance, the Donoghue approach stubs its toe now and then, but it does so infrequently. If a fund is a consistently good performer, our tracking system will pick it up, and we will continue to recommend it as long as it delivers a relatively attractive investment result. On the other hand, if one of our buys ceases to perform and stumbles badly, our tracking system will quickly flag it, and we will recommend that you move out of that fund. The beauty of the system is that it is dynamic —it moves you in and out of funds based on how they are performing. Our system helps you avoid painful losses and those sleepless nights that come from investing in a fund before it slumps, and waiting—perhaps forever—for it to rebound just so you can break even.

It's important to note that the Donoghue Strategy is not built on a hair trigger. Based on our extensive testing, we know that the system does not change its buy and sell list with every twist of the stock market. The Donoghue Strategy is by nature geared for long-term investment profits.

### Moving in Time

The mention of market twists and turns brings us to the final component of the Donoghue Strategy: our system for timing major stock market moves. There has been a lot written lately about this business of timing the market. Magazine articles attempt to describe this or that timing system (they come in a variety of shapes and sizes). Often, readers are left confused about what "timing the market" really means. Let's set the record straight. The purpose of market timing is to take advantage of two important investment techniques: avoiding losses and improving the efficiency of compounding investment returns. When we say timing, we refer to an investment strategy that tries to allocate money, either totally or partially, in the stock market at the most lucrative times. Obviously, you want to load up on promising stock funds just when the bull is about to take off. (Remember, a bull market can last months or years.) At such a time, share prices are relatively low and you stand to earn substantial profits. The trick, however, is to sell out near the top and preserve your capital. If you can do that, you avoid the big decline and, more important, are prepared to buy back in at bargain prices after the market has dropped. That way, your money compounds its investment returns at higher and higher rates.

When the bull is tuckered out, you want to seek shelter in the money market, where the value of your principal does not fluctuate and your money earns current money market rates. At such a time, the idea is to avoid painful stock market declines and get your money earning a decent return in the money market—not the negative returns produced by a retreating bull. This is the essence of market timing: adding incremental return to what would otherwise be gained through the old buy-hold-pray approach.

Finally, when the market is, as they say on Wall Street, trading sideways (going neither up nor down but fluttering a lot), you may want to have some portion of your money in the stock market and some in the money market. When the U.S. stock market is looking shaky and/or trading sideways, and there are indications that economies overseas may offer strong investment rewards, you may also want to have some of your money invested in an international growth stock fund. Such a fund invests in promising companies in other countries. (Worried about being an unpatriotic investor? Isn't that a Honda in your driveway?)

"But how," you ask, "can you tell when the time is right to move money in or out of the U.S. stock market?" That's the key question for all market timing systems. You should realize that no system—including ours—can perfectly call every market top and bottom. A good system, however, based as it should be on sound economic principles and managed by market experts, can help get you in the stock market when strong gains are possible and out when the weather turns nasty. Based on extensive testing of past market performance, we know that the Donoghue Strategy should do the trick. It has shown that it can beat the performance of the S&P 500, a traditional benchmark, and we are confident that its underlying indicators, when analyzed by our team of experts, can identify long-term market trends.

While we believe the Donoghue Strategy will help you become a successful and confident investor, we want you to keep in mind that, like all systems, it has been tested against past market results. There's no way to guarantee that the market will always perform as it has in the past. Any system that tries to entice you with such guarantees is a fraud.

### The Technicals of Timing

Here's how our system works. Our calls are based on an analysis of three long-term indicators of major stock market moves. By major, we mean moves that represent at least a 10 percent fluctuation in the Dow Jones Industrial Average. A 10 percent change in the Dow, by the way, would include so-called market corrections. (Other timing systems, which try to catch every small turn of the market, are really only appropriate for the "pros" who work for institutional investors such as pension funds and brokerage houses.)

Every indicator has its own strengths and weaknesses. Some are good at predicting market tops (sell signals), others are good at market bottoms (buy signals). We chose a mix of indicators that would enable us to call both market tops and bottoms. Our indicators have also shown, through extensive testing, an ability to give clear signals. In other words, when we signal that the bull is ready to go on a rampage (or, conversely, slump down in the grass), we're really sure about it. When a market surge is about to occur, we tell you to invest 100 percent in equities. When that bull market is on its last legs, we tell you to move 100 percent into the money market until a new bull appears on the field. Finally, when our indicators disagree, we know that we're probably in for a spell of sideways trading. At such a time, we recommend that you allocate various portions of your money between the stock and money markets. International stock funds may be recommended as well. The ultimate goal at such a time is not only to have some participation in the stock market but also to maintain a healthy margin of safety by sheltering some of your dollars in the money market.

Our technically minded readers will want to know what indicators we chose. Here goes. (You do not need to understand the underlying technicals, or what they do, to use our system; you just have to follow its advice.) The three indicators are: (1) mutual fund cash positions, which are excellent predictors of market bottoms; (2) the relationship between long-term and short-term interest rates, known as the yield curve, which is very good at calling market tops; and (3) the average maturity index of institutions-only money market funds, a fine tool for calling both tops and bottoms. Given what we know about the direction of the market at any time, we assign a certain weighting to each indicator to come up with clear and comprehensive timing signals.

Readers of all three previous Donoghue books will recognize the phrase "money fund average maturity." Our original SLYC system recommended investment positions based on where interest rates were headed. It was, and remains, our view that the direction of interest rates drives the stock market. When we used SLYC to time the market, we knew where interest rates were heading by watching for changes in the average maturity of money funds.

The Donoghue Strategy described here builds on that tradition—one of its indicators is the average maturity figure for institutions-only money funds. (These special money funds are only available to large institutional investors.) We chose that indicator over the average maturity figure for all money funds because we have found, again through extensive testing, that it is much more sensitive to interest rate trends and, therefore, a better predictor of imminent stock market moves. You can see that the Donoghue Strategy, which was unveiled in late 1986, has its roots in our earlier work.

How can you put the Donoghue Strategy to work for you? First, decide how much you can afford as an initial investment, then get your hands on a current copy of *Donoghue's MONEYLETTER.* On page 1 you will find a list of the stock mutual funds that we feel offer the strongest potential returns. Check page 3 for the box entitled "Current Advice." This tells three types of investors (conservative, active, and venturesome) exactly what percentage of money should be placed in U.S. stock funds, in international stock funds, and in a money fund. Our economic commentary offers a detailed rationale for our current positions. (By the way, when you subscribe, you fill out a "risk questionnaire," which helps you decide whether you're a conservative, active, or venturesome investor.)

It may sound as though we're just pushing you to subscribe to our newsletter. While we certainly like to see circulation increase, the fact is we sincerely believe that many mutual fund investors can't achieve superior investment results without expert help. Many people don't have the time, energy, or wherewithal to study the economy and the relative performance of mutual funds on a regular basis. They also lack the confidence to act on their own.

Our original SLYC system was very much "do it yourself." In past books, we taught you how to gauge interest rate trends by watching for changes in a very special number: the average maturity of money market mutual funds. The Donoghue Organization compiles that statistic weekly, and it is published in newspapers nationwide. As we mentioned earlier, the financial markets have become extremely complex and volatile—today, you need more than the average maturity number. Quite frankly, the only way you can keep on top of things is to receive regular, expert advice on market trends and fund performance.

### Other Market Indicators

Interest rates on three-month Treasury bills (rates are quoted in the financial pages of newspapers) are a good indicator of short-term interest rates. Longer-term Treasury bonds give you information about long-term interest trends. (Again, the figures will be in the paper.) In "normal" times, the rates for T-bonds should be higher, because lenders usually demand extra return for tying up their money for longer periods.

When both T-bills and T-bonds move down, this is a "bullish" indicator, suggesting stock prices will rise (and also suggesting that you may want to be invested in the stock market). When T-bill rates top T-bond rates, it's a "bearish" signal. That's because this interest-rate pattern hints that corporations are borrowing heavily in the short term, fearing a later rise in interest rates. If they're right, you'll want to be in the money market, because then, in effect, you'll be a lender and will be able to profit by higher interest rates.

### Reading Mutual Fund Tables

If you're moseying through the financial pages anyway, and you'd like to read the mutual fund tables, here's how:

- The table has four columns—the abbreviated name of the fund or fund family is the first.
- The second column gives the NAV (net asset value) per share as of the close of trading on the preceding business day.
- The third column is the "asked price"—what you'd have to pay if you bought a share. In a no-load fund, the asked price equals the NAV; in a load fund, it equals NAV plus sales charges.
- The fourth column gives the change since yesterday: up ⅛ of a dollar, down 1¼ dollars per share, or whatever.

### You Prefer to Fly Solo?

There are, no doubt, some readers who want to try managing direct market investments. If you think you can achieve a better return than that available through funds, then you may be interested in more advanced (and riskier) investment techniques than those we've already described.

You may want to buy and hold, or buy and trade, individual stocks and bonds. You may be interested in tangible investments, such as real estate, gold, or collectibles. If you find risk more amusing than terrifying, you may want to trade stock or commodity options. Chapter 15 is an introduction to the perils and pleasures you'll encounter—but only an introduction. Be sure you understand what you're doing before you commit your money.

A word of advice: if you're 100 percent invested in stocks, be sure to check your holdings at least once a month. If your portfolio is down 10 percent from its recent top, think seriously about selling (you'll probably still have profits—you're just selling because there is a downward trend, not an actual loss yet). You may want to wait until things look better before making any further equity investments. This piece of advice, of course, can also apply to investors who decide to invest in the stock market through mutual funds.

Another idea for readers who want to experience the thrill of direct market investing: before you make the big leap, spend six months or a year managing a "paper portfolio": pick an amount to be invested, decide how you'd invest, and follow the daily financial pages and see how you'd have done if you had invested real money. The exercise will show you if you're adept or all thumbs when it comes to picking investments and knowing when to switch. It'll also reveal your attitude toward the work involved in active portfolio management. Do you grin or groan each day when you settle down to review financial facts and the status of your hypothetical portfolio? Do even imaginary losses strike you as tragedies? Don't forget to consider taxes and transaction costs in your paper portfolio—many a real investor has earned profits, only to see them wiped out by brokerage costs or taxes.

## CASE HISTORY
### *Investment Basics*

"Aw, c'mon, Pauline," Nick Donato said. "It's not like we're going to go to Las Vegas gambling the money. Come to think of it, we didn't do that badly that time we went to Vegas."

"Remember all those articles in the paper about young kids preparing for retirement, and how they can afford to take some risks because they've got lots of time to make up for it if they fall on their fannies? Well, you *are* retired, and I'm getting ready. We can't afford to take the risk."

"We can't afford to take a *lot* of risks," he explained. "But we have all the money in a tax-exempt bond fund. Hell, we're not in that high a bracket anyway, and we get lots of tax breaks for being senior citizens. Lets say we leave most of the money right where it is. But I think we should buy some stocks, and some other bonds, and try to earn some more money."

"I'm still not happy about the chance we could lose money," Pauline said.

"Then maybe we should start out real easy and cautious. Suppose we do some research, read some books, maybe call up that radio show that gives advice to the seniors. Don't get me wrong. First of all, I'm not too hot on the idea of waking up broke at my age. Second of all, we don't have to do all the picking ourselves. We can invest in some mutual funds. That way, it's like we send one check, and we have a whole bunch of different investments. And there's somebody who's supposed to know what to do, picking them out."

"If he knows what to do," Pauline asked darkly, "why is he still working for some mutual fund somewhere?"

"I don't know. Maybe it's a girl, and no one will give her a job like being in charge of a bank, even though she's this financial genius, because they're prejudiced. But when I was out fishing last week—" a pause for a groan from Pauline—"Jerry Millman from down the street was out on the boat. He was telling me that he has shares in a couple of different mutual funds, and he just switches back and forth when one of them isn't so good, so he can make more money. And he told me how much he started out with, and how much he has now. Even if I double the first amount and cut the second one in half, it still sounds pretty good."

"And if this financial genius can pick a good fund, how come he was so dumb he picked the bad one in the first place?"

"He says it's not really a question of good and bad. It's just that the stock market changes. Sometimes business is good, and the stock market is way up, and then you want to own a lot of stock. Sometimes business isn't so great, or everybody's running out borrowing money, so you want to own bonds so that basically you're lending them money."

"Well, there's a lot of financial stuff in the public library," Pauline said, beginning to warm to the idea a little. "I guess we could study and read all about it, and learn what to do. You remember Mrs. Antonucci, from Henderson Street? Well, her son Johnny is doing very well as a stockbroker."

"I bet you'd get to like it, once we started investing," Nick said. "You were never much of a sports fan, so you don't understand how I feel when I root for my teams. Once we pick out some mutual funds, or if we go on and buy some stocks, you know, separately, then they'll be our teams, and we'll root for them."

"I just hope we don't lose too much," Pauline said. "I know perfectly well that you used to bet five or ten bucks on the football pools at work! And it wasn't a big deal if you lost—*when* you lost—because it was for fun, just like going to the movies. But we can't gamble with the money we have to live on."

"Guaranteed, no gambling," Nick said. "We won't buy any of those brand-new stocks that claim if you pay a dollar today some other nut will buy it from you tomorrow for fifty dollars even though the company doesn't know when they're going to finish inventing a cure for cancer or whatever. We'll just get mutual funds that buy good, solid stocks; or that buy bonds so we'll get a check every month."

"Maybe I should call Mrs. Antonucci's Johnny and ask him for the name of a broker down here. His firm might have an office."

"We don't even have to do that. Millman says that he buys all his funds through the mail, right from the fund, and it costs less because there's no fee for the stockbroker."

"And it's not like buying, you know, sweaters through the mail? You don't have a lot of annoyances?"

"He says not, they're very reputable. And, anyway, I bet everything goes through some central computer somewhere. So they could just as well take your instructions from the mail, or from the telephone, and put it in the computer."

After many hours spent reading about investments—the library had a great collection, and it comprised some of the best-circulated books and magazines in town—and many hours on the phone with their kids, they chose a no-load fund family.

They decided to leave one-third of the money already invested in tax-exempt bonds in the bond fund; they considered that their "bedrock" money. They split the remaining funds in half, between a money market fund with check-writing privileges (which allowed them to cut down on the balance in their non-interest-bearing checking account) and a growth-and-income fund. After all, they had a life expectancy of at least fifteen years, and hoped that they could benefit by continued growth in the economy. They also hoped that they would be able to leave a comfortable inheritance for their children, and growth stock fit into their estate plan.

Investing successfully calls for a little elbow grease. If you are willing to develop your own investment personality—represented by a custom-fit balance between risk and reward—you'll be better equipped to choose appropriate vehicles.

# 5

## Shopping the Financial Supermarkets

Money . . . well, money is like a car. You can't get around without it, and you sure can be driven by it. You can buy money (by working or investing success-fully), rent it (by borrowing . . . and most of the day, you have to park it. This chapter tells you something about the available "parking spaces" for your money. Today, you can bank at home, on your computer terminal; get cash from a machine in the lobby of your bank, or even in a shopping center or commuter railway station; get financial services in a department store. (One pinstriped wag suggested a slogan for Sears Financial Services: "If you lose your shirt, we'll sell you a new one.") You can establish a central account that gives you a single statement for your savings and investments, and "sweeps" extra cash into high-yielding accounts. It's a far cry from the old days, when you could get a (low-interest) savings account, a (no-interest; high charges) checking account, and nothing more, in a marble-walled building during bank-ers' hours only.

The change from a bank monopoly to a vast spectrum of financial super-markets gives you new opportunities to earn a better return on your hard-earned money. But you also need more information, to pick the right services —and choose the vendor that offers the most economical package of services.

### What's a Bank?

The earliest banks were really a kind of giant safe-deposit box: they'd hold on to your money (at least until the James Gang dropped over), and hand it back to you if you asked nicely. Even today, one of the major functions of banking is safeguarding money (and other valuables, in safe-deposit boxes).

Later, banks began to offer other services. For one thing, they realized that the bulk of the money deposited sat around in the vaults most of the time: most people didn't demand their money back for a while, and then only a small part of it. So the bank began to lend out the money, charging interest for this accommodation. And then the depositors began to get wise, and soon they wanted to get some interest on their deposits. The second bank function is to lend out the depositor's money (well, a small fraction of it is the bank's own capital), and pay the depositors interest on their accounts—not, of course, as much as the borrowers pay. In fact, until 1986, banks were forbidden to pay more than a certain amount (5.5 percent in 1985) of interest on savings accounts.

The third major banking function is the creation of money in the form of checks. Instead of bringing a cartful of alfalfa, or even silver dollars or dollar bills to the general store, depositors eventually found that they could write checks. A check is a promise to pay a certain amount of money in an existing bank account, to the person named on the check. The receiver can just deposit the check in his own account—he doesn't have to go to the trouble of getting cash for the check, then depositing the cash.

By the mid-twentieth century, a system of legal regulation had been developed, classifying institutions that you might be tempted to call "banks" into several categories:

- Investment banks involved in capitalizing new businesses and issuing stock.
- Commercial banks, whose main business was offering checking accounts. Originally, it was illegal to pay interest on checking accounts; to add insult to injury, most banks extracted a panoply of charges from checking account customers: for maintaining an account; for letting the balance fall below a certain amount; for each check written; for bouncing a check.
- Savings banks, whose main business was offering savings accounts (with maximum interest rates set by federal law) and Christmas clubs (with no interest at all—what a happy holiday present for the bank!).

- Savings and loan associations (S&Ls)—similar to savings banks, but operating under different charters and watched over by a different set of regulators. The people who were into S&L were basically involved in long-term lending for home mortgages. That's why they had such gruesome troubles in the seventies and eighties. They had a nice, fat portfolio of twenty- and thirty-year home mortgages—at 5, 6, maybe 7 percent interest. And to get anyone to deposit any money during the high-flying seventies, the S&Ls had to offer competitive interest rates. It's tough to make a profit when you buy something for $8 and sell it at $5—which is, in effect, what the S&Ls were doing by earning 5 percent interest on mortgages and paying 8 percent (or even double digits) on certificates of deposit to attract new deposits.

### CDs NOW!

That might be the slogan of the Savers' Liberation Movement, a consumer group that came to power in the seventies. You see, banks had developed a way to pay higher-than-passbook rates to the wealthy, corporations and other depositors who were willing to tie up large sums of money for six months, a year, or several years. These *certificates of deposit* (CDs) came under a different set of federal regulations than passbook savings accounts. It would make a nice Ph.D. thesis for a financial historian to track all the changes in regulation, but suffice it to say that, by the mid-seventies, depositors with $10,000 who were willing to keep it in the bank for six months could earn rates of return much higher than passbook-account rates: sometimes three times as high.

### NOW Accounts

At first, commercial banks could offer checking accounts, but couldn't pay interest on them; savings banks could pay interest on deposits, but couldn't offer checking accounts. Then a clever Massachusetts banker thought of the NOW account, which, for all intents and purposes, was an interest-bearing checking account. NOW stands for negotiable order of withdrawal. You see, they open a savings account for you; you can take out your money by using an "order of withdrawal" that looks exactly like a check, and it's "negotiable" because you can make it payable to anyone you like, and he or she can "negotiate" (cash) it.

Eventually, both commercial and savings banks in all states were permitted to offer NOW accounts. Before complete bank deregulation, limits were set on minimum account balances and maximum available interest (passbook rates). As of March 1986, banks can—but are not obliged to—pay market rates of interest on these "checking" accounts, and need not demand that any minimum balance be maintained. This is not to say that banks *will* offer higher interest rates; that they won't impose a raft of Mickey Mouse conditions on the account; or that they won't offset the interest rate you do receive by zapping you on charges for writing checks, making deposits, or maintaining the account.

The 5.5 percent passbook rate isn't sacred (in fact, it started around 2 percent, then crept up, with bank regulators setting *maximum*, not minimum, passbook rates). With a declining prime rate, bankers have less incentive (and less willingness) to pay high rates on CDs and NOW accounts. However, those accounts are going to look pretty sick unless they pay a noticeably higher rate than passbook accounts. Post-deregulation bankers have a right to *drop* passbook rates—and they will, too, unless they fear shouting and screaming from depositors.

Another new development: the *money market deposit account* (MMDA), invented to counter some of the challenges posed by the competition that money market mutual funds offered the banks. An MMDA pays market or close to market rates on deposits, and permits limited liquidity: usually, you can withdraw as much cash as you like (as long as you maintain the minimum balance), and write as many checks to yourself as you like—but you can write only a limited number of checks to other people (say, three a month). Furthermore, MMDA checks are usually required to be at least a minimum amount (e.g., $100), so you can use them for high-ticket items, but the MMDA is not a substitute for an ordinary checking account.

### Money in Motion

Everyone needs some "liquid" funds—cash in the pocket, and checks that can be written in small amounts. It's not practical to put *all* your money in long-term, illiquid investments such as real estate or stocks. You'd be surprised how unimpressed the bus driver is by your brokerage account—if you can't deposit the fare in the fare box, you can't get on the bus. Although the IRS will happily accept a check drawn on your money market or central asset account, your local supermarket probably won't. And you can't pay a $78.09 utility bill with a check on an MMDA that sets a $100 minimum on checks.

Therefore, you'll need at least one "convenience" bank account. The best choice is a NOW account with a low required balance, that allows you unlimited free checking with no minimum check size. It helps a lot if the bank offering it has *automated teller machines* (ATMs) so you can get cash and make deposits when the bank is closed. If this is not possible, you'll need a bank with branches conveniently near home, office, or, preferably, both—so you won't have to make a major expedition to deposit your paycheck. Hint: if you use the bank your employer uses, your paycheck will be credited to your account faster.

Some banks will give you a better deal on a mortgage or auto loan if you maintain several accounts there; if you plan to borrow, consider "relationship banking." And if you're affluent, some banks offer "personal banker" service, providing financial advice, fast and courteous consideration of loan applications, and other goodies. Just like any other bank service, the question is what it costs, how much convenience it provides, what you get for your money, and how the cost compares to similar services available elsewhere.

How much liquidity do you need? You need an account or accounts (savings, checking, or both) large enough for you to draw your weekly cash needs until your paycheck clears; and you need a checking account large enough to pay your bills without bouncing any checks. If you're careful and willing to spend some time on it, you can keep your checking account "lean and mean" by depositing enough each month to meet your bills from your money market mutual fund, MMDA, or central asset account.

But this strategy can backfire if you get careless, encounter a few unexpected expenses, or if you write checks on an account before the deposited checks have cleared. And before you start, compare the real costs and returns —it's not worth an extra $100 a year in per-check charges (imposed because the average daily balance in your checking account is so low) to get an extra $50 a year return by keeping most of your money at work in a money market fund or MMDA.

Another tip: many investors are so intent on finding worthwhile long-term investments that they forget they may need extra cash at tax time. To pay the IRS, they have to sell off investments that they wanted to hold for the long run. Remember, if you have a good year in investments, you may have to pay quarterly estimated taxes or play "catch up ball" on your 1040. (See chapter 16.) So make sure you have the cash as well as having the money to meet your tax bill.

### Parking Lots

Some people are too conservative and safety-oriented to invest in stocks or bonds (although we'll show you safe, high-yielding investment choices in later chapters). Other people focus their attention on long-term investments, but need a safe place to store surplus cash (say, a year-end bonus; a tax refund; profits from stock sales) while they decide what the next investment should be. For both groups, "parking places" are an essential part of the overall financial plan.

What's a parking place? It's a way to earn higher-than-passbook (or NOW account) rates on money. Some parking places you might consider:

- Certificates of deposit (CDs) offered by banks
- Money market mutual funds
- MMDAs offered by banks
- Central asset accounts offered by banks, brokerage houses, or mutual fund families

All of these alternatives are safe and can give good returns. It's up to you to explore the differences between these four types of accounts, and the individual differences among specimens of the same type, to pick the best one for you (see table 1).

**Certificates of Deposit**    In effect, a certificate of deposit is a contract between a depositor and the bank. The depositor agrees to take a chunk of money and leave it in the bank for a specified period of time. If the depositor wants the money back before the period elapses, he, she, or it must pay heavy interest penalties. Before deregulation, the penalties were set by federal law; postderegulation, banks have discretion—but you can be sure that the penalties will be painful enough to discourage most depositors from getting their money back early.

In the early seventies, CDs were pretty much limited to $10,000 and over, and typically had six-month or longer periods. Today, some banks will give CD terms on much lower amounts, and some will even let you "design your

**Table 1.    Recent Interest Rates for Short-Term Money Market Investments**

| Wednesday, October 1, 1986 | Rate (percent) |
| --- | --- |
| Money market mutual funds | 5.30 |
| 3-month Treasury bills | 5.34 |
| 6-month Treasury bills | 5.60 |
| Money market deposit accounts | 5.39 |
| 6-month certificates of deposit | 5.66 |
| 1-year certificates of deposit | 5.93 |
| 2½-year certificates of deposit | 6.42 |

Source: Donoghue's Money Fund Report, BANXQUOTE ONLINE, New York.

own" CD by choosing a term—perhaps the 89 days until you have to pay the caterers for your daughter's wedding, or the 192 days until your son enters college.

One of the most important factors in shopping for a CD is the rate of return. But be careful: the advertised rate may not tell the whole story. For instance, the big print may claim that a six-month CD earns X percent annually. The fine print may say that this figure is based on the assumption that you "roll over" the CD when it matures—and that you get the same rate of return. But interest rates may have plummeted six months from the date of your investment; or, if rates are high, you may want to invest in a money market fund or a bond fund instead of rolling over the CD. Not all banks compound interest on the same schedule—daily compounding means a much higher yield than annual, quarterly, or monthly compounding.

The key word here is "shopping." Because you won't be tapping the money before maturity (except in an emergency), you don't need to go to the bank around the corner. An out-of-state bank might offer the most tempting terms. (You may see their ads in your local newspaper, or a financially oriented publication like the *Wall Street Journal* or *Money* magazine.

Here are some of the questions to ask when you're considering a CD as a parking place, or as an investment vehicle:

- What is the minimum deposit?
- What is the yield, based on the assumption that the entire amount remains on deposit until maturity, but is not rolled over?
- How, and how frequently, is interest compounded?
- Is the interest rate a "split rate"—X percent on, say, the first $1,000, Y percent on the rest of your deposit?
- What are the penalties for premature withdrawal?
- Can you add more money to your CD? What interest rate will you get on additions—your original rate, or the market rate at the time of the addition (which could, of course, be higher or lower than the initial rate)? Can you withdraw the additions from the original funds without penalty, or must they remain for six months, a year, or whatever the original term was?
- What happens when your certificate approaches maturity—will you be notified? Will the money be rolled over automatically, or unless you give other instructions?

If the rates offered by an out-of-state bank put a gleam in your eye, check with the bank before you invest. They may discourage out-of-state investors, or may impose a giant minimum deposit such as $100,000. Find out who insures the deposit—any one of the federal agencies is okay, private insurance is bad news. Is the selection of maturity terms as generous as that of banks near you? If not, can you live with the limited selection of maturities offered?

**Out-of-State CDs**     To invest in an out-of-state CD, either wire the money (which will get it there faster, but will cost a few dollars) or send a registered letter with your check; the name the account is to be held in (yours; yours and another person's as joint owners; yours, in trust for someone else, who will get the funds if you die while the certificate is in force); your Social Security number; the term and amount of the CD you've chosen; your address, phone number, and signature. If you plan ahead, you can ask for the number that will be assigned to your account—then you can endorse the check to start the account with the correct account number. (Mark it "for deposit only"—otherwise, anyone who gets hold of the check could cash it.)

There are two tricky points about the timing of out-of-state CDs: which date will be used to determine your interest rate—the date you call to ask about the account? The date your money arrives? The date your check clears? The other question is when does the interest (at whichever rate bank policy prescribes) begin to accrue? There's a simple answer to that one—it should be the date your money arrives (a potent argument for wiring the funds, as long as wire charges are within reason).

Certificates of deposit are considered bank accounts; if you buy a certificate from a federally insured bank, you're insured up to $100,000 per "name." That is, you are insured up to $100,000 for an account in your name; $100,000 for an account in joint names; $100,000 for an account in trust for someone else; and so forth. If (our mouths to God's ear) you have a couple of hundred thousand dollars in CDs, you can either establish joint, etc., accounts, or simply go to several banks. There's no limit on insurance on accounts in different banks.

In short, if you're prepared to tie up your money, CDs can give you an absolutely safe way of earning high rates.

**MMDAs**     Many banks offer money market deposit accounts, paying rates theoretically set by the money market. The yield will probably be somewhat lower than you could get by buying a CD; in return, you get some liquidity. Usually, you agree to maintain a minimum balance (often set on the high side, perhaps more than you'd want to keep in a bank) in your MMDA. As long as you maintain the balance, you'll be allowed to make as many withdrawals of cash, and checks made payable to yourself, as you like. You'll also be allowed to write a limited number of third-party checks each month, usually with a minimum amount—three checks a month of $100 or more each is typical.

MMDAs are bank accounts, and, if you choose a federally insured institution, the normal insurance rules apply. So MMDAs are absolutely safe, and offer the chance to use your money without tying it up the way you would in a CD, but less freely than if you opened a simple checking account or a NOW account with a lower minimum balance.

The banks started MMDAs because they were getting killed by competition from . . .

**Money Market Mutual Funds**    The money market mutual funds were started to give small investors a chance to benefit from rising interest rates. The funds could accept many small investments and use them to buy large CDs, Treasury and other government obligations, commercial paper, or any other short-term investment permitted by the money fund's charter, and which the fund's investment manager considered a good buy.

Although the money funds are not insured, they are still very safe (in fact, no one has ever lost any principal invested in a money fund, although there's no guarantee how high the return on a money fund investment will be). That's because they invest largely in government obligations, and in any case stick to short-term investments so they can bail out of any investment that seems likely to turn sour.

The typical money fund requires an initial minimum investment (usually lower for IRAs and Keoghs), although some funds do not require any set minimum. Then you can add money to your account (usually with a minimum additional investment) at any time, and can withdraw money by using "checks." (In technical legal terms, they're not checks, but there's no functional difference.) Most funds place a minimum check size—usually $100 to $500 —and restrict the number of checks you can write per month. Some funds let you transfer money—to your bank account, or to another fund in the family the money fund belongs to—by telephone.

In the early eighties, with interest rates going through the roof, money funds were excellent primary investments for a portfolio. If you can get super high returns with absolute safety, why not go for it? Today, with interest rates tamped down (but not so's you'd notice it, when your Visa or MasterCard bill arrives), money funds are great parking places. For everyone except the most conservative investors, though, they are better choices for primary investments.

**Central Asset Accounts**    CAAs are offered by a variety of sponsors: brokerage houses, mutual fund families, and banks. The purpose of a CAA is to streamline and centralize your financial planning by placing all your transactions under one umbrella. (Not coincidentally, all the fees accrued in the course of the various transactions go to one organization.) The financial products and services included in the CAA arrangement may include:

- Brokerage—either discount, full commission, or somewhere in between; similarly, financial advice, research, and analysis may be available to a greater or lesser degree. (Bank CAAs handle this by setting up an arrangement with a brokerage house.)
- A choice of money market, equity, and bond mutual funds to invest in.
- A credit or debit card. A debit card is similar to an American Express, Visa, or other credit card, but when you "charge" something, the amount is removed immediately from your account. You don't get a monthly bill —and you don't have a chance to withhold payment to straighten out a dispute, or to choose how much of the bill you'll pay right away.
- A checking account.
- Automatic bill paying. You explain whom to pay, on what schedule (e.g., your kid's college; the bank holding your mortgage), and your account is automatically debited. In one sense this is certainly a convenient arrangement—but do you want to give up that much control over your financial affairs?
- A "sweep" feature. If your account contains any amounts that are not producing income—say, you've directed your broker to sell some stock or a bond, and the transaction has been carried out—the extra money is "swept" into an interest-earning account (usually a money market fund). CAAs differ greatly in their sweep policies—some sweep daily, some weekly. Some have different policies based on the amount to be swept—the more money, the more frequent the sweep.
- ATM access—that is, you can use a magnetically coded card to get cash from "cash machines." Be careful—some CAAs treat these withdrawals as credit card cash advances, with high interest (imposed as soon as the withdrawal is made, not delayed until a month after the bill) and minimum fees.
- Monthly statements and analysis. Some CAAs allow you to write code

numbers on your check; you then get a monthly statement showing how much you spend on groceries, how much on shelter-related expenses, and the like. Some CAAs include a thirteenth, end-of-year analysis, which can be very helpful for matching the year's actual figures to your goals, and in setting goals for the future. Watch out: Not all CAAs automatically return your canceled checks. Canceled checks are an important part of your record keeping—you don't want to discover that you never got the canceled check the day before your appointment with the IRS auditor.

Bank CAAs established in federally insured banks are insured to the normal limits. It takes some watching—you're not too likely to have over $100,000 in a deposit account, but you might very well have more than this amount in securities plus cash. Brokerage CAAs are insured by the SIPC (Securities Investors Protection Corporation) against the possibility of the broker going bankrupt or tampering with your account. Unless you are an active stock or bond trader, you're likely to do better with a bank CAA —for one thing, brokerage accounts can take several months to close, because the brokerage has to make sure that all your transactions have been processed.

The typical fee for CAA services ranges between $30 to $100 a year, plus commissions on any trading you've done, sales load on any load funds you've invested in, and back-end loads if you've disinvested in a fund with a charge of this type. However, some CAAs don't have any annual fee; others charge as much as $500.

Some things to consider when you're shopping for a CAA:

- What is the minimum amount to open an account? The minimum addition that can be made?
- What are the basic annual charges?
- Which services are included? Are any services you particularly want missing? Are there many services that are useless to you?
- Look at a sample monthly statement—can you understand it, or does it look like a cross between a New York subway map and the federal budget?
- Which mutual funds are available as investment options?
- How frequently will your account be swept, given your normal balance?
- Is the amount and level of investment advice that suits *your* needs included in the package?
- Does the schedule of brokerage commissions fit *your* trading pattern?

If you have several parking places and several investment vehicles, the CAA can be an excellent (and economical) way to "put all your eggs in one basket—and watch the basket."

## How Safe Is Your Account?

Gee, wouldn't you think it would be impossible to lose money by running a bank? It would be like the casino losing money at roulette. (On the other hand, Dana once operated a toy roulette wheel at a charity bazaar—and lost money.)

Remember, banks are in the business of taking money in at one window and lending it out at another (sometimes to the same people—if they have both a mortgage or car loan and deposit accounts at the bank). So they run two risks. First of all, they can make loans that are simply no good—to Third World countries, owners of dry oil wells, bankrupt corporations, and the like. They also run the risk of "lending long and borrowing short": they may have a portfolio of long-term, low-interest mortgages, while they have to pay depositors higher rates to attract their money away from the stock market, the money market mutual funds, and other competitors.

If you've read a newspaper in the past ten years, you've noticed that bank failures didn't end with the Depression. Banks—and especially savings and loans—can wind up over their heads in shark-filled waters. Furthermore, because banks participate in loan guarantees, and participate in large loan transactions originated by other banks, if one bank makes a few spectacularly stupid loans, many other banks can suffer.

That's why you're smart to stick to federally insured institutions. The best-known is the FDIC (Federal Deposit Insurance Corporation), which insures national banks and state-chartered commercial banks and mutual savings banks that have agreed to be regulated by the Federal Reserve Board. Savings and loans that belong to the Federal Home Loan Bank Board are insured by the FSLIC; credit unions belonging to the National Credit Union Administration are insured by the National Credit Union Share Insurance Fund. An institution insured by one of these federal agencies will mention the fact in its ads and on statements—look for it before you commit your money.

Not all S&Ls are federally insured. Some have bought their own insurance. In ten states (California, Colorado, Iowa, Kansas, Maryland, Massachusetts, North Carolina, Ohio, Pennsylvania, Utah), banks and S&Ls can be "state-insured"—that is, the state creates and regulates private insurance schemes for banks. If the bank fails and the insurance company can't cover the total amount owed, the bank's customers are out of luck—the states don't dip into their treasuries to make up the difference. An easy answer is to avoid these institutions like the plague.

The insurance limit for federally insured institutions is $100,000—not $100,000 per account, but $100,000 per depositor. So if you have $105,000 in an account, only $100,000 is insured. If, God forbid, your bank goes under, the federal agency is responsible for paying your $100,000; for the rest, you're just (another) creditor of the bank. If the bank's debts are settled for twenty-five cents on the dollar, you get only $1,250 of your $5,000. However, if you have $100,000 in an account, your spouse has $100,000 in an account in the same institution, you have a joint account for $100,000, an in-trust-for account for $100,000, they're all fully insured. Now, as to whether the federal insurance agencies will be able to stay afloat if there are lots and lots of bank failures . . . it's the same kind of financial soap opera as the Perils of the Social Security Trust Fund.

When an FDIC-insured bank fails, there are two ways the FDIC can handle it: by merger or liquidation. If the FDIC can find a merger partner, the healthier institution takes over all the accounts; your account simply becomes an account in the surviving bank, and you can have immediate access to all your funds (insured or not).

However, if the bank is liquidated, the FDIC takes over the obligation of paying back the depositors up to the $100,000 limit—if you exceed the limit, you'll get back only what the other creditors get, after a delay to get things straightened out. Furthermore, your account will be tied up until the liquidation is completed. Some theorists feel that the FDIC will start to favor liquidation over merger, to show bankers that it means business, and that they can't count on a merger to save them from the consequences of bad business practices.

The safest policy is to diversify—don't keep all your money in a single bank, and stay away from banks with either a habit of engaging in so many loan participations and guarantees that they can't keep track of them; of making high-flying (and unrepayable) international loans; or an oversupply of long-term, low-interest mortgages in their portfolios.

But you don't want to keep *all* your money in the bank, anyway. Bank interest (including CD and MMDA interest) is taxed as ordinary income. If you want long-term growth and a chance to beat inflation, or if you want tax-exempt income, you'll have to supplement your savings with other investments.

## CASE HISTORY
*Shopping the Financial Supermarkets*

It was two weeks before the wedding, and Helen Donato and Edward McGarry ("Teddy" to his parents) were sitting in her condo. It would soon be theirs. He was sipping Scotch and filling out change-of-address forms; she was polishing her engagement ring with jewelers' rouge (a pretty domestic routine that soon went by the board).

"I know we decided how to divide up our money between the joint account and individual accounts," he said. "But we've got to decide where to have the joint account, so we can get the account opened and the money transferred and this and that."

"I don't know, I never thought about it," Helen said. "I guess we need a bank that has branches near here, and also near both our offices."

"That doesn't matter so much, if we get the kind of account that lets us use those teller machines."

"I'm not crazy about those machines," Helen said. "I mean, if it's late at night you don't want to use them in case there's a mugger right outside. Also, it's okay if you just want cash, but if you put a deposit in there, and for some reason the machine doesn't get the entry, then it's really tough to prove you did deposit it. If you deposit a check, it's not so bad, because the person who wrote the check can swear up and down that they wrote it. But if you put in cash . . . well, I can understand their point, it's an easy thing to lie about . . . but if I'm making a deposit, I want a receipt from a real person who can be blamed if something goes phlooey."

"You really save those things?" Ed asked. "You know, the receipts? Every once in a while, I find a bunch of them all crunched up when I send my topcoat to the cleaner, and I throw 'em out."

"Well, *I* keep them," Helen said righteously. "I just keep a business envelope in the desk, and I file them in the envelope."

"Okay, what about MonsterBank?" Ed asked. "Lots of branches, cash machines, lots of ads telling you what a great place it is to bank."

"I hate MonsterBank," Helen said. "I went in there once to cash a check . . . admittedly, it was lunchtime, but it took *sixty-nine minutes* just to get to the front of the line. And the teller was nasty to me."

"Right. MegaTrust?"

"They're a little better. Should we have a savings account?"

"Well, mostly we'll be using the account to write checks. So let's try to get a NOW account, and be sure we keep the minimum balance in it, so we don't get stuck with a lot of check charges. And let's make it a rule, an absolute rule, that we won't make more than . . . hm, two cash-machine withdrawals a month each, and not more than a hundred dollars. *And* that when we do, we'll put the receipt . . . oh, on the kitchen counter, or stuck to the refrigerator with one of those magnets that looks like an Oreo cookie, or someplace where the other one can see it. I tell you, when I was living with Patti, we got into trouble with that all the time."

"You *lived* with Patti?" Helen asked ominously. "I didn't know that."

"Well, it's not strictly relevant. Maybe we can even get a money market account, and get some higher interest."

"I think we're better off with a plain NOW account," Helen responded, not entirely mollified by his answer. "I don't think we should keep all that much in the bank anyway. We should just keep in enough to pay our bills, and concentrate on investments with some long-term potential, if there's anything left over. Not now—'cause we don't have enough money—but later on, I think it would be a really good idea to get one of those central all-in-one accounts. Then they'll make sure all our money earns some interest, or gets reinvested."

"Where are you going to have your account?" Ed asked. (Remember, they had decided to maintain separate individual accounts in addition to a joint account for family bill paying.)

"Right now I have two accounts," Helen said. "A NOW account at the bank across from my office, and a money market fund, which is where I put the real money. Every once in a while, when the balance gets too low in my checking account, I just deposit five hundred or a thousand dollars from the money market fund. But I'm not sure I should keep the money in the money fund . . . the interest rate has really gone down since I got it. So I'm thinking about switching over to their tax-exempt fund. Not that I'm in such a hoity-toity tax bracket, but it's earning about the same amount as the money market fund. Either that, or a growth-and-income fund so I can take advantage of both high interest rates and what the stock market is doing. And, talking about hoity-toity tax bracket, where do your parents do their banking?"

"They have one of those your-own-personal-banker deals at what's-its-name: you know, the Blue Bloods Bank and Trust Company. I went there with him once. It's a real hoot. They have these hushed little rooms with walnut paneling, and red leather chairs, and whole strings of under-lings who bow you in and bring you coffee and little glasses of sherry and yucky cake with caraway seeds in it. It's very English. Actually, they don't give you such a great deal, but my dad loves it. He says that his broker makes the real money for him, and anyway you can't buy that kind of pampering anyplace else, in these decadent days."

Unless you have wads of money, banks, brokerages and mutual fund companies can seem ominous and impersonal. All the more reason to take it upon yourself to learn how products and services differ. Financial services come in all shapes and sizes (*read:* varying prices and potential value). Smart consumers have a good sense of what they're looking for and what the market offers.

# 6

## When to Bring In the Professionals

There are several reasons why people get professional advice or service. First, they may be in a situation that is simply outside the ken of a nonprofessional: they may need open-heart surgery, drafting of elaborate trusts, or installation of a new electrical system in the house. Second, they may have a good idea of what they want to do, but need another perspective on the decision. Third, they may be *able* to do whatever it is they need, but it's too much trouble or not an economical use of time.

In a financial climate that's frankly confusing, it helps to have a team of advisers to help you use the information you get from all sources.

We hope to convince you that you need a will. Unless your will is of the very simplest, you certainly need a lawyer—not just to write the will, but to integrate it with an overall estate plan. You'll also need a lawyer if you start a business (even a business that you carry on while "moonlighting" from your regular job) or get a divorce.

Business owners know that they need an accountant. Many other people can benefit by accounting services: people with complicated tax returns; people who need valuation of stock in a small business, or of marital assets in a divorce; people trying to pick the best estate plan.

But although lawyers and accountants have valuable professional training, their training is restricted to a narrow range of traditional skills. An accountant may be able to assess the balance-sheet effect of any action you can take, but that doesn't mean s/he can select the best insurance settlement option for you or give you sound advice about investing your IRA money. A lawyer may understand trial strategy inside out, or may be able to negotiate a charging rhino to a standstill, but won't necessarily be able to pick stocks or tell you whether a real estate limited partnership is a better deal for you than an aggressive-growth mutual fund. Lawyers and accountants *may* be knowledgeable about investments, just as they *may* be terrific tennis players—but if they are, it's because they've taken the time and trouble to learn and practice, not because it's part of their professional training.

Stockbrokers make money by selling you stocks and other financial instruments and also when you sell stocks or borrow using your portfolio as collateral. They make money when you trade—not when you buy a few securities and keep holding them. Sometimes a broker's recommendations are based on a profound knowledge of an industry and a particular firm's status within the industry, supplemented by insight into economic trends. Sometimes they're based on stale research reports, or simply a desire to move a stock that's a real dog. A discount broker doesn't give investment advice—just executes trades as ordered by the customers. The costs of running a firm without an expensive research department are lower, so discount brokers can charge lower commissions than full-service brokers.

We're going to spend a chapter showing you that you probably need insurance—not just life insurance, but also health insurance, disability insurance, auto insurance, and insurance for your home. Although you can get some of these policies at work (paid for partially or entirely by your employer) and some through groups you belong to, you'll probably buy most insurance through an agent or broker.

Generally, insurance people handle either life insurance or property and casualty insurance, but not both. An agent handles policies from a single company; a broker handles the policies of several companies. The trade-off is that there are a lot more agents (the insurance company would rather have wholehearted devotion than a cold-eyed appraisal), so it's easier to find one. CLUs are Chartered Life Underwriters, who have taken technical insurance courses and passed an exam. The CLU designation is a good sign; at least it means that its owner is serious about life insurance, not a part-timer trying to pick up a few bucks until his or her pork belly contracts come due.

These four groups—lawyers, accountants, brokers, insurance agents—all have a specific professional perspective. They're trained to think in certain ways and to use certain tools. Who pulls it all together? In the final analysis, you do, of course; it's your money and your life-style, and you have to make the ultimate decisions.

In the short run, a financial planner can be very helpful. Although there are no legal restraints—anyone can call himself or herself a financial planner —there are well-trained individuals who know how to integrate a multitude of financial instruments into a "symphony" that's right for your family's particular needs. Certified financial planners (CFPs) have taken a two-year course from the College for Financial Planning in Denver, Colorado. Many CFPs and other professional financial planners belong to professional organizations. These include the International Association for Financial Planning (IAFP), the Institute of Certified Financial Planners (ICFP), and the National Association of Personal Financial Advisors (NAPFA).

### Getting Referrals

The best recommendation comes from a satisfied customer—someone who has had comparable services performed. You have to be careful of two things: a professional can be very good at some things, very bad at others; and a person can start out, young and eager, and end up old, jaded, and careless. A client who seems like a dazzling path to fame and fortune at the beginning of a career can be considered a boring waste of time later on.

Professional organizations also give referrals. The problem with these is that the organizations usually refrain from making any judgment of quality. They'll tell you who's available in your area—but won't distinguish between the diligent and competent and the alcoholic and neglectful.

The legal and customary barriers have come down: professionals can now advertise, and many of them do. As a bonus, many ads include the promise of a brief free consultation. This will give you the chance to meet the professional, see his or her office (palatial or pigsty?), and talk long enough to find something about his or her manners and mannerisms, style, and professional approach. The ad will tell you something about the professional style: is the ad restrained or flamboyant? Are there any claims in the ad that seem dubious to you? If so, can the professional substantiate them fully?

### Questions to Ask

Once you've gotten a referral, it's appropriate to telephone and ask a few questions to decide if it's worthwhile to set up an appointment. The first question is how much an initial consultation—just to learn about the professional and his or her skills and style—will cost. After the initial consultation, you can (and should) break off the relationship if there's a conflict of objectives, or if you don't think you could work comfortably with the professional.

On the phone or in the office, you're trying to find out the professional's background; if his or her training is up-to-date; experience in handling situations like yours; and what it'll cost to do what you want done.

General questions:

- How long have you been in practice?
- What was your professional training?
- What continuing professional education have you had since then (advanced degrees or certificates; seminars; courses)?
- How many matters of this type have you dealt with before? How many are you dealing with now?
- How many other professionals work with you? How many support staff (paraprofessionals, secretaries, investigators)?
- Do you have a computer? What kind?
- How do you set your fees—a flat fee, a contingent fee, a commission (who pays it?), an hourly fee? If it's an hourly fee, how many hours do you estimate this matter will take?
- How often do you bill? Do you charge interest on bills that have been outstanding a certain length of time? (Actually, this practice, while unpleasant for nonpaying customers, shows a desirable businesslike approach.)
- Have you ever worked with your other team members before? What is your impression of them? (You probably can't expect much in the way of candor, but you may get a useful involuntary reaction.)

Overall, what you're looking for is a competent, well-trained, articulate, well-organized person who is not so busy that your interests will be neglected. Either recent professional training or continuing professional education is a plus. The financial conditions, laws, and regulations affecting your family's financial plan change so often that a professional must work hard to stay current.

Be sure to ask life insurance agents if they have—or are studying for—CLU designation. The Million Dollar Roundtable and similar organizations are of less interest to you; all they mean is that the member is very good at selling large amounts of insurance—not necessarily a plus, as far as you're concerned.

Ask financial planners about their financial philosophy, and what they think about index funds, OTC funds, and junk-bond funds. It doesn't much matter what the answer is—you're just interested in an articulate answer. Also be sure to ask financial planners if they're registered as investment advisers under the 1940 Act; if not, which exemption they fall under. Again, you're not interested in the specific answer so much as a confirmation that the planner understands the applicable law and can discuss it intelligently.

### The Temptations

If the only tool you have is a hammer, you tend to see everything as a nail. Each profession equips its members with a particular perspective; a particular body of information; and a way of looking at the world and handling problems. It's difficult for anyone to escape this professional orientation, even if the client would be better off with a different approach. Lawyers, for example, may keep pursuing elaborate procedural devices in a case that both clients would rather settle and have done with.

We hope you'll be dealing with people of the highest ethical caliber, and you won't have to worry about inflated bills, being charged for work that was never done, or that was unnecessary. But there are subtler temptations in the path of the honest professional.

- No one would become a life insurance agent unless s/he thought life insurance was important (or unless s/he was unusually cynical). Since life insurance agents get commissions on selling policies, there's a natural tendency to believe that a large life insurance policy fits into every financial plan. Furthermore, since commissions are highest in the first year, there's a natural tendency to believe that a new, more elaborate, and larger policy is necessary at intervals (especially if your old policy was issued by another company).
- Anyone who charges by the hour has an incentive to treat your matter ve-e-e-ry slowly, with great deliberation and consideration of every feasible alternative, and some that are barely possible.
- Anyone who charges a flat fee, on the other hand, has an incentive to dispose of the matter fast—even if it really needs more time or more creativity.
- Many lawyers use will drafting as a "loss leader." They figure that they can get you into the office, charge you $50 or $100 for filling in the blanks on a form will, and then keep you as a client if you ever need any

more elaborate (and lucrative) services. You don't just want the blanks filled in; you want a honest-to-goodness estate plan which uses all the appropriate financial techniques. This takes a lot longer, costs more than the "fill-in-the-blanks" approach—but is worth infinitely more to you.

- Brokers get a commission on every transaction; some mutual funds assess a redemption charge, others a purchase charge (or both). In these cases, the more often you buy and sell, the more often they make money. Outright "churning" (inducing customers to buy and sell just to generate commissions) is illegal, but there are gray areas. A person who lives on commissions can, genuinely and reasonably, believe that you should sell Fido Industries and buy the new issue of Paragon Moneyspinners. It would take a saint not to be influenced by the possibility of making money on the deal.

- Accountants, of course, are just as subject to temptation as anyone else. There's the temptation to hurry through a minor account to give A-1 service to a larger customer. The primary temptation, though, is not one that concerns us here: the urge to give a major client the benefit of the doubt on its assertions made in its books and records. That's a real problem for the stockholders of the major client, but not for us, in this context.

- Some financial planners earn their living by commissions on insurance sales, stock sales, real estate, etc. Like anyone else who earns commissions, the tendency is toward rose-colored glasses for commissionable investments, a jaundiced eye toward anything else. Other financial planners earn hourly rates or a fixed fee, with concomitant temptations: to drag out the analysis forever, or rush you out the door, respectively.

### Getting Help

If you feel overwhelmed by your financial choices (even after our lucid explanations), if you need a complex tax return prepared or a separation agreement drawn up, if you're too busy making money and raising a family to devise or carry out plans for that money and that family, you can and should get professional help. It's lucky that the expansion in the number of professionals means that you'll probably be able to find skilled help at a convenient location, at prices you can afford. (Find out if the charges for getting the advice are tax deductible—they probably will be if they involve tax advice or the production of taxable income.)

Don't forget the importance of convenience. After all, people don't go to fast-food restaurants because hamburger cookery is an arcane art mastered only by a few. They're hungry, tired, and in a hurry. Although computers have speeded things up a lot, there's still no "fast finance." But with the right team of advisers, you can say, "Hold the pickle . . . lots of lettuce."

## CASE HISTORY
### When to Bring In the Professionals

"Look, I understand your problem," Neil Milner said. "But the fact of the matter is, I don't really know a lot more about it than you do. Hey, I'm an accountant, not a clairvoyant. You want to know if the stock is going to go up? If I knew that stuff, I wouldn't be talking to you, because you better believe I'd be drinking vermouth on the Champs-Elysées instead of doing your tax return right here. I can look at the balance sheet they gave you in that prospectus, and I can tell you what you probably already knew. It's a start-up company, they don't have any product yet, they owe money to everybody in the solar system, and they have what they say is a real hot idea for cancer therapy via genetic engineering. So if they're right, and you buy this stock now, you're really going to make a fortune after everybody in the company wins the Nobel Prize. Or even if they're wrong, you could make a nice little bundle if enough other people think the stock is worth it."

"Then what should I do?" Carolyn Stillwood asked. "Who should I ask?"

"Don't go by me," Neil said. "I have a money market account, some zero-coup bonds, I own a co-op and part of a shopping center, because to me, real estate is safe. But, then, if I didn't think a lot about being safe, I'd be a secret agent instead of an accountant. But, look, as your accountant, I'm in a good position to advise you about your tax position, to tell you the best market timing so you can save money on your taxes —but I can't tell you what to buy or when to sell it so you can *make* money. For that, I guess you could read about the market, subscribe to a newsletter, watch 'Wall Street Week' ask your broker—if you go to the kind that gives you advice instead of the discount kind."

"I have a discount broker," Carolyn said. "I can't even stand to buy a pair of nylons retail, so I just can't bring myself to pay all those commissions to a broker. Besides, my brother used to listen to everything his broker told him, and now my brother's down twenty-three grand and out of the market."

"At least the broker made a nice living on those commissions."

"Yeah, but he blew it all on stock index futures. It all comes down to: who're you gonna call?"

Neil began to hum, then broke off when he realized he was humming "Send in the Clowns." He then responded, "You're probably going to think that I'm just saying this so *we* can get rich and *you* can get poor, but I really think that, if you have a respectable amount of money—or even if you don't, and you want to get there—you need a team. I'm on the numbers end of it—but, basically, all I can tell you is what you have and what it would look like if certain assumptions turned out to be for real. And your lawyer can tell you how to set things up so you won't get into any trouble with the courts. If your lawyer knows anything much about taxes, you probably don't need *me* in on the deal—unless you're concerned about business valuation, or if you want to make sure your business uses accepted accounting conventions, or something like that.

"And unless you think you can plan your own market strategy, I'd turn to a broker—a better one than your brother had!—to talk to you about that."

"Isn't there anybody who can pull it all together?"

"Basically, you have to," Neil said. "Whose money is it, after all?"

"What do you think about financial planners?" Carolyn asked.

"Some good, some bad . . . some of them are really sharp, really sophisticated, and have a good view of the forest that doesn't keep them from seeing the trees. And some of them are a bunch of turkeys who couldn't make it selling insurance, or selling bonds, and figure that now they have something else to sell. It's the luck of the draw. You have to find somebody who really knows what he's doing, and someone who isn't just trying to unload some junk that he's going to get a commission for selling."

"But there's the problem of what you said before," Carolyn told him. "If they know anything, why would they tell me?"

"Well, if you pay them enough . . ."

"Then is it worth it?"

"Sure it is, if you save enough money in taxes, or if you stop thinking about one piddly little transaction at a time, and get some perspective about your money and where you want to go with it."

"So there really isn't anything anybody can contribute that you can't do yourself?"

"Well, I can't claim that I'm such a giant brain that my clients couldn't learn accounting if they decided to do it. But a lot of times, it helps just to have someone else tell you something. Maybe you had a perfectly sensible plan, but you need someone else to tell you to do it. Or maybe you keep having these big fights with your husband, and you need a referee, or someone besides your mother to give you some new investment ideas."

"I guess I don't mind reading the racing form before I go to the track," Carolyn mused. "It's not like the handicappers are right all the time, but if I'm going to get on a horse, I want to make sure it doesn't have three legs. And the same thing goes for investments."

There's a lot to be said for the do-it-yourself approach. But there are times when having a team of pros working on your behalf pays off. The trick is selecting the team. Don't be shy about asking sharp questions —after all, you will be paying the freight. You deserve the best advice you can find and afford.

# 7

## Get Poor Slow: Using Credit Sensibly

Part of your financial plan consists of saving, accumulating assets, and making investments that will increase family wealth. However, if you're at all like the average American (or the average American government), you're in hock up to the earlobes most of the time.

Before you can even think about increasing family wealth, you have to take care of the bills and make sure that friendly looking chap coming up the front walk isn't intent on foreclosing the mortgage or repossessing the VCR.

The old joke is that a banker is someone who will lend you money if you can prove that you don't need it. When you already have adequate resources, credit will help you get wealthier. For instance, if you can get a low-interest loan—perhaps by borrowing against the cash value of an insurance policy—and invest the funds at a higher rate, or at the same rate but tax free, you win in two ways. First, you make money, and, second, you get an interest deduction which offsets any tax bite on the investment. But be careful: in any year, you can deduct interest on amounts you borrowed to invest—but not more than your investment income. Until 1990, some of the excess of investment interest over investment income will be deductible. There is also a complex minuet involving the way the new rules on passive investment activities interact with the rules about investment interest. In a really bad investment year, you might not be able to deduct all your investment interest (but you can carry the excess forward to later tax years). All we can say is: if you think you're in this situation, check in with your accountant.

Using credit can also help you lock in savings: if you *know* you can afford a new stereo, and a store you can trust is having a fabulous Columbus Day sale, you can save plenty of money by charging the purchase at the sale price, and paying the bill the next month. The simple point is that there'll be no interest, or only a little interest if you pay within a month or so—interest won't have had much chance to accumulate.

### Personal Cash Management

Credit can also be a tool for cash management. If you've just received, and paid, your credit card bill, so that your balance is zero, and you charge something else today, you won't get the bill for almost a month. You'll probably have about a month as a "free-ride" period, when you can pay without incurring interest. So you can get almost two months' free credit. Note: some merchants are particularly sloppy about reporting credit transactions, so you can get three months' or even more free credit.

Naturally, this strategy works only if you can guarantee that, once the bill finally appears, you'll be able to pay it.

If you've owned a house for a while—especially if your neighborhood has been the site of a real estate boom—you probably have a lot of equity built up. Home equity is the appraised market value of your house, less the amount outstanding on your mortgage. Traditionally, the only way to get at this equity was to sell the house. Later, the second mortgage appeared, but was considered disreputable if not outright disgraceful. Today, second mortgages and revolving credit lines based on home equity are added devices in your credit arsenal.

The term "arsenal" is chosen deliberately—these weapons, known as "home equity loans," can blow up in your face if you're not careful. Using home equity is an excellent financial move if it allows you to borrow needed funds (e.g., college money) at a favorable rate, or if you can use the money for productive investments. However, using home equity is a very bad idea if you risk your house for ephemeral consumption, or if you respond to advertising and borrow against your home equity when another form of credit would save you money in the long run.

Sure, there's more to life than paying taxes, but you must assess the tax impact before entering any major transaction. TC '86 places limits on the amount of home equity loan interest you can deduct. Here's a summary:

- You can deduct "qualified residence interest"—interest on a mortgage, second mortgage, or home equity loan on your first or second home.

- In any case, you can't deduct interest on any part of a loan that is more than the fair market value of your home (even if you can get someone to lend you that much). If you have a $150,000 loan on a house worth $100,000 on the open market, you can't deduct more than the interest on $100,000—and you may not be able to deduct that much. Another limitation on the deduction: the largest loan whose interest you can deduct equals your cost basis in the house, plus the cost of improvements to the house, plus certain medical and tuition bills for your family. Your cost basis is the amount you paid for the house. If you had to adjust the basis because you bought this house after selling another one (see chapter 16), you don't have to worry about it.

Why the special treatment of medical and educational expenses? Because Congress wants you to be able to tap your home equity to meet these "emergency" expenses—but also wants to make it tougher for you to get around the phaseout of consumer interest deductions.

It's not impossible to use a home equity loan to buy a new car or other consumer goods and still deduct the interest. But is it worth it? For one thing, you're putting your home on the line. If hard times visit your doorstep and you can't make the payments, you could lose the roof over your head. For another, applying for a home equity loan involves sheaves of applications and stacks of application fees—perhaps $1000 or $2000. That's a reasonable price to pay to take care of medical bills or send a kid through college—but much too much for new furniture or a vacation.

But, let's face it, not every use of credit is justifiable in strict cash-management terms. Sometimes you'll borrow or buy items on credit because it's an emergency, and you'll worry about repayment later. Sometimes you'll want new clothes, consumer goods, or a vacation, and you'll figure that something will turn up between now and the time they send someone around to break your thumbs.

In this chapter, we'll discuss the legal and practical ramifications of your credit alternatives, and how to make choices among the often bewildering selection.

## Your Credit Rating

Once upon a time, a righteous individual paid cash for everything, or did without. Today, a person like that would be considered odd, if not subversive. Many stores would *rather* have your credit card than your check, or even your cash, because it makes it less necessary for them to trust you—or investigate the value of your check—and to keep large sums in cash on the premises.

Anyway, you never know when you'll need credit: for a hospital bill that isn't covered by insurance; to buy a house or car; to take advantage of some special bargain; to take a necessary trip. Your best bet is to establish a credit rating as soon as you reach adulthood, and to devote a fair amount of time and attention to keeping the credit rating polished and glowing.

Oddly enough, a person who has never borrowed any money or incurred any debts is usually considered a poor credit risk rather than a good one. So the key is to incur a series of small, manageable debts and pay them all. One way to do this is to get a number of store credit cards, gas credit cards, or other cards that are easy to get. Some of them come to you involuntarily, through the mail.

Also oddly enough, the accounting system for most of these cards is set up to reveal your current balance, but not account activity. That is, they can find out if you owe them money at any given time, but not whether you've *ever* owed them money or even used the card. They can't tell if you're a star customer who charges $500 a month and pays it immediately on billing, or if you wouldn't be caught dead in the store.

If you can't get a store card, you may be able to start with a very small personal loan from a bank. The interest rate will no doubt be painful, but you can deposit a corresponding sum in an interest-bearing bank account, and use the interest to offset some of the interest you pay on the loan. The key here is that your current payments will boost your credit rating.

Once your basic reliability is established, you'll probably want a national credit card such as Visa or MasterCard. To get these cards, it helps to have a history of stable employment at a decent salary—though you may be offered the cards if you graduate from a prestigious college or graduate school—and a good credit history. If you have an all-in-one account with a bank or brokerage firm, you may be offered a national credit card.

Usually, the card issuer charges you a yearly fee, and imposes an interest rate on your average daily balance remaining unpaid after the "free-ride" period. Minimum interest charges are also common. You'll be given a credit limit, which may be increased periodically if you are reasonably prompt about paying your bills. You may also be able to use the card to get "cash advances" —in effect, unsecured personal loans, albeit at high interest rates. This can be very useful if you need cash away from home, in a state, city, or country where it's hard to cash a personal check. But be careful about reading the fine print: cash advances seldom have a free-ride period, and usually carry interest from the date of borrowing.

If you're very responsible, you may also qualify for a "gold" or "preferred" card, which probably carries a higher credit limit and may carry additional tangible benefits plus whatever intangible satisfaction you derive from the prestige.

An intellectual distinction should be made between credit cards and "travel and entertainment" cards such as American Express and Diners Club. The travel and entertainment card issuers normally expect you to pay your bill each month as it's presented. There are exceptions made for some big-ticket items such as airline tickets. If you normally pay the full balance on your credit card every month, the difference has no practical significance. But if you usually stretch out payment for a few months, the difference is of great practical import.

Travel and entertainment and credit cards are especially useful for business travelers. For one thing, corporate cowboys and cowgirls don't have to worry about trying to cash personal checks away from home. For another, they don't have to carry large amounts of cash. Traveler's checks are another way to deal with both problems, but, if you worry about your image, beware: traveler's checks carry a sophomoric stigma among the fast-track crowd. The clincher for many business people is that the credit card receipts provide excellent documentation of expenses for tax purposes. After all, why not let a financial giant like American Express do all your paperwork for you? Finally, it may also be possible to charge a business expense, put in a reimbursement claim, and get the money back from the employer or client before the bill has been paid. Now that's what we call a cash management double play!

## Monitoring Your Credit Rating

Because credit ratings are so important, and mistakes and misstatements can be so damaging, credit users have substantial protection from federal law. For one thing, disputed amounts on credit card bills are not permitted to damage a person's credit rating. For another thing, a law called the Fair Credit Reporting Act permits individuals to inspect any credit files maintained on them; to challenge the notations in the files; and to get mistakes corrected.

Ever been turned down for a loan because a total stranger with a similar name was a deadbeat? It may pay to use the Fair Credit Reporting Act procedure routinely, every year or every few years, to make sure that your credit rating is as good as you deserve. As we discuss in chapter 11, the Equal Credit Opportunity Act protects women against credit discrimination based on marital status.

### A Smorgasbord of Credit

A history of responsibility with short-term credit such as credit cards is helpful if you ever apply for a bank loan, especially a long-term loan such as a mortgage. Generally, a *secured* loan—one which gives the lender the right to sell some of your property and keep the part of the proceeds representing your overdue debt—will have a lower interest rate than an *unsecured* or *personal* loan. When you take out an unsecured or personal loan, the banker has nothing to rely on but your personal probity—and fear of being sued for the overdue balance. If you have a "relationship" with a bank—that is, if you've been banking there for a while and/or have several accounts—you may qualify for lower rates or a "yes" on a loan that would otherwise have been turned down.

### Credit Terms

If you have a reasonably decent credit rating, you'll have a dazzling and confusing variety of alternatives if and when you want credit. You may qualify for some or all of these:

- Personal loan.
- Secured loan.
- Home equity loan.
- Home mortgage.
- Credit card.
- Credit card cash advances.
- Travel and entertainment card.
- Asset-based loan (e.g., borrowing against a cash-value life insurance policy or your stock portfolio).
- Dealer financing (e.g., you buy furniture or a car).
- Overdraft checking (i.e., you are allowed to write checks larger than your checking account balance, up to a defined limit; in effect, the bank preapproves personal loans up to the credit limit).

When you're considering the use of credit, you may have several alternatives. For instance, you may be able to charge a purchase; get financing from the dealer who sells you the merchandise; get a cash advance; write an overdraft check; use an existing revolving-credit line based on the equity in your home; or even dig into your savings or cash in some of your investments. Which is the best choice?

Many factors are involved. If you dig into savings or realize (sell) an investment, you have to worry about *opportunity cost*—that is, you're losing the return the investment would have continued to earn if you left it undisturbed. If, for the sake of argument, you sell some stock or bonds, you may also have to pay a capital gains tax on your profits.

On the other hand, if you undertake some form of plain or fancy borrowing, you'll have to pay some form of plain or fancy interest. One fundamental distinction is the one between *open-end* and *closed-end credit.* If you use a form of closed-end credit (such as a home mortgage or a car loan), you buy merchandise on credit, or borrow a certain amount of money; you agree at the outset on a payment schedule (although you may be able to extend or refinance the loan). Open-end credit, such as credit cards and revolving credit based on home equity, gives you more control. You agree on credit limits and interest rates; you decide when you'll buy merchandise, get check overdrafts, or otherwise get credit. You also decide (within agreed-upon limits) how much you'll repay in each payment, and how long payments will continue. As you can imagine, the longer it takes you to repay, the more overall interest you'll pay on the transaction.

You'll also have to consider:

- How long the payments will continue (as an elementary practical consideration, the loan should not last longer than the item financed).
- How much you'll have to pay overall (you may end up paying several thousand dollars for a color television set).
- How high the true interest rate is when interest charges are imposed.
- If there are any late charges.
- What the seller or lender can do to you if you're late or stop making payments (add a late charge; sue you; repossess the property financed; sue the person who acted as your guarantor or surety).
- When the lender considers you to be in default.

If it makes you feel any better, interest costs are tax deductible. Of course, if interest rates decline, this advantage becomes smaller.

Not all credit has a fixed interest rate. Recently, variable-rate credit has become popular. If your interest rate can vary, you'll have to understand the events that will cause a change. These include: a change in the yield of Treasury bills; a change in a particular bank's prime rate; and a change in the Consumer Price Index. You'll also want to know if there are any limits on the amount interest can increase or decrease. Some loans are written with a limit of $X$ percent in a six-month period or $Y$ percent over the life of the loan.

Sometimes the monthly or other payment itself is *capped:* that is, if the initial payment is $229 a month, you may be guaranteed that the monthly payment will never go over $350. The problem with that is, if rates go through the ceiling, you may face *negative amortization:* that is, the monthly payment is smaller than the interest charge for each month. The upshot? You never pay off any of the principal. Instead, you keep getting deeper and deeper into the hole.

For that matter, not all closed-end credit has uniform payments. You may encounter a transaction with a *balloon* payment. In this case, you agree to make a certain number of payments of X dollars each, and a final payment of Y dollars each.

Especially in times of high interest rates, lenders and credit sellers may offer especially attractive terms for the early part of a credit transaction. Make sure you understand the way the deal works. It can be an unpleasant surprise to be billed for mortgage payments at 14 percent after a year of payments based on a 9 percent rate. Ouch!

### Federal Truth-in-Lending Laws

Luckily for borrowers, the federal truth-in-lending laws require lenders and credit sellers to disclose, quite explicitly, what the true interest rate on a transaction is; what the down payment is; how much is being financed; how many payments must be made; how large each payment must be; any possible variations in payment; for closed-end sales of goods, the total amount that must be repaid over the life of the transaction; any late charges that can be imposed; for open-end credit, the method used in computing the balance on which interest can be charged. These federal laws replace state laws that are less rigorous (but not state laws that give consumers *more* protection). What's more, federal laws apply to nearly all credit transactions you might enter into. The most common exceptions are loans over $25,000 that are not secured by the borrower's home and business loans.

The federal laws (Congress's Truth-in-Lending Act and Regulation Z issued by the Federal Reserve Board) are just concerned with disclosure. They force credit sellers and lenders to tell you enough to compare various kinds of credit, but don't regulate interest rates. The states have the job of setting maximum interest rates. However, some states have abolished their usury laws, and *any* rate of interest is legal. Many other states have set usury ceilings so high that any rate a banker can dream up is acceptable.

The sad fact of this matter is that bankers, in many states, are getting away with murder! With the prime lending rate (the rate bankers charge their best corporate borrowers) now hovering around 7.5 percent, consumers are being bludgeoned with annual finance charges on credit cards to the tune of 18 to 21 percent. New Jersey bankers lead the pack.

### Interest Rates

There are several reasons why lenders charge interest. First, they're greedy devils. But let's be fair about this. Wouldn't you, in all honesty, do the same thing in their place? Probably—unless you're a medieval Catholic theologian or a devout Moslem, both of which have philosophical objections to the practice of charging interest.

There's also the fact that if they didn't lend you the money—or let you have some of their merchandise on credit—they would have other opportunities for profit. For instance, they could invest the money safely in something like Treasury bills, or sell the merchandise to someone else for cash. The longer you keep the money tied up, the more profit they sacrifice. Remember, this business of *opportunity cost,* also expressed as the *time value of money,* is the keystone of sound financial planning. And isn't that why you're reading this book?

A final reason why lenders charge interest: risk. A bird (or $50 bill) in hand is worth two in the bush. In other words, either bird or bill can disappear by the time of final reckoning. You may stop making payments; therefore, the lender—stupid they're not!—wants to protect its interests by requiring a down payment, getting a security interest in some of your property, or adjusting interest rates and late charges to compensate for the risk.

Some transactions involve a *prepayment penalty,* an extra sum you have to cough up if you make payments in advance. This is illogical, because there isn't always opportunity cost involved, and there's certainly no risk once your debt is paid in full. The only way to explain this weird banker behavior is by reference to our first principle.

### Computing Interest

There are several ways of computing interest, and of quoting interest rates. However, for consumer transactions, all interest rates must be quoted in a uniform manner, using the *annual percentage rate* (APR). Therefore, whether the transaction involves simple interest, add-on rates, or discount rates, you can compare the rates because a uniform APR is used to describe all of them.

The APR is the real rate of interest, because it includes the vital factor of the amount of money you can use at any time. For starters, the simplest possible loan is a one-payment loan with simple interest. For example, you might borrow $1,000 for a year, with 10 percent simple interest. At the end of the year, you give back $1,100—the $1,000 you borrowed (the principal) and $100 interest.

However, if you were supposed to make monthly payments of $100, after the first payment, you would only have the use of $900, because you gave back $100. Therefore, your second payment would include $9 in interest; the third payment would be $100 principal plus $8 interest, and so on, until the entire $1,000 was repaid.

It's more common for loans to have uniform payments, and for interest to be computed using either the *add-on* or *discount* method. In the add-on method, the total amount of interest for the entire loan is added to the loan principal. This amount is then divided by the number of payments to determine each individual payment. In the discount method, all the interest is subtracted from the amount borrowed; the borrower gets only the difference between the two (or, if the transaction is a credit sale, the borrower can get merchandise worth only the difference). The add-on method gives a higher APR than the theoretical rate of interest, because you have use of less than the total amount borrowed for most of the loan term. Furthermore, the discount method gives a much higher APR than the theoretical rate, because you *never* have the use of the full amount borrowed—in fact, you may have to increase the amount of the loan to compensate.

Most loans and credit sales are *self-amortizing*. That is, a schedule of payments is set up so that by the time you've made all the scheduled payments, you've paid all the principal and all the interest. However, some loans have a final, extra-large balloon payment. A balloon mortgage on a home may have such a large balloon payment that it's virtually inevitable that the home buyers will have to refinance at the end of the mortgage term.

An amortization schedule is based on the assumption that all payments will be made on time, and not prepaid. If you prepay, you may be entitled to a *rebate* (refund) of some interest. This occurs because the payments are set up on the basis that you'll have the use of the money for the full loan term. If you repay early, you had less use of money, and therefore less interest accrued.

Don't worry—the federal laws require the lender or seller to tell you if you'll be entitled to get an interest rebate if you repay. It's quite possible for the same transaction to involve both a prepayment penalty and an interest rebate—one of them is a result of the way amortization schedules are created; the other is part of the contract between borrower and lender.

When you get a disclosure statement about credit, you won't find the terms "principal" and "interest." The approximate equivalents are *amount financed* and *finance charge.* The difference comes about because some costs that you would not think of as principal are included in the amount financed, and the finance charge includes costs other than interest.

### Credit Insurance

One important item is credit insurance. The seller or lender can exclude this item from the disclosures as long as you are informed that credit insurance is optional, and as long as you get an honest explanation of its cost.

The term "credit insurance" is something of a misnomer. Actually, it doesn't insure your credit worthiness. Rather, it protects the creditor if you die or become disabled, and therefore become unable to pay; or if the collateral is lost, stolen, or damaged. Credit insurance is usually much more expensive than comparable coverage under your own life, health, or homeowner's insurance, and frequently the creditor "sells" the coverage, offering another chance to fatten what can be an already excessive profit.

What to do? You don't need credit insurance if the debt is small compared to your total assets and you have plenty of cash to cover it if you die or become disabled. Nor do you need credit insurance if you have adequate insurance coverage otherwise. If you're very short of cash, and if your age or physical condition prevents you from getting ordinary insurance at tolerable rates, credit insurance can be worthwhile.

**Other Credit Costs**    The amount financed and APR don't reflect some of the real costs of getting credit. You are entitled to a separate disclosure, but the lender doesn't have to include these in the APR:

- Costs that would be charged in a cash transaction (e.g., dealer prep fees for an automobile, delivery charges).
- Amounts that you are required to keep in escrow (this is a frequent requirement in mortgage transactions; you may also have to keep a compensating balance in an account with a bank lending you money).

- Charges for overdrawing a checking account.
- Late charges.

Good news about late charges: a recent Federal Trade Commission rule (also adopted by federal bank regulators) prevents lenders and sellers from "pyramiding" late charges. That is, if you miss a payment or make the payment late, the lender or seller can go ahead and charge the late charge provided by the agreement. But if you make your next payment on time, the lender or seller can't "create" a default by subtracting the late charge from the timely payment, then claiming the second payment is late and imposing another late charge.

As we mention in chapter 14, there is a raft of costs involved in getting a mortgage: all sorts of surveys, application fees, fees for looking at the surveys, fees for looking at the applications, and so on. Most of these costs will not be included in the amount financed or the APR, but they'll have a major effect on your cash flow for the year of the transaction.

### Mortgage Refinancing

Home mortgage rates have started to descend from the dizzy heights of the early eighties. On the other hand, credit card rates zoomed up when the prime rate went through the ceiling—and stayed up when interest rates gained a degree of modesty.

Time out for an important cultural anecdote: the point about credit card rates is a subcase of Butz's Law, promulgated by the former, and unregretted, secretary of agriculture Earl Butz. Butz's Law states, "When farm prices go up, food prices tend to go up. When farm prices go down, food prices tend to stay up."

In that vein, many hard-pressed homeowners are now thinking seriously about refinancing the mortgage.

There are two important factors in mortgage refinancing: how much can you save over the full term of the mortgage (adjusted for tax deductions) and how much cash will you pay up front to arrange the refinancing?

As a rule of thumb, the longer the mortgage, the more you'll pay overall. And, a long-standing nugget of Americana has been the goal of paying off the mortgage. John Wayne and Maureen O'Sullivan, thank you.

However, if you're in a high tax bracket, you may not mind having a mortgage too much. Why? Even if it seems as if the mortgage payments will never end, part of each payment is deductible as interest. You may even want to refinance a fifteen-year mortgage as a twenty- or thirty-year loan, even if the rate isn't much lower. On the other hand, if you have cash but want to save money overall, you may want to refinance a twenty- or thirty-year loan over fifteen or even ten years.

But even if interest rates have sunk since you got your mortgage, and even if several banks offer you mortgage funds, you may have a few surprises in store. The bank is likely to charge you *points*—3 or 4 percent of the face amount of the loan—as a loan origination fee. It's true that the points can be deducted in the year you pay them, because they're considered prepaid interest for tax purposes. But you'll still have to come up with the money.

You may also face a prepayment penalty for paying off your original mortgage. Some states, such as New Jersey, forbid prepayment penalties; other states allow them (New York takes this position). There may be other processing fees, depending on the bank. So one cost of refinancing a mortgage is the time and annoyance involved in phoning or visiting banks to find out if you qualify for refinancing, what the rate will be, and what the other costs will be. The calculations get tougher if the original mortgage, the proposed substitute, or both, are adjustable rate loans.

One guideline is that it doesn't pay to refinance unless you can reduce your interest rate by at least 2 percent (or otherwise improve your position—say, by eliminating the risk of negative amortization). Another is that it doesn't pay to refinance unless you can recover the up-front costs of refinancing within two years through your savings on mortgage payments. You should also look at how fast you'll be building up equity in your house—especially if you plan to get a home equity loan later.

### Keeping Your Head

Sometimes it seems that half your mail consists of people trying to give you credit cards, lines of credit, overdraft checking, or other "easy credit terms." And the other half consists of bills for the stuff you've already *received* on easy credit terms.

Some experts suggest that your credit debts (excluding a home mortgage and car payments) should not exceed 10 percent of your take-home pay. For some people, this is a breeze; others would find it impossible. But since housing sets most people back a quarter to a third of their take-home pay— and there may be $100 a month or more for the car payment—that leaves very little for grocery bills, clothing and entertainment *not* charged, utility bills, much less a program of savings and investment.

If you're afraid that you might get into debt trouble, here are some guidelines:

- Once you've established a good, solid credit rating, don't have more cards than you need—get rid of the cards that merely provide temptation.
- See if you can reduce your annual fees. For instance, you may be able to trade in a card with a $35 annual fee for a free card offered as part of a banking relationship or all-in-one account.
- If money (and credit cards) burn a hole in your pocket, don't carry the cards unless you've planned in advance to make a purchase. If necessary, keep the cards locked up in a home file or your safe-deposit box, and don't give them an outing more than once a month.
- Make long-range plans, and don't use the cards at any other time unless there's a real emergency.

For instance, you could decide to use the card once in March, to buy winter coats for the kids at a spring sale; once in April for a short vacation (with costs strictly controlled); twice in June, to buy new business suits for you and your spouse, and to replace the worn-out lawn furniture; and so on through the year. If you get a big tax refund, you can use this amount for credit card bills.

### Leverage and Taxes

Even after TC '86 has done its worst, many forms of interest are deductible. However, nobody is in the 100 percent bracket, and tax rates are a lot lower now than they used to be, making the deductions that remain worth less. So don't let yourself lose control of credit spending and call it tax planning.

Sometimes leverage is the financial equivalent of a blowtorch: a useful tool, but very dangerous in the wrong hands. The theory of leverage is that you use a small amount of your own money, and lots more borrowed money (the proverbial OPM, *other people's money),* to invest. Your interest cost is deductible. When it finally comes time to repay, you can take advantage of inflation by repaying in cheaper dollars. Your profits, measured by the small amount of your own money invested, will be dramatic.

What's wrong with this picture? For one thing, inflation seems to be under control. For another, even if inflation is rampant and unchecked, you can never guarantee that you'll keep up with it and have enough cheap dollars to meet your obligations. It's harder than ever to qualify for large loans and find profitable projects that can be leveraged. So if anyone presents a deal to you in terms of leverage, take an even closer look than you usually do. And don't expect real estate sellers to leap enthusiastically if you offer a "nothing down" deal.

## Summary

It's no longer a disgrace to borrow. Very few families could ever buy a house, or even a car, if they couldn't borrow. And most families can enjoy consumer goods a lot sooner by making sensible use of credit than by insisting on saving every penny before buying anything.

The key is "sensible" use of credit. Choose a form of credit that offers the most favorable payment terms and the lowest overall costs. Find one that matches payments to the family's cash flow, and make sure that total payments can be met without sucking up funds that are needed for other things.

### CASE HISTORY
### *Using Credit Sensibly*

"Well, what do you think?" Johanna Mikulski asked her husband, Gary. "Are we serious, or are we just looking at all these houses because it's a cheap date?"

"C'mon, you're the carpeting voyeur, not me," Gary said. "I'm just the wheelman. I do the driving, you do the looking. But, look, I grew up in a house, and my father wasn't exactly rich as Rockefeller." (The elder Mikulski was a steelworker; the younger, an insurance agent.)

"But he paid nineteen thousand dollars for that house. And when he signed the papers for a six percent mortgage, your grandmother wailed for a week, because he was crazy and he'd delivered the family into the hands of the loan sharks. Now, all the houses we're looking at are close to a hundred thousand dollars, and *maybe* we could get a twelve percent mortgage. That's if we put down a lot of money, assuming we had a lot of money."

"I think that agreement you signed with Blue Cross is really going to help us out," Gary said. (She was a nurse-midwife, and Blue Cross had agreed to reimburse her directly for her fees; a couple of sympathetic obstetricians were referring their least complicated cases to her, and she was referring her most complicated cases to them.)

"But we can't count our babies before they're hatched. And it's not like either of us has a steady salary we can count on."

"Last year we made more money than *anyone* in either of our families ever made. And I've got two big, healthy commissions coming in soon, and I think the Hopgood Corporation really liked that presentation I did."

"What a salesman. You've really convinced me. Let's take a look at one more house."

They really liked the trim, modest bungalow—not too spacious, but there was an extra room that would make a good child's bedroom, and a good study in the meantime. The house would be easy to heat. It had a new roof, but the plumbing needed some work (see chapter 14). They liked the people who were selling the house, and they believed them when they said that they were selling because Paul had gotten a new job. Of the houses they'd looked at, it seemed as if they were being sold because the *termites* had gotten a new job, and were about to take the house with them. Ninety-three thousand dollars seemed like an awful lot to pay for a bungalow, but, well, that's what things cost these days.

One night, the Mikulskis sat down with their financial records, a programmable calculator, and the first in a series of steaming pots of fresh coffee.

"Last year, our monthly take-home was thirty-two hundred dollars," Gary said. "This year is going to be even better."

"We can't guarantee that," Johanna said. "Let's stick to the facts."

"And we're paying seven hundred a month rent on this—uh, this palace."

"We also have a car loan to worry about, and we haven't finished paying off my college loan."

"That's about another two hundred a month, and that won't last forever either."

"We've got two years to go on the college, and another year on the car. But, frankly, the car may not make it through the year, and it sure won't make it through two more years. Then we'll have to get another car."

"We don't have to buy a Rolls. We could get another used car for a thousand, maybe two thousand."

"And have as much trouble with it as with this one. That reminds me, we also have a whole fistful of credit card bills. We owe some money on the gas card—"

"Big deal. Two hundred dollars. We could pay them right now."

"Not *right* now—the check from the Bradys hasn't cleared yet, and I just paid the gas company and we have to pay the telephone bill. And you should see the bill from the Visa card, it's enough to gag a moose."

"We can send them a hundred dollars a month, no problem."

"A hundred dollars a month *forever,*" Johanna said, melancholy.

"I still think we did the right thing," Gary said. "We both love to listen to music—"

"Yeah. I think Record City is going to make us stockholders."

"And we *had* to have that vacation last year. No question in my mind. It was cold, it was snowy, the car was in the shop, you felt awful because the woman with the heart condition lost her baby, I felt awful because two of my biggest policies lapsed. If we hadn't gotten away, it's touch and go whether we would have been divorced by now, or in the loony bin, or whether one of us would have taken a hammer and murdered the other while we were locked up in here with cabin fever. So I'm really glad we had those credit cards."

"Maybe now we should declare a moratorium," Johanna said. "We had that real big deduction for interest on the taxes last year, you remember?"

"I think that's great," Gary said. "It was about the only deduction we did have, except for your Nursing Association dues and your malpractice insurance, and except for a couple of crummy bourbon-and-branches I bought for clients, and some gas mileage on the car."

"But we really need the money we're spending on interest a lot more than we need the deduction."

"Fine. Lock up the credit cards. Of course, you need a new winter coat, and there's practically nothing in the checking account, and about this time of year you always say that we should start doing the Christmas shopping so it won't be so crowded and everybody won't have had time to jack up the prices yet. . . . "

"You have convinced me yet again, O Great Persuader," Johanna said. "But there's a really great coat sale at the Liberty Mall, if the clutch will hold out that far, and I have a half-day off next Tuesday. I think I can hold the line on the coat price."

"I think we can get them to come down on that house," Gary said. "The plumbing really needs a lot of work."

"They already came down eight thousand dollars. Anyway, what would it cost us to keep up a house like that?"

"If we really clean out the savings account, we can put down five thousand dollars."

"That's not much for a house that's more than ninety thousand dollars."

"I know, but maybe we can get a second mortgage, or maybe your Aunt Klara will lend us some money."

"Fat chance. Listen, do you want some more coffee?"

"Yeah. Is there any of that slivovitz left?"

They did make an offer, and the Macneils agreed to come down a thousand dollars, just for the look of the thing. They exchanged contracts, contingent on the Mikulskis getting a mortgage commitment within six weeks.

The Mikulskis went to four banks and a credit union; paid several hundred dollars in various kinds of application fees; and got turned down five times. The banks refused to lend more than 80 percent of the house's appraised value—and the appraisers, who were not the world's greatest fans of bungalows, appraised the house at only $80,000. They wouldn't lend more than $64,000, and they wouldn't lend a nickel to the Mikulskis anyway. As far as the banks were concerned, they were a poor risk. Although both of them were working, neither had a steady, reliable salary; they had a couple thousand in credit card debts to pay, a college loan, and an auto loan.

By the time these glad tidings had been passed along, the Macneils were living in a house filled with packed boxes; they had filed a change-of-address notice with the post office, and had gotten the cable TV connected at their new house. They were less than enthusiastic about the idea of finding another buyer—particularly long-distance. The Mikulskis' lawyer came up with a last-ditch method of saving the deal. She suggested that the Macneils give the Mikulskis a mortgage. After all, their new house cost only $70,000, and $30,000 of that was an assumable 7 percent mortgage; with the assistance of Paul's new employer, they had gotten a $30,000 adjustable-rate mortgage with a special first-year rate of 10 percent. They did have a small mortgage on their old house, with a due-on-sale clause, but they needed only $10,000 cash to pay off that mortgage.

The Macneils had been more than disappointed lately by the performance of their money market fund, and didn't have much confidence in their ability to pick stocks (or even mutual funds). They liked and trusted the Mikulskis, and *everyone* was having a baby, so they figured that both midwifery and insurance were pretty safe occupations. So the Mikulskis scraped up $5,000 cash; Aunt Klara did, finally, lend them $5,000 more —but she demanded a note, monthly payments, and 14 percent interest; and the Macneils gave them a mortgage for the rest. They decided that it was a safe investment; that the yield was at least as good as they could get elsewhere; and that, if the worse came to the worst, they could foreclose and sell the house at a profit.

The outcome of the deal? The Mikulskis were proud homeowners. The mortgage payments came to about $900 a month—more than they were paying in rent, but they were building equity in the house, and they felt it was a good investment. They were short of savings and strapped for cash for several years, but their predictions of increasing income *were* correct. In due course of time, they did get the college loan paid off; the car did just about manage to live out its life expectancy, and they got a good deal on an only slightly used 1978 Toyota; and the credit card bills every month continued to be enough to gag a moose.

The Macneils continued to get their mortgage check on time every month (and so did Aunt Klara). Part of the mortgage check went to pay off their own mortgages; part was placed in Carole's Keogh plan to make up for the loss of her teachers' pension; the rest was invested for the kids' eventual college costs.

When it comes to credit, more often than not, there's more than one way to skin a cat. People who take a realistic view of the debt they can afford often discover they have more flexibility than they thought existed.

# 8

## Funding Your Retirement

There's more to a job than a salary. One element of a job is the working conditions—whether you enjoy your job and like the people you work with; whether you have opportunities for training and career advancement. But, you say, we are living in a material world, and you are a material girl (or boy)? On that level, your salary is only part of your total compensation for your work.

Your salary (and bonuses, and cash profit-sharing, and benefits) are *current* compensation: you get paid now, for this year's work. For most employees, the job also involves an important element of *deferred* compensation. That is, part of the compensation for the work you do now is invested, and paid to you later—generally, after you leave the company or retire. The element of deferred compensation makes it possible for you to plan a reasonably prosperous retirement. It also allows your employer to promise you X dollars in the future without having to spend the entire X dollars (because you get to benefit by the appreciation in the invested funds). Finally, deferred compensation has favorable tax consequences for both the employer and the employee—because, if the employer follows the rules, it gets a tax deduction for the amounts it spends on deferred compensation; and the employees won't have to pay tax on the deferred compensation until they receive the funds. However, the '86 tax law changes make deferred compensation less attractive. For one thing, tax rates are lower; for another, most people remain in the same tax bracket throughout their lives, so there's not much point in deferring income (that you could be investing now) in the hopes of a lower tax rate in your later years. Finally, there's a degree of well-justified skepticism about the permanence of these changes to the tax law. A person who deferred income today (passing up investment opportunities or just the chance to enjoy spending the money here and now), only to find that tax rates had shot back up when the money was finally paid, would be mad as a hornet.

The rules for pensions are among the most complex and technical in accounting and tax law, so forgive us for oversimplifying a bit. We won't address every issue, and we'll omit some of the exceptions to the exceptions. If you need the full technical treatment, talk to your employee benefits coordinator (if you're an employee) or your accountant (if you're the boss).

In this chapter, we'll treat two basic methods of funding retirement: the pension and other plans provided by your employer (though some of these plans allow employees to make contributions); and the plans you set up yourself—the Keogh plan for the self-employed; the IRA for anybody with earned income.

### Employer Plans

In the good old days, employees were expected to work until they dropped; or, perhaps, when they were too old and feeble to produce much profit for the employer, they might be taken in by a charitably minded relative or the county poorhouse. A few benevolent employers set up a scheme to reward a few of the faithful employees who had outlived their usefulness to the employer.

Then, after World War I, the United States enacted an income tax. (There had been a short-lived income tax during the Civil War, but red-blooded Americans had not been willing to sit still for it.) It now became worthwhile to find ways to accumulate money that were not subject to income tax. Life expectancies gradually increased, too.

Taken together, these factors made pension plans more attractive. Then, Henry Ford had the seminal (and subversive) idea that, if he paid his factory workers more, they would buy Ford motorcars and other luxury goods. He was absolutely right; but his revolutionary $5-a-day wage had a tremendous impact on the way workers valued their own labor.

What's the situation today? We have a large older population, many of whom have come to expect a retirement on a company-paid pension; we have labor unions, which are fairly strong in some industries; and we have a group of highly taxed top executives who desperately need a way to increase their overall compensation without also increasing their current tax bills. We also have a complex of laws (and "complex" is putting it mildly) aimed at making sure that a company's top management can't manipulate the company's pension plan too much, or use it entirely as a private reserve and keep the rank-and-file workers from receiving benefits.

Unless you work for a very small (or very unenlightened) company, there's probably some kind of pension plan. Remember, the funds contributed to the pension plan on your account are part of your compensation, just as much as your salary. It's vital to understand the plan. If you have control over the investment of your pension, it's vital to make intelligent choices.

## Defined Contribution or Defined Benefit?

When an employer sets up a conventional pension plan, it has a fundamental choice to make. Should it have a *defined contribution* plan, which obligates it to contribute a certain amount (either a dollar amount or a percentage) each year to a separate account for each employee—or a *defined benefit* plan? If the employer chooses the latter, it maintains a single account for the whole company, and determines how large a retirement benefit each worker will eventually receive (usually a percentage of the employee's final salary, times the number of years he or she worked for the company).

Whichever choice it makes, the company is limited in its generosity to top management. First of all, to qualify for tax deductions, the plan must be *nondiscriminatory:* it must use the same formulas for setting benefit levels for all employees. (The exception is that benefits can be *integrated* with Social Security—that is, the employer's Social Security taxes, or the benefits a pensioner receives from Social Security, can be taken into account in setting the employer's contribution level, or the level of retirement benefits.)

Second, there's a limit on the amount an employer can contribute each year to a defined contribution plan ($30,000, or 25 percent of the employee's salary, whichever is smaller) and a limit on the total amount of defined benefit a plan can provide ($90,000 or 100 percent of the employee's average salary for his or her three highest-paid years). Starting in 1988, these limitations will be adjusted to account for changes in the cost of living. Somehow we doubt if these limits will create much of a problem for you.

## Pension or Profit-Sharing?

Sometimes the term "pension plan" is used to include profit-sharing plans as well; technically, the difference is that an employer, once it establishes a pension plan, must make contributions to the plan every year, no matter how inconvenient this may be. A profit-sharing plan, not unreasonably, involves sharing of profits only; the employer doesn't contribute in years in which the business shows a loss.

Just to make the whole thing more confusing, the term "profit-sharing plan" refers to two completely different kinds of plan. One involves a distribution of cash to employees in good years, to motivate them to make sure all following years are good ones. The other kind, the one we're discussing here, is a plan whose primary purpose is providing deferred compensation for employees. A profit-sharing plan of this type must involve recurring, substantial contributions from the employer. The employer must also have an "allocation formula" that decides how the contributed profits will be allocated among the employees who are plan participants. Most profit-sharing plans don't require a "contribution formula" (the exceptions: certain Keogh plans). That is, if an employer adopts a profit-sharing plan, it need not commit itself to contribute a certain percentage of profits each year; but it must have a plan for dividing up the contributions, whatever they turn out to be.

### SARA Sings a CODA

Most pension and related plans are strictly plans of deferred compensation. However, the Internal Revenue Code does allow certain plans to maintain "CODAs"—cash or deferred arrangements. The employer allocates a certain amount for each employee; the employee has a choice of taking the cash (and paying income taxes on it right away) or allowing it to be deferred until retirement, death, disability, or until he or she needs the money on account of hardship, or reaches the age of fifty-nine and a half.

In technical terms, a cash or deferred arrangement is a "tax-deferred profit-sharing plan" if the employer gives the employee the choice of taking the profit-sharing in cash or having it deferred. The employer gets a tax deduction for both the amount deferred by the employee and any employer matching funds, because both amounts are compensation for the employee. On an average, companies surveyed in 1985 matched 50 percent of the amount deferred by their employees.

### The 401(k) Appeal

The SARA (salary reduction arrangement), also known as the 401(k) plan (after the section of the Internal Revenue Code authorizing it), is a popular variation on the CODA. By December of 1984, 80 percent of the Fortune 500 companies, and many smaller businesses, had adopted these plans; and participation among eligible employees was even higher than IRA participation. Popularity was immediate: the current provisions have only been in force since 1979.

A 401(k) plan allows employees to defer part of their salary tax free. That is, the employee agrees *not* to be paid part of his or her salary; the IRS agrees not to expect tax withholding on it, and doesn't require the employees to pay income tax on the deferred amounts until they receive them. However, the deferred amounts *are* subject to Social Security (FICA) taxes. The maximum the IRS will permit to be deferred is the smaller of 25 percent of salary or $7,000 (Congress can permit cost-of-living increases in the $7,000 figure), but most salary reduction plans are written to permit only 5 to 6 percent deferral.

Most 401(k) plans give the participants a choice of three or four investment options—generally, participants can invest in the employer's own stock, an equity fund of some kind, a guaranteed investment contract based on something like CDs or Treasury bills; some plans also permit investments in bond funds, or a wider variety of equity funds. It's good for participants to have the opportunity to control the investment of their retirement funds—but most of the investment vehicles are not insured, and the participant has the investment risk and loses money if he or she makes bad choices.

It's less than clear from the text of the new law, but probably a 401(k) plan will be treated like other plans offered by an employer—and if the 401(k) owner (or his or her spouse) is a plan participant, the rules explained below apply and the IRA deduction is phased out, based on taxable income. (So if the employee is married and files a joint return, both spouses' incomes trigger the phaseout.) Furthermore, participation in the employer's plan triggers the phaseout rules if the employee moonlights or has a sideline business and uses this income to open an IRA.

Employees can get payouts from their 401(k) accounts without tax penalties once they reach fifty-nine and a half, stop working for the employer maintaining the account, or become disabled. However, they will have to pay income taxes on the money. If they want to pass up both use of the cash and the taxes, they can roll over the 401(k) distribution into an IRA. *Red flag:* Like all IRA rollovers, you must act within sixty days of getting your mitts on the cash, or the transaction will be treated as a taxable distribution, not a tax-postponing rollover.

What if you prefer to take the money? If you're over fifty-nine and a half and haven't already taken a lump sum, you can use a special averaging provision. Depending on your date of birth and other factors too complex to go into here, you may qualify for either ten-year or five-year forward averaging. Even if you qualify for the ten-year, the five-year plan may be a better deal—advice from your employee benefits coordinator, financial planner, or accountant will help.

### 401(k) Loans

A 401(k) plan can be written to allow participants to borrow against their accounts without getting the plan into trouble with the IRS or Department of Labor—as long as loans are available to all participants on nondiscriminatory terms and provided that the loan terms call for repayment within five years (or a "reasonable time" if the loan is made so that the participant can buy himself or herself a principal residence). The '86 Code tightens up the earlier requirements; loans to buy a second home, help a family member buy a home, or re-hab a plan participant's principal residence fall within the five-year rule.

The loan itself is not treated as taxable income to the participant—as long as the loan amount, plus the maximum amount the participant had outstanding in loans from the plan during the preceding year, is not more than $50,000. However, 401(k) plans are not supposed to be used as piggy banks: not only does the participant have to pay interest on the borrowed funds, he or she may not be able to deduct the interest.

### Withdrawal Symptoms

Tapping those 401(k) funds is not supposed to be easy and painless, but it's not supposed to be impossible, either. Withdrawals without tax penalties are permitted in case of hardship—defined as immediate, heavy, bona fide financial need where no other resources are reasonably available to satisfy the need. To add insult to injury, regular income tax is due on the amounts withdrawn.

Now the really bad news: current law restricts tax-free hardship withdrawals to the amount actually deferred from the employee's salary. If the hard-up employee withdraws the employer's matching funds, or investment earnings from the deferred amounts, the withdrawals are treated as premature distributions, and an extra 10 percent income tax penalty is assessed.

### Salary Reduction Plans for Public Employees

Section 403(b) of the Internal Revenue Code allows government employees, public school teachers, and employees of not-for-profit organizations to have their own salary reduction plans. These plans come in two varieties—one invested in annuities, the other invested in mutual funds. The money can come from two sources: additions to salary contributed by the employer and salary deferrals elected by the employee (in a fashion similar to conventional corporate cash-or-deferred arrangements).

The maximum that can be contributed in any year is the employee's "exclusion allowance," which, in turn, equals 20 percent of the employee's salary multiplied by the number of years the employee has worked full time for that employer and minus the annuity premiums the employer has already paid. But if this amount is higher than the ordinary limit on defined contributions, that limit applies—that is, 25 percent of salary or $30,000, whichever is smaller. There's also a limit on the amount of salary the employee can defer. Current law sets it at $9,500 a year, but it will be raised each time the limit on 401(k) plan deferrals is raised.

As a bonus, the IRS allows higher "catch-up" contributions for some employees who made low contributions in earlier years. But that's beyond our scope here; ask your union rep or benefits adviser.

### Stock Plans

Usually, the employer contributes money to the pension or profit-sharing plan. However, the employer may be a little short on ready cash, but have plenty of its own stock available, and may want to motivate employees by tying their own fortunes more closely to the price of the company's stock. The Internal Revenue Code allows employers to maintain various kinds of plans funded with the employer's own stock rather than with cash.

A *stock bonus* plan is similar to a profit sharing plan, except that the employer has to make contributions whether or not it has profits. The contributions are made in the form of shares of the employer's stock. It's permissible for the employer to make distributions from the plan in cash—as long as all plan participants have a choice of getting cash or shares of stock from the plan.

An *ESOP,* or employee stock ownership plan, is a special type of stock bonus plan. The employer can use the ESOP as a way to raise funds for its operations. The plan borrows money (usually from a bank; and the employer frequently guarantees the loan) to buy the employer's stock, and pays for the stock with the borrowed money. Employers like ESOPs, because they can provide benefits with a small cash outlay (the interest—and that's deductible).

## Simplified Employee Pension Plans

An employer—especially a small company—may want to motivate its employees by providing deferred compensation but may not want to endure the hideous complexity or high cost of setting up a conventional defined benefit or defined contribution pension plan. In such a situation, the employer has several choices. It can give the employees more money, telling them that it's their problem what they do with it. Or the employer can bite the bullet and establish the conventional pension plan. There's another choice, however, one which is likely to appeal both to employees and the employer: a SEP (simplified employee pension plan).

In effect, the employees set up their own IRAs, and the employer makes contributions to them. Employees must be allowed to participate in the SEP if they're over twenty-one and have worked for the employer in the current year and in at least three of the preceding five years. The employees can still make their own contributions to IRAs, and deduct them according to the rules explained later in this chapter.

The employer doesn't have to make contributions every year—but if it makes contributions in a particular year for any employee, it must contribute for all participants. The maximum annual contribution is $30,000 or 15 percent of compensation, whichever is smaller (not 25 percent of compensation, as in other defined-contribution plans). Another 1986 innovation: SEP participants can choose to have some of their income deferred by placing it into the SEP; here the limit is $7,000, as in a 401(k) plan. This limit will go up each time the 401(k) limits do.

SEP amounts are excluded from gross income, but the "elective deferrals" are counted as wages for Social Security and unemployment tax purposes.

Unlike most conventional plans, the entire amount in the SEP is fully vested immediately. Nor can the employer write the plan to forbid withdrawals from the plan. But any amount the employee withdraws is taxed in the year he or she withdraws it, and there's a 10 percent penalty for premature withdrawals. If the employee keeps the SEP funds intact until reaching age fifty-nine and a half, the SEP funds are taxed like IRA funds.

The employee is allowed to make one rollover per year from the SEP to another SEP or another IRA. The employee can transfer the SEP between different types of investments (e.g., from a growth mutual fund to a high-tech sector fund) as often as he or she likes without tax penalty—as long as the employee doesn't actually get access to the money in spendable form.

### Conditions for Qualification

In order to be a qualified plan (that is, for the employer to have the right to deduct its contributions to the plan), a pension or related plan must meet a number of technical tests. The purpose of the tests is to make sure that the plan really is a valid plan aimed at providing deferred compensation for *all* eligible employees, not just a favored few. The cumulative effect of all these rules is to make a lot of employers frantic, a few accountants and lawyers rich, and many more employees eligible for a pension when they reach retirement age.

**Participation**   Under the integration rules, employers are allowed to exclude employees from plan participation if their salary is less than the Social Security wage base. (Most employees earn less than the Social Security wage base.) The rationale for this gaping hole in the pension safety net is that the employer pays hefty FICA taxes each year, and thus contributes quite a bit to employee retirement security.

If the plan is not integrated, the employer can't require more than two years of employment as a condition of plan participation. In fact, if the employee is required to work for the employer for more than a year before becoming a participant, each participant must be 100 percent vested immediately. Under earlier pension law, employers could require employees to be at least twenty-five before becoming plan participants; current law requires that twenty-one-year-olds can be plan participants. And if they start work between eighteen and twenty-one, those years must be counted toward vesting credits. What are vesting credits? We're getting to that momentarily.

In short, employers are limited in their ability to exclude workers who are "too young" from plan participation. What about workers who are "too old"? No one can be excluded from participation in a defined contribution plan at any age. However, workers who are hired by employers who have defined benefit plans can be excluded from participation if they're within five years of normal retirement age when they're hired. The reason for their distinction is that a defined benefit plan provides a fixed benefit for employees, and the employer would have to contribute an enormous amount to make this benefit available for older workers.

**Vesting**   It's perfectly legal for an employee to have a certain amount in his or her pension account (or to be theoretically entitled to certain benefits), yet to be unable to collect all or part of the funds. This can happen because the employee is less than fully *vested.*

It used to be a common practice for employers to draft pension plans so that all of the top executives, but none of the rank-and-file workers, could collect pension benefits—because the ordinary workers would get fired before they were fully vested. Now, tax and labor law require employers to set up vesting schedules in a more equitable fashion.

The IRS sets limits on vesting schedules permitted for qualified plans. The plan's vesting schedule must be at least as generous as the two IRS minimum schedules.

One permitted alternative is for the employees to be completely unvested for five years—but to be 100 percent vested as soon as they've been working for the employer for five years. The other OK alternative is 20 percent vesting after three years, 40 percent after four years, 60 percent after five years, 80 percent after six years, and 100 percent after seven years.

Top-heavy plans—plans in which 60 percent or more of the benefits go to officers, stockholders, and top employees—must provide extra-rapid vesting for rank-and-file employees. They must either be entitled to participate in the plan as soon as they reach twenty-one, and be fully vested after three years, or vesting must be phased in over six years, with participation required for employees over twenty-one with one year of service. Many small businesses' plans are top-heavy, simply because there's a small group of owner-managers, and an even smaller group of employees: say, a chemist, a sales person, and a finance person own the business jointly, and they have one secretary-receptionist and a person working in the stockroom.

If you're choosing among several job offers, think carefully about the vesting rules the various companies offer, as well as the generosity of the employer's contribution to the pension fund. If you change jobs frequently, you could find that you missed being vested in *any* of the plans, and won't be collecting any pensions from any of your employers.

**Breaks in Service**    A year of "service" for your employer (it does sound a bit military, or a bit "Upstairs, Downstairs," but it *is* the technical term) is a twelve-month period in which you worked at least one thousand hours for the employer. A break in service is a twelve-month period in which you worked less than five hundred hours for the employer.

The reason it matters is that, under certain circumstances, an employee who has a break in service can lose vesting credit for *all* the years before the break—say, an employee who worked for two years gets laid off, or leaves to have a baby, or goes to work for another employer, but is eventually rehired. We won't open this can of worms here—ask your employee benefits person or union rep, and allow plenty of time for the explanation. We just wanted to alert you to the fact that a 1984 federal law called the Retirement Equity Act gives employees a large measure of protection against losing credit due to breaks in service—especially those caused by maternity or paternity leave, or leave occasioned by adopting a child.

**Employee Contributions**   Some conventional employer-sponsored plans—not just SEPs—allows the employees to make their own contributions to the plan. In fact, some plans *require* employees to make contributions as a condition of participation.

In order to prevent discrimination in favor of the highest-paid employees, qualified plans are not allowed to set the level of mandatory contributions over 6 percent of compensation. The reason for this rule is that your average Carrington or Colby can easily afford to spare 6 percent of compensation— that's just the champagne bill, after all—but most people find it hard to defer that much compensation and still pay the bills. Qualified plans are not allowed to accept voluntary employee contributions in an amount over 10 percent of compensation.

Before TC '86, some voluntary contributions made by employees were deductible. Sorry, that possibility has been removed—now QVECs (Qualified Voluntary Employee Contributions) are *never* deductible.

**Forms of Retirement Benefit**   Thanks to 1984's Retirement Equity Act, spouses of employees have more protection. This bill makes the normal way for a married person's pension to be paid the *joint and survivor annuity*. That is, benefits will be paid to the worker and his or her spouse—and to whichever of them survives.

As you can imagine, the employer's responsibility to pay benefits over a longer time means that each benefit check will be lower—but the employer is not allowed to reduce the joint and survivor annuity below 50 percent of the benefit for the worker's life alone.

The normal provisions must also include a *preretirement survivor annuity*. That is, if a worker who has vested pension rights dies before retiring, his or her surviving spouse must be paid a pension.

But these two options don't suit the financial plans of all married couples. Those who want a larger benefit check can choose to have retirement benefits paid in the form of an annuity over the life of the working spouse only. But both spouses have to sign the consent form—the working spouse can't make a unilateral decision.

Depending on the way the plan is structured, and how the individual plan is written, employees may also have the choice of receiving retirement benefits in a lump sum, rather than continuing annuity checks. Much more about this in the retirement chapter; later, we'll tell you the tax and financial factors that should guide your choice.

**Early and Late Retirement**    The traditional assumption is that the "normal" retirement age is sixty-five. However, as our country's demographics change—and there are more and more surviving retired workers to be supported by a smaller number of active workers, it's understandable that financial incentives are being developed to encourage people to keep working longer. As we'll explain in chapter 17, the Social Security retirement age for receiving full benefits is being extended.

Under the same rationale (and using the same numbers), the benefits provided by defined-benefit plans must be reduced for those who retire before the normal Social Security retirement age. The reduction must be actuarial: that is, it must take life expectancy into account and reflect the larger number of years over which benefits will be paid. If the employee retires before sixty-two, the benefits payable at sixty-two must be actuarially reduced to reflect the earlier retirement.

As we'll show you in chapter 17, the IRS has twin concerns in this area: first, that people will take advantage of the tax breaks inherent in pensions, drawing funds out of pensions too soon or too generously; second, that they'll opt for endless tax deferral and *never* take the money out of the pension fund. So the IRS prescribes the slowest and fastest permitted pace for making withdrawals and imposes penalty taxes for those who step over the lines.

The general rule is that all distributions from qualified plans, IRAs, tax-sheltered custodial accounts, and annuities must begin no later than April 1 of the year after the year in which the plan participant reaches the age of seventy and a half. (We don't know how they dream these things up either.) This is true whether the participants have already retired or not, or whether they ever will. However, a "grandfather" clause (an appropriate name under the circumstances) allows rank-and-file employees who reach the age of seventy and a half before January 1, 1988, to delay retirement payouts until they actually retire. Again, as chapter 17 will show, the employee usually has a choice of taking the distribution in a lump sum (and paying taxes on the whole mass, though with a few special tax breaks allowed) or setting up a payout schedule that either meets the IRS requirements or is subject to penalty taxes.

**Investment Choices for Your Pension**    More and more plans are being written (or amended) to provide employees with some control over the investment of their pension accounts. Part of this is due to an upsurge of workplace democracy, and part of it is due to employers' increasing distaste for being sued by disgruntled pensioners as a result of poor investment performance.

The choices open to you depend on the way the plan is written; the best choice for you depends on your own needs, and your predictions about long-term trends in the economy. Most plans that do give you investment control let you choose among the employer's own stock, some kind of equity fund, some kind of income instrument (say, certificates of deposit or a bond fund), and perhaps something more risky but zingier such as real estate investments. You may also have several choices within the general equity or income category.

The choices are similar to, but more restricted than, the choices you'll face investing in an IRA or Keogh (see the rest of this chapter), but you may also have the option of investing in your employer's stock. In any of these cases, some experts advise that you can take more risks earlier in your career, because you'll have more time to recoup any losses. And everyone warns that a diversified portfolio offers the best chance of a prosperous retirement—and don't get too carried away with the opportunity to buy the employer's stock. Unless your employer's stock outperforms the market every year, it should be only one element in an investment plan.

### Do-It-Yourself Retirement Funding

If you own a business (even a small one), you can shelter a generous portion of your income by using a Keogh plan. (Of course, if you have employees, you also have to make Keogh contributions for them, which is a lot less amusing.)

Whether or not you own a business, and whether or not your employer makes contributions to a qualified plan for you, you can maintain an IRA and deposit up to $2,000 a year in it (as long as you earn at least $2,000 a year). If your spouse is also employed, you can deposit $4,000. If your spouse is not employed, you can deposit up to $2,250 by using a spousal IRA. You can also use an IRA as a "parking place" if you collect a lump sum from a pension plan but don't want to pay taxes on it right away.

Note that we said *deposit,* not *deduct.* Under the 1986 law, taxpayers with a moderate or high income lose the right to deduct part or all of their IRA contributions. Tough new rules about withdrawals and taxation of post-retirement payouts have also been added. But a definite IRA advantage remains: accrued interest on, or appreciation in value of, the IRA account won't be taxed until the payouts are received.

We'll start this section with a quick look at Keogh plans—and advise that if you're self-employed you talk to your accountant or financial adviser right away to see if a Keogh plan fits into your plans. It's a great tax shelter and a very nice benefit of working for yourself.

Then we'll conclude this chapter with a more detailed look at individual retirement arrangements. Reports of the IRA's death have been greatly exaggerated. Before the 1986 tax changes, IRAs were a star-spangled great deal, and we strongly urged that everyone open one and make the maximum contributions each year.

Then, legislators proposed to tinker with, or even remove, the IRA deduction, but taxpayers voiced their complaints in no uncertain terms. The legislators backed down, sort of, and IRA contributions are still permitted—although many taxpayers will not be able to deduct them. The party's over, but IRAs are still important for those who are not qualified plan participants and can't qualify for, or don't want, a Keogh plan. Even for plan participants, IRAs can provide a useful source of "forced savings" and guarantee that funds will be undisturbed until they're needed for retirement.

Are new-style IRAs for you? It depends—you may be able to get similar effects by opening an account in a top performing mutual fund (see chapter 4) and earmarking the money for retirement. You may also do well by assembling a portfolio of tax-exempt municipal bonds. But be careful: thanks to tax reform, not all bonds issued by government or quasi-government agencies are tax-exempt. Those used for essentially private purposes, such as building a profit-making sports stadium, provide a taxable yield. The income from tax-exempt bonds won't be taxed (though it may trigger taxation of some Social Security benefits if you receive the income after retirement), and there are no restrictions on the amount you can invest or when or how you use the money.

## Keogh Plans

At first, qualified pension plans were limited to corporations, which made contributions to the plan for their employees. That left out business owners (who were not considered employees) and unincorporated businesses.

Under current tax law, any self-employed person is allowed to maintain a Keogh plan for himself or herself. This is true even if the person also has a "straight" job, and is covered by the employer's pension plan.

A Keogh plan can be set up either as a defined benefit or a defined contribution plan. The defined benefit plan allows the self-employed person to defer tax on a lot of income, and to provide himself or herself with very generous retirement benefits: the maximum permitted is the amount needed to fund an annual benefit equal to the smaller of $90,000 or 100 percent of the average salary for the highest-paid three years. The closer the business owner is to retirement age, the more income s/he can defer (at the cost of tying up the funds for several years).

The limit on a defined contribution Keogh is the smaller of 15 percent of compensation or $30,000. If the self-employed person also has employees, the Keogh plan can be set up either as a profit-sharing plan, based on the business's income, or as a money-purchase plan, if the calculations are based on a percentage of the rank-and-file employees' compensation.

It's okay for rank-and-file employees to borrow from the Keogh plan, but it's a "prohibited transaction" for the owner of the business to borrow from the Keogh plan, and, if detected, will mean that the plan will be declared disqualified and past tax deductions denied.

### Individual Retirement Arrangements

The most popular name for the IRA is "individual retirement account," but technically there are several kinds of arrangements that qualify for this. Last year, in our original draft of this book, we said that the IRA was one of the few tax breaks available to the middle class and a great way to build retirement funds. Well, the enfeebled IRA is still one of the few tax breaks available to the middle class. Don't automatically discard the idea of continuing to open IRAs or make contributions to existing IRAs. Just be sure to balance the costs, inconveniences, and returns against other investment choices open to you.

### The IRA Deduction

Before the 1986 Act, anybody with earned income (whether or not he or she was a participant in a qualified plan) could open an IRA and make deductible contributions. Now, the contributions are permitted, but the deduction is phased out based on the taxpayer's earned income if he or she is a participant in a qualified plan. (If an employee also owns a small business and opens a Keogh plan based on this moonlighting income, the Keogh plan counts as a qualified plan for this purpose.) In all, what counts is participation—not vesting or the likelihood of ever collecting Nickel One from the pension plan. And if either spouse is a plan participant, both spouses' IRAs are subject to the limitation on deductions.

The IRA deduction is phased out based on taxable income for plan participants. Single taxpayers with an adjusted gross income over $35,000 are not entitled to *any* IRA deduction; those with AGIs under $25,000 are entitled to deduct their full contributions (up to the $2,000 limit, of course). The deduction is phased out for singles with AGIs in the $25,000–$35,000 range. For married taxpayers, the full deduction (up to the $4,000 limit) is allowed if the couple's AGI is under $40,000; deductibility stops at $50,000. In between, a partial deduction is allowed. The $2,250 limit on spousal IRAs is also subject to the reduction. Married couples filing separately don't get IRA deductions.

The IRA owner has a number of choices: s/he can buy individual retirement annuities from insurance companies, or set up individual retirement accounts with banks or savings and loan institutions (usually, but not always, invested in savings certificates or money market accounts), brokerages, or mutual funds or money market funds (see figure 3).

It's important to remember that the owner can open a new IRA every year (or, indeed, can contribute to more than one IRA in a particular year, as long as s/he doesn't exceed the $2,000 or $2,250 limit for the year). It may make sense to diversify by maintaining several IRAs, and allocating contributions according to each year's economic conditions.

Once you open an IRA, you don't have to contribute every year; you can skip years when you're short of money; or, you can contribute every year, but less than the maximum. However, they don't let you play catch-up ball: if you contribute only $1,000 a year, you can't contribute $3,000 the next year. And you can't make extra voluntary contributions to your IRA, even if you don't try to deduct them; there's an excise tax of 6 percent per year on excess contributions, and earnings on excess contributions, accruing as long as the excess contributions stay in the account.

**Spousal IRAs**    The basic purpose of the IRA is to allow employees to save part of their current income for retirement. But homemakers work, too, even though they don't get paid (and even though they don't get to retire—someone has to put away the golf clubs and make the iced tea leisurely sipped on the porch).

However, the tax code does permit homemakers to have a retirement plan of sorts. A married couple with one employed spouse and one homemaker spouse is entitled to contribute up to $2,250 to a spousal IRA. There are two

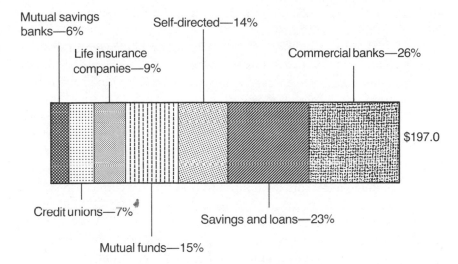

**Figure 3** Where IRAs are deposited (in billions), December 1985.
(*Source:* Investment Company Institute)

ways to handle this: either there can be one account for each spouse, or a single account with a subaccount for each spouse. The tax laws do not permit IRA accounts to be owned jointly by two spouses; but if there's a single account with two subaccounts, it *is* permissible for each spouse to have a right of survivorship in the other spouse's account. (If the couple consists of two working spouses, the maximum IRA deduction for the couple is $4,000—but they must have separate accounts.) What if the homemaker spouse later gets a job? Then the spousal IRA or subaccount simply becomes a regular IRA, and the contribution limit increases to $2,000 a year.

The $2,250 maximum deduction for a spousal IRA can be allocated between the accounts (or subaccounts) as the couple decide—it needn't be $2,000 in the working spouse's account, $250 in the homemaker's. However, the maximum allocation to either spouse is $2,000—no fair allocating $2,200 to one spouse, $50 to the other. You don't have to itemize to claim an IRA deduction, but you must file a joint return to claim a spousal IRA deduction.

As we'll discuss in the retirement chapter, there's a tax penalty for IRA owners who fail to start withdrawing their money by age seventy and a half (and a penalty for withdrawing the money too slowly). However, if the employee spouse is seventy and a half or older, but the homemaker spouse is not, the employee spouse can continue contributing to the spousal IRA—and can continue to claim the deduction. And the homemaker spouse, like the employee spouse, must wait until age fifty-nine and a half to start drawing out IRA funds without a tax penalty.

You'll find out in a moment that the IRA rollover—movement of funds from one retirement plan to another, using the IRA as a medium—is a powerful tax-planning tool. You can use the tax rules as a finely tuned instrument: become a veritable rollover Beethoven.

But a word of caution here: it's not fully resolved, but the working spouse will probably not be permitted to roll over half of his or her lump-sum distribution from another retirement plan into the homemaker spouse's spousal IRA. And if the couple has a single IRA with two subaccounts, the employee spouse must be careful to make sure the lump sum goes into the correct subaccount.

**Rollovers**    In essence, the rollover is a way of using an IRA as a "parking place" for funds that aren't needed immediately, and that would create tax trouble if they were received (and taxed) immediately. There are various reasons why a person might get a lump-sum distribution from a retirement plan: s/he might have changed jobs, and have a healthy chunk of vested benefits. The plan could terminate. The employer might have gone out of business, or been acquired by another business that terminates the original retirement plan and substitutes its own. The employee might even have retired and chosen to take his or her benefits in lump-sum form—but might want the money to grow tax free for several more years.

The basic rule is that retirement funds—whether in the form of a $250,000 lump sum or a $100-a-month pension—are taxed when they're received. (See our retirement chapter for a discussion of the exceptions to the rule, and how to use them.) The IRA transfer (a version of the rollover that moves your money directly from one qualified plan to another) gives employees a chance to avoid receiving the money—and therefore to avoid paying tax on it.

Rollovers can also be useful on the family-law front. For example, one spouse may be awarded a share of the other spouse's retirement benefits— either as part of the financial arrangements attending a divorce, or to deal with arrears of alimony or child support. Amounts received in connection with one of these "Qualified Domestic Relations Orders" (QDROs) can be rolled over to an IRA. If an employee's surviving spouse gets a lump-sum payment of the deceased employee's retirement benefits, s/he can roll the lump sum over into an IRA (but if anyone *other* than the surviving spouse—say, a son or daughter —inherits the lump sum, rollover treatment is not available). A private ruling from the IRS allowed one surviving spouse to contribute $2,000 to a spousal IRA for the year the employed spouse died.

Rollovers should be planned carefully. When you use a rollover, you actually take physical possession of your funds, for no more than 60 days, and in most situations, only one rollover every twelve months will be permitted before tax trouble arises. (Check with your employee benefits coordinator or tax adviser for details.) The exception to the rule: changes of *trustee*— where you do not take possession of the funds—say, shifting an IRA from a bank to a brokerage house—are not considered rollovers. Such shifts are called transfers and can be made as often as you like. But watch out for nontax transaction costs: if you have to pay a fee for opening and closing each account, plus, perhaps, some penalties for cashing in certificates of deposit before the due date, you'll hurt your IRA performance severely, and deplete your eventual retirement funds.

An IRA owner who receives a distribution from a qualified plan, or from a Keogh plan, escapes tax if s/he rolls over the entire distribution, or at least 50 percent of it, into an IRA within sixty days of receiving the funds. The distribution won't be taxed as current income, and it won't be penalized as an excess IRA contribution, either. If the plan permits it, an IRA can also be rolled over into a qualified plan, without incurring early-withdrawal penalties. (One warning: an IRA that contains any rollover funds from a self-employed person's Keogh plan can never be rolled over to a qualified plan.)

## Individual Retirement Annuities

People have very different financial priorities, tolerance for risk, and willingness to spend time on financial planning and portfolio monitoring. That's what makes horse racing. (Sorry—we're not allowed to mention gambling and the sacred processes of Wall Street in the same breath.)

For people who don't want to manage an IRA account themselves, individual retirement annuities—sold by insurance companies—can be a good choice. The IRA owner opens the IRA with the insurance company as trustee, and spends up to $2,000 a year ($2,250 for a spousal IRA) to buy annuities from the company.

There are two available kinds of IRA annuity. The *fixed* annuity is invested in the insurance company's general investment fund. The fixed annuity guarantees a certain annual return, albeit a low one (typically, in the 4 percent range), and will pay more if its investment performance exceeds that level. Many fixed insurance annuities now manage to return over 9 percent a year.

The *variable* annuity is invested in a stock, bond, or money market fund managed by the insurance company; the return, which is not guaranteed, depends on the performance of the fund.

There are a few reasons to be cautious about IRA annuities. First, you may be able to get much zippier performance, at a tolerable risk level, by managing your own IRA funds assertively. Second, the tax code favors all annuities, letting funds accumulate tax free until withdrawal; some experts question whether it's really necessary to use tax-sheltered investments (such as municipal bonds or annuities) in an IRA or Keogh plan, which is tax-sheltered itself. Third, make sure the transaction costs are competitive. Typically, the insurance company assesses an annual fee for maintaining the IRA annuity; there may also be a "front load" for opening the annuity arrangement, and a "back load" for withdrawing or transferring your money. (The back load may decline over time, as an incentive to you to keep the arrangement in force.)

## Individual Retirement Accounts

Outside the annuity context, there's a dazzling variety of IRA options available to you. You can open an account with a credit union, bank, or savings and loan. Most of these accounts are invested in certificates of deposit, but banks and related institutions are beginning to experiment with offering money market or equity accounts to IRA owners. You can open an account with a money market, equity mutual, or bond fund—your IRA contributions are invested in the fund. You can open an account with a brokerage house, make your contribution, and have it invested according to your broker's recommendations; or, you can instruct your broker how to invest.

However, there are some limitations on your freedom. First, IRA contributions have to be made in money, not stock, Czarist bonds, or gold bullion. Then, you can invest in almost anything—but not *quite* anything. An investment in tangibles—such as art, collectibles, or rare wines (what you might call a sousal IRA)—will be treated as an excess contribution, and you'll have to pay the excise tax on excess contributions as long as the tangible property remains in the account.

The rules for IRA investment are more or less like the rules for any investment, and we've already given you *those.* The only difference is that you have to take a long-term view for your IRA, and you won't have to worry about taxes for a good many years. Depending on your personal priorities, the IRA could be a place to experiment—because you have several to many preretirement years to catch up—or a place to be utterly cautious—because you'll need the money after retirement, when other sources of income may be scarce.

Like any other investment, IRAs tend to trade off between risk and return. If you buy bank certificates of deposit or Treasury bills, you *know* what your return will be—but you may find your money locked into a low return. (And, by the way, just because you can withdraw your money at fifty-nine and a half without paying a tax penalty, that doesn't mean the bank can't penalize you for early withdrawal if your certificate is not mature when you're ready to retire.) Another thing to consider: bank accounts, including IRA accounts, are insured by the FDIC up to $100,000 per depositor. There's nothing to stop you from having several accounts in several banks, if your IRA comes perilously close to the magic $100,000 mark.

There are other good reasons for having several IRA accounts. If you have only one account—let's say you've invested in a bond fund—you may find that the excellent climate for bonds when you opened the account has soured. If you opened the account with a family of funds that includes both stocks and bonds, and that offers you switch privileges, you can move part or all of your money—including the current contribution—into a stock fund.

But if you bought bonds directly, you might resent having to buy more bonds when you'd rather have stocks. Well, you could switch trustees—move the whole amount into equities—but the transaction costs could be high. The smartest technique might be simply to open a new, equity-based IRA, for the current year—and perhaps a real-estate-based IRA later; then you can contribute each year to the IRA that seems likely to yield the best results. Furthermore, once you're ready to retire, you don't have to use the same withdrawal schedule for all your IRAs—as long as you meet the IRS withdrawal rules (i.e., adequate withdrawals starting no later than age seventy and a half.) You might want to take all the money out of a small IRA in a lump sum, and use it for home repairs, medical bills, or a great vacation—and draw monthly checks from the others.

In 1985, the majority of IRAs were in banks or related institutions (26 percent banks, 23 percent savings and loans, 13 percent in credit unions and mutual savings banks combined). Nine percent were annuity plans from life insurance companies; 15 percent invested in mutual funds; and 14 percent were self-directed (allowing the owner full investment discretion). Will you follow the crowd, or do you have confidence in your investment skills?

**Timing Tips**    If you qualify for an IRA deduction, you must make your contribution on or before the due date for your tax return—not including extensions. (You used to be able to get an extension of time to file, make the IRA contribution at your leisure, and take the deduction for a mid-summer contribution.) For nearly all our readers, then, that means that you can make a 1987 contribution (and take it off your 1987 taxes) up to April 15, 1988. If you *do* make a contribution for one year after December 31 of that year, make sure you make it clear to the bank, brokerage, mutual fund, or wherever you keep your account *which* year the contribution is being made for; otherwise, they could inform the IRS it was made for the following year, and your deduction could be questioned.

At first glance, it seems that the best strategy is to hang on to your IRA funds, making the contribution at the last possible moment. In fact, this is sound strategy—but only if you're seriously cash-poor. If you can possibly spare the money, the really smart move is to make your IRA contribution *early* in the year. Why? Because that way, you can take maximum advantage of compounding, and if you're entitled to any tax advantages, you can enjoy them for as long as possible.

In fact, according to figures provided by E. F. Hutton, an investor who makes maximum IRA contributions each year on January 1, and manages an 8 percent return each year, would have $244,692 at the end of thirty years. If s/he made the same contribution on April 15 of the *following* year for each preceding tax year, s/he'd have only $219,610. If you don't qualify for an IRA deduction, be sure to compare the IRA with other investments you could make. How does their after-tax return compare with the after-tax return achieved by making an early IRA contribution?

Apropos of coming out ahead: many young people are hesitant to open an IRA, because they don't want to tie up money for twenty, thirty, or even more years. But the penalty on premature withdrawals, though stinging, is not necessarily fatal. If you withdraw IRA funds before reaching fifty-nine and a half (unless you're disabled), you'll have to pay ordinary income taxes on the amount withdrawn, plus a nondeductible penalty of 10 percent of the amount withdrawn. But you've had tax advantages in the meantime; and depending on your tax bracket and the investment performance of your IRA, you might even come out ahead, after paying the penalty.

**Investment Choices**    Probably the most conservative choices are annuities and insured bank CDs—low-risk choices that call for little management on the owner's part. However, if you choose CDs as a funding vehicle, don't fall asleep at the wheel—it's not necessarily a good idea to have the bank automatically roll over your CDs as they mature. You might get a better deal with savings certificates of a longer, or shorter, maturity than the one you originally chose. The bank, spurred by competition, might be offering higher-yielding but still safe accounts of other types. You might also want to take the opportunity to switch your money from CDs into another medium—perhaps a bond fund, stocks, or a real estate limited partnership. However, remember that stocks and bonds not only are not insured, but you risk losing part of your capital as well as losing additional amounts you could have earned through better performance.

Unless you're a real cynic, you'll agree that government bonds and government-guaranteed obligations are pretty safe. This safety sometimes means anemic yields. Outside of the IRA context, low yields on government bonds are balanced by tax exemptions; but IRA appreciation is tax free anyway. So think carefully about government obligations; by all means add them to your IRA portfolio if safety is your first objective, or if their yields are competitive with other investments you're considering.

But keep in mind that the government guarantees interest payments, and that your principal will be returned if you hold the bond or other instrument to maturity. The government doesn't, and can't, guarantee that you won't lose money if you sell the obligation before maturity. However, this is less of a problem for IRA investors, with their long-term orientation, than for short-term bond investors.

You can probably tell by now that we favor no-load mutual fund families (or low-load families with performance that justifies the extra costs), we also favor them for IRAs. We stress fund families, because you may be able to juice up your investment performance by intelligent switching—investing in initial public offerings through a fund when the field is hot; moving into sector funds; or shifting from the money market into equities and back.

Depending on the wisdom of your picks, and the level of your transaction costs, buying individual stocks or bonds can also be a good IRA choice. Zero-coupon bonds are a special case. "Zeros" give some investors very unpleasant surprises, when they're called on to pay taxes on so-called "phantom interest" that was deemed to them but that wasn't paid because the bonds sell at a deep discount instead of paying interest. IRA owners who invest in zeros, however, don't have this problem because the appreciation on their accounts is tax free. The prices of zero-coupon bonds fluctuate a great deal, in response to changes in interest rates, and you can really get burned—unless you're sure you'll hold the bond to maturity. In that case, you may be disappointed because you locked in a low rate of interest, but at least you won't lose your capital.

Some IRA owners even use mutual funds to speculate in options—some of them are high flyers, and some of them are high fallers. Enough said.

The Tax Code of '86 changes the guidelines for IRA investors. Before the Act, some investors were hesitant to put growth stocks into an IRA. Their reasoning was that the IRA funds, when they were finally withdrawn and taxed, would be subject to ordinary income rates—so the investor would be sacrificing the preferential treatment given to long-term capital gains. Of course, tax reform eliminated such preferential treatment—so if you find the risks tolerable, why not go for the growth?

By the same token, many IRA owners used to shun tax-exempts, figuring that it would be silly to put tax-exempt investments in a tax-exempt IRA. But as of this writing, economic trends make the yields of some safe tax-exempts attractive indeed. The lesson: explore the alternatives in light of the new tax law.

### Summary

Most American employees are participants in some sort of pension or profit-sharing plan sponsored by their employers. The pension provided by the employer probably won't be enough for comfortable retirement, and the Social Security system may have crumbled by the time today's young workers are ready to retire.

Keoghs and IRAs to the rescue. Almost everyone can use one or both of these tools to build a retirement fund in the hundreds of thousands of dollars (perhaps even over a million—if you make maximum contributions for thirty years or more, early each year, and manage a double-digit rate of return each year.) Supplement your Social Security benefits (if any) and employer-paid pension with IRA or Keogh funds and enjoy the results of a lifetime investment program—the result is likely to be financial security and a solid foundation for an estate plan.

### CASE HISTORY
#### Funding Your Retirement

It was Parents' Night at Christopher Columbus Grammar School, and the classrooms and halls were filled with a milling throng of parents— some in car coats and jeans, some fresh from the 6:52 commuter train, laden with unread newspapers and briefcases bulging with files that would never be looked at until they were lugged back to the office. Once the parents outside a particular room established the names of their neighbors' kids, and tried desperately to remember if their own kids were lifelong enemies or passionate partisans of the kids in question, there was nothing much to do but chat. Politics and religion were too controversial; but money is a perennial topic of conversation. So first they rehearsed how much everyone had spent for their houses; how shockingly high real estate taxes were; and how shockingly high income taxes were.

After that, the next step was to talk about tax shelters. Dave Lipsky mentioned, with a furrowed brow, that he owned interests in two real estate limited partnerships. He didn't really understand the provisions of the new tax bill, but he was sure that they would bring bad news. His participation contract in the limited partnership called for him to put in more cash in a few months, and he wasn't sure whether to make the payment, hope that the promoter would accept a smaller payment in light of the reduced tax benefits, or just walk away from the deal and hope the promoter wouldn't sue. That touched off another round of real estate talk.

Beth Dartnell said that they had just loved their IRAs but now weren't sure if they should make further contributions. Their earnings ruled out a deduction. They weren't sure whether to keep making contributions to their IRAs (hers, a high-growth mutual fund that had a good track record; his, divided between a junk bond fund that had a high yield but didn't match the overall return on her growth fund and an over-the-counter stock fund that met with disaster one year but rebounded the next). Should they forget about the IRAs and instead favor other investments that do not restrict input and withdrawals?

Dr. Jerome—he was an optometrist, but insisted that you call him "Doctor"—had a Keogh plan. He praised its tax-shelter ability even higher than the Dartnells praised their IRAs. He was able to put away —ahem—a substantial sum. He contributed 6 percent of his income to his Keogh plan. He would have been able to contribute much more without violating the law. But there were two things to think about: he and his wife enjoyed good restaurants and exotic vacation trips, and their kids were old enough to savor the phrase "charge it," but not yet old enough to go to college. So Dr. Jerome managed to spend much of his after-tax income on these pleasant pursuits. Then again, he had an office receptionist and an assistant who helped with eye exams. Although Dr. Jerome liked both of them, he had no intention of being any more lavish to them than he really had to be. Increasing his own Keogh contributions would also mean that he would have to increase Keogh contributions on their account.

Frances Dunbar was next on line to consult with Mr. Barrow, the fourth-grade teacher. So she mentioned, literally in passing, that her employer's salary reduction plan allowed her to defer up to 6 percent of her salary each year. She always directed that 5 percent—a nice round number—be deferred. Her company, a large business that continued to be closely held by the family that founded it, was somewhat paternalistic, and specialized in more than generous employee benefits but provided salaries that were somewhat below the industry norm. Because the company was family-owned, there was an endless supply of brothers-in-law and third cousins to take over when a top management job opened up. The limited possibilities of advancement, and the lowish salary, made her more responsive to the blandishments of headhunters. But she wasn't sure whether she would be better off if she left before her ample pension benefits vested. Just before she went into the classroom, Lilly Venegas mentioned shyly that she was a financial planner, and proffered her card: Ms. Dunbar might want to come to her office and discuss the financial implications of a career change.

(If you're wondering about Mr. Barrow, the local teachers' union had won a number of concessions during a bitter strike a few years earlier —including the establishment of a 403(b) salary reduction annuity plan as a supplement to the defined benefit pension plan already in place.)

Lilly Venegas was nearly mobbed; she was surrounded by people asking questions, and gave an impromptu seminar on IRA rollovers, culminating in a frantic, octopuslike distribution of business cards.

Some of the parents were pleased by what they heard about their kids; some were disappointed; some were angry at the teacher, the school system, or the kids. The ones with adequate retirement plans felt smug; the ones without felt that dammit, there was something *else* to feel that they had lost a status game about. Some of them just held on to and hugged the resentment; others took concrete steps to make practical retirement plans—by establishing IRAs or Keoghs; by making full use of the plans offered by their employers; by monitoring investment performance of the self-directed plans they already had. They were the lucky ones. Well, not really lucky—fortune favors the prepared mind.

Don't be left in the dust. Get going on your retirement plan today —you'll feel better about yourself as you build the foundation for financial security in your golden years.

# 9

# Insure Yourself, Don't Bury Yourself

Nobody, except a murderer with precognitive abilities, can tell whether a particular person will die during a particular year. And only a burglar with excellent contacts with other burglars knows whether a given house will be hit in a given year. But anyone with the supporting data and a flair for mathematics can tell, with a high degree of accuracy, about *how many* people in a given age group will die this year or next year, and so on; and can tell about how many houses will be burglarized, how many cars will be stolen, how many people will become disabled, and so on.

This phenomenon is known as the *law of large numbers,* and it makes the insurance industry possible. By calculating about how many insured events will happen, and how many policyholders there are, and by estimating the investment return available on premiums paid by the policyholders, insurance companies can set policy premiums. Sometimes they're wrong—especially if there's a stock market slump, or a rise in the cost of providing certain types of insurance, such as medical malpractice. When that happens, the papers are filled with discussions of the "insurance crisis," and, of course, premiums go up.

### Your Income: Wanted Dead or Alive

Life insurance provides two major functions. First, and most important, it provides a substitute for your income if you die while the policy is in force.

Furthermore, handled properly, life insurance benefits qualify for favorable tax treatment. You can also get disability insurance to replace your income if you're unable to work, property insurance to replace property that is damaged or stolen, and liability insurance that will provide you with legal representation if you are sued under certain circumstances, and pay part or all of any judgment against you.

The second function of life insurance is providing liquidity. That is, even if you leave a sizable estate, the value of the estate may be tied up. Let's say you leave a house and a portfolio of stocks that your survivors don't want to sell now, and a half-interest in a profitable, thriving business. Your son wants to take your place as president of the business. He's well qualified, and your business partner agrees.

In the long run, you've left your family well provided for. But in the short run, they may be short of cash to pay day-to-day expenses, including the expenses of probating your will and administering your estate. Without life insurance, your family might have to sell assets they'd rather retain. With life insurance, the proceeds of the policy can meet the immediate needs for cash.

Life insurance is very important for small businesses, too. First of all, the business itself may want a "key man" policy to compensate for the loss it suffers when the business founder dies. Then, the owners of the business are likely to want a "buy-sell agreement" that makes sure the business can continue and helps the family of a deceased owner. Under a buy-sell agreement, the business itself (or other owners) agree to pay a specified price for the dead person's interest in the business. Usually, the money comes from life insurance.

If you have either of these needs, you need life insurance. If you don't have these needs, or if they're met in other ways (if you're leaving plenty of cash to your family, for instance), then you need less, or no, life insurance.

### How Much Do You Need?

Some people want to have enough life insurance so that their families will not suffer a decline in standard of living if the insured person dies with the policy in force. That's a valid decision, as long as they can afford the premiums without impoverishing themselves.

Others feel that the insurance is a backstop, and they carry enough to make sure the family will not suffer financial hardship, but won't depend entirely on insurance either. These people figure that their wealth-building program, rather than life insurance, is the major tool for family financial security. Is this good strategy? It depends on how realistic their financial plans are.

One thing is clear: you don't want to be worth more dead than alive. So what you have to do is figure out your family's basic needs (being sure to deduct the cost of your own food, Brooks Brothers suits, and commuter tickets—expenses that end when *you* do). Then think about the resources that will be available: any life insurance provided by your employer; any death benefit payable from your pension plan; the monthly income from your income-oriented investments; any Social Security benefits payable to your spouse and surviving children. One way to fill the gap is with life insurance.

There are two major kinds of insurance (and innumerable variations of these themes): *term* and *whole life.*

Term is pure insurance: your premiums buy nothing except your survivors' right to receive the face value of the policy if you die while the policy is still in force. The major disadvantage of term insurance is that it gets more expensive every year (because older people are more likely to die, so it's more expensive for the insurer to provide the coverage). Furthermore, it may be difficult or impossible for an older person to get term insurance at all. (Some term policies are guaranteed renewable; others are convertible to whole life policies.)

Whole life insurance combines term insurance with some kind of cash value or investment feature. Your beneficiary receives the face value of the policy (less any outstanding policy loans) if you die while the policy is in force. You may also get dividends on the policy, the ability to borrow at low rates, and increases in cash value based on investment returns. Again, it depends on the terms of your policy.

Most whole life policies can't be cancelled as long as you keep paying the premiums. The premium is level throughout the life of the policy. Cynics say this means you're paying too much in the early years, and the policy may not even be in force later on, when the level premium would be a bargain. Anyway, most people's income increases over time, so they can afford higher insurance premiums a lot better as they reach their mid-forties.

You *can* borrow against the cash value of a whole life policy, and interest rates are a lot lower than market rates. But, remember, if you die before you've fully paid off a policy loan, the loan balance is taken out of the amount otherwise payable to your beneficiary. In effect, the loan reduces the amount of insurance you have. If you need the insurance for your family's security, why reduce their protection? And if you *don't* need that much insurance, why not reduce your coverage to the appropriate amount and reduce the premium you have to pay while increasing your funds available for investment?

Forty-nine of the states (all except Montana) have adopted some version of the Model Policy Loan Interest Rate Act. This state law gives you a choice between an 8 percent rate on policy loans and a variable rate, with a maximum rate limited by Moody's Corporate Bond Index monthly averages. However, this choice applies only to new policies; insurers who issued old policies permitting loans at 6 percent or even lower rates are stuck with them.

### Term or Whole Life?

A term policy is best if:

- You have very limited funds, but *must* have some insurance.
- You have a sound investment program, but also need pure protection.
- You have good financial self-discipline.

Whole life insurance is best if:

- You envision that term insurance will be unavailable or too expensive later on.
- You have *no* financial self-discipline, and recognize that forced savings are better than no savings.
- You have a bad record of investment performance, and the return on a variable life or universal life policy is better than your investment record.
- Your brother-in-law, or someone to whom you owe a favor, is selling the whole life policy.
- Your estate planning or tax strategy calls for owning or transferring a whole life policy.

### Kinds of Term Insurance

The plain-vanilla term policy provides pure insurance for a certain number of years, and nothing else. You may also be able to buy convertible policies, which can be converted to whole life insurance without taking a medical exam or otherwise proving that you're insurable, and renewable policies, which guarantee the right to renew (usually only until age sixty-five or seventy-five) without proof of insurability.

Usually, the face value of a term policy stays the same (although the premiums go up) as long as the policy is in force. However, there are *increas-*

*ing term* policies whose face value increases (useful if your obligations increase over time) and *decreasing term* policies. Decreasing term policies are useful if you want to insure payment of a constantly declining sum: for example, your mortgage.

Some employers pay for group term insurance for their employees, as a fringe benefit. Others offer the employee the right to pay part of the insurance premium, with the employer picking up the rest. Most plans that offer group term life insurance as an employee benefit should qualify under the new 1986 rules, so the employee will not have to pay income tax on the value of the insurance coverage. Other groups you belong to (e.g., bar association, civic association, religious group) also offer low group rates on policies.

If you decide that term insurance is for you, shop around for the best deal. You may be able to get a discount for paying your premium for an entire year at once, instead of quarterly or monthly (as long as the discount is greater than your investment return, this is a good deal). Nonsmokers or nondrinkers can get lower rates. A company may cut premiums on very large policies, or for policies that have been renewed several times by a policyholder who can prove good health.

### Kinds of Whole Life Insurance

Here we enter a realm of dizzying variety, and will give you only the basic description of the most common variants and options. An insurance agent can give you an explanation of the policies offered by one company; an insurance broker, on the other hand, can give you a comparison of the policies of various companies.

One basic distinction is between participating (also called par and dividend-paying policies, issued by mutual insurance companies) and nonparticipating policies. Participating policies pay dividends (sometimes only if the policy has been in force for a year or two), at the discretion of the insurance company. The dividends can be applied toward the premium on the policy, used to buy more insurance, or invested by the insurer and added to the cash value of the policy. Nonparticipating policies don't pay dividends, but their premiums are usually lower.

Usually, whole life policies run as long as the insured person (or someone on his or her behalf) keeps paying the premiums, and premiums continue to be due throughout the policy life. However, there are also policies designed to be paid off at a certain age, with insurance protection continuing but no further premiums due; policies which can be converted into smaller paid-off policies if the policyholder is unable to pay the premiums or simply stops paying them.

*Endowment* policies run for a certain amount of time, or until the insured person reaches a certain age. When the time limit is reached, or if the insured person dies earlier, the face value is paid to the beneficiary. Although endowment policies have higher premiums than conventional whole life policies, they can be good for meeting special needs: a lump sum for college expenses for your kids, for example, or funds needed to enter a retirement community.

The "plain vanilla" whole life policy provides a constant premium, a constant death benefit, and a buildup of cash value. Of course, in effect, the insurance company is playing with your money: the more cash value builds up, the less risk they're taking because much of the eventual payout on the insured person's death comes from the cash value. There are also modified whole life policies, with a low premium in the early years—when family resources are usually lowest—increasing to catch up in later years.

Variable life insurance and universal life insurance policies were designed to meet the criticism that whole life policies were a bad financial choice because their returns were too low. The underlying theme of various kinds of variable and universal life is that they separate the pure-insurance element (similar to term insurance) from the investment element. Depending on the type of policy and the insurer, you may be able to change the premium; change the amount of death benefit payable; change the way the funds are invested —for example, by shifting among investment portfolios.

Once you understand the way a policy works, the best comparison is between that policy and a package you assemble yourself, using term insurance and your own investments. If the variable or universal life policy, after the insurer's charges and fees, has a lower cost than your term insurance plus investment costs, and yields a higher return, the life insurance policy is a better bet.

### Comparing Policies

Once you've decided what *kind* of policy you want, which insurer is the best choice to buy it from? For one thing, you want a company that'll be around when your beneficiaries need it. Check *Best's Insurance Reports* at a reference library. A company rated excellent or very good is fairly likely to be solvent when it counts.

The *interest-adjusted cost indexes* are valuable tools for comparing the cost of policies with similar terms. There's an interest-adjusted index for term policies, and two for whole life policies. One of them measures net cost (it's also called the surrender index): it's what you would pay if you held the policy for a certain amount of time, usually measured at ten and twenty-five years, then turned it in for the cash value. The other index, the net-payment index, measures the cost of hanging on to the policy until you die. Both indexes are important in figuring out costs.

The indexes are quoted in terms of dollars per thousand dollars of insurance: you might be told that the index is $2.50 at twenty-five, $4.37 at thirty-five, $8.03 at forty-five. These are *not* the actual premiums you'd pay, because the indexes are adjusted for various features. But if two policies are really comparable, and the insurers are equally reputable, and one has a higher index, the other is a better buy.

State laws where you live probably require insurers to furnish this information about their policies. Even if it doesn't, make it clear that you'll give your business to the agent or broker who provides the best service—including the greatest amount of useful information.

### Insurance Riders

In addition to disability insurance (discussed below), there are two *riders* (additions to a life insurance policy) dealing with disability that may fit into your financial plans.

- Waiver of premium—your insurance stays in force, without the need to pay premiums, during any period of time you are completely disabled.
- Disability income. after you've been disabled for a certain amount of time, perhaps, six months, the disability income option pays you a certain amount per month, for a certain number of months.

Other riders you may be interested in:

- Double indemnity: the face value of the policy is doubled (or, in a triple indemnity rider, tripled) if your death is accidental and occurs within ninety days of the accident.
- Guaranteed insurability: this rider is available to younger policyholders, and allows them to buy increased insurance coverage on a defined schedule, without having to prove that s/he is still insurable. This can be a good choice for people with a family history of chronic illness.

## Choosing the Beneficiary

The most usual choices for beneficiary are your estate (so the policy proceeds can be administered in the way you've chosen for your estate), your spouse or live-in, one or more children, other family members. The choice, of course, is a personal one. As we'll discuss in chapter 18, estate and income tax considerations make a difference.

For one thing, if insurance is payable to your estate, the proceeds of the policy will be part of your taxable estate. That's no problem if your estate is too small to generate estate tax, but can mean a big tax bill otherwise. The proceeds of a policy will also be included in your estate if you had "incidents of ownership" such as the right to change the beneficiary, when you died. So to get the policy out of your estate, you have to give up the incidents of ownership. You can't wait too long, either—if you make a gift of an insurance policy within three years of your death, the policy proceeds go back into your estate.

If the policy proceeds are payable to a person (a "named beneficiary") and not to your estate, the beneficiary does not have to pay income tax on the proceeds themselves. However, if the proceeds are left with the insurance company and invested under a settlement option, the *income* on the proceeds is subject to income tax.

If you divorce, or if your spouse dies before you do, you'll want to change the beneficiary or name someone as alternate beneficiary.

If a beneficiary or alternate beneficiary is a minor, the insurance company won't be happy about paying out lots of money to a minor. One way to deal with this is to make sure the minor beneficiaries have a legal guardian who can receive and take care of the insurance proceeds. Another way is to set up a trust for the minor beneficiaries and have the proceeds paid to the trust.

You can also set up a living *(inter vivos)* trust, or a trust that is part of your will, and either give the life insurance policy or policies to the trust or have the insurance proceeds paid to the trust after your death.

## Health Insurance

For most working people, health insurance provided by the employer is a major fringe benefit. Some employers continue to provide health insurance to retirees; a 1985 law called the COBRA (Comprehensive Omnibus Budget Reconciliation Act) makes such coverage more widely available.

If you don't have health insurance at work, or if it isn't enough, you may qualify for a fairly low-cost group policy from an occupational or affinity group you belong to. You may even be able to form your own "group" of as few as three members, and get better rates on health insurance.

Otherwise, you're on your own, and you'll probably have to shell out a hefty premium for medical insurance. In this case, "medical" insurance is something of a misnomer. It's tough to get insurance that covers ordinary visits to a doctor, or prescription drugs. Some comprehensive employer-paid plans, and some small-group plans, offer insurance for dental care, but most policies don't cover this. Most private "medical" or "health" insurance policies really cover the costs of hospitalization. There are three main kinds: basic hospitalization; basic medical/surgical; and major medical.

- Basic hospitalization policies pay for hospitalization (in a semiprivate room), for nurses, operating-room fees, and other services billed by the hospital, for a certain number of days (say, twenty-one days). As you'd imagine, policies paying for a larger number of days of hospitalization charge higher premiums. If you have to be hospitalized several times, most policies are written so that you can't collect unless there's a waiting period between hospitalizations (say, three months).
- Basic medical-surgical coverage supplements basic hospitalization coverage by paying the bills doctors charge when you are hospitalized or have surgery. The amount paid by the policy may not be as high as the doctor's actual fee. If so, you are stuck having to pay the difference.
- Major medical insurance takes over where basic hospitalization and medical-surgical policies end.

Major medical insurance pays some of the cost of catastrophic illness. A typical major medical policy covers hospital and related fees and doctors' bills above a certain amount (the deductible). A "first-dollar" policy has no deductible, and is correspondingly more expensive. Most major medical policies cover only a percentage of the bill (say, 75 to 80 percent). The rest, or "coinsurance" amount, is the policyholder's responsibility. However, some policies have a "stop-loss" amount: once you pay this amount in a given year, the insurer pays the rest. Major medical policies usually have a policy limit, say, $150,000, or even $1,000,000; others have no policy limit. As you'd expect, a higher policy limit (or a lower deductible) means a higher premium. Furthermore, if a given expense could be covered either by a basic policy or by major medical, you can't collect twice; you have to choose between the two.

### Medicare Part B and Medi-Gap

Most people over sixty-five are automatically covered by Medicare Part A, which is roughly equivalent to basic hospitalization coverage. Those who are not automatically covered can buy into the system, but it's expensive.

Medicare Part B, which is roughly equivalent to medical-surgical insurance, is automatically available to senior citizens who have Part A coverage, unless they *refuse.* Part B is free for people receiving Medicaid or Supplemental Security Income; otherwise, there's a monthly premium, deducted from Social Security checks. (The 1985 premium was $15.50 a month.)

Medicare covers only the cost of acute illness. It *doesn't* cover chronic illnesses requiring long-term nursing home care. Nor does it cover checkups, routine dental care, routine foot care, or prescription drugs—all of which can be major expenses for older people. Medicare also imposes both deductibles and coinsurance. So Medicare is very far from being a solution to senior citizens' problems of paying for health care.

About two-thirds of Medicare beneficiaries have some kind of private supplementary insurance (usually called "Medi-Gap" policies). Medi-Gap policies are designed to supplement the Medicare coverage by paying for things that are not paid for by the federal program, or by paying the deductible and/or coinsurance amounts.

The National Association of Insurance Commissioners has drafted model standards of Medi-Gap policies. Policies that meet these standards, that conform to state regulations, and that pay out at least 60 percent of premiums (75 percent of group premiums) as benefits to their policyholders can display a special seal. Look for the seal, and be very suspicious of Medi-Gap policies that *don't* have it.

As an alternative to Medi-Gap, you might consider buying and maintaining good major medical coverage before you reach retirement age. You may be able to get better coverage for lower premiums. See if your employer-paid policy can be continued after you retire. Also be aware of dropping employer-paid and major medical insurance after retirement—there may be a period of years when your spouse has no insurance of his or her own, is no longer covered by your policies, and is too young for Medicare.

## Health Maintenance Organizations (HMOs)

An HMO is a prepaid group medical plan. An individual or family can join by paying a premium; a person's employer can pay for HMO membership; the government will also pay for a senior citizen's HMO membership if an HMO is available and s/he wants to join.

In return for the premium, HMO members get services varying according to the HMO's rules. The most comprehensive HMOs provide *all* kinds of medical, surgical, and hospital care; others provide only doctors'-office visits and outpatient surgery.

The advantage of an HMO is that it provides all or most of an individual's or family's medical-care needs for a single premium. The disadvantage is that, to take advantage of this, the HMO members must use only the HMO's facilities and its personnel. This has been a major sticking point for employers trying to get workers to convert to an HMO—after all, who wants to give up a trusted family doctor simply because he or she does not happen to partici- pate in a certain HMO.

Some people feel that HMO care may be impersonal, or even substandard, if the personnel aren't up to par or if the HMO puts cost cutting above bedside manner. On the other hand, people who go to private doctors echo many of the same complaints—and pay higher medical bills.

## Disability Insurance

For young people, the risk of becoming disabled is much greater than the risk of dying. Disability insurance provides income at a certain level, for a certain number of weeks, once the insured person has been disabled for a certain length of time.

The most important consideration in choosing a disability insurance policy is its definition of "disability." Some policies are keyed to inability to do *any* kind of job; others will provide benefits if you are unable to do your *normal* job. The latter policy is much better because it will help you afford an adjust- ment to a new career, should you be unable to resume your old job. Also look for a policy that obligates the insurer to provide you with rehabilitative therapy so you can learn to perform as many tasks as possible.

Disability insurance is also important for small businesses, which can founder or go out of business if a key person is temporarily or permanently disabled.

### Home Insurance

The most familiar form of home insurance is homeowner's insurance. But tenants don't like to lose their property to fire, flood, or theft any more than homeowners do. Home insurance is available to both homeowners and renters.

Homeowners with mortgages *have* to carry at least fire insurance, and in an amount equal to at least 80 percent of the home's value, in order to stay out of trouble with the lender. In addition to this mandatory coverage, lenders are likely to want coverage on the structure of the house and its contents in case of flood, falling objects, electrical damage, and theft.

There are a couple of tax issues that could affect your choice of homeowner's insurance. For one thing, if you suffer a casualty loss that is not related to business (for instance, the pipes freeze and burst, and the water ruins your sofa and carpet), you are entitled to a tax deduction only if your casualty loss is over $100 *and* if all your casualty losses for the year exceed a whopping 10 percent of your adjusted gross income. (Mama always said there'd be years like that.) Since you fervently hope that things won't get bad enough to justify a tax deduction, you'd better beef up your insurance coverage to compensate.

If you do qualify for a tax deduction, the '86 Code says that you can't get a deduction for an amount that *would have been* covered by your policy if you *had* made a claim. Why would people pay insurance premiums for ages, then not make a claim once something goes wrong? Because making a claim tends to lead to an increase in premiums or to cancellation of the policy; some people prefer to "save up" the policy in case something *really* bad happens. Some courts agreed that they should be allowed to do this without a tax penalty—but Congress cracked down. Now, no deduction is allowed for amounts you could have recovered from the insurance company.

Homeowner's policies vary widely. The relevant factors are:

- Covered "perils"—things that can lead to a covered claim.
- The amount of coverage. Usually, personal property is covered for half as much as the structure of the house. Then again, some policies provide a higher payoff for fire than for other perils.
- The amount of deductible—that is, the amount of damage you have to absorb before making a claim. A lower deductible means a higher premium. Some experts suggest that one week's salary is an appropriate deductible.

- The standard for paying claims. A cash value policy pays the value of the property in the condition it was in at the time it was destroyed. A replacement value policy pays what it would cost to buy a new object. As you can imagine, a brand-new couch is worth quite a bit more than an eight-year-old suede beanbag that's been the favorite resting place of the family dog.
- Whether all articles are covered or not. Many policies expressly exclude very valuable items like furs, jewelry, and computers. To get coverage on such items, you'd need to buy a *floater* at extra cost.
- Amount and conditions of liability insurance. If someone slips on your rug, or the painter falls off your roof, you could face a major lawsuit and a major jury verdict or court judgment.

Remember to increase the amount of coverage you have regularly. The idea is to keep pace with inflation, increases in the value of your home, and increases in the value of your possessions as your style of life improves.

Tenants in apartment buildings and in two- and three-family houses can buy renter's insurance, covering their own personal property, but not the structure of the building.

### Federal Programs

Thirty-one states have federal flood insurance programs at low rates. Furthermore, if you live in one of the eligible communities, and if you *don't* buy the insurance and your property is damaged in a flood, your federal disaster relief will be reduced by the amount you could have gotten from flood insurance.

What if your neighborhood is dangerous, so insurers don't want to issue policies? About half the states participate in the FAIR plan, which means that homeowners who want fire insurance are assigned to insurance companies that must provide fire insurance though they need not provide full homeowner's policies.

Other kinds of dangers are covered by federal crime insurance. Ask your insurance agent or broker whether this inexpensive coverage is available in your area. If it is, you can get burglary, robbery, and other crime coverage for your home, apartment, or business.

### Automobile Insurance

Unless you're an outright scofflaw, you *have* to have automobile liability insurance, in at least the amount required by your state's financial responsibility laws. The required amount is usually much too low, so you'll want more. Liability coverage is described by three figures, e.g., 100/200/50. That is, the limit is up to $100,000 for injury to one person, $200,000 for injuries caused by one accident, and $50,000 for property damage.

Liability insurance gets you off the hook if you are in an accident and potentially face liability for damage to someone else. There are other categories of auto insurance that protect you and your property:

- Collision insurance pays for damage to your car caused, logically enough, by collisions. If you have a really terrible car, the cost of collision insurance may be more than the value of the car.
- Comprehensive insurance pays for damage to your car inflicted by other causes.

    (Both collision and comprehensive coverages usually have a deductible; again, a week's salary is a ballpark figure. (Other experts suggest 5 percent of the value of the car.) You may be better off dropping collision and comprehensive coverages on an old clunker, and depositing the cost in your money market account or in a special "repairs" account.)

- Medical coverage pays the bills of people injured in *your* car in an accident. Liability pays the bills of people in the *other* car or cars.
- DOC (drive other cars) coverage handles your liability incurred while driving a borrowed or rented car.
- Uninsured motorist (or family protection) coverage deals with a situation in which you're in an accident with a hit-and-run driver or an uninsured motorist. In some states, uninsured motorist coverage is mandatory; if so, it'll be included in your liability insurance premium.

### No-Fault

Before the no-fault system was developed (and to this day, in states that do not use the no-fault concept), a serious automobile accident would involve negotiations about whose insurance company would pay for what. If the negotiations didn't result in a settlement, there would be a long, complex, and expensive trial, and much of the eventual recovery would go to law-yers.

The idea behind no-fault was to simplify the process, and make sure that the money paid out would go to victims of accident and injury. Approximately one-third of the states now have some kind of no-fault system. But state laws vary. Sometimes, a very serious accident can still give rise to a fault-based claim, so drivers in these states still need liability insurance. In the other no-fault states, and in these states where the amount in question falls below the limit, injured drivers make an application to their own insurance company for compensation rather than suing the other driver.

### Shopping for Auto Insurance

Car dealers often sell auto insurance, but this convenient system seldom offers the broadest coverage or lowest rates. See if you can get a discount, often available for policies purchased by a group; for policies covering several cars in the same family; for nonsmokers and nondrinkers; for those who do a limited amount of driving; for young drivers with good grades, especially if they've passed a driver's ed course; and for senior citizens. However, you can expect your premium to be *increased* if your car is overpowered—that is, too high a horsepower or weight ratio—or has a bad repair record.

*Caution:* If you're switching auto insurers, hold on to your old policy for at least sixty days since auto insurers usually reserve the right to cancel a policy for *any* reason whatsoever in the first sixty days. After that, you're probably safe from cancellation, as long as you pay the premiums and your driver's license hasn't been lifted. But an insurer can refuse to *renew* your policy when it expires, or it can zap your rates. Even if no insurer wants you, you can still buy the state-mandated liability insurance. You'll be assigned to one of the insurers, but the liability insurance premiums will be high. So preserve a good driving record, for your financial as well as physical well-being.

### Summary

You *have* to have automobile liability insurance if you drive; if you have a mortgage, you *have* to have adequate homeowner's insurance. After that, it makes sense to protect your family's financial security by assembling an ade-quate insurance portfolio.

Life insurance is invaluable for young families because it creates an instant "estate" before the family has had time to accumulate many other assets. But there's no point in overinsuring or in taking on premium payments that are so high that no funds are left for investment.

Similarly, there's no point in buying "first dollar" coverage against accidents that may never occur—it makes more sense to reduce premium payments and accept a moderate deductible.

## CASE HISTORY
### *Insure Yourself*

For Gary Mikulski, it was the beginning of the day: 9:20 A.M. For Marjorie Ricks, the day wouldn't really start for a while—her first class at the community college where she taught history wouldn't start until 1:00. For Ed Ricks, it was the end of a very, very long day—he was a first-year resident in family practice. He was supposed to have gotten off work at midnight, but there had been one of those regularly scheduled emergencies, and he had been one of a group desperately trying to pull through a four-year-old with liver cancer. She hadn't made it, and now he was exhausted, unshaven, and rumpled. He had managed to get out of his stained greens and into the jeans and shirt he had tossed into his locker—how long ago?—but he looked nothing if not disreputable.

Marjorie put a cup of coffee into one of his hands, and squeezed the other. "Gary, would you also like a cup of coffee?"

"Yes, please. Do you have any Sweet 'n Low?"

Gary and Ed had been fraternity brothers, and Ed had agreed, if warily, to listen to Gary's presentation about insurance.

"I'm sure that you, as a doctor, understand that health can end abruptly, and that even the life of a young person can be cut off."

Ed's face clouded. He had managed to forget about the girl with cancer for almost a minute. He also suffered from the common medical syndrome of believing that one suffers from all the diseases one studies, and at any given minute he was morally certain that he had at least four terminal diseases. Wasn't he exhausted all the time, with poor muscle tone, bloodshot eyes, and a coated tongue?

"So you, better than anyone, should understand the need for insurance."

"I really don't know, Gary," Marjorie said. "First of all, we have *no* money—I mean, zilch—but we're both working, so if one of us, God forbid, died, the other one would still be self-supporting."

"Okay, if you're short on money, insurance can be part of a comprehensive financial plan," said Gary, who had definitely heard *that* one before.

"Marjie's right," Ed said. "Between the two of us, I guess we have about three thousand a month. I don't want to bitch about it too much, I know lots of people would be grateful for it, but this goddamn apartment costs a thousand a month, and we're putting almost five hundred a month toward paying off our education loans, and that leaves us only about fifteen hundred a month for everything else. And we eat out a lot —I mean, neither one of us really feels too much like cooking at the end of the day, and we have this godawful car which we bought for cash, but between the insurance and the gas and the parking . . ."

"Andrew Tobias wrote a book called *Getting By on $100,000 a Year and Other Sad Tales,*" Marjorie said mordantly. "We're not up to a hundred thou' a year, but we certainly manage to take a lot of money and make it disappear."

"Yes, but, fortunately, you have much more income potential than most couples," Gary rejoined. (Part of an insurance agent's training is overcoming objections.) "Those loans won't be forever, you know. And when Ed finishes his residency . . ."

"In three years, if I live . . ."

"You'll have much more income, free and clear."

"Don't get your hopes up," Ed said. "I've got an offer from an HMO, and I'm almost sure I'll accept it. But it's a salaried job, with none of those big, juicy fees."

"And none of those big, juicy malpractice insurance premiums," Marjorie said. "Whoops, sorry, Gary."

"No sweat, I'm strictly on the life insurance end. Okay, but, look, what would happen if you died tomorrow, Ed?"

"Well, first of all, Marjie would be able to file a joint return for two years, and she wouldn't have any of my expenses to worry about, and she could tell the bank to go whistle for my loans. . . . I'm probably worth more dead than alive."

"Then what if Marjorie died?"

"Look, I love my wife very much, but I don't exactly think of her as a cash cow."

Gary decided to go for the jugular. "Then it sounds to me like you don't have much of an estate. Not much in the way of savings; you don't own your own home; probably not many investments."

"Only too true," Marjorie said.

"Life insurance is a tax-favored way to build an estate instantly. I'm sure that by the time you're forty or forty-five, you'll have your debts taken care of, Marjorie will probably have tenure, you'll have a very comfortable income, probably some real estate, securities . . . but right now, there's just no other way for you to accumulate a substantial estate. I'm not saying that you're going to enjoy paying the premiums, but if you buy a cash-value whole life policy on each of you, enough to replace a year's income, then you've provided the survivor with a tax-free source of funds in the year after a death. And if you keep the policy in force for a while, you have an inexpensive source of borrowing power."

Gary showed them the rate tables, made a few calculations, accepted another cup of coffee and a slice of raspberry coffee cake (assuredly not homemade—from the gourmet takeout place down the block), and left with a binder on two whole life policies: one on Ed for $50,000, and a matching policy on Marjorie's life. Originally, they were going to insure Marjorie for only $35,000, but the premium for a thirty-one-year-old female was lower than that for a twenty-nine-year-old male, so they opted for the larger amount of coverage.

Ed and Marjorie each got a $50,000 term policy a few weeks later. They were impressed by Gary's argument about the need for insurance; about liquidity; and the need for an estate. They were willing to help out an old college buddy, but not to the point that they felt their own financial health was being jeopardized. The thought of having a taxable estate at all brought snorts from both of them, so they didn't devote much thought to the problem of beneficiary designation: each one paid for the policy on his or her own life, and named the spouse as beneficiary.

They continued to maintain both the whole life and term policies in force, more out of habit than anything else. After Ed finished his residency, they became enthusiastic (though not uniformly successful) investors. Their foray into commodities would have been disastrous except that, when Marjorie found out she was not going to get tenure, she was offered (and accepted) a very nice job with a firm that made econometric models of commodity trends.

In effect, they won their gamble: neither of them died young, or at a time when the other spouse was economically dependent. Eventually, they had substantial assets, both liquid and illiquid, to make up an estate. They did borrow against the cash value of the whole life policy, once, when they had a chance to get into a shopping center venture. The policy loan was duly repaid. Insurance was the least exciting part of their financial plan, but it *was* a part, and it wouldn't have been wise for them to leave it out entirely.

Buying insurance is not a task most of us look forward to. We do not like to face unpleasant issues like, illness, disability, and death, especially if we are young. Moreover, insurance policies and terms are not always the easiest to understand. But investing some time and diligence in choosing the *right* insurance policies for you will pay off in the long run.

# 10

## Creative Singlehood

Although you may continue to receive help (even substantial help) from your parents, at some point you have to leave the financial nest and take off on your own. The postcollege period of getting your first full-time job and first apartment is an exciting one. If you made a few financial mistakes, you'll have time to "catch up" later; but if you start out the right way, establish good financial and investment habits, and learn to live *below* your income, you have a very good chance of living well during your prime years, and of retiring comfortably.

However, it's tempting to go overboard with your new financial identity. After years of living with your parents or in a dormitory or in a scruffy apartment with a mattress on the floor and posters Scotch-taped to the wall, and after years of "dressing up" by putting on a T-shirt with no obscene words in its caption and leaving off your earphones, the thought of a closet full of Brooks Brothers suits and upholstered furniture is an attractive one. No dues, no debts (well, maybe a sheaf of student loans), no responsibilities—it seems easier and more fun to go out every night and buy drinks for all your friends, to run up the balances on your shiny new credit cards until they threaten to repossess your ten-speed bike and your VCR, to study water-skiing in Waikiki if you can get two weeks off from your job.

We're not exactly preaching the good old-fashioned American values of thrift, hard work, and self-denial. After all, you owe it to the American economy to do your share as a consumer. We're just suggesting that you cool it for a while, establish a practice of investing regularly, and *later on* enjoy the rewards of having a comforting balance-sheet figure and a portfolio of assets to fall back on.

### Oh, Those Loans!

With scholarships harder and harder to get, many families turn to student loans as a way to handle college costs. Federally insured student loans typically offer bargain-basement interest rates, with repayment deferred until after the student finishes school and (at least theoretically) starts to earn a living.

Unfortunately for the Department of Education, many borrowers simply never bother to repay their student loans. And it can be hard for the government to trace someone who graduates from the University of Wisconsin and moves to Memphis.

However, in the summer of '85, the Department of Education announced that it was bringing in the Doomsday Bomb: faced with a total default of over $4 billion, the education agency said it would mail out notices of default. If no payment arrangements were made within sixty days, the defaulters would find their tax refunds seized by the IRS and paid to the Department of Education.

For this reason, and to protect your credit rating, one of the first things to do with your paycheck is to start repaying any student loans in your name. If relatives have loaned you money for college, they'll certainly appreciate repayment—especially in light of the fact that they have to report as income the "interest" you would be paying if you had borrowed the money at a commercial rate of interest. (See chapter 16 for a discussion of intrafamily loans.)

### Career Plans

Now that you have a job, we hope it's exactly what you want. But, this being the real world, we assume you had to make some compromises. If you're like most people, you have many working years ahead of you—at least thirty, maybe even fifty. This is the time to make long-range (though flexible) plans for your career.

If you want to stay with the same company, start thinking about the qualifications that are needed for internal promotions. Are there in-house training courses available? How can you sign up? Will the company pay for college or graduate courses? Which areas of the company are likely to see growth in the years ahead, and which are likely to contract? (The odds of long-term growth in the telecommunications division are greater than those in the horseshoe division, though you never can tell.) What skills will be needed in the future? (If the company does a lot of business with Japan, an engineer who is fluent in Japanese is more promotable than an engineer who isn't.)

Does long-term promotion depend on frequent transfers? If so, is this a plus or a minus for you? Some people enjoy seeing the world; others hate to be uprooted. Of course, it's easier for a single person to transfer than for a family to uproot a houseful of kids and perhaps a spouse who needs to find a job in a new town in a hurry.

If you're not happy with the corporate culture in which you find yourself, or if you think your employer is headed for a shake-out, think about the company (or industry) you'd like to move to. Once again, the questions to think about include long-term economic trends; the skills you think will be needed for good jobs in the future; and what kind of company you'd like to work for.

Also consider your long-range personal plans. Many people want to have children some day; and in most families, this means that the mother will take some time off from work (ranging from six weeks to ten years) or will reduce her commitment to work while the children are growing up. That means that she'll need some skills that are easily transferable; must be able to work for herself and set her own hours; or must be so indispensable that employers will hire her on her own terms and suit her hours to her child-rearing obligations. (If the father is responsible for most of the parenting tasks, of course the same thing applies to him.)

Flexibility is the key here. There are plenty of engineers who've been bounced from prosperity to indigence back to prosperity by the fortunes of the aerospace/defense industry. There are lots of computer programmers tossed out of work by increased sophistication of computer hardware. Factory workers who confidently expected their kids and grandchildren to work for the same employer find that factories are shutting down forever or moving to Asia or Latin America. High-paid corporate executives have been given a day to clean out their desks if they lose an intracorporate political struggle, or if the company is acquired. To succeed, you can't be too dependent on one company, one geographic area, or even one career. You must be ready to learn new skills and seek new opportunities as they arise (or as your rowboat springs a leak).

So, make a five-year career plan. It should include where you want to be, what you're looking for in terms of working conditions as well as compensation. Decide what you'll have to do to get there. Then make a schedule and stick to it. Review the plan regularly, and nudge it back into line when it drifts away from reality. Remember, this is the time for advanced training. Sure, it's a relief to get *away* from school for a while, but just think: if it's tough to go to night classes now, when you'd rather relax, think of how tough it'll be when you've put in a full day, you have a home to take care of, a hard-working and long-suffering spouse, and a couple of kids who've forgotten what you look like.

Studies have shown that people who *have* career plans get further ahead, faster, than those who are content to let their careers drift. But no plan is forever. Just as there's no longer such a thing as a "one-decision" stock, there's no such thing as a viable career plan engraved in granite and never changed. Always keep your eyes open for golden opportunities.

### Pay Yourself First

If you develop a habit of investing when you're twenty, the habit will be ingrained when you're forty. If you develop the habit of saving part of every paycheck, and of investing part or all of every raise (after all, you did without the money *before* your raise), you'll have a nice nest egg for your wedding and honeymoon, for kids if and when they come along, for a first house (whether or not you marry).

If your employer offers a 401(k) or other payroll deduction plan, think very seriously about participating. Once again, if you never see the money, you won't miss it.

Another way to save is to stop making interest-free loans to the U.S. government—which is what you do if your paycheck is overwithheld. Many people pride themselves on getting a big refund or think that a big refund means that their tax preparer did a great job. Instead, they should be kicking themselves for acting like prize saps. Your goal in tax withholding is to pay *exactly* what you owe, not a penny more. If you're a risk-taker, your goal is to pay *exactly* 90 percent of what you owe, and not a penny more; there's no penalty for 10 percent underwithholding, as long as you make it up with your tax return each year.

When you start a new job—or start to cope with tax changes—you'll have to file a new or amended W-4 form to determine the number of withholding allowances you claim. Most single people claim just one allowance and leave it at that. But you're definitely entitled to at least two allowances as a single —one to deal with the personal exemption, the other to deal with the standard deduction. You may be entitled to additional allowances if you own a home or have a deductible IRA or other deductions. The more allowances you can claim, the lower your withholding and the bigger your paycheck. (Note to tardy taxpayers: if you don't file a new W-4 form before October 1, 1987, your employer will withhold based on only *one* allowance, cutting your paychecks. So get those pencils ready.)

### Tax Planning for Singles

Which brings us to another point. If you're single, whatever your income, you'll pay higher tax rates than a married couple, filing a joint return, would pay on the same income. You, dear friend, need tax planning.

One of the smartest tax moves you can make—as well as one of the smartest financial moves you can make—is to buy a house, co-op, or condo. (More about that in chapter 14).

Another thing you can do: take a good look at tax-free mutual funds or money market funds. Even if you're only in the 15 percent bracket, 0 percent tax on income can look a lot better than 15 percent tax on the same amount of income. The big question is whether the after-tax return on a taxable investment beats the return on a tax-free investment.

IRAs are a lot less fun now that deductions have been limited. However, since you're just beginning your career, you may earn less than $25,000 and thus qualify for the full $2,000 deduction. (Of course, the less you earn, the tougher it is to find the $2,000.) Does it pay to lock up income all the way until retirement? Probably . . . you'll be very grateful later on for the funds in your IRA account.

If you're thinking about a career change, or about going into business for yourself, it may pay on both the career and tax levels to moonlight a little in self-employed status and sock some of the proceeds away in a Keogh plan. (On the other hand, unless you earn enough in your job to have paid the maximum Social Security tax on your salary, you'll pay a painful chunk of Social Security tax on your self-employed income.)

### Estate Planning for Singles

It's hard to get too excited about estate planning at this stage of the game. It's not that young, single people *don't* die; it's that, to put it crudely, their loss to the world is apt to be a purely emotional one, with no financial consequences. If a single person dies intestate, his or her court-appointed administrator may get a few nasty letters from creditors, and the estate may not be large enough to pay all the bills, but there won't be a widow and orphans tossed out into the cold to starve.

That's one reason that Dana—like a surprising number of lawyers—doesn't have a will. As far as she's concerned, they can stage a Viking funeral and heap up all her possessions and burn them after she dies. It might be nice to leave a few mementos to her friends, but it's not a high priority; she wouldn't mind providing for her parents, except for the melancholy fact that they're likely to die long before she does.

But if you have a lot of assets, or if you care passionately what happens to them, or if you want to make sure your debts and funeral expenses will be paid after your death, it does make sense to have a simple will and a modest amount of insurance.

### Developing a Good Credit Rating

If there's one area where youthful indiscretions will haunt you forever, it's your credit rating. All too many people have taken advantage of easy credit and immediately charged an apartment full of beautiful furniture, a wardrobe of great clothes, a refreshing vacation, dinners out when they're too tired to cook . . . you can imagine the rest. Later, when the same people, fiscally more prudent, want a mortgage or a car loan, they often find themselves turned down flat because they took so long about repaying these early debts. They get caught in a vicious cycle, needing to rely on credit financing but not qualifying for it.

On the other hand, the crusty Yankee, determined to make it last or do without, is at just as much disadvantage in the modern world. The person who has always paid (frugally hoarded) cash for everything can't get a loan either . . . because he or she has no credit record.

Your mission, if you choose to accept it, is to steer between these two extremes—get a prudent portfolio of credit cards and perhaps a loan or two, use them sensibly, and pay them off quickly. That way, you'll have a sound credit rating, and you'll be able to match expenses and income levels.

College seniors (especially those at prestigious colleges) often find themselves inundated with credit card applications. It makes sense to take advantage of at least some of these offers. Paradoxically, it makes sense to select some of the *least* attractive credit cards: ones at department stores you'd sooner die than enter, gas credit cards when you don't have a car. That's because credit reporting bureaus typically look only at your outstanding balance, not at the activity on the card. They can't distinguish between the customer who charges $1,000 a month and pays it off promptly, and one who never uses the card. The latter group gets credit for the commercially desirable behavior of the former.

Technically speaking, there are three kinds of cards that are commonly referred to as "credit cards":

- True credit or charge cards (e.g., department store cards, Visa, Master-Card): you agree to pay at least a minimum amount every month (typically, five or ten dollars), and to pay interest on all balances that are *not* paid off the first month.
- Travel and entertainment cards such as American Express and Diners Club: you agree to pay your balance in full every month, except for some large purchases such as airline tickets. If you don't, hefty interest charges await you. Travel and entertainment cards are typically harder to qualify for than credit cards, and often charge higher annual fees.
- Debit cards are a recent development. A debit card can be used to make withdrawals from automatic teller machines—and can also be used to pay for purchases if the retailer has an electronic terminal that can be used to withdraw money directly from your bank account. Understandably, merchants love this: they don't have to wait for the money, and don't have to worry about rubber checks. Customers are a little less enthusiastic, because of the possibility of computer malfunctions (to err is human . . . to really screw up, you need a computer), and simply because they'd rather keep the money in their own accounts, earning interest, as long as possible. Many people have learned the hard way that a checkbook is also a more convenient record-keeping device than a pile of debit-card confirmation slips.

### Which Cards? How Many?

As we've said, you may want a few perfectly useless cards, just to establish a credit rating. (If you still have trouble, join your employer's credit union, if one is available, and establish an account that can be used as security for borrowing; get a life insurance policy with cash value as a possible loan source; or even take out a small loan from a bank in which you have an account. Don't use the loan money—deposit it in an interest-bearing account and make payments as they come due. You'll spend a little extra interest on the way, but you'll establish a reputation for repaying your debts.

If you happen to qualify (and have expensive tastes) *and* you can pay the entire bill every month, travel and entertainment cards can be very helpful. For the rest of us peasants, credit (charge) cards do the trick. They are accepted by most merchants, and offer the flexibility of paying off the entire balance each month (escaping interest charges) or making payments in a number of installments (at the cost of high interest rates). Many of these cards also offer the possibility of cash advances—in effect, automatic, unsecured personal loans. Here again, the benefit is the convenience. The disadvantage, however, is comparatively high interest rates.

Some gas station chains and department stores will accept their own credit cards . . . but no one else's. So, if you're a regular customer, a credit card application makes sense.

In the palmy years of the sixties and early seventies, not only were credit cards free of service charges, the banks practically threw them at your head. Today, of course, most credit cards have an annual fee in the neighborhood of $20 to $35. Some charge a small fee for every transaction, or for every cash advance. Sometimes, if you want the card, you'll just have to bite the bullet and pay the fee. On the other hand, there's no point in getting four or five credit cards if your annual fees exceed the amount you charge each year.

You may be able to get credit cards with no annual fee if you maintain a number of accounts at a bank that offers free credit cards as an incentive; have a cash management account; or belong to an organization that includes service-charge-free credit cards as a benefit.

### Credit Cards and Cash Management

If you plan a solid day's shopping, you may prefer credit cards to cash, even if you're floating in the green stuff. The less cash you carry, the less attractive you are to a mugger or pickpocket. (On the other hand, don't tempt fate: keep your credit cards separate from your wallet. That way, the person who steals your purse, steals trash . . . or $38.19 and a roll of Tums, not your checkbook and credit cards too.)

If you incur a potentially deductible expense, you'll prefer credit cards to cash as well. The credit card receipt, and your monthly bill, will furnish evidence to the IRS that you really spent the money when and where you said you did. If you pay cash, the IRS has nothing but your word and your personal records (easily manipulated) to go by. If you pay by check, you have your cancelled check. But, from the seller's point of view, a credit card is better—they don't have to worry about your honesty the way they would if you paid by check. From *your* point of view, a credit card is better, as long as your balance stays within tolerable limits.

Every credit card monthly statement indicates a posting date—the last date on which charges will be billed for that month. Let's say your posting date is the fifteenth. If you buy something on the fourteenth, you can expect to see it on the next bill. If you buy on the sixteenth, though, it'll take an extra month to show up. The credit card company generally gives you almost a month to pay before interest charges accrue, so you can get almost two months' free credit by judicious timing of purchases. If you have several cards, you can fit the purchase to the posting date of each. Some stores and restaurants are notoriously inefficient about reporting transactions to credit card companies, so you can get a month's, or even two months', extra free credit.

Credit cards really come into their own when they allow you to lock in bargain prices on things you really do need and can afford. If your old winter coat has had it, you can buy a new one at the end-of-season sale in March, and string the payments out until the snows fly again. If you've decided that you want a VCR, and that it fits into your budget, you can take advantage of Nutty Nick's Columbus Day sale, instead of waiting for your Christmas bonus to come through. Similarly, you can use cash advances for sudden bargains that require cash, or for irresistible investment opportunities—as long as the transaction is worth the interest charges you'll incur, and as long as you're sure you can repay.

*If* you use them sensibly—confining yourself to things you do need and can afford—credit cards are the greatest things since sliced bread. If you can't use them responsibly, and suffer from the common delusion that easy credit means you'll never have to pay for the stuff, they're the worst thing since moldy bread. And you can't even make penicillin out of them.

### Strategies for Semisingles

There are millions of people who are more than roommates, and less than married (at least to each other). The Census Bureau calls them POSSLQs—Persons of Opposite Sex Sharing Living Quarters. (Some of them are Persons of Same Sex Sharing Living Quarters, but the Census Bureau hasn't figured that out.)

If you're living together, you *don't* get the tax advantages of the joint return

—but you don't have to worry about the marriage penalty either (see chapter 16). If you have joint accounts with your live-in, the inheritance and tax consequences are entirely different than those for married couples' joint returns. If the joint accounts are substantial, we urge you to seek legal advice about this.

If a married person dies without a will, his or her spouse and children are automatically entitled to a large portion of his or her estate. In fact, if there *is* a will and it leaves little or nothing to the spouse, most states let him or her challenge the will and get a statutory percentage of the estate. If a cohabitant dies without a will, the other cohabitant has no such right to a share of the estate.

As we'll discuss in chapter 12, it's far from automatic that the poorer spouse will get alimony when a marriage breaks up. On the other hand, it's all but inevitable that the couple themselves will make an agreement, or the judge hearing the case will issue an order, dividing the couple's property along equitable lines.

There are no equitable distribution laws for cohabitants, and "palimony" is a journalistic invention. There *are* cases that will divide an unmarried couple's property based on a written or oral contract between them, and some courts will hold that a couple's behavior (for example, pooling their assets, working together in a business) was the equivalent of a contract to share property. There are also cases holding that people who do anything so immoral (or at least as chancy) as living together can't expect the courts to give them any help.

If you are living with someone, it makes a lot of sense to have a written agreement. It needn't be formal—just sit down and agree which items belong to each of you as an individual (which you can take guiltlessly if the relationship breaks up); which items are joint property, and how you'll divide them if worst comes to worst. If you have joint accounts, you should agree how much each will contribute, and how you plan to divide the household expenses. Make it clear who gets to keep the apartment in case of a split. If you own a house together, make it clear how much each contributed, and the ownership percentage of each of you.

On the other hand, the relationship may continue harmoniously until one of you dies. In that case, you'll want to protect your faithful partner by making provision for him or her in your will, and by maintaining adequate insurance coverage. (The insurance coverage doesn't give a hoot about your relationship to your beneficiary, as long as the premiums get paid. They *may* make a fuss if your live-in partner wants to buy an insurance policy on your life—they may claim that s/he doesn't have an insurable interest in your life. In that case, all you have to do is buy the policy yourself, name him/her as the beneficiary, then make a gift of the policy to your cohabitant.)

On the other hand, the relationship may progress so well that you decide to do something *really* radical and get married. Which brings us to our next chapter.

## CASE HISTORY
### *Creative Singlehood*

Cornflakes after midnight. Patsy Cline sang about walking after midnight. But Dale Robichaux preferred cornflakes when he had trouble sleeping (which happened fairly often) and when he was unaccompanied in bed (which happened more often than he'd like you to believe). He would stare at the illuminated dial on his clock radio for a while, then get out of bed, pad into his tiny kitchen, and fix a bowl of cornflakes. He loved the privacy, the sense of doing something secret, something he would never have been permitted to do when he was a kid.

Dale was a man indelibly marked by the sixties—both eighteen and nineteen. The latter could be discerned in his rectangular wire-framed glasses, droopy mandarin moustache, and slightly thinning blond hair swept back and over his collar, and in his habit of addressing everyone as "man," whether this was chronologically or chromosomally appropriate. The former appeared in his great-great-great-granddaddy's pocket watch, which he wore year round, and in the vests he wore during the winter and the starched white piqué waistcoats he wore during the summer.

His $850-a-month one-bedroomer had a fireplace with gas logs (any attempt to use real ones would burn down the building), but there was no room for a table in the kitchen: just enough room for a counter and a Louis XIV barstool. The counter could just about fit a toaster oven, an espresso machine, a bowl of cornflakes, and a yellow pad, so Dale could worry about money in graphic form.

Two years earlier, he had quit the District Attorney's office to start his own law practice. Although the number of death threats against him had diminished noticeably, now they came from his own clients rather than those he had helped put behind bars, which was disagreeable. More to the point, Dale wasn't sure about the financial wisdom of the change.

When he quit, he was earning $34,000. He didn't expect to make any money in his first year in practice, and he hadn't. In his second year, he had grossed $47,819 (a figure etched in his memory), which sounds more like it, doesn't it? But as an assistant district attorney, his only working expenses were replacement waistcoats and a *Wall Street Journal* subscription.

As a sole practitioner, he had to worry about office rent (not very high —a more established lawyer rented him a room for $100 a month, in exchange for Dale's taking over some of his least interesting and lucrative cases); telephone bills; enough law books to make the shelves look impressive; and he even had to buy his own yellow legal pads instead of filching them from the supply room. Sometimes he thought that Daddy was earning more than he was.

Daddy was not the senior Robichaux—who had passed on some time earlier—but Dale's secretary, whose full name was Trinidad Gonsalves. He depended heavily on her skills in typing, pacifying hysterical clients, and remembering where things had been filed and when things were due. Any further involvement was short-circuited by the fact that Daddy's husband was not merely a police sergeant but a jealous man; it was his way of injecting a little romance into the prosaic métier of desk sergeant.

Every month, Daddy's salary, the office rent, and the Keogh plan took a big chunk out of the incoming cash. He had established the Keogh plan with an eye toward his own, very eventual retirement—he was thirty-three when he shook the dust of the DA's office off his feet; but he had to make contributions for Mrs. Gonsalves, which rather cramped his style. Then there was the rent, the electricity bill, the cleaning services (he had a great, though abstract, respect for order; left to his own devices, both apartment and office would turn into sties).

The upshot was that, after everyone got paid, after the American Express bill (for the occasional dinner and evening at a jazz club with the latest girlfriend) was satisfied, there wasn't much money left over. Furthermore, he had to keep more money in his checking account than he would have preferred: because his income was unpredictable, but the bills arrived steadily, and the IRS was heard from four times a year. It wasn't much of a strategy, but he pretty much dumped all his incoming money into the checking account and helplessly watched it flow out.

Well, it was at least a free checking account paying 5.5 percent on the rather modest balance.

In the assets column, he had inherited a picturesque and moldy clapboard house in Jackdaw Couch, Louisiana, from his aunt Honoria. He had never sold the house, both out of sentiment for the old home place and the virtual impossibility of finding a buyer for the damn thing. Aunt Honoria had left him $11,000, most of it spent, the rest invested in stock. Unfortunately most of them were airline stocks—Dale thought airlines were romantic. He had also bought some municipal bonds that were doing better—but a reliable 11 percent yield on $5,000 isn't exactly enough to buy a BMW.

Dale was a pretty good poker player, and usually managed to win a couple of hundred dollars at a throw, but this was hardly a dependable source of income.

As he scratched over the figures on the yellow pad, he pondered the chances of improving his financial situation:

1. He could start making more money. This seemed possible—his practice was expanding; he was working on a very promising case on a contingent fee that could be as much as $50,000 (*if* he won the case, and it would take more than a year to get the case to trial, and it might be appealed after that). He thought he might be able to gross $60,000 this year, and perhaps $70,000 the next. Now, as to how much he could keep . . .
2. Cut his business expenses. That didn't seem very plausible—he didn't see how he could cut his office expenses below $100 a month: his furnishings were not exorbitant; the thought of desertion by Daddy filled him with panic, and in fact he'd probably have to give her a raise in the near future. Come to think of it, if he kept on litigating and doing estate planning, he'd probably need an office computer. Certainly, the computer would make it easier to get out the bills on time (but only God knew what would make the clients *pay* the bills on time). That would be an additional expense, but certainly not a frivolous one. If he bought a copying machine, he could cut down on the hideous bills from the copy shop. Would it be worth digging into a slenderish checking account to the tune of $700 or $1,000, to save $65 or $70 a month? Probably. He added a note to the pad to remind himself to ask Daddy to call around and get some price quotes on copying machines.

3. Cut down on personal expenses. Ridiculous. True, the apartment was tiny and the rent exorbitant, but it was conveniently enough located so that he didn't have to keep a car. Sure, he could save some money by moving into some *hovel* somewhere, but he declined to engage in such extremism. And he wanted to dress well, and eat well; he had no intention of coming home after a day at the frontiers of the law to hunch over a hot stove.

4. Improve investment results. He decided to sell the worst of the airline stocks, put the cash into his Keogh plan, and take the tax loss. Sure, he hoped to earn more money next year (making a tax loss more valuable), but he also devoutly believed that the new tax bill would keep his tax obligations within tolerable limits.

He concluded, as he had concluded several times before, that he wasn't going to get rich any time soon. The best bet seemed to be to increase his practice. That seemed practical. He made a note to be sure and send in his racquet club membership (and accompanying fee). Not only was it fun and good exercise, but it was a good way to meet potential clients and/or sexual partners, and he had literally hammered out a number of settlements in his cases while playing racquetball. Although Dale was an agnostic, he was a vestryman of the local Episcopal church —another source of clients.

A rumor, so far unaccompanied by a red herring (preliminary prospectus), held that Dale's apartment building was going to go co-op. If that happened, he would have two important decisions: whether or not to buy his apartment—and, if he wanted to buy, where the heck he would get the money (and if he didn't buy, where the heck he would move that would offer comparable amenities for "only" $850 a month).

He had a theory, abetted by advice from his stockbroker (who had been a sixth-grade classmate), that over-the-counter stocks in the health care field would yield both short-term and long-term profits. He decided to take the fee from a case he had recently settled, use part to pay the Brooks Brothers bill, and the rest to buy the stock.

He was reasonably pleased with his decisions, and was guardedly optimistic about his financial situation and prospects. He put away the yellow pad, checked to see that the appropriate file folders were stashed in his attaché case, ready for the morrow, and leafed through the latest *Sports Illustrated.* At last, feeling sleepy, he put the cornflakes bowl into the minuscule dishwasher, and padded into the bedroom.

The lesson here? The smart folks at Kellogg's don't fool around when it comes to cereal. Take a hint—you have a better shot at creating a lifetime of financial security if you start early, approach financial matters with confidence and maturity, and follow through on your plans.

# 11

# Preparing for Marriage

We won't be dealing with the emotional aspects of marriage here; there are any number of authorities, from Barbara Cartland to Edward Albee, to inform you about *those*. Instead, we'll be talking about marriage as it affects your financial life-style. Two bank accounts that beat as one . . .

The most usual situation today is that both spouses will be working at the time they marry, and will continue working for most of their lives, at least until they reach retirement age. If they choose to have children, one spouse (usually the wife) may spend some years exchanging paid employment for unpaid child rearing. In this situation, the couple will have to adjust from having two incomes to meet the needs of two people, to having one income to support both spouses and one or more very expensive little strangers.

As we've discussed in chapter 2, the key is to have open communications between both spouses; to have a workable budget and the discipline to stick to it (and the sense to amend the budget when conditions change). In addition to the budget tasks that face every single person and every family, there are special legal and tax consequences of marriage.

## Should You Have an Antenuptial Agreement?

At one time the exclusive province of Orthodox Jews and suspicious heiresses, today's antenuptial (or premarital) agreements are a sensible choice for financially independent singles about to marry.

An antenuptial agreement, like a cohabitation agreement, defines the couple's separate property that they bring into the marriage, and outlines the financial regime they'll follow after the marriage. Many antenuptial agreements contain a waiver or limitation of alimony, if the couple ever divorces. They may also contain a provision under which one spouse gives up all rights, or limits his/her rights, in the other spouse's estate. These provisions are most likely to be used if one party is much richer than the other, the other a possible fortune hunter; or if the spouses-to-be have been married before, and want to protect their own children by earlier marriages.

In addition to these purely legal provisions, many antenuptial agreements contain less tangible provisions that are still important to the people involved. For example, they may agree to divide housework tasks in a particular way; may agree to spend at least one evening a month going over the financial records and working on the household exchequer; or may decide minimum and maximum visits with in-laws.

It's also important to discuss when (in fact, whether) they plan to have children, and how it will affect the mother's work life. Many a young parent has blithely *assumed* that the spouse would stop working, or keep working, only to find out that the spouse in question had very different ideas. Although no court in the world will *order* someone to do the dishes while his or her spouse is taking night-school classes, it's important for the couple to work these issues out. Can't agree on anything? Well, at least you can send back those godawful wedding presents. Where did Aunt Felicia *get* that atrocity— in a box of soap powder? At the town dump?

Which brings us to the question of whether antenuptial agreements are enforceable—will they "stand up in court"? Most contracts (a classification that includes antenuptial agreements) never *get* to court, because the parties obey the contract, or at least they don't think it's worth going to court. However, enough cases have been decided to be able to state some rules about antenuptial contracts:

- In general, a contract *will* stand up in court, if it's fair; if both parties had equal access to legal advice; and if both parties were open and aboveboard about their assets and liabilities. If you "forgot" to mention a $3 million trust fund or a $100,000 debt, don't be surprised if the court "forgets" to enforce contract provisions in your favor.
- Most states *will* allow a spouse to give up or limit his/her interests in the other spouse's estate, at least if s/he had adequate legal advice about his/her "right of election" (right to take part of the spouse's estate if s/he

doesn't think the will's provisions are adequate) and had a fairly good idea of the size of the spouse's estate.
- States are split about antenuptial contracts that limit or forbid alimony, saying that these contracts encourage divorce and therefore violate public policy. Others say that a properly advised adult can agree to do without alimony if s/he wants to. A lawyer with domestic relations expertise will be able to tell you which kind of state you live in.

Do you need a lawyer if you decide to draw up an antenuptial agreement? Maybe not, if your net worth consists of a '79 Duster and $4,000 in an IRA account, and if you and your spouse-to-be agree on all major issues. Definitely, if you each have substantial assets and the prospect of acquiring many more —in fact, each of you should have a lawyer in that situation. Somewhere in between, both of you can share a lawyer.

### Not Too Much Togetherness

You may decide to deposit most of your paychecks into a joint account, and to have credit cards that either one of you can use, based on both your incomes. This is a personal decision; it's up to you.

However, it's crucial that *each* of you maintains at least a small separate account, and that each of you maintains a good credit record based entirely on personal earnings. It's also a good idea for each of you to execute a durable power of attorney (see chapter 18), naming the spouse or some other responsible person as your attorney-in-fact to act for you if and when you are disabled.

If you do these things, you'll be prepared for any eventuality. Many widows and divorced women find it impossible to get credit, because they never established a personal credit history, and their husbands are unable or unwilling to help them out. A joint account can be tied up for crucial weeks or months after a death, or while a divorce is in process—times when quick cash is imperative. An accident or serious illness can make it impossible for a person to make decisions for him—or herself, and the legal process of appointing a guardian is lengthy and expensive. A durable power of attorney makes it unnecessary.

We hope you'll have a blissful, 120-year marriage. But it never hurts to be prepared for the things that could go wrong with this scenario.

### Wedding Announcements

Not only will you want your family and friends to know about your newfound happiness; you'll want to inform various people, corporations, and agencies about your marriage:

- Review your insurance coverage (or, more likely, get some).
- Inform your employers so that you can add your new spouse as an insured person on your health coverage, and make him/her the beneficiary to your retirement plan funds. If you decide *not* to have a joint and survivor option on your pension, produce the necessary waiver from your spouse.
- Inform the sponsor of your IRA if your new spouse will be the beneficiary if you die before retirement, or while payments are being made.
- Women: if you'll be using your new husband's name, get a new Social Security card, driver's license, credit cards, etc. If you'll be keeping your birth name, there's an argument for *not* notifying anyone, especially credit card issuers. Although the Equal Credit Opportunity Act made it illegal to cut off a credit account just because a woman marries (or divorces), issuers have been known to do just that—why expose them to temptation?
- If you aren't living together before the wedding, be sure to change addresses on magazine subscriptions; if one of you will be moving out of an apartment, make sure that the telephone company and utility company know about it, and stop sending you bills incurred by the next five tenants.
- Talk to your union rep or employee benefits coordinator about the way your health benefits fit in with your new spouse's and how to make a claim and avoid duplication.

### Yours, Mine, and Ours

Whenever two or more people share ownership of property, there are three basic ways this can be handled:

- Tenants in common—the "tenants" can leave their share of the property by will.
- Joint tenants—the surviving joint tenant(s) automatically inherit a deceased joint tenant's share of the property.

- Tenants by the entirety—a special joint tenancy limited to married couples. Tenants by the entirety get special protection against the joint
  property's being seized by creditors of one of the joint tenants.

If a person owns property before marriage, and has the property put into
joint tenancy or tenancy by the entireties, or deposits it in a joint account, s/he
is really making a gift of half the property's value to the spouse. Luckily, since
1981, such a gift has been free of federal gift tax. However, transferring
property into joint ownership is not always the best estate-planning move;
discuss it with your lawyer before you take action.

Sometimes people who are afraid of losing large amounts of money in
business, or who think they may lose large lawsuits, will transfer property into
their spouse's individual name. Once again, this is a gift, and once again,
there's no gift tax to worry about. But the maneuver doesn't always work to
keep the transferring spouse's creditors away from the property. The transfer
may be held void as a "fraudulent conveyance." The stratagem can also
backfire if the spouse sooner or later develops less-than-warm feelings toward
the transferor, and sells the transferred property and uses it to finance a more
agreeable life-style without the transferor.

Older couples should consult a lawyer about the best way to hold property
in order to protect assets against Medicaid requirements (more about this in
chapter 17).

In short, there are a lot of questions to think about when you have to
decide how title will be held (that is, whose name property will be in). It's an
important part of the legal advice you should get before any major transaction.

### Marriage and Taxes

We have some good news and some bad news. Married couples who file joint
returns get to take advantage of the lowest tax rates for any level of income.
Paradoxically, however, many middle- and upper-class couples face a "marriage penalty," and pay more tax as a married couple than they would if they
were living together. (One *Wall Street Journal* reporter took this into account,
and delayed her winter wedding until after the following January 1, so she and
her fiancé could have one more year of comparatively low taxes.)

These seemingly irreconcilable facts arise because the income tax system
is "progressive." That means "progressive" as in progressive disease, not
progressive as in left-wing. In a progressive tax system, you don't pay taxes
at all until you reach a minimum income; you pay higher tax rates on a larger

income. A regressive system—like Social Security taxation—imposes the same rate on everyone, but stops collecting once a maximum is reached. Thus, in effect, rich people pay a *lower* effective rate of Social Security tax than poor people.

To understand the effect of progressive taxation on a married couple's income, it helps to think of a wedding cake. Imagine that the Uncle Sam Bakery creates a wedding cake by starting out with three layers of cake, each fourteen inches in diameter. Then the cake decorator pares away one inch from the outside of the bottom layer—that's the tax on the first few thousand dollars the couple earns. Next, the decorator pares away three inches from the outside of the middle layer—the tax on the next few thousand. As the pièce de résistance—or the *coup de grâce*—the cake decorator slices away five inches from the top layer. The net result is a perfect, three-tier wedding cake —and an awful lot of cake for the tax man. A lot more was carved away from the top layer than the bottom layer—a higher percentage of the *last* dollar of income goes to taxes than from the first dollar of income.

When a person earning $15,000 marries a person earning $17,000, the couple's joint income is $32,000, so the marginal tax (the tax on the last dollar of income) is higher than on either of the single incomes. The tax bill is much lower than it would be for a single person earning $32,000—but quite a bit higher than the total tax bill the two would pay as single people. The so-called marriage penalty is really an effect of the progressive tax system. (A common delusion is to claim that the wife's income accounts for the entire marginal tax rate, and to claim that the family "can't afford" for her to work. Meanwhile, the cost of the husband's business suits and commuter tickets is conveniently ignored. This is bad accounting as well as sexism—the tax burden must be allocated between the two of them.)

For a while, a few people tried to get around the marriage penalty by getting a divorce each year so they could file as single persons and remarrying once again after January 1. Apart from the fact that it costs more to keep getting divorced than to shut up and pay the two dollars, the IRS will simply disregard any divorce it believes was purely a tax dodge. The alleged divorcés will be treated as married people filing separately, which wipes out the tax advantages.

### Contingency Day

Lynn Caine, author of *Widow*, writes movingly about the combination of emotional and practical problems that beset a surviving spouse. The problem is intensified if the spouse who dies is also the one who had sole control over the couple's finances. The survivor then has the task of figuring out what the family owns, who the bills are owed to, on what schedule, and must cope with insurance proceeds and administering the estate.

As an antidote to the practical problems, Ms. Caine suggests that couples have a regular "contingency day"—a frank discussion of things that could happen (a sudden death, a disabling accident) and what the family's financial response should be. Each spouse must know the amount of insurance coverage the other carries; must know where the policies are kept, who the beneficiaries are, how to make a claim. Each spouse must know the whereabouts of the other spouse's will, and it doesn't hurt to pick a lawyer or law firm who can be consulted in connection with the estate.

Contingency day can also be a good time to review financial plans. Is the trust for the kids going to be large enough to handle educational expenses? Is it time to switch out of equities and into the money market? Considering the way house prices have increased, isn't it time to increase insurance coverage on the family home? Would it be worth selling some stock and using the profits to lower the balance on the MasterCard?

Spouses can complement one another: a prudent spouse acts as a check on a reckless financial chance taker, or a methodical spouse can ride herd on one whose financial methods are slapdash. They can also work harmoniously together if their money styles are compatible. Two can't live as cheaply as one —but a couple or a family can work together to create wealth.


## CASE HISTORY
### *Preparing for Marriage*

Edward McGarry was holding the clipboard, while Helen Donato was poking ineffectually at the mounds of shredded newspaper, excelsior, straw, and packing peanuts that littered the floor.

"How are we on thank-you notes?" he asked.

"Fully up to date. We're not supposed to put all this garbage back in the boxes with the presents, are we?"

"I don't think so," Teddy said. This was going to be his first marriage, and he didn't have any sisters, so he wasn't fully conversant with all the attendant rituals. In fact, the only way he could cope with the situation was to impose a structure of schedules and goals—hence the clipboard.

"Flower arrangements ordered?"

"Check."

"Did you get the quotes on the champagne?"

"Yeah. They're in the blue folder on the desk."

"When are we going to go in for the wills?"

"Week from Tuesday at three o'clock. I already checked with your secretary. You didn't have anything scheduled and she's going to keep the rest of the day open, unless there's some kind of real emergency. And if there is, I can go by myself for my will, and you can make another appointment."

"Okay. I was supposed to call the insurance guy. I made you the beneficiary of my policy last year when we got engaged, so all I had to do was increase my coverage and add a disability policy. He's going to call you at the office to set up a time to see you and give you his ideas about your coverage."

"I don't really think I need any more. It's not like I'm keeping you, or anything; I mean, if I dropped dead tomorrow, I hope you'd be horribly upset, but it wouldn't stop you from making a living."

"It's not like I'm keeping you either. But I think we both should have some insurance, especially disability, and it'll be nice for the kids, once they come along."

"Did we get the bank statement?" Helen asked. Although they weren't living together, and were old-fashioned enough to avoid doing so until *after* the wedding, they had opened a joint account after the engagement.

"Sure. It's on top of the refrigerator."

"Well, what kind of place is *that* to put it?"

"That's where my mother always put the bank statement so my dad would know where to look for it."

"From now on, let's put it near the computer, okay? That makes a lot more sense."

He acceded, with bad grace, but he had to agree that it did make more sense. Each had deposited two thousand dollars in the joint account, and they agreed to deposit half their paychecks—after IRA contributions had been made—to the account. (It was a special account keyed to money market rates; in exchange for a fairly high minimum balance, they were entitled to write up to eight checks a month without charge, with a fifty-cent-per-check charge for subsequent checks. They figured that they might lose some interest by keeping several thousand dollars in the account instead of in a cash management account; but they were willing to trade off the convenience of having a handy bank and cash machine for the extra return.)

By this point, Helen had swept up the packing materials and stuffed them into plastic trash bags—it took three. "Some of this stuff is really the pits, you know?"

He agreed, but his private feeling was that it would be embarrassing to get wedding presents in the form of money rather than potentially hideous gifts. Helen would have preferred money—even if it isn't the right size, it's always the right color.

"I hope we get lucky at the casino," she said moodily, thinking of the island paradise where they would be spending their honeymoon. "Otherwise, we're going to be spending all our bonuses."

"It's definitely worth it," Teddy said; he had gone so long without a vacation that his co-workers were beginning to suspect him of masterminding an embezzlement plot. "And, after all, it's the last honeymoon we're ever going to have. Well, maybe a second honeymoon, together. But definitely not with anyone else."

"I sure hope you're right," Helen said. "Not only do I love you and want to spend the rest of my life with you, but I sent that lawyer away with a flea in his ear when he said something about us signing an antenuptial agreement. If I didn't think I could trust you about money, I wouldn't be marrying you."

Teddy was a little uneasy, but didn't want to mention it. In the Victorian novels he loved to read, every marriage came accompanied by a marriage settlement. Dammit, both money and marriage were serious (he was about to think that both were sacred, but stopped himself in time), and should be handled with due stateliness. Anyway, as a tennis buddy of his (who happened to be a lawyer during the less interesting of his waking hours) pointed out, if they did get a divorce, no court would give Helen a plugged nickel anyway.

He returned to the clipboard. "Tickets for honeymoon."

"Plane tickets, check, in the green folder. Hotel reservation confirmation, confirmed by phone, they said it's been sent out, hasn't arrived yet. Listen, want to do the bills tonight?"

"Okay, if you've got those presents under control."

"All logged in. I got my phone bill—did you get yours?"

"No, I'm on a later billing cycle. Oh, yeah, I called the phone company and told them when to disconnect my phone. And I have the electricity bill, too."

Their plan was that they'd sit down at least one night a month, and pay bills and have the computer kick out a financial statement. They agreed that they'd pay the mortgage and assessments on her condo, the telephone and utility bills, and other bills that appertained to them as a couple, from the joint account. Each one would maintain separate accounts with the other half of his or her aftertax income, and would use those accounts for personal bills—like their wardrobes; entertaining friends the other couldn't stand; his opera subscription and her basketball tickets.

They agreed that, as soon as they got back from the honeymoon, she would transfer the condo from her name into their joint names. That would be a sizable gift, but not a taxable one—there's no gift tax on gifts to one's spouse. He agreed to transfer his account with his commodity broker to their joint names, though at the moment, there wasn't enough in the account to get excited about: he'd been on the wrong side of a couple of market moves.

The honeymoon was a bit more expensive than they'd thought it would be—they had no luck at all at the casino, and a very low resistance to temptation in the forms of native handicrafts, duty-free French perfume, a Swiss watch for Teddy, and sweet rum drinks with vegetation sprouting from them (a possible factor in their lack of luck at the casino). They agreed to pay the credit card bills from the joint account—except for the perfume and watch, which came from their separate accounts.

As their marriage progressed, they did sometimes fight about money (Edward calculated that 11 percent of their arguments were about money, but, then, he's that kind of person). However, the arguments were about differences in style and temperament, not about bounced checks (because they kept the checkbooks in exquisite balance), and not about relentless hounding from their creditors (because they paid their bills on time) or mad extravagances (because their occasional extravagances were not really fatal to their financial plans).

Money didn't really come between them often because they generally stuck to the rules and plans they had designed together. Teddy and Helen maintained a healthy respect for the financial aspect of their union.

# 12

## Planning for Divorce

Marriage is about love, support (financial and emotional), raising a family, growing together—and it's also about compromise, accommodation, and money. Divorce is about guilt, greed, resentment, revenge, animosity—and money. The typical scenario is that a couple, after years of arguing about money, discover that the income and resources that wouldn't support one household now have to stretch for two households. Once, unhappily mated couples stayed together for the sake of the children; today, they may stay together just because they can't afford to split up. The sobering fact is that a divorce may not hurt a man's standard of living (may even improve it), but almost always causes a severe decline in the standard of living of women and children. Plunges from comfort to welfare are not uncommon.

The process of getting a divorce itself can be expensive. You may do all right with a do-it-yourself divorce if you're reasonably amicable and have no children and no assets worth mentioning. Otherwise, you are probably making a mistake by forgoing the services of an experienced divorce lawyer. Even an amicable divorce can leave a wake of bad financial and tax decisions.

Sometimes it's possible for a couple to use the same lawyer. This is emphatically not recommended. It's close to impossible for a lawyer to represent two clients equally well when their interests are opposed. Every extra dollar that client Ramona gets comes out of client David's pocket; and what about that affair that client Alex confessed in confidence—shouldn't client

Suzanne know about it if state law gives her a bigger share of the marital assets where a spouse is guilty of fault?

Therefore, you'd better plan on having a lawyer for each spouse. Some of the legal fee may be deductible—the part attributable to tax advice or the part attributable to getting and collecting taxable income (i.e., alimony). The deduction won't be allowed unless it, and other miscellaneous deductions, exceed 2 percent of adjusted gross income. But, if, as is common practice, the husband pays the fees of his wife's lawyers, he doesn't get the deduction, even for her tax and alimony advice. Be sure to ask your lawyer for a detailed bill that gives you evidence for any deduction you're entitled to take.

But it doesn't stop there. In addition to lawyers, you may need to hire accountants (for tax and valuation advice), appraisers, and business brokers. After all, how else can you tell what a small business or an art collection is worth? Naturally, each spouse will have a different opinion about the value of a major asset.

### Three Kinds of Money

Potentially, three kinds of money are involved in a divorce. First, there's a division of the marital assests. In nearly all states, this will be done on *equitable distribution* principles—the judge handling the case either approves the arrangements the parties made in their separation agreement, or divides the property according to statutory guidelines and the judge's own sense of fairness. (A recent survey of California cases showed that the average was 70 percent of the overall marital assets to the husband, 30 percent to the wife.) This process creates two important questions—What's a marital asset? And what is a fair division of these assets?

The second kind of money is alimony, maintenance, or spousal support. The spouse with more assets can be ordered to pay the spouse with fewer— usually it's the husband who's ordered to pay, although needy husbands are entitled to alimony on the same terms as needy wives. If complicated tax rules are followed, alimony can be deducted by the paying spouse, and is taxable income for the receiving spouse. However, if the receiving spouse has negotiating power, he or she can specify in a separation agreement that the amounts paid will *not* be alimony, so s/he won't have to pay tax on them.

The third kind of money is child support, paid by the noncustodial parent to the custodial parent. When child support is paid (and it often isn't— compliance is miserable, in both senses of the term), it has no tax effect. The paying spouse doesn't get to deduct it, and the receiving spouse doesn't have taxable income. Before 1984, if monthly payments were not allocated between child support and alimony—say, if an ex-husband was paying $150 a month to his ex-wife—the whole amount would be treated as alimony. As a result of the 1984 tax reform act (DEFRA), even if there's no allocation between alimony and child support, an amount will be treated as child support if it depends on some possibility involving a child.

*Tip*: It's still better to allocate—that gives *you* control over the tax treatment of the amounts.

## The Separation Agreement

A separation agreement is a contract between spouses, settling financial matters like property distribution, alimony, custody, and child support. In some states, it's literally a vital document—you can't get a no-fault divorce without one. Wherever you live, it's an important document. It gives you a chance to negotiate a settlement and get the terms *you* agree on, not terms imposed by a court.

Sure, it costs a lot of money to sit around and argue with two lawyers sitting there (and charging by the hour). But if you go into court without an agreement, you can expect to spend *real* money—on a trial that could last weeks, naturally with the lawyers charging all the time; on expensive expert testimony; and on forfeiting the financial and tax benefits you could have gotten from a properly drafted separation agreement. If there's a particularly juicy bit of financial or sexual scandal involved, you could find your name all over the papers—not a bit of publicity you're likely to enjoy.

You have two choices to make once you have a separation agreement, and once it has been approved by the court. (It probably will be, unless there's something obviously and monstrously unfair about it.) The separation agreement can either *merge* (become part of the court's divorce decree) or *survive* (maintain an independent existence). The paying spouse usually wants it to merge; the receiving spouse usually wants it to survive. That's because, once a decree merges, it becomes part of a court order, and an appropriate court can modify it. If the paying spouse violates the merged agreement, s/he can be punished for contempt of court, but that's not the most terrifying threat in the world. If the agreement survives, it's a private contract, and a disobedient spouse can be sued for breach of contract. Furthermore, courts can't modify the contract—that has to be done by mutual consent.

### What is "Equitable"?

Nearly all the states have equitable distribution systems. Therefore, a major objective of the separation agreement is to set up a division of marital property that will be approved by the relevant court as equitable.

The various states have criteria developed by state laws and court cases. In general, the factors that will be considered in dividing property include:

- The financial contribution each spouse made to the marriage.
- The nonfinancial contribution of each—e.g., housework, child care.
- The personal financial assets each has outside the marriage.
- The age and work experience of each—a fifty-six-year-old homemaker who has never held a paying job is in a very different situation from a twenty-nine-year-old computer programmer.

The theory is that the split is supposed to be fair, and to reflect the financial contributions and needs of each—not necessarily a 50-50 split.

### What Is Marital Property?

Theoretically, the job is to divide the marital assets, not separate property belonging to spouses individually. However, state law may require a spouse to transfer separate property if there isn't enough marital property (or enough liquid assets) to make a fair division.

One of the major areas of controversy is the "PHT degree" (the initials stand for "putting hubby through"). In the archetypal case, a woman drops out of school or gives up her plans for future education so she can get a dead-end job that will pay for her husband's professional education. Then he dumps her, after he has his degree or professional license, but before he has enough salary, or enough professional income, to make a decent-sized equitable distribution or alimony award possible. Will she have to pay the penalty of backing the wrong matrimonial horse, or will the courts find a way to help her out?

Very few states would go all the way and call his degree or professional license a marital asset, and divide its value between the spouses. On the other hand, few states would simply shrug and say she's out of luck. Various approaches have evolved:

- The courts could make him pay her tuition in college, graduate, or professional school, so they'll have a more equal earning ability.

- The courts could say that the degree and license are not marital assets, but a professional practice (like a small business) is, thus ordering him to pay her a part of the professional income for a number of years.
- He might be ordered to support her for several years, in compensation for her years of supporting him.
- The equitable distribution award might be adjusted to take her unusual financial contributions into account.

Of course, the matter won't have to go to court if the parties can arrange a separation agreement that's acceptable to both, and that deals with the "PHT" situation.

### What's Alimony?

Don't let the phrase "permanent alimony" get your hopes up too high (or down too low). Permanent alimony doesn't mean forever. It just means alimony payable after a divorce, as distinguished from temporary maintenance or alimony *pendente lite* (pending the trial) payable after separation but before divorce.

Alimony usually ends when the receiver remarries (though a couple could agree on a single lump sum for all alimony, or for payments for a certain number of years regardless of marital status). Some states forbid courts to order alimony for anybody who is capable of self-support; even in the other states, the trend is toward short term "rehabilitative" alimony designed to allow a spouse to get training to become self-supporting. So not only can't anyone count on alimony payments being made as agreed (or as ordered), but no one can count on substantial or long-term alimony being ordered.

For practical purposes, alimony is any payment for the support of an ex-spouse, so alimony is distinguishable from equitable distribution settlements and from child support.

For tax purposes, alimony (deductible by the payor, taxable income for the receiver) must meet *all* these tests:

- It must be payable in cash.
- It must stop when the payee dies.
- It must not be reduced for any reason having to do with children.
- If it's over $10,000 a year, it must be due for at least six years (fat chance —unless the receiver is elderly, ill, or otherwise unlikely to be self-supporting, courts would seldom order alimony for as long a period as six years). It's okay if the payments stop when the payee remarries.

- The payor loses tax benefits if the first year's alimony payments (whether by agreement or simple failure to pay) are more than $15,000 greater than the average payments in the second and third years, or if the second-year payment is more than $15,000 greater than the third-year payment. The paying spouse has to include in income the excess alimony, minus the $15,000 measuring amount; the receiving spouse gets a deduction based on the extra income tax he or she paid on the excess. But, frankly, the chances you'll find yourself in this situation are only slightly greater than the chance that Bobby Ewing will turn up in your shower.
- Even if the payments do meet all these tests, the divorcing couple can agree that the amounts will *not* be alimony; the IRS won't object as long as the payor doesn't take the tax deduction.

### Who Gets the House?

The usual outcome is that the custodial parent will get to live in the house with the kids, at least until they grow up. This is not inevitably the case; if there are no kids, or no substantial assets other than the house, the best thing to do may be to sell the house and split the money. Some other strategies include:

- The custodial parent gets to live in the house, and is assigned full ownership—but s/he has to make all the payments.
- The custodial parent gets to live in the house (perhaps paying rent), but it belongs to the paying spouse, who pays the mortgage, etc.
- The custodial parent gets to live in the house, perhaps paying a specified share of the expenses. Once the kids grow up, the house is sold, and the proceeds divided.
- The house is sold, and one spouse gets an amount attributable to the original equity; the other gets the profits on the sale.
- In a two- or multi-family house, each spouse lives in a separate apartment. This is great for preventing disruption in the lives of the kids, but check to see if it harms your tax status. For example, some people who are separated (but not yet divorced) are allowed to file as single people, with tax rates lower than married people filing separately. But different courts take different views of what it means to be "separated"—some say that if the spouses live in the same house, they're not really separated, even if they can't stand each other.

### The Negotiating Process

Once a couple has decided to divorce, just about everything is open to negotiation. To reverse the slogan: somebody walks, and money talks. The amount of assets to be transferred, on what schedule, the form the assets will take, custody and visitation, and tax matters are all up for grabs.

One of the most powerful factors is time. If one spouse is in a hurry to divorce and remarry an impatient (perhaps a pregnant) paramour, but the other still cherishes hopes of getting back together, obviously the hopeful spouse has a strong incentive for staying married at least until a satisfactory settlement is produced. A spouse who has been guilty of fault in a state that uses fault as a criterion in setting equitable distribution or alimony awards may be in a hurry to arrange an amicable settlement before the facts come to light.

Timing also matters when it comes to making a divorce official. A couple can file a joint return as long as they are legally married on December 31 of that year—even if they hate each other, and even if they live apart. But a joint return requires the signature of both spouses. If the lower-income spouse refuses to sign, the higher-income spouse can face a painful tax bill, because the rates for married taxpayers filing singly are quite a bit higher than the rates for joint returns. The disparity becomes greater if the lower-income spouse is

| Richer Spouse Wants | Poorer Spouse Wants |
|---|---|
| * The smallest possible overall package | * The largest possible package of financial transfers |
| * Nothing down, low monthly payments | * As much money as possible up front, generous continuing payments |
| * High proportion of tax-deductible alimony | * High proportion of tax-neutral child support |
| * No provision for ex-spouse and children after payor's death | * Generous insurance and/or will, trust provisions for ex-spouse, or at least for kids |
| * Dependency, medical expense deductions for kids | * Ditto |
| * Ex-spouse gets appreciated assets | * Ex-spouse keeps appreciated assets |
| * Alimony terminates ASAP (unless high-bracket taxpayer needs to pay for six years to lock in the deduction) | * Alimony continues as long as possible |
| * Separation agreement merges | * Separation agreement survives |

making a home for the children, and qualifies for lower head-of-household rates. If the lower-income spouse has any sense, s/he won't sign the joint return without getting concessions in return.

Every divorce is different, of course, but, in general, the negotiating parameters for the couple are outlined in the table on page 177.

As you can see, their objectives are usually diametrically opposite, which makes for some interesting negotiating sessions. However, there are some areas where their interests can be harmonized. Alimony can be a tax shelter for a high-bracket tax- and alimony-payer, and s/he can actually end up with more aftertax income by paying alimony that reduces his or her tax bracket. No matter how much the divorcing couple hate each other, they usually love their children, and want to see the children well provided for. A payor can consent to high alimony, knowing that the ex-spouse will remarry quickly and end the alimony obligation.

## Appreciated Assets

Let's say that a couple agrees that the marital assets are worth $100,000, and that he should get $60,000 worth, she should get the remaining $40,000. That doesn't end the negotiations—because they will still have to decide who gets what assets. Part of the question is practical—as we've said above, the custodial parent usually gets the house, or at least gets to live in it; if one spouse uses the pickup truck or the computer in his or her business, it doesn't make sense to award it to the other spouse.

Cash and money market funds are also easily divided. But what about stocks, bonds, and other assets that could have appreciated (increased in value) since they were acquired? On the practical level, it's only fair to treat this property as if it were worth its present value, not its original value. So if the couple bought stock for $10.50 a share, and it's now worth $19 a share, five hundred shares should be treated as worth $9,500. (If the stock was owned jointly, it will probably be treated as if only half is being transferred—the transferee spouse already owned half of it.)

The tax situation has changed dramatically since 1984. Before that time, a spouse who transferred appreciated property would have to pay tax on the appreciation. The theory was that s/he sold the appreciated property, then traded it for marital rights worth exactly the same amount. The "exchange" was tax free, but the transferring spouse had to pay capital gains tax on the appreciation. (No tax losses were allowed for the transfer of depreciated property.)

However, as a result of DEFRA, the spouse who transfers the property no longer has to pay tax on the transfer. But don't think the IRS has cheerfully given up a source of revenue. Instead, the tax burden has been shifted to the transferee spouse. The tax bill is not immediate—it's deferred until the transferee spouse sells the appreciated property. Then a capital gains tax is due, on the difference between the sale price and the original price at which the spouses (or the transferor spouse) acquired the property. In our example above, let's say the transferee spouse keeps the stock for another year and a half, then sells for $21 a share. S/he has to pay capital gains tax on $10.50 per share.

Therefore, it makes a lot of difference whether you get cash, property with a stable value, or appreciated property in a divorce settlement. The choice depends on your tax bracket as well as your priorities. If you would have to sell the property for immediate cash, you'll also get an immediate tax bill (but at least capital gains rates are lower than ordinary income rates). If you take on appreciated property, you're also taking on market risk—the stock that's worth $19 a share today could be worth $3 a share when you want to (or need to) sell it. But if you can afford the risk, and can afford to delay the sale until the right moment, taking appreciated property could be a good deal for you (and for your spouse, who can increase your assets without depleting his or her own correspondingly).

### Divorce and Estate Planning

It's a normal reaction for a married couple to want to provide for each other and their children, by drafting wills and trusts and getting adequate insurance coverage. (More about this in chapter 18.) It's only understandable that this reaction lessens or disappears when the spouses are estranged.

In most states, once a couple is divorced, any will provisions relating to that spouse (leaving him/her money; appointing him/her an executor or trustee) are invalidated. The will itself remains valid, but those provisions are treated as if the ex-spouse had died before the testator. These state laws only apply if there has been a divorce—not a separation, or even a decree of legal separation. So once a couple separates, it makes good sense for each of them to draw up a new will. But separation, or even divorce, won't revoke your designation of an insurance beneficiary. So talk to your insurance agent about changing the beneficiary, unless maintaining an insurance policy for the benefit of your ex-spouse or children is part of the divorce settlement.

The payee spouse is probably going to want a guarantee that alimony payments will continue for the specified number of years, and that child support will continue until the kids grow up—even if the payor spouse has died in the interim. So the payee spouse will push for insurance coverage, a testamentary trust, or a bequest. However, the usual rule is that people can change their wills as often as they like, so the provision may be in the will one day, out the next. There *is* such a thing as a contract not to revoke or change a will, but states differ in the amount of enforcement clout such a contract has.

Until a couple is divorced, a spouse who gets less than the statutory elective share (usually about one-third of the estate) has a right to challenge the will and collect the statutory share. A divorced spouse does not have this "right of election," but separated spouses should know that election against the will is a real possibility if they die before the divorce goes through.

## Pensions After Divorce

Most states take the position that a working spouse's pension rights are a marital asset, and can legitimately be divided as part of a divorce settlement. This is most likely to be true if the rights have already vested (if the pension is already unconditionally payable to the worker sooner or later), less likely if the funds have not vested yet—after all, the worker could quit, get fired, or become disabled before vesting.

The general rule is that benefits from a pension plan can't be assigned to anyone except the worker. This rule is designed to protect workers from having their pensions signed over to their creditors. However, the Retirement Equity Act of 1984 changed this rule to a limited extent: pensions can be assigned based on a "qualified domestic relations order"—basically, a court order that deals with equitable distribution, alimony, or child support. The order has to specify the schedule for payments to the worker's spouse or ex-spouse, and the amount or percentage of the payment to be paid him/her. The order can specify that payments to the spouse or ex-spouse start on the earliest date on which the worker could retire and receive benefits—even if s/he keeps working after that time. It's a very good idea (at least from the receiving spouse's viewpoint) for the order to specify that payments will be made to the ex-spouse if the working spouse dies before the earliest normal retirement age. If this isn't specified, the payments won't be made.

The amount to be paid to the worker's spouse or ex-spouse will be adjusted to account for the likelihood of the worker receiving the pension, and also for the number of years that the worker was both married and working for the employer. If a man worked for a company for twenty-one years, only seven of which were during the marriage, then one-third of the pension will be the starting point for the computation.

Courts take two general approaches. Either a lump sum is awarded at the time of the divorce, to take care of all rights in the working spouse's pension, or the spouse gets a share of the working spouse's pension "if, as, and when" it is payable.

A spouse who is awarded rights in the other spouse's pension can roll the funds over into his or her own IRA, but is not entitled to use ten-year forward averaging or treat the funds as capital gains.

### Who Gets the Exemption?

The general rule is that the parent who provided a home for the kid for most of the year gets to claim the child as a dependent on his or her tax return. The test is one of time, not of who provides the most money. However, the parents can change that if they agree. The custodial parent fills out IRS Form 8332 (or a similar statement), and the noncustodial parent attaches it to his or her tax return. They might do this if the noncustodial parent is in a higher tax bracket, and needs the exemption more.

The decision doesn't have to be made once and for all; it can be made each year. In fact, annual renewals can be a negotiating point: the custodial parent can just refuse to sign if the child-support payments are in default. On the other hand, the ex-spouses may not even want to talk to each other once a year.

Either parent (custodial or noncustodial) can deduct medical expenses for the kids (if, of course, the overall medical expenses are high enough to be deductible). And just because the noncustodial parent gets the exemption, it doesn't mean that the custodial parent can't claim head-of-household status, the earned income credit, or the dependent care credit, if s/he is otherwise entitled.

### Collecting the Payments

A person who is in a hurry to get divorced in order to remarry (or simply because the marriage has become so distasteful) is likely to agree to a deal that a cooler-headed person would spurn.

Years after a divorce, one or both ex-spouses may have remarried and started new families. It's understandable that the adorable baby just born to an adored new spouse would get more attention than the possibly sullen, unmanageably adolescent offspring of an ex-spouse one would prefer to forget.

For one reason or another, compliance with alimony and child-support orders is dismal. An April 1984 study released by the Bureau of the Census in July 1985 shows that about half of the single mothers were supposed to receive some payment from the kids' fathers. Of those, three-quarters received at least *some* of the required child support, but only half received the full amount ordered. The full amount ordered is nothing to write home about— average payments in 1983 were $2,341, *down* from $2,746 in 1978, and down even more in real (inflation-adjusted) dollars.

A payee spouse has various options, before and after the divorce, to make sure that s/he gets the amount agreed on and/or ordered by the court:

- Don't make unreasonable demands. It's tough enough collecting *reasonable* amounts; if you extort an unreasonable agreement, you'll never see that money.
- Get as much money as you can up front—a motivated spouse is more likely to make one payment right now than monthly payments for years.
- Try to have a trust set up to fund alimony and/or child support. A neutral trustee is far more likely to make the payments on time than a hostile ex-spouse.
- Try to get life insurance (especially paid-up policies) involved in the settlement—again, the insurance company is less personally involved.
- If all else fails, various steps can be taken to collect overdue support payments: garnishing the payor's (or, in this case, nonpayor's) salary; putting a lien on his/her property; having his/her tax refunds diverted to pay the overdue amounts.

No one ever said that getting a divorce would be fun, or easy. But if the soon-to-be-ex-spouses and their lawyers are willing to behave maturely and responsibly (not always the case—and the lawyers can throw even bigger tantrums than the clients), a way can probably be found to allocate their property and set up an appropriate schedule of continuing payments, with the least damaging financial and tax consequences.

## CASE HISTORY
### *Planning for Divorce*

Marsha Blumbaum drew back her arm and, with a vicious hiss of air, slammed the black rubber ball against the wall of the court. "That's what we're gonna do to your crummy client," she said.

"That's what you think," Dale Robichaux said. "Hey, by the time we're finished with your client, he isn't going to need his tennis racket."

"Why not? No, never mind, I figured it out. Forget it. Your client is going to get *zip. Zilch. Nada.*"

"My client is going to get the house, the car, the joint accounts, and substantial child support."

"I'm glad you don't have the effrontery to ask for alimony," Marsha panted, scooping a difficult shot off the floor.

"It just isn't a great idea for her," Dale said. "She makes a pretty nice income, and if she gets alimony, it's just going to give her tax problems. Anyhow, the kids are young enough that she's going to need child support for quite a while, and she might remarry in the next couple of years."

"The psychiatrist, hmm? The co-respondent?"

"Will you cut out this crap with the psychiatrist? He isn't a co-respondent, assuming that there was such a thing anymore."

"But we have that letter she wrote him. I mean, no way is she gonna get any alimony in this state with that letter in the file."

"I don't know why you people can't figure out that the reason your client could find that letter in the desk is that she never sent it. I mean, do you have an envelope? A cancelled stamp? A postmark? All you have is this dippy letter about how crazy she is about her shrink, which is not illegal in this state or any other."

After the game, as Dale sat with a cane-covered Breuer chair cutting into the backs of his gym-shorted legs, Marsha brought some much-needed cold drinks. She handed Dale his grapefruit juice, and pressed the cold, dappled can of Foster's Lager against her forehead and the back of her neck. Then she opened the can, tore open a small paper packet of salt, and sprinkled a few grains of salt into the beer. "Replaces the electrolytes," she explained. "Okay, my client offers seventy-five a week child support."

"Let's not insult each other's intelligence, okay?" Dale said. "That won't even pay their tuition, and he's the one who wanted them to go to that snob school in the first place. Does he seriously want them to go to public school? And does he really want his kids to have to go without just because he and his wife can't stand each other anymore? I mean, we can't stand them, and we've only known them for a couple of months. They've been married for fourteen years."

"Dale, we've got you over a barrel. You've seen the numbers at that pretrial disclosure hearing. We have two more months to come up with a settlement. If we don't, I assure you my client has no problem with letting the case go to full trial. And I think that the case is going to come up in front of Open Mind Kelley."

"Why do you call him that?"

"Because he *thinks* that every pope since Pius IX is a direct agent of the devil, but he's willing to keep an open mind about it. You go up before Kelley with a client who's a working mother, you're screwed already. *His* mother never worked, she stayed home scrubbing the floor and baking angel food cakes, or whatever, and *his* wife got a job teaching school and ran off with the school psychologist. Hey, that's right, once Kelley hears this routine with the headshrinker, your client is going to be lucky if he doesn't order her summary execution."

"Talking about over a barrel," Dale said, chewing the last ice cube in the grapefruit-juice glass, "I hope you've filed for an extension of your client's 1040, because you're going to have to come up with something awfully good to make my client sign a joint return. And I figure that your client will have to pony up an extra two grand to file a separate return —that's assuming that my client pays half the tax on a joint return, which I assure you she has no plans to do."

"I'll have to stop negotiating now," Marsha said. "I'm going to go take a shower. Give me a call at the office once you guys are willing to be a little reasonable."

Three days later, Dale's client, Michelle Parran, shuffled a handful of bills. It reminded Dale of a poker hand; he would far rather have had a pile of poker chips in front of him than the analysis pad and financial calculator.

"I can't believe what it costs to heat that barn," Dale said. "And are you sure those quotes were for fixing your roof or restoring the Sistine Chapel?"

"We were very involved in Gracious Living when we bought it," Michelle said. "As far as I'm concerned, if I never see another piece of crewelwork again, it'll be too soon. And the commuting is brutal." (She was an art director at a magazine.)

"The outline of a Machiavellian scheme appears," Dale said. "Okay, let's go over those child-support figures again."

A little later that day, Richard Parran was telling Marsha, "I don't want her to have that house, dammit, I love that house. It's a beautiful, gracious home, and now that it's the way I want it, I want to live in it. And it's convenient to the office, and it gives me a setting for entertaining suppliers and customers. She's the one who doesn't want to be married, let her find some apartment someplace."

"You both agree that she's going to have custody, don't you?" Marsha said.

"Sure. She's a rotten wife, but not too bad of a mother."

Marsha's private opinion was that her client had no intention of

dealing with kids except in limited doses, when they were freshly pressed
and starched, on their best behavior, and when they could be taken
either to a restaurant of Richard's choice or to an interesting sporting
or theatrical event or could be displayed to his advantage. "Right, then,"
Marsha said. "Usually, in a situation like that, the custodial parent either
gets the house as her part of the settlement, or gets to live there until
the children are emancipated."

"But that isn't the law, is it?" Richard said. "I mean, it isn't illegal
to do it the other way. My friend, Dr. Manus the ophthalmologist—he's
very well known—*he* got the house. It's a sixteen-room center-hall
Colonial. Very gracious."

"We'll work on it," Marsha said. "Now, about your business."

"There's nothing to talk about," Richard said. "I built that business
up from the ground, she had nothing to do with it. It's mine."

"Her statement is that when you first started the business, she did all
the bookkeeping and billing, without pay."

"So what else is new about the Dark Ages? When I was nineteen, I
was peeling potatoes in Fort Ord. Does that mean I get to call up the
federal government and have them send me a couple of tanks?"

"She also says that she contributed to the business's success by giving
dinner parties and holiday parties."

"She's my wife, what did she expect to do?"

"However you feel about it, the law of this state is that a business
owned by one of the spouses is a marital asset, and we'll have to take
it into account."

It took several more sessions with the clients, a few more racquetball
games, and a lot of time on the telephone and hunched over financial
records, but the Parrans (and their lawyers) eventually came to an agreement, and it was duly approved by Judge Timpkins (it turned out that
Kelley was temporarily appointed to a higher court).

As everyone wanted, Michelle got custody of the two children, Nina
and Paul. Richard got custody of the house—he got the right to live
there as long as he wanted, on two conditions: that he pay Michelle $400
a month rent, and that, if he decided to sell it, he would notify her of
any offer (she would have the right to find a bona-fide better offer) and
pay her half the net proceeds of the sale.

Richard agreed to pay $150 a week child support, and, after a look
at his tax return, $100 a week in alimony. Various propositions were tried
out about transferring some of the stock in his business to Michelle. But
Dale realized that owning a minority of the stock in a closely held
business—the majority of whose stock is held by someone who can't
stand you—is not a very valuable asset. You don't have enough voting

power to affect corporate decisions and there's no way you're going to get any dividends on the stock. Worse, no one wants to buy the stock, so you can't even sell it.

Instead, the soon-to-be-ex-spouses agreed to a one-time payment of $15,000 in return for all rights Michelle had in the business and in Richard's retirement benefits under the company's pension plan. She also got their art collection, half the money in the money market account, and about a quarter of their stock and bond investments. Richard got the rest of the stocks and bonds, and also kept their time-share in a vacation condo and their share in a real estate limited partnership.

Michelle was very concerned about the kids' further education. Richard agreed to continue paying their private-school tuition. He also agreed to transfer a healthy chunk of change into an irrevocable trust; his brother, a banker, agreed to act as trustee. The purpose of the trust was to use its income for the kids' personal, medical, and educational needs. The trustee could also accumulate the income, if it wasn't needed, or distribute part of the principal if the kids really needed it. According to everyone's best estimates, the trust would be large enough to pay for two college educations by the time the kids were old enough. Any leftover principal would be divided equally between Nina and Paul when Paul (the younger) finished college or reached the age of twenty-five.

Richard didn't like this very much, but Marsha was adamant that money be available for college costs. After examining Richard's rather sketchy estate plan, she discovered that he was likely to face substantial estate taxes (especially since, as a divorced person, the unlimited marital deduction would not be available). The assets in the irrevocable trust were removed from his estate, saving lots of estate taxes. However, they were also removed from his control: he couldn't use them or enjoy the income from them. No pain, no gain.

It was a good thing Richard got that extension. They did, eventually, sign a joint return, and Michelle reimbursed Richard for one-third of the taxes for the year. He paid the rest.

Richard revised his estate plan, leaving most of his estate to the children, but adding not-insubstantial provisions for his two sisters (if they survived him) or his nieces and nephews (if they didn't), and adding bequests to two of his favorite charities. That will didn't last long—he remarried fourteen months after the divorce. He also agreed to maintain a $75,000 insurance policy on his life for each of the children.

Michelle had a will drawn up (she had never had one before) dividing her estate, such as it was, equally between the children. She also bought as much insurance as she could afford.

Richard also agreed to pay the hearty legal fees the entire process had generated. It was some consolation that he would get a tax deduction for the part of his (but not Marsha's) bill that was itemized as representing tax advice. He had enough money to need lots of tax advice.

The bottom line? Richard got to remain in the house he loved, at the cost of a modest monthly rental payment, and with the proviso that he could keep only half the proceeds if he sold the house. The heating and utility bills became his responsibility. He was also stuck with the roof repairs and other, future maintenance, but the agreement provided that his share of the sale proceeds would be adjusted to take these expenses into account.

He agreed to pay (and, as it turned out, was pretty good about paying) $250 a week to Michelle—$100 of which was tax deductible. Under the agreement, the alimony payments were to continue for four years, which was probably longer than a court would have awarded. The child-support payments continued until each child reached eighteen. The state in which Richard and Michelle lived did not take the position that a parent's duty to support his or her children included the obligation to provide a college education; however, the trust took care of that.

Michelle used the $15,000 lump-sum payment for her interest in the business to make a down payment on a two-bedroom condo. She let the kids have the bedrooms, and slept on a pullout couch in the living room. The kids really cost more than $150 a week to raise, but she had her salary. She had to pay taxes on the $100 a week alimony payments, but the alimony decidedly came in handy. She was also careful to make the maximum contributions each year to her IRA (even though not all of the contribution was deductible), because she could no longer count on Richard's extensive deferred compensation for retirement security.

Michelle had always had her own credit cards, so she continued maintaining these accounts (and paying the bills). They analyzed their joint credit card bills, and she agreed to pay the part of the bills that represented her own clothing and part of the money spent on the kids' clothes. He paid the part that represented a family vacation (a last-ditch try at reconciliation), having the living room sofa reupholstered, car repairs, and some restaurant meals.

Once the dust settled, Michelle found herself with a noticeably lower standard of living, but there was no danger that she'd starve. Overall, she felt it was all worth it to see the last of Richard. Richard had transferred $15,000 cash and had divided the money market and bank accounts. He had paid significant legal fees and agreed to pay $650 a month as rent, alimony, and child support. He was somewhat less affluent, though his expenses as a single man would be lower than they were when he was married and rearing children. He emerged with a better estate plan, at the cost of setting up a large and quite irrevocable trust. He felt it was all worth it to see the last of Michelle. Both lawyers were happy to see the backs of their clients.

Richard and Michelle had lost "that lovin' feeling," but once they buckled down to the negotiations, they kept their wits. Divorce is very painful, but mature financial planning can prevent utter disarray.

# 13

## "Minor" Adjustments: Kids and Your Life-Style

Someone asked Commodore Vanderbilt how much it cost to keep a yacht. He said that if you have to ask, you can't afford one. Let's face it, you *can't* afford to have kids. Depending on who you ask, it costs either your entire income or the external debt of the Third World to raise a kid; so if you want 'em, have 'em anyway.

### The Baby Bonanza

Merchandisers slaver at the prospect of a couple having their first child. They know that most parents-to-be go completely mad, buying everything in sight . . . and the ecstatic future grandparents go beyond madness into fiscal recklessness. (By the time the second child comes along, everyone is much more blasé about the whole thing.)

You can save a lot of money by keeping your head. Despite what the salesperson tells you, your child will *not* be illiterate and unemployable merely because you refused to blow $2,000 on "educational" crib toys. As long as you observe common sense precautions about baby furniture (impossible to stick an infant head through; not covered with yummy toxic paint) and clothing (not marinated in cancer-causing chemicals), your well-fed, well-loved baby should be fine. But be wary of secondhand furniture: it may not meet current safety standards.

If the pregnancy is normal and there are no high-risk factors, you can save a lot of money by having a midwife rather than an obstetrician deliver the baby. Your health insurance will very likely pay the midwife's fee, or the fee for a "birthing center" (both more comfortable and less expensive than a hospital) if the appropriate licensed personnel and facilities are available in your area. And your health insurer may actually pay you in cash to leave the hospital as soon after the delivery as you can manage, rather than staying the conventional three days. One of Dana's friends recently had a second child. She told Dana that she stayed in the hospital until they kicked her out—she said it was her only chance for a little peace and quiet until the kids are ready for college.

In the financial realm, babies have one inestimable advantage over children. Babies know if they're full or hungry, dry or wet, coddled or ignored—but they don't know if they're fashionably dressed, or if their strained peaches are the brand *everybody* eats. Once your kids are big enough to walk, talk, and imitate, you will be besieged by requests for toys seen on TV, for "normal" $100 running shoes instead of those gross sneakers, for designer jeans, computer software, and much, much else, with threats of everything from suicide to turning you in for child abuse if you don't comply. If you're like most people, you'll give in occasionally—to budget-crunching effect.

### Teaching Kids About Money

Part of the problem is that kids really do think you're made of money; part of it is that things like mortgage payments and college tuition ten years down the line seem impossibly remote and uninteresting compared to this year's Christmas presents.

Kids usually have to be six or so before they really understand time; before that, the idea of saving up for next year's birthday present or next month's winter coat is probably beyond them. When you think of it, the concept that a tiny dime is worth more than a big nickel is really a pretty sophisticated one.

Then again, in the old days, either kids observed their parents working on the family farm or could see Daddy shoeing horses at the village smithy. The connection between work and food, warm clothing, and shelter was strong and direct. How do you explain to a little kid that Daddy is a commodities trader and Mommy sells insurance? A visit to the parental office reveals neither an understandable product nor a connection between work and the family's standard of living.

There are also psychological problems involved. Divorced parents are notorious for trying to buy love; competitive grandparents jockey for positions with gifts of escalating expensiveness; and many parents hate to admit that they can't afford something that other, neighboring families can afford, because it seems like a confession of failure.

One thing is clear, as observed by everyone from child psychologists to *Reader's Digest* anecdotalists. Kids may be prodigal with *your* money, but they tend to be anything from careful to miserly with their own. Give a kid an allowance, and watch him (or her) turn from secretary of defense to Scrooge McDuck. There's virtual unanimity among experts that kids *should* have an allowance, so they can learn budgeting and wise use of discretionary income. There are two areas of controversy: whether kids should be paid for chores (or expected to do them as part of family life), and whether allowances should be purely discretionary income, or should include an obligation to buy clothes, school supplies, lunches, etc.

One solution is to make part of the allowance unconditional, the rest in return for work above and beyond the call of duty. For example, parents who come home from work to find the house cleaned and dinner simmering away on the stove may well be inclined to provide generous allowances; it's sure cheaper than hiring a housekeeper. Parents also have a responsibility to shut up about clothes, records, and makeup purchased with such allowance, except in the rare case where their opinion is solicited. The point, after all, is to teach kids about using money intelligently—a lesson that will be blunted if the money must be used to satisfy someone else's taste, or if bailouts are available.

If your kids are entrepreneurially minded, you owe it to them to treat their ventures seriously. It doesn't help to gush about how "cute" it is, then provide the lemonade stand with below-cost materials and an endless supply of customers. If the venture isn't practical, kids should learn why, and be helped to make it workable.

However, the rule of nonintervention may have to be suspended for teenagers when drugs and alcohol are freely available in the community. Parents owe it to their children to find out if the kids are spending their allowance (or money stolen from the parents) on liquor and drugs. Sometimes the kids don't really want the drugs—they want to know that someone cares about their well-being and their activities.

### Kids and Taxes

No matter when in the year a baby is born, he or she is a dependent for the whole year—you don't have to prorate. (On the other hand, you can't take a fetus as a dependent, even if you *do* believe that human life begins at conception—the IRS is not amused.) The personal exemption is $1,900 for the 1987 tax year, $1,950 for 1988, and $2,000 in 1989; after that, the amount will be indexed for inflation. However, high-income taxpayers lose the benefit of part of the personal exemption (which is one reason why *real* tax rates are higher than the much-advertised 15 percent and 28 percent). The personal exemption is phased out completely somewhere around income of $100,000. Just thought you'd like to know. A widow, widower, separated, or divorced person who maintains a home for a dependent child or children may qualify as a "head of household." The tax rates for heads of household are lower than those for single people, and quite a bit lower than those for married people filing separate returns. TC '86 also allows heads of household to use a larger standard deduction than single people; earlier tax law assigned the same standard deduction to both.

If you own or control a business, and your child is old enough to do worthwhile work (say, working in the stockroom; making deliveries), you can hire your child. As long as s/he really does the work s/he's paid for, and the compensation is reasonable, your business gets a deduction for the salary; the salary is subject to income tax withholding (unless the kid can claim enough exemptions to wipe this out) but not FUTA or FICA tax (either employer- or employee-paid), and you're not bound by the minimum-wage laws. It's also a great way to find out if the kid really is interested in inheriting the family business, and what kind of job s/he'd do as a full-time employee.

### Kids' Income—Income Splitting R.I.P.

Gee, it used to be so peaceful doing tax planning in the good old days. You'd defer compensation; make sure that money coming in was capital gain rather than ordinary income; and you'd find simple ways to transfer income from high-bracket members of a family to lower-bracket members (e.g., kids and retired parents).

It was too good to last. Most of those techniques are now thoroughly obsolete. As to whether the reduction in tax rates is worth it, only time will tell. And surely new loopholes will be found. . . . Those wonderful folks who brought you the cattle-feeding tax shelter won't rest on their laurels.

Unfortunately, there's no "zero-bracket age" for paying taxes: anybody who has income has to pay taxes unless taxable income can be reduced to zero by using the personal exemption, standard deduction, itemized deductions, and credits. So if your children earn money by working, or if they receive gifts or interest on bank accounts, or if they're beneficiaries under a trust already set up, you are the proud parent of a potential taxpayer. (The slightly puritanical phrase "unearned income" means investment profits, as distinguished from money earned by the sweat of your brow.)

You're also the parent of a person with a Social Security number, if your child is over five years of age. For returns due after January 1, 1988, you must list the Social Security number of everyone over five whom you claim as a dependent. If you fail to do this, you're subject to a $5 penalty—big deal!— but the far greater risk is that the IRS may try to deny dependency exemption if the Social Security number is missing.

TC '86 has tough new rules about kids' income. In effect, Congress has made it pointless to try to shift income within the family (at least from the income tax standpoint—it might be worth doing to save estate taxes). If assets are transferred to a child under fourteen, the income on those assets will probably be taxed at the parents' highest rate—not at lower, "kid-sized" rates. (You may have read or heard that the crack-down applies only to assets transferred by parents, not by other relatives. Not true—whoever told you that was using an earlier version of the bill, not the one ultimately adopted by Congress.)

You've probably also heard that up to $1,000 of the child's unearned income can be taxed at the lowest, 15 percent rate. That's something of an oversimplification. The tax law really refers to "net unearned income." To compute net unearned income, you start with total unearned income, then subtract $500. You can also subtract $500 worth of standard deduction or $500 worth of itemized deductions. (The distinction means something, because, as explained below, there are limitations on kids' use of the standard deduction.) If the kid somehow manages to scrape up more than $500 worth of allowable deductions directly connected with producing the income, and if these deductions, plus the kid's other itemized deductions, exceed the 2 percent "floor" on miscellaneous itemized deductions, they can be deducted over and above the basic $500, instead of the $500 of standard or itemized deductions.

To see how this works, consider a child with no earned income and $1,300 unearned income. The kid can use $500 worth of standard deduction. That means that the net unearned income is $800. The first $500 is taxed at the child's rates, but the deductions have been used up by then; the remaining $300 is taxed at the parents' top rate. (How about an IRS training film called *Top Rate,* with Tom Cruise as a hot-shot trainee and Kelly McGillis as an expert in combating abusive tax shelters?) But for a kid with no earned income, and only $400 in unearned income, the $500 standard deduction reduces taxable income to $0, so no tax is payable at anybody's rates.

Children who file tax returns usually can't claim the personal exemption, because the tax laws say that a person who could be claimed as a dependent on someone else's tax return can't take the personal exemption. (It's only fair: anyone claiming the dependent is already taking a personal exemption for him or her.)

Children (all minors, not just the under-fourteen crowd) are also limited in the amount of standard deduction they can claim. If they have earned income, they can use the standard deduction to offset part or all of their earned income; if they don't, they can still claim a standard deduction of $500.

Just so the IRS won't have to spend a lot of time auditing piggy banks, kids won't have to file tax returns unless they have unearned income over $500, or unless they are not allowed to use the standard deduction to offset all their gross income.

Are asset transfers and income-shifting dead, then? A few useful planning techniques survive. Consider an extended family with a couple of rich members (desperately trying to reduce their taxable estates) and lots of hard-pressed young parents. If the rich relative gives the money, stock, or real estate straight to the parents, any income from the gift is, of course, taxable to the parents. If, however, the rich relatives give the stuff to the kids, the income may also end up taxed at the parents' highest rates. But if the rich relative pays tuition or medical bills for the kids, the rich relative's estate is reduced; there's no gift tax (because amounts paid directly for anybody's education or medical expenses are exempt from gift tax) and the parents and kids don't get any income, so they don't have to pay any taxes on the transaction.

### UGMA, No Cavities!

Even if giant tax benefits are unavailable, there still may be good reasons to give money or property to your kids, grandkids, nieces and nephews, and other relatives and friends. But the practical problem with giving kids large sums of money, or valuable property, is that if the gift is string-free enough to help out with estate planning, the youngster can do whatever he or she likes with the gift. You may disapprove of motorcycles, or sports cars, or trips to Marrakesh, but you're out of luck once the assets have been transferred.

Even apart from the tax side of life, legal principles have evolved to deal with the special problems of the interaction between minors and money.

The legal problem is that, while minors can own things, they have legal problems in administering and disposing of them. If a minor enters into most kinds of contracts (say, a contract to sell a house), s/he can walk away from the contract as soon as s/he reaches majority, claiming that the contract was a product of immaturity and shouldn't be enforced. Therefore, no one in his right mind will deal with a minor.

There are several ways to cope with this. One way is to have gifts or bequests to minors made in the form of a trust. The trustee takes control of the property, manages it in the minor's behalf, and eventually distributes the property to the eventual adult. A less formal variation is the power in trust: let's say you want to leave your art collection to your nephew, who is now four and a half. You leave it to his mother, ordering her to keep the collection intact until he reaches eighteen (or twenty-one), then turn it over to him.

The Totten, or tentative, trust is another informal mechanism for making gifts to minors (or anyone else, for that matter). The most common Totten trust is the "passbook" trust: a person opens a bank account in his or her own name, "in trust for" someone else. The person who opened the account can add to it or withdraw money freely; when s/he dies, whatever is in the account goes to the person for whom it is in trust. If that person is a minor, a guardian may have to be appointed.

Appointment of a guardian is time consuming, and expensive; further-more, the court-appointed guardian may have to go back to court (at further expense) whenever the minor's property is transferred. If the property is left to the minor in trust, there's no need for a guardian. What if it's too much trouble, or too expensive, to set up a trust? UGMA to the rescue.

UGMA is the Uniform Gifts to Minors Act. Depending on the version of this law your state has adopted, it may be possible to make gifts of money, stocks, and real estate to a minor, *without* setting up a trust, and without appointment of a guardian. A person (frequently, the minor's parent) is named as the UGMA custodian. Then, money, property, etc., can be given to the custodian, who will take care of the property, using it for the minor's benefit, and distribute the remaining property when the minor reaches majority. (In some states, including New York, the property can be held until the kid reaches twenty-one—even if the legal age of majority is eighteen. This is a good choice if you don't believe the kid has mature judgment.) In New York again, and in some other states, it's okay for a will to specify that a sum of money left to a minor is to be deposited in a particular bank, which will take care of it for the minor, under the supervision of the probate court.

You can set up an UGMA account, naming yourself as custodian, for each of your kids; and you can encourage relatives to make additions to that account instead of giving the kid some tacky toy, hideous sweater, etc., on birthdays and other festive occasions. Make sure you appoint a successor custodian in case you die while the kids are still minors. Check with your lawyer—it may not be a good financial or tax move to appoint yourself as custodian.

### Child Care

Good, responsible, safe child care is a necessity for single parents, for couples both of whom work, for couples consisting of one worker and one full-time student—or just for beleaguered parents who need a little time off. Good, responsible, safe child care is also difficult to find.

Some good news: if your employer offers child care (or reimbursement for your child-care costs) as an employee benefit, you don't have to pay tax on the value of this fringe benefit. However, the amount involved is limited to the *smallest* of these amounts:

- Your earned income.
- Your spouse's earned income.
- $5,000 ($2,500, if you're a married person filing a separate return).

San Francisco has an ordinance requiring employers to build child-care facilities in exchange for permission to develop a site; other cities may follow suit.

You can use IRS Form 2441 to claim a tax credit for some of your expenses of caring for a child (or a disabled dependent—say, an elderly, ill parent). The credit is available if the child-care expenses are necessary because both spouses work, or if the children are being raised by a single parent. The credit is based on a percentage of your adjusted gross income, going *down* as your income increases. For 1984, the amounts ranged from 30 percent (for AGI between zilch and $10,000) down to 20 percent for AGI over $28,000. The percentages can be applied up to a maximum amount—$2,400 for one dependent, $4,800 for two or more in 1984, so the maximum credit is $1,440 (30 percent of $4,800).

### Education Expenses

We've now led you painlessly up to the most painful issue: the cost of education and how to cope with it. Once your kids reach school age, the school system will take care of your child-care needs for much of the day. (You may still need help between the time the kids leave school and when you and your spouse get back from work.)

Some people think it's important for their kids to attend high-status nursery schools, so they'll have an inside track to prestigious private schools, and eventually to classy colleges. If that's the way you feel, be prepared to pay royally for the privilege.

If you're a brownstoner, you may find that any place you can afford to buy a home is a place you wouldn't want to send your kids to school. So you may have to include the cost of private schools in your calculations when you pick a house. On the other hand, if you live in an area with good public schools, be prepared for breathtaking property taxes.

Then there are music lessons, summer camp, tutoring, special SAT courses . . . but the biggest problem in family financial planning is dealing with the cost of college.

Want to project college costs of the future? As Mark Twain pointed out, if his contemporaries had projected recent increases in height backwards, they would conclude that the soldiers at the Battle of Hastings were about four inches high. But, as a safe minimum, figure on needing at least $10,000 per year, per kid—and, with your luck, you could have kids who want to become dentists or radio astronomers or something else calling for endless graduate school years (see figure 1).

### Basic Plans

Well, first of all, you can go to your kid's high school graduation, shake his or her hand, and wish him or her luck in all future endeavors, including somehow raising tuition for college. This won't make you popular with your kids right away, but perhaps they'll always be grateful for the lesson in self-reliance. Maybe not.

There *are* alternatives to attending a four-year college full-time. Maybe the kids can start out at an inexpensive two-year community college, then transfer to a four-year college. They could get full-time jobs during the day (preferably working for an employer who provides tuition assistance) and go to school at night. They could enroll in a four-year college, and work part-time on weekends and at night. Some part-time jobs (for example, night word-processing operator for a law firm) can be quite lucrative.

The kids *could* attend your state's university, and continue to live with you, thus qualifying for lower in-state tuition and saving dormitory costs. On the other hand, some of the most educational aspects of college years come from having one's very own dormitory room, hundreds of miles away from the nearest parent.

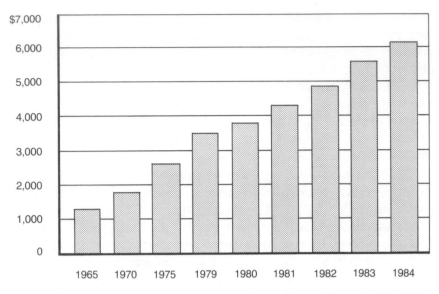

Figure 4    The rising cost of a college education—tuition and required fees for a full-time student and at a four-year university. (*Source:* U.S. National Center for Education Statistics, *Digest of Education Statistics*)

But maybe you want to go first cabin—you agree with your offspring's desire to attend a private four-year college. If you're hideously rich, you can just peel off a few thousand-dollar bills every semester, and never look back. If you're like everyone else, you'll need a systematic program of investment (preferably starting when the children are in diapers rather than sheepskin), combined with financial aid from the college, federal grants, federally insured loans, and private loans.

### Financial Aid Packages

Middle class: noun or adjective describing a person who is too rich to qualify for financial assistance, and too poor to qualify for a bank loan. Well, things aren't *quite* that bad. You may be able to qualify for federal or state financial assistance; for scholarship grants; or for private loans. By reducing college costs (as we've described above) and by using the financial strategies we'll get to in a moment, you should be able to make ends meet.

The federal government provides two kinds of grants for college students (grants are funds that don't have to be repaid) and two kinds of student loans. There's also a federal work-study program that permits students to earn some of their educational costs.

The grants are the Pell Grant (based on financial need), ranging up to $2,100 a year (1985–86 figure) and the Supplemental Educational Opportunity Grant, also need-based and ranging up to $2,000 a year. The Department of Education gives colleges enough money each year to cover all Pell Grants for which eligible students have applied. Schools get a defined amount of money for SEOGs, so it's vital to apply early, before the money runs out.

Work-study jobs paying at least the minimum wage are available for students who can demonstrate financial need. Again, it's important to apply early before the good jobs are snapped up. Some work-study jobs are on campus, others off-campus for nonprofit, public-service agencies. Kids who don't qualify for work-study should not necessarily despair—they may be able to get more lucrative jobs in the private sector.

As soon as the college lets your kid in, it will furnish you with a raft of financial aid forms. Much of the information needed for the forms comes from your income tax return; W-2 forms, bank statements, mortgage escrow statements, and your personal budget records may also come in handy. If you decide to apply for federal financial aid (and why not? You have nothing to lose but a few hours of swearing at the forms), four to six weeks later you'll get a Student Aid Report (SAR). The SAR recaps the information you provided, and includes a very important number: the Student Aid Index Number. In this case, a low number is good—if the number is under 1,900, your kid can get a Pell Grant; if the number is higher, it's no go. Other programs may use the SAR in their calculations as well.

Before you give up on scholarships and grants, put in some research time. There are scholarships for academic achievement not based on need. Some of them are based on high school grades or standardized tests; others focus on a particular area of achievement, such as science or humanities. The college may have scholarship funds available. An organization you belong to (say, the Masons or Rotary) may have scholarships; your employer may provide grants for employees' children.

Of course, you're familiar with athletic scholarships. These are not limited to major sports such as football and basketball—there are fencing scholarships, lacrosse scholarships, crew scholarships—and an athletic daughter might find that the school of her choice is eager to encourage female athletes (or anyway to prove that they're a great bunch of fellas who would never *dream* of committing sex discrimination). There are also music scholarships for singers, orchestra players, band players, composers . . . and even weirdo scholarships for people with particular last names, left-handed chem majors, and goodness knows what else. Your kid's high school guidance counselor should be able to help; also try the reference room of your local library. Your ever-helpful Congress pounded another nail into the coffin by decreeing that if your child manages to get a scholarship, any scholarship funds in excess of tuition and course-related expenses (e.g., books and lab fees) are taxable income. So are any scholarship funds specifically earmarked for other purposes (e.g., room and board). On the other hand, the scholarship money is treated as "earned income" for the purpose of deciding whether the kid is allowed to use the standard deduction on his or her tax return.

### Student Loans

If what you've got is an ordinary, non-needy kid with an inauspicious last name? Next step, student loans.

The two federal programs are Guaranteed Student Loans (GSL) and PLUS loans. No, it's not guaranteed that your kids can get a loan—it's guaranteed that, in the not-too-unlikely case that s/he defaults on the loan, the bank making the loan will get paid by the federal government.

Technically, the GSL is made to the student, and is his or her debt. (The bank will cheerfully accept repayment from the student, you, Jack the Ripper, or anyone else with a solvent checking account.)

The good news is that GSLs have a low interest rate (between 7 and 9 percent), and repayment need not start until after the student graduates or quits school, with five to ten years to pay. It's up to the student to contact the lender after leaving school to set up a repayment schedule.

The bad news is that the amount of the loan depends on financial need, and can't be more than $2,500 a year for undergraduates, $5,000 a year for grad students. Talk about your basic drop in the bucket. The total amount an undergraduate can borrow is $12,500, and the most a grad student can rack up is $25,000 (including loans when s/he was an undergraduate). There's also a 5 percent "origination fee" deducted from the amount borrowed—it goes to the federal government as a little thank-you for taking the trouble to insure the loan.

The PLUS loan is, indeed, an addition to the GSL. There's no requirement of need. PLUS loans go to the parent (up to $3,000 per year, $15,000 per kid) or to undergraduates who are financially independent of their parents (up to $2,500 a year; but the PLUS and GSL can't add up to more than the GSL limits). Grad students can get up to $3,000 a year, $15,000 overall, *in addition* to their GSL money. PLUS loans don't have origination fees, but the agency guaranteeing the loan may charge up to 1 percent as an insurance premium.

Again, there's bad news: 1985–86 interest rates are 12 percent, and parents who get PLUS loans must start repayment within sixty days of the loan. Student borrowers can defer principal payments, but must begin paying interest within sixty days of the loan unless the lender agrees to defer that too.

What if you don't qualify for GSL funds, and the PLUS funds just aren't enough? Fortunately for you, banks are actively seeking customers for loans. Some are offering premiums for students who borrow, and the Chase Manhattan Bank is installing computer terminals in schools throughout the country so students can borrow from Chase. As a benchmark, the *Wall Street Journal* for August 20, 1985, reports that Chase offers parents of undergraduates, or graduate students, up to $10,000 variable-rate loans to supplement GSL funds, or for parents who are shut out by the $30,000 family-income limitation of the GSL program.

Of course, if you're a qualified borrower, you don't have to get a loan earmarked as a student loan. You could get a second mortgage on your house; use a line of credit secured by the equity in your home; get a mortgage larger than you need when buying a home; other methods include getting a policy loan on your life insurance and using the cash advance provisions on your credit cards. Your job is to find the credit source that provides the most favorable repayment terms, with a monthly payment you can live with. The higher your tax bracket, the less painful the interest charges, because they're deductible.

### Planning for College Funds

Suppose you're already borrowed up to the nostrils, but your kids don't qualify for any known scholarship, grant, or GSL; and suppose that a PLUS loan is not only too small for your purposes, but would add a monthly payment that stands in for the straw that broke the camel's back.

Or, on the other hand, suppose that your kid has a package of financial aid; a part-time job; and you have one or more loans, and you're still short on tuition and dormitory fees—not to mention clothes, transportation, collect calls home asking for money, textbooks, the computer the college demands or expects, and all the other expenses of college life.

Or—Well, we're out of hands, but imagine the situation where *your* parents sent you off to carefree college days with all expenses paid and a guitar and Frye Boots thrown in, and you want to do the same. Or, contrariwise, that you couldn't afford college or had to pinch pennies and work two jobs to get through, and you want something better for your kids.

In any of these cases, you'll need to have funds available for some or all of the cost of college. The sad fact is that, for most middle-class families, a large part of the cost of higher education must come out of family resources accumulated before the kids reach college age.

If your investments have been fantastically successful, then, what the hey, you can just sell off a few shares of a little stock you picked up at $3\frac{1}{8}$ that now sells for 72 $\frac{5}{8}$. But then you'd be paying college costs with aftertax funds, and that's no fun.

Building a college fund is like building a retirement fund with an IRA or Keogh plan: it really helps to start early. (By the way, for those who have children late in life, or for people who remarry and start a second family, IRA and Keogh funds may be a very viable source of college money, if your kids are in college after you reach fifty-nine and a half.)

You can simply open a savings account, Totten trust account, or UGMA account for each kid, and make regular deposits. If you ignore our advice and continue being overwithheld in order to get a large tax refund each year, this is a good use for that tax refund. You can also ask relatives to make deposits into these accounts instead of buying the children another wool scarf (which they'll probably hate) or another toy (which will probably be left someplace underfoot).

If you think you know what will happen to interest rates (a delusion that has confined many economists to Amusing Agricultural Establishments), and if you're *sure* you won't need the money, you can buy zero-coupon bonds for each child. The advantage is that you'll know exactly how much will be in the college funds when it's needed (unless the bonds are called in the meantime). The problems? You may lose money if you sell the bonds before they're due; unless they're tax-free zeros, taxes are due on the "phantom interest" each year even though no cash is paid.

Colleges are really crying the blues nowadays. . . . They say that lower tax rates make charitable contributions less desirable. That cuts one source of their income. The temptation to make up for it by zapping the already hard-pressed tuition payers may be irresistible. With any luck, lower tax rates will make it easier for *you* to accumulate assets.

But we'd be lying if we claimed to have simple, foolproof strategies for beating college costs. The very affluent can just write a check for college tuition without much pain; or they can sell assets they won't really miss. For the rest of the world, the key is understanding the available benefits, starting an investment program far in advance, and choosing the best loan package available.

## CASE HISTORY
### *"Minor" Adjustments*

"Ladies, start your engines," Johanna Mikulski announced, and twenty-seven pregnant bellies rose and fell rhythmically. "Coaches, get ready. We're going to practice our cleansing breath, then move on to the panting."

For Johanna, this was work; she was teaching this class. For the class members and their husbands, it was preparation for a frightening and exciting new series of responsibilities.

Trinidad ("Daddy") Gonsalves (due date December 3) tried not to worry about all the things that can go wrong when you have your first baby at thirty. According to Johanna and the obstetrician she worked with, the baby was normal, healthy, and vigorous. According to the amniocentesis, he was slated to become Francisco Paulo Guimaraes Gonsalves instead of Dorothy Angelica Gonsalves. Daddy had heard varying stories about what childbirth was really like. Her aunt Giulia regaled her with stories about the days of agony the birth of each of her five children had caused her; her friend Tricia said that having a baby wasn't any tougher than running a 10k race on a medium-hot day. (To Daddy, who wasn't too big on exercise anyway, the two statements seemed more or less equivalent.)

The birth, even if it wasn't physically traumatic, was likely to become financially traumatic. Daddy planned to leave her job a month before the due date, and to take at least two months after birth to recover. After that, she knew she could return to work whenever she wanted, in fact, her employer, Dale Robichaux, was tremulous at the thought of having to fend for himself for three months.

They had worked out a compromise: she agreed to return as soon as she felt physically ready, but she would work less than full-time. She would set her own hours, and if necessary would take typing and transcription tapes home with her. They agreed that she would get paid half her usual salary, and would not be expected to work more than twenty hours in any week. However, she would be setting her own hours and controlling her own work, which would make her an independent contractor, not a regular employee. Dale would stop making payments of Social Security tax and withholding income tax from her salary, leaving her responsible for paying Social Security self-employment tax and making estimated tax payments. He would also stop making contributions to this Keogh plan for her, because she was no longer a full-time employee.

Luckily, her husband's job as a police sergeant entitled them to excellent health benefits, including complete coverage for prenatal care and delivery. So that was no worry. Equally luckily, her mother was retired and loved taking care of babies, so she could be relied on to handle much of Francisco's care while she was in Dale's office. When Paulo worked the four-to-midnight or midnight-to-eight shift, he would be able to handle some child care, and Dale had agreed that she could bring Francisco with her to the office on days when no clients were expected.

But having the baby would definitely put a crimp in their financial style. The Gonsalveses had agreed that Daddy would not return to full-time work until Francisco was in kindergarten. There was not much Paulo could do to increase his income: his salary was dependent on the police union contract. He planned to take the test for promotion to lieutenant the next time it would be given (two years away), and he knew that even if he passed the tough exam, it could take years to get appointed as a lieutenant. Sure, he could quit his job and go to work for a private security outfit, but he loved his job. He was also looking forward to the generous pension he could collect after twenty years on the job —only eight years away. (He had volunteered for the Navy, served a hitch as an MP, then gone immediately into the police force.)

They had a nice-enough four-room apartment; the dinette was about to become Francisco's bedroom. The location was convenient enough for both of their jobs, but the local schools were nothing to write home about (other than to complain). But the rules specified that police officers had to live within the city itself. Plenty of Paulo's brother officers flouted the rules, and lived in the suburbs (some of them in a suspicious degree of luxury), but he believed in abiding by the laws as well as enforcing them. That meant that, in a few years, they'd face some tough choices: buying a hideously expensive house, co-op, or condo in the city itself; sending Francisco to private school; breaking the rules and moving out of the city; or changing jobs to the private sector. A move to the private sector might mean a better salary, but it might also mean a cut in health insurance benefits—which would be a problem if Francisco ever acquired a little brother or sister. Both families had a history of bad teeth, and the Police Department paid for dental care; a corporation might not.

The Gonsalveses had already spent almost $1,500 on baby furniture, a folding stroller, baby clothes, and toys and accessories for the nursery. They knew that babies grow out of their clothes awfully fast. They could count on some hand-me-downs from Francisco's older cousins, but they knew that wouldn't be enough. Maternity clothes were another $600 expense, but Daddy planned to pass them on to her sister Luisa, who had just had her pregnancy confirmed.

Daddy had a year of community college credits; Paulo had completed a B.A. in Police Science after five grueling years of night classes. They both resolved that Francisco would never have to go through that. He would be an educated man, and he would be able to attend any college he liked. A look at college costs led them to amend that plan, but they wanted him at least to be able to attend the state university full-time, during the day, without having to worry about holding a job. So they resolved to deposit at least twenty dollars a week in a special bank account in their joint names, in trust for Francisco, and to transfer the money to a money market or mutual fund account as soon as it reached a large-enough sum to meet the minimum deposit requirements.

It would be tough, but they resolved to live on Paulo's salary while Francisco (and any future siblings) were growing up. This was more than okay with Sergeant Gonsalves, who felt better about himself when he could think of himself as the sole support of his family. They would save Daddy's part-time salary, and use it for their IRAs, for Francisco's college fund, and for "extras" like summer camp and music lessons for the kid(s).

So, on balance, they would have financial problems as parents, but none they couldn't solve. Daddy's income would decrease quite a bit, but they wouldn't have to spend much on medical care or child care. They'd get a new dependent for tax purposes, but their bracket wasn't high enough for tax planning to be much of a priority for them. They'd made the decision that Paulo should keep his job and try for a promotion, because job satisfaction was more important than the higher salary he might be able to earn working for a private company. Anyway, he'd be eligible for retirement at forty-five, and could get a private-sector job then.

They could get more involved in local politics, and try to improve the public schools; they resolved to do this, but wanted to keep their options open about private schools. Paulo thought St. Anne's, the local parochial school, was the best choice, but Daddy was concerned that the discipline might be too rigid (her brother had gotten kicked out of St. Anne's) and there might be too much emphasis on rote learning.

Francisco was in no hurry: he emerged a week late, on December 10, at eight pounds three ounces and in perfect health. He was even more of a delight than his parents had expected, and even more expensive than they had planned—but his proud parents still thought they had the best of the bargain.

Daddy and Paulo had done their best to plan ahead and use what resources they had wisely. The financial adjustment to parenthood was jolting but not insurmountable. By taking a realistic view of how their finances would be changed by the baby's arrival, these parents coped rather well.

# 14

## Major Commitments

Let's move into some examples of the way you'll integrate all the planning techniques in some of the largest financial decisions you'll ever make. Throughout your life, much of your paycheck will go either into your home or your wheels—how can you get the best value for your dollars? How can you understand the lengthy, complex documents offered for your signature? Even if you understand the basic terms of several deals, how can you pick the deal that forms the best fit with your own needs?

You've heard a lot about real estate investment; everybody has at least one friend or brother-in-law who's made (or claimed to make) a killing in occupied apartments or shopping mall development. Maybe that's your path to personal wealth, too; but right now, we're looking at the best way you can pick the apartment, co-op, or house to serve as your own personal residence. If you choose well, you can have a pleasant home; either see your equity in the home zoom year by year, or see the money you saved by renting an apartment appreciate as part of your investment portfolio. If you're a homeowner, you also get very meaningful tax savings. (In fact, as we'll discuss in chapter 16, owning a home is one of the best tax shelters available to ordinary working people.)

Naturally, you won't spend all your time at home; even if you don't have a job to go to, you're likely to be chauffeuring the kids to ballet class or just cruising down the freeway. Remember that little deuce coupe you bought for

$170 when you were in high school? Well, forget it; once your present clunker or cherry goes to the Big Used Car Lot in the Sky, you're facing a five-figure investment for a new car, and well into the thousands for another used car. We'll give you some strategies for keeping the cost of driving from driving you up the wall. Most people spend much of their lives either at home or in the car anyway, so it's sort of appropriate that many of the same financial strategies are useful for both:

- Careful shopping based on your needs and preferences.
- Picking the right down payment for your financial picture.
- Considering the cash-flow consequences of a loan.
- Shopping for the best deal you can get on interest rates, loan fees, and other credit costs.

Let's face it, it's much more fun to think about redecoration, or getting a brand-new car with additional vroom, than it is to worry about mortgage payments or how much an overhaul of the carburetor will cost. And most people would rather think about almost anything else than about funerals (especially their own or that of someone they love). But, nevertheless, we hope we can prove to you that a funeral is one of the major expenditures any family can expect, and that buying a burial plot is a real estate deal you may never have thought about, but may well have to make. We'll also give you some tips for making the sad occasion less traumatic in both emotional and financial terms.

Financial tools and a financial strategy aren't much good if they only help you with minor problems. The real challenge comes when you confront the most important personal and financial decisions. That's the big league. So let's start now.

## House Versus Apartment

At one end of the social spectrum are bag ladies, derelicts, and others with no fixed address; at the other, jet-set spongers who drift from yacht to mansion as professional guests. In the middle, there's everybody else, concerned with selecting the best housing value and making the house, apartment, co-op, or condo as pleasant as possible.

Most Americans—and especially most American families—want to own their own homes, and many people make accumulating a down payment a major objective of their investment program. Congress wants Americans to become homeowners, allowing taxpayers to deduct mortgage interest and real estate taxes and providing tax breaks when homeowners sell their houses after age fifty-five, or sell a house at any age and reinvest in a more expensive home. (The tax breaks are just as good for co-op apartments and condominium units.) The tax deal is even sweeter for those who become part-time landlords by living in part of a two-, three-, or four-family house and renting out the rest. They get a generous allowance for depreciation; can deduct the cost of repairs to tenants' apartments; and can use improvements to the tenants' apartments to offset the potentially taxable profits on sale of the house. (However, they lose some of the tax break available on sale and "trading up.")

If you rent an apartment, you're at the mercy of rent increases as often as the law will allow. If the building goes co-op or condo, you may find yourself having to move or buy your apartment at the least convenient time for you. If you're a homeowner, you can look forward to living in a fully paid off, free-and-clear home—which can be especially important if you're living on a fixed income after retirement. Once you build up substantial equity in a home, you have an asset you can borrow against if necessary. Older people can consider a "reverse mortgage"—a bank either makes a lump-sum loan or provides a lifetime annuity, in exchange for part or all of the equity in the house after the homeowners die.

After all this buildup, you can see that owning a house (or co-op or condo) can be a great idea. But it's not for everybody. Renting an apartment has advantages. When the plumbing leaks, you just call the super or the managing agent. It may take ages to get the repairs, but you don't have to pay for them. If the building is in a declining neighborhood, you don't have to worry about the value of the property holding stable—you just pick up stakes and move when your lease is up.

Renting may be your only choice if you've just left school or gotten married, and have just started a savings program. Even if you have a healthy money market fund and a well-balanced mix of mutual fund investments, renting may still be the best choice for you. Buying your own home can be a sound investment, but maybe your investment results are much better.

Maybe you hate to paint, tinker, and garden, and you have a nice apartment convenient to work, and the only house you can afford is a "handyman's special" in the middle of nowhere. Maybe your plans are uncertain—your company could transfer you, you might go back to school, you might marry your old boy- or girlfriend halfway across the country, and you don't want to be tied down to owning a house.

The price of houses *usually* increases over time, and you can *usually* find a buyer and sell at a profit—but if you buy at the top of a cycle and sell when real estate prices are going down, or when your area has fallen out of fashion, you'll have to wait a long time for a buyer or drop your asking price.

After all these warnings, you still want to become a homeowner (or sell your present home and buy a better one)? Great. Just be sure that you keep three important questions in focus. First, can you afford the initial costs of buying a new home (down payment, fees, and closing costs)? Can you afford the costs of making the home livable, or more pleasant (cash payments to contractors, cost of materials and new appliances, payments on a rehab loan)? Can you afford the monthly payments (mortgage, maybe a second mortgage, real estate taxes, water bills, utility bills, oil bills if you have an oil furnace)? If the answer is yes, it's time to set out the welcome mat.

### House, Co-op, or Condo?

The Dick and Jane readers always show a free-standing house, with a lawn and a white picket fence. That's the American dream. It's great to have a lawn for the kids to frolic, but remember that you have to mow that lawn, and that the more property you own, the higher your real estate taxes.

A co-op is usually an apartment building converted from rental units to units covered by a special "proprietary lease" giving the co-op owners rights over the building. If you buy a co-op, you *don't* buy an apartment—you buy shares of stock in the corporation that owns that building. Usually there's a "co-op board" that has the right to veto sales of stock—a fact that Gloria Vanderbilt and Madonna found out the hard way. More prosaically, if you buy a co-op and later want to sell, the co-op board may refuse to let a would-be buyer move in. Also beware of the "flip tax." Some co-ops, trying to prevent "insiders" from buying co-op shares at a low price, then turning them over at a hefty profit, insist that sellers turn over part of their profits (it could be as much as 25 percent) to the co-op board.

If you become a co-op owner, you'll have to pay a monthly maintenance charge that covers the provision of services such as heat and elevator service. If you can't pay cash for your shares, you'll also have monthly mortgage payments. Depending on whether or not the co-op association has enough funds to make repairs, you may get stuck with special assessments—to put in a new roof or an alarm system, for example.

If you buy a condo (whether it's an apartment or a townhouse), you really are buying real estate, not shares of stock. You own your particular unit, and have a right to use the common areas (halls, recreation areas, etc.). You'll have to make mortgage payments (unless you paid cash) and there may be a fee similar to the co-op owner's maintenance payments.

Co-ops and condos offer many of the satisfactions (and tax breaks) of owning a house, with fewer maintenance and repair obligations. It's also a matter of location—co-ops and condos tend to be located in or near cities; houses tend to be in smaller cities or suburban areas. Real estate agents say that the three most important things about a home are location, location, and location—so, once you decide where you want to live, you may already have made the decision about whether to buy a house, co-op, or condo.

### Old House or New House?

Many would-be buyers have the choice between a recently built house and an older house. Part of the decision is simply a matter of personal taste: do you think an oak floor is warm and traditional, or old-fashioned and tacky? Are original plaster medallions on the parlor floor a source of pride, or something to get rid of at the first opportunity? The problem with new houses is that they tend to be skimpily constructed, with small rooms. The problem with older houses is that they tend to be eccentric, the impact of age, wear, and unstandardized building techniques coming home to roost. You can't tell what lurks behind those walls: very possibly, the plumbing is exhausted and ready to collapse, the wiring system hopelessly inadequate, the furnace going down for the third time. It's essential to have an engineer look over an older house you're planning to buy. (A tip from a veteran: there's no way on God's grass-covered earth that the engineer is going to climb up on the roof, but you definitely want to know the condition of the roof. Bring binoculars.)

Many new houses come with a Homeowner's Warranty (HOW), a program that provides repairs in exchange for either a lump-sum payment or monthly payments. Investigate this very valuable feature. For older houses, you're on your own. You'll probably find that your neighbors will be glad to talk about their own experiences with plumbers, painters, carpenters (misery loves company). Unfortunately, it's easier to find out whom to *avoid* than whom to patronize.

### Brownstoning and Sweat Equity

You'd probably *prefer* to live in a quiet suburb or an exciting metropolitan residential neighborhood. But if the only house you can *afford* is in a rotten neighborhood, you may be better off buying the house, fixing it up, taking a profit, and moving to the area you wanted to live in the first place.

The good news about being an urban homesteader: you can probably buy a larger house for less money than you could in a more desirable neighborhood; and, once others follow the pioneers, you will probably find yourself living in a house that appreciates greatly in value, in a neighborhood that keeps getting better and better. Moreover, if you live in an urban area, your access to your job, shopping, entertainment, and other amenities will probably be easier than if you lived in the suburbs (but don't count on finding any amenities in your new neighborhood). The bad news: you could guess wrong, and find yourself in an area that continues to deteriorate. Even if the neighborhood eventually improves, you face years of rehabbing a house that might have been divided into single rooms, allowed to deteriorate for twenty years, or been abandoned by its owners. And, in the meantime, you may have to put bars on the window and alarms on every door, and spend every fine Sunday morning scrubbing graffiti off your front door. If you have kids, and the neighborhood schools are unspeakable, you'll either have to budget for private schools or find some way to send them to school someplace else.

Brownstoning, in short, is not for everybody. But if you can't afford a house any other way, want to stay in a metropolitan area instead of the 'burbs, are handy or have enough money to fix up the house, this high-risk, high-return strategy can give you a fine home (eventually) and a dramatically improved family balance sheet.

### Very New Homes

If you buy a co-op, condo, town house, or unit in a development, you may be buying a home that hasn't even been built yet. There are definite advantages: you can save money by having the builder eliminate the features you don't want, or have the unit customized to your taste. Furthermore, you can check on the progress of the work, or have an expert check for you.

The possible disadvantages? An inefficient developer can be slow getting everything finished, leaving you with home payments but no home for months or even more than a year. A crooked developer can take your money and simply walk away. A stupid developer could have forgotten to check the local water table (so your new home is underwater) or legal formalities (so the project is tied up in litigation). Even if your home is ready on time, little niceties like streets, roads, and sewers may be delayed.

A final caution: if you fall in love with the plans or the model unit, remember that what you see is not necessarily what you get. Go over the contract with a fine-tooth comb. Will your unit have the same layout? the same carpeting? the same lighting features? How much extra will you have to pay to get what you want?

## Home Improvements

At one extreme, there's the "shell," where you're basically buying four walls, a roof, and the opportunity to scoop out everything inside and replace it so you'll have at least a minimally livable house. At the other extreme is the dream house built to your personal specifications. But even dreams change over time, and a house can need repairs, or you can need an extra bedroom for the baby, a darkroom for a photographer, a separate entrance for a home business.

So you'll be making at least some home improvements sometime during your life in the house. If you can swing it, and the improvements are needed right away, it may pay to get a larger first mortgage than you need and apply the extra to fixing up the house. That's because second mortgage rates are usually higher than first mortgage rates, and rehab loans written as personal loans come even higher.

If the improvements are made once you've lived in the house for a while, you may have enough equity to get a comparatively inexpensive second mortgage, or to refinance your first mortgage for a high enough sum to pay for the improvements.

If you plan to live in the house forever, you can personalize your home. If you plan to sell the house and move on (or even think it's likely that your plans will change), be careful: that creative floor plan, the built-in laser light show, the sunken bathtub (and corresponding depression in the living room ceiling) may *lower* your house's resale value, not raise it. As a rule of thumb, *whatever* you do will infuriate potential buyers. Builders say that the kitchen is the most "overimproved" room in the house, with many families spending a fortune that they'll never recoup. If *you* spend a lot of money on avant garde stainless steel, the buyers will want stripped pine, and vice versa.

Keep careful records of all improvements made throughout the life of your house; they'll affect the cost basis (tax value) of your house. A higher basis means less potentially taxable profit. Keep especially careful note of money you spend to refurbish your house to make it more attractive to buyers: these "fixing-up" costs may also affect your basis. Most of all, keep a record of the amount of gain that you postponed taxation on: it will lower the basis of the *next* house you buy. (More about this in chapter 16.)

## Senior Homeowners

By the time a couple is ready for retirement, there's a good chance that the home mortgage will be paid off, or nearly paid off. That gives them several planning possibilities.

For one thing, they can just stay put, enjoying the freedom from mortgage payments; their housing cost will be restricted to property taxes, repairs, and utilities. However, this strategy can backfire if the house is too large for them to maintain, if they simply feel that they're rattling around in an oversized environment, or if it's a large, open-plan house with impossible heating bills (in the frost belt) or air conditioning bills (in the sun belt). If the rooms are smaller and can be closed off, the problem can be dealt with more easily.

Keeping the old house may be an emotional struggle for the survivor after one spouse dies. A suburban home can be difficult for a person whose visual or other physical problems make driving difficult or impossible. A sprawling, three-story house can create barriers for a person with visual problems, or one who is wheelchair-bound or uses a cane to get around. A compact ranch house or an apartment would be a better choice under the circumstances, although a lot can be accomplished with a chair lift on the stairs or other modifications that an architect can suggest.

Some people want to retire near family and friends; others want to explore. Some feel more comfortable with familiar things, others want to start a new life in a warmer climate. Luckily, the IRS provides a one-time tax break for home sellers over fifty-five (see chapter 16 for a fuller discussion): $125,000 of profits from home sales can be taken tax-free. The untaxed profit from the home sale can buy a life-care contract, an annuity, be invested in safe but high-yielding income investments, and can pay a lot of apartment rent.

However, senior homeowners should think carefully about selling the house and not replacing it with another house or co-op or condo. That's because a family home is considered an exempt asset for the purpose of Medicaid. Therefore, if an elderly person needs chronic custodial care and has to apply for Medicaid, the value of the home will *not* be counted in determining Medicaid eligibility, as long as the sick person's spouse continues to live there. (However, after both spouses have died, the local Medicaid agency may be able to collect part of the value of the home, cutting down on the possible inheritance of other family members.) If, like most people, the older couple *might* need long-term care, and can't pay $20,000, $50,000, or more a year, hanging on to the family home—or even *buying* a home for the first time—

can be a very useful strategy. If the old house is too big, too expensive to run, or too inconveniently located, the answer might be to buy a *smaller,* more convenient, but more expensive home—thus turning cash that might have been spent on medical bills to qualify for Medicaid into an exempt asset.

Another housing strategy for seniors: let's say that an older person or couple needs a place to live. Perhaps they've been living in an apartment in a deteriorating neighborhood, or their rent has been raised sky-high. If one (or several) of their children want to provide financial help but can't quite manage to have Pop and Mom move in with them, and if the kids are in a high tax bracket, everyone's needs can be met. The kid or kids buy a suitable house, co-op, or condo for the parents. The kids are the owners; the parents live there, and pay rent that is a fair market rent, and that covers, or nearly covers, the monthly mortgage payments and upkeep of the property. The kids lose the investment return they could have gotten on the down payment and closing costs, but they have little or no out-of-pocket expense (the rent covers all that). When the parents die or move, the kids own a property that, with any luck, will have appreciated nicely. In the meantime, the parents had a nice place to live and were protected against eviction.

### The Part-Time Landlord

How would you like to live in a house you own, without paying a cent out of your own pocket (and maybe even making a profit)? How would you like to turn dollars in your pocket into a tax loss—legally? How would you like to start a modest real estate empire for the price of *one* down payment on *one* house? All of these are within your reach, if you have the funds—and the personality—to become a part-time landlord. If you buy a two-family, three-family, or even a larger apartment house, live in one unit yourself, and rent out the rest, you can have low-cost or free housing, get income each month, and watch your investment appreciate (in the real world) while it depreciates (giving you enjoyable tax deductions).

As we go to press, TC '86 is still too new for the IRS to have promulgated regulations. But it seems that small-scale landlords (unlike real estate investors, who are less actively involved in their projects) will qualify for the "active manager" exception to the new "passive activities" rule. (The phrase "passive activities" is kind of like "honest lawyer"—it strikes you as being a little strange after you look at it for a while.) That is, if the rental part of the property produces a tax loss (say, if allowable tax deductions exceed rental income), the landlord can deduct up to $25,000 in tax losses. These losses "shelter" other income—that is, the loss reduces the amount of income that would otherwise be taxable.

Because the landlord is an active investor, the losses can shelter any kind of income, not just income from other passive activities. This rule is modified for active landlords whose income is over $100,000 a year. Those whose income is over $150,000 can't use any tax losses to shelter non-real-estate income. Note that the tax break is completely phased out by 1991 for those in the $100,000–$150,000 income range.

Not only does the Internal Revenue Code favor home ownership, it favors businesses of all kinds. Therefore, although you can't depreciate a privately owned one-family house—because it's just a personal expenditure—you *can* depreciate apartments you rent out. Say you buy a two-family house for $75,000, and let's also say that the tenant's apartment occupies half the house, and that $60,000 of the price is attributable to the house, $15,000 to the land. You can take depreciation deductions on an opening basis of $30,000. (Sorry, no depreciation on land.) If you make repairs to the tenant's apartment, you get an immediate deduction (no deduction for repairs on your *own* house or apartment). Other business expenses—like ads to attract new tenants—are also deductible. Congress has spent the last few years stretching out the length of time over which real estate must be depreciated, so the available deduction each year is smaller than it used to be. However, Pollyanna would be glad to point out that *that* only means that deductions are available in more years. If you sell the house without letting a year pass without rental income, you may have to pay back some of the depreciation deductions you took (discuss the subject of "depreciation recapture" with your accountant).

In short, living in a multifamily house gives you terrific tax benefits, and can help you afford a house when your monthly income would be much too small to make house payments without a boost from the tenants. And once you own a multifamily house with a reasonable amount of equity, you can use that equity to buy another piece of property (again making sure that the cash flow will turn a profit, or at least cover the monthly payments) . . . and take it from there.

There's got to be a catch somewhere. Well, for one thing, multifamily houses are generally, and not unnaturally, more expensive than single-family houses, so you'll need a hefty down payment (or a wraparound or other creative financing device). Remember all those times you tried to get the super to fix something in your old apartment, or tried to figure out whom to call with a complaint? If you're right downstairs, your tenants will have *no* problem figuring out whom to call with a complaint. Since they don't have far to go, they probably won't hesitate to let you know what's on their minds, at 2:00 A.M.

In the good old days (from the landlord's perspective) tenants *had* no rights. Now, all those laws you applauded when you were a tenant can work to your disadvantage. Your tenants may have a legal right to withhold rent if repairs are not made, or may have a right to spend their money on repairs instead of rent. Tenants may be late with the rent, or fail to pay it altogether, without a shred of legal justification—and it's no picnic evicting anyone, even someone without a legal leg to stand on. Depending on the number of apartments, and on state and local laws, you may have to install hideously expensive fire escapes, sprinkler systems, security systems—the hits just keep on coming.

If your tolerance for frustration is low, and your economic aspirations can be lowered correspondingly, your best strategy may be to buy a two-family house. Two-family houses occupied by the owner are usually exempt from laws about discrimination, many provisions of the building code, and, best of all, from rent control. (But check with your lawyer—and don't buy the house unless you're sure that it's a legal two-family in the first place. The conversion from one to two family could have been illegal—and just because *they* got away with it doesn't mean that *you* will—or it could have been legal if and only if the second apartment was inhabited by a family member.)

### Mortgage Versus Alternatives

Well, you *could* pay cash for the house—if you're awfully rich or the house is awfully cheap, or if you've just sold another house and you think the mortgage rates you'd have to pay far outstrip the investment return you could get on your money. But for most people, buying a house means getting at least one mortgage of some kind.

A potential homeowner (or a person buying a new house after selling the old home) has several considerations to keep in mind:

- How large a down payment can I afford?
- If I *can* afford a large down payment, should I use it all for that purpose, or keep some of it for investments or home improvements?
- Given that down payment and the cost of the home I choose, what will my monthly payments be? (Or, if you haven't chosen yet, how large a monthly payment—and how expensive a home—can you afford?)
- How much appreciation in value can I expect each year?
- In addition to principal and interest on my mortgage, real estate taxes,

and homeowner's insurance premiums, what other costs will I encounter each month (e.g., heating; extra commuting costs if you move to a remote location; extra child-care costs if it takes longer to get home from work)?

- How much will it cost to get the home into livable shape? How much will I expect to spend later on improvements to make the home more comfortable or increase its resale value?
- Can I get any income from a rental apartment? If so, what are the associated costs and tax benefits?
- If I have a home office, what tax benefits can I expect?

The down payment and monthly payment you can handle help determine the kind of mortgage you can get; if you have several options, they help determine which is best for you. That's one reason why you should start shopping for mortgage terms even before you begin house hunting. First of all, you may find out that you can't swing the home purchase (so why tear your heart out by falling in love with a little center-door Colonial?). Second, you'll save a lot of uncertainty and stress by knowing that you want to apply to the Second National Bank for your mortgage, and that you want the Extra-Super-Special-Adjustable-Flip-Cap Special, or whatever.

### Mortgage Types

The traditional mortgage—the kind the villain in the melodrama was always threatening to collect—was the interest-only mortgage. The mortgagor (the person borrowing the money and buying the house) paid interest throughout the life of the mortgage, when the entire principal was due. As you can imagine, this led to a lot of defaults. However, interest-only mortgages, though now rare, haven't entirely disappeared. Sometimes a seller in a hurry to sell will offer an interest-only mortgage to the buyer. It can be a very good option if the interest rate is tolerable, and if the buyer can absolutely count on a large sum of money when the mortgage is due (e.g., a lump-sum retirement payout, an inheritance from an estate tied up in probate).

The next development was what is now called the *conventional* mortgage: a long-term (fifteen- to thirty-year) mortgage with a fixed rate. At the beginning of the term, nearly all the payments go to interest; later on, equity builds up at increasing rates. The interest rate never changes over the length of the mortgage—but don't forget that the monthly payments are almost guaranteed to go up as tax rates and homeowner's insurance premiums climb. Also remember to increase your insurance coverage as the value of your house increases. Not only is this a commonsense move, but if you read the fine print, you'll see that you have a legal obligation to maintain insurance on a large percentage (usually 80 percent) of the value of the home. If you don't, you're in default, and the lender could, technically, begin foreclosure proceedings. (They're more likely to lecture you than foreclose.)

Mortgages usually run for a long time, and interest rates fluctuate in the meantime. One way the savings-and-loans got into the deep pasta in the early eighties was by writing long-term loans at what turned out to be low interest rates. Other banks learned the lesson, and during the late seventies and early eighties, adjustable-rate mortgages became popular. The borrower gets the loan at an initial interest rate (which might be below the market rates). Later on, the rate is adjusted to account for market interest rates. Adjustable-rate mortgages (ARMs; also called variable-rate mortgages) differ widely in their terms. It pays to take the time to compute the monthly payment based on the lowest interest rates you can expect. Most ARMs have a *cap,* or limit on rate increases. But watch out for *negative amortization:* if your monthly payments don't even equal the interest as it falls due, you can't reduce the balance of principal you owe, and you'll actually owe more at the end of the mortgage than at the beginning!

Sometimes a loan is written as a *balloon* mortgage. Your monthly payments are based on a twenty-or thirty-year mortgage, but the mortgage runs for only a short term (say, three, five, or ten years). At the end of the short term, you owe the "balloon": the original principal, less the comparatively small amount of equity you've accumulated. You must either pay the balloon or refinance. A balloon mortgage is a good choice if you *know* you'll have the money (for example, you'll be collecting a lump-sum retirement benefit; are confident you can refinance at a favorable rate—or, preferably, both, so you can decide whether to spend your cash on paying off the mortgage or invest it and refinance.)

The *rollover* mortgage is a variation of the balloon mortgage. Again, the monthly payments are based on a long term, fixed-rate mortgage, but the balance is due in a short term (less than ten years). At the end of the short term, the homeowner is guaranteed the right to refinance for an equal term, at the interest rates then current. The homeowner gains because s/he doesn't have to take out a new loan, and doesn't have to pay the (considerable) fees involved in getting a new loan.

Among the bewildering variety of mortgage options, there are a few others you might try. The GEM, or *growing equity* mortgage, is a fixed-rate mortgage, but the monthly payments increase each year by a fixed amount (let's say, 3 percent). However, the extra payments go directly to reduce your principal, so the mortgage gets paid off faster. Instead of the ordinary monthly payments, some banks will bill you every two weeks. In effect, you make thirteen monthly payments each year (twenty-six biweekly payments)—once again, the effect is to get the mortgage paid off faster.

### How Much Down?

Banks have rules about how much they'll lend, and whom they'll lend it to. One of the most important factors is the ratio between your monthly income and the mortgage payment; many banks also look at the relationship between your monthly income and *all* your long-term debt, including car loans and credit card balances.

Another vital factor is the amount of the down payment. Banks seldom lend more than 80 percent of the value of the house determined by the bank's own appraiser. You may well be paying *more* than the appraised value of the house, so you'll either need to put up at least 20 percent of the purchase as a down payment, or seek alternatives or supplements to a first mortgage from a bank.

- The federal government to the rescue: you can buy a house with only 5 percent down if the house is inexpensive and if your lender is approved by the FHA (most lenders are). If your house falls within the FHA limits (from $67,000 to $90,000, depending on location), the FHA will provide insurance; if you default, the FHA pays up.
- Uncle Sam again: if you're a veteran (or the widow of a veteran whose death was service-related), you may be able to get a VA mortgage with *no* money down. FHA and VA mortgages are assumable.
- Bad news on the federal front: effective October 15, 1985, the Federal National Mortgage Association ("Fannie Mae") tightened up its rules. Fannie Mae buys mortgages from banks; a lender is less willing to lend if the mortgage can't be resold. Fannie Mae raised its income requirements for home buyers who put down less than 10 percent; started looking harder at appraisals; and refused to buy adjustable-rate mortgages without "caps" or *with* unrealistically low interest rates in the early months.
- SAM to the rescue (no Uncle): some lenders will offer a *shared appreciation* mortgage. The home buyer gets a low interest rate, but has to share

some of the profit on the eventual sale of the home with the lender. The mortgage may be written *demanding* that the home be sold at a particular time.

- Uncle (or aunt, grandma, dad) to the rescue: the *partnership* mortgage involves a would-be homeowner who borrows part of the down payment from a relative or other friendly person (and maybe part of the monthly payment too). When the house is sold, they share the profit in an agreed ratio. They'll also have to work out, in advance, who decides when the house is sold and what are acceptable terms. Would-be partners should also be aware that the IRS has cracked down on loans within the family. The borrower is allowed to deduct interest at the fair market rate—even if the family lender doesn't *want* any interest. The bad news is that the family lender has to pay income tax on this "phantom" interest.

- Family member or seller to the rescue via the "reserve account mortgage." Somebody puts about 5 percent of the house's appraised value in an interest-bearing account in the lender's bank, and agrees not to use the money for a certain number of years. The money acts as security against default, so the buyer can put down a smaller down payment. If, after the number of years has passed, there's been no default, the family member or seller gets back the money, plus accrued interest.

- The seller may agree to loan the buyer the full purchase price, with nothing down; or much of the purchase price. Either the seller can hold the mortgage as a long-term investment, or can sell it to a bank or real estate company at a discount, realizing immediate cash.

- In rare cases, the seller may have a long-term, low-rate mortgage that the buyer can assume (take over and make the payments on). However, most mortgages have a *due-on-sale* clause. In other words, the mortgagor has to pay the balance as soon as s/he sells the house—the mortgage can't be assumed. Federally chartered banks are allowed to write mortgages with due-on-sale clauses. Some states forbid due-on-sale clauses, so it may pay to apply for a loan at a state-chartered bank (or choose a house with an assumable mortgage). Even if an assumable mortgage is available, it's not always the best choice. Naturally, the mortgage you can assume will be much smaller than the sale price of the house. You'll either have to arrange a wraparound (see the next paragraph); put down a *very* large down payment; or get a second mortgage from a bank (at rates even higher than first-mortgage rates, which are no picnic).

- Under a *wraparound,* the seller keeps paying the old mortgage (let's say,

$750 a month); you pay the seller an amount large enough to cover the mortgage plus the appreciation in house values (let's say, $1,100 a month). For your own protection, you should arrange with the seller's bank to notify you if the seller defaults, and to let you pay the defaulted amount yourself. Of course, a wraparound won't work if the seller's original mortgage had a due-on-sale clause.

### Closing Costs

You already *know* about the down payment and the fee for your lawyer. There are many other costs involved in buying a house. Most of them have to be paid at the time of the closing, so you'll need several thousand dollars in cash to swing the deal.

The costs you may encounter include:

- Loan application fee.
- Loan origination fee.
- Title insurance—you'll *need* one policy to protect the lender; you'll probably want one to protect yourself.
- Cost of recording deed.
- Cost of title search.
- Credit report fee.
- "Points"—a point is 1 percent of the total amount of the mortgage, and buyer, seller, or both may have to pay points.
- Fee for mortgage insurance.
- Assumption fee if the seller has an assumable mortgage that the buyer assumes.

You'll also have to pay for fuel oil that is delivered with the house, and for any personal property of the seller's that goes along with the house. Be sure you know how much money you have to bring to the closing, whom the checks should be made out to, and whether the checks must be certified. (In some states, you don't even have to go to the closing—the title company handles everything; in this case, your lawyer or the title company will tell you which checks to autograph.)

### Does Refinancing Pay?

Several years down the road, and you're a happy homeowner. Your balloon mortgage is about to come due; or your renewable mortgage is up for renewal, or you bought when mortgage rates were at an all-time high and you wonder about getting a new mortgage at a lower rate. You may have plenty of equity in your house, and you're thinking about getting a second mòrtgage on this equity for college costs or home remodeling. We've already discussed the tax implications of using a home equity loan to lock in interest deductions—see chapter 7 for the whole story.

The decision to refinance is a very personal one, but here are some of the factors involved:

- If you *can* pay off your mortgage, is there a prepayment penalty? How much? Is it worth paying it to avoid later interest payments? (Some states, such as New Jersey, forbid prepayment penalties.)
- Suppose you do repay. You *won't* have to keep making payments, so your cash flow will improve. On the other hand, you won't be able to invest the amount you used to pay off the mortgage, and you won't get a tax deduction for interest paid. If you prepay, will you really be better off after taxes, or are you just trading dollars?
- If you want to refinance a high-interest mortgage, will you face a prepayment penalty? What kind of fees will you have to pay for credit investigation, loan application, etc.? The fees can add up to several thousand dollars, some experts suggest that refinancing isn't worth it unless you can cut your mortgage rate by at least 2 percent.
- If you want to use the equity in your house for college, retirement, or rehabbing the house, can you get the money you need on better terms elsewhere?

As we've said, you have to live somewhere. Millions of people have stopped paying rent and started investing in homes of their own. A co op, condo, or house can be an investment in privacy, security, and pleasure—and can also be the first step in building family wealth.

For the typical family, the biggest expenditure they'll ever make is for a house; the next biggest for the family car. On one level, a car is a strictly practical means of transportation. On another level, it's a dream machine. We wouldn't even try to talk you out of buying a car that symbolizes luxury, or excitement, or glamour to you—and we couldn't do it if we tried.

Just be aware that you'll have to pay extra for your dreams, and that transportation is only one of the functions your car serves.

### Buying a New Car

There's nothing like it . . . a shiny new car, just the options and trim package you want . . . hot off the assembly line. (As long as your car wasn't made on Friday, when the workers were in a hurry to leave for the weekend, or a Monday, when they're back, sullen and hung over.)

Once you've chosen a make and model (based on your own experiences and preferences, and reviews in auto magazines and consumer magazines), some factors to consider:

- What's the price, after applicable discounts and rebates?
- How good is the warranty?
- Where can you get your car serviced if there's trouble?
- Can you use cheaper regular gas, or do you need more expensive premium or superpremium?
- What's the car's fuel economy like?
- Do you have enough space inside for your family (some cars are crowded enough in the backseat to turn the Jolly Green Giant into Yoda) and the groceries, sports equipment, and other cargo you'll be carrying?
- Can you see the road fully when you're driving, or are there dead spots?
- What kind of trade-in can you get on your old car? If the amount is laughable, you may be better off selling the old car privately and using the cash as a down payment on the new one.

On the painful subject of car loans, we'll merely remind you to shop as carefully as you would for any other loan; to explore alternatives like credit union loans (if you belong to a credit union) and insurance policy loans; and to make sure that the loan doesn't last longer than your car.

### Buying a Used Car

A used car can be either a great value or a horror that disintegrates the minute your check has been cashed. It helps a lot to hire a reliable mechanic to look at any used car you're serious about buying. If you buy from the car's owner, there's no way you're going to get any warranty, and if the car breaks down, that's your problem. A used-car dealer may help out in either or both of these ways. Remember, however, that for years the most damning thing anyone could say about Richard Nixon was that he didn't even live up to the high moral standards expected of a used-car dealer.

The *Kelley Blue Book* is the used-car buyer's Bible: it gives information about the resale value of just about every model imaginable. There's no real reason to buy a car above the *Blue Book* value unless there's something special about that car you just *have* to have. (Dana is looking forward to buying a cream 1963 Caddy convertible with a maroon interior—as soon as she learns how to drive.)

Some considerations about used cars:

- For unusual or early models: Can you get parts anywhere? Does anyone know how to fix it?
- How's the fuel economy? Don't go overboard, though; you can buy a lot of gas for $2,000.
- For old cars, does the car have the currently mandated safety and anti-pollution devices?
- How much would it cost to fix the dents, dings, and rust spots?
- Are the defects that have appeared over time dangerous, or merely annoying?
- What's the *real* reason the seller had for getting rid of the car?

### Upkeep and Maintenance

There are several arguments for buying a really terrible-looking car, and keeping it looking that way. Custom detailing costs a lot more than a bucket of soapy water and some Turtle Wax (or a car wash). Thieves would much rather steal (or strip) a gleaming, expensive, late-model car than a bucket of bolts. If there's at least one rotten driver in the family, you'll be less homicidal if s/he crunches up a clunker than a cream puff.

But if you're like most people, your car is your pride and joy, so you'll want to keep it looking great and riding smoothly.

- Cultivate the services of a good mechanic (and encourage any penchant your kids have for tinkering with cars).
- Learn to tune up the car yourself, or get it done at the appropriate intervals.
- Review your driving habits—jackrabbit starts or the dread Lead Foot Syndrome will wear out your car.
- Check the alignment regularly; replace wiper blades, shocks, brake linings, change oil at least as frequently as your owner's manual recommends.

If your household includes a teenage driver, be prepared for excruciating auto insurance premiums. Some insurers will ease the pain a little if the young driver maintains at least a B average in high school, or if s/he passes a driver's ed course. By the way, you can get your own premiums on some policies reduced if you're a nonsmoker, a nondrinker, or both. The worse your car is, the less inclined you'll be to carry collision insurance, or to lower your deductible and increase your premium—so you should save on insurance that way.

## Funerals

Again for most families, the third-largest expenditure, right after cars, is for funerals. The death of a family member unlocks a collection of accumulated guilt, unspoken love, resentment, and a desire to make up for real or imagined slights. It's easy for a family to spend resources needed for the surviving family members on an elaborate funeral. Some elderly, poor people will go through terrible deprivation to make sure they have enough of an estate to provide a splendid funeral.

As a result of a recent Federal Trade Commission rule, funeral homes *must* disclose their prices for various services; must discuss prices over the telephone; and must provide itemized bills on request. A remote family member, friend, or member of the clergy can get much of the necessary information, sparing the immediate family this task.

A person can make an anatomical gift of his or her own body to a medical school for educational purposes, or can donate kidneys, corneas, or other transplantable organs. After death, a member of the immediate family can make the anatomical gift. An ordinary funeral can take place after organs have been removed for transplantation.

Some unscrupulous directors will claim that embalming is legally required in all cases, or that elaborate coffins are required for bodies that will be cremated. In fact, embalming is legally required only if the funeral will be delayed or if the body will be shipped a long distance; and a simple, inexpensive container can legally be used for cremation. After cremation, the ashes can be scattered or placed in an urn and given to a family member or placed in a niche in a columbarium. (There's a cost for buying or renting the space.)

A burial plot is, in many ways, an ordinary piece of real estate; it has to be bought, and can be sold or devised by will. If the family prefers that the dead person be buried, there'll also be a charge for continued upkeep of the grave, and for placement of a tombstone or other marker. Above-ground "burial" in a mausoleum is also a possibility.

Some people try to spare their families grief (and expense) by making prearrangements for their own funerals. One way to do this is by prepaying for a funeral meeting your wishes at a particular funeral establishment. Be sure your family is aware of this arrangement, and don't do this unless you're sure you won't move far away—a prepaid funeral contract in Teaneck won't do much good if you die in Pensacola.

Another way is to join a memorial society, which is sort of a "funeral co-op."

It will probably (though not necessarily) be less expensive to have cremation, followed by a memorial service, instead of a traditional funeral and burial.

You *should* make your family aware of your funeral instructions (difficult as this topic is to discuss). Your will is about the worst place to do this. There's a pretty good chance that no one will even look for the will until *after* your funeral. A better alternative: a letter of instructions that your family knows where to find when you die.

There's just no way that it can be pleasant to think about your own death, or the death of people you love. Still, maybe when the unhappy day comes —by 2099?—they'll arrange things differently.

# CASE HISTORY
## *Major Commitments*

"It's not natural," Gary Mikulski said. "When we watch *Magnum, P.I.,* you don't drool over Tom Selleck, you drool over the house."

"Big deal," Johanna said. "You drool over the Ferrari. But, sure, I'd love to have a glorious, big, beautiful house. A mansion. Why not? We deserve it."

"Definitely, we deserve it. But that doesn't count for a whole lot. As Jimmy used to say, life is not fair."

"Okay, not a mansion. But I'm sure we could get a house. A sensible house."

"What's the most important thing we should look for?" Gary asked, and answered his own question at the same time Johanna spoke. He said, "That it should be a good investment"; she said, "That we can afford it."

"Sure, a house is a place to live and bring up the kids," Gary said. "But we have to look at it as our major investment. Basically, it's not only a tax shelter, it's an important part of our retirement fund, and it's also

a way to build up an estate. Apart from our insurance, of course."
(Because he was an insurance agent, they both had lots of insurance.)
"So, even if we have to extend ourselves a little, maybe go without some
things for a few years, the main thing is that we pick an area that has
some potential for appreciation. Maybe we should take a look in the
South Maple section."

"It's not just an investment," Johanna said. "It's miles from nowhere,
those old houses are drafty as heck, and I don't think it's really safe there.
Sure, we could probably get a place for forty or fifty thousand dollars,
but we'd have to spend a fortune fixing it up. And the first thing we'd
have to put in would be a burglar alarm system. I think we should get
a smaller place, but a new house—maybe one of those three-bedroom
town houses that Asterisk Developments just put up. They're attached,
so the heating bills wouldn't be all that much, and they're practically
brand-new, so we don't have to worry about the plumbing rotting out,
and the gutters being no good, and the new furnace to be put in, and
all that stuff Lou and Donna always bore us with about their oh-so-
authentic Victorian house."

"You get it at the other end," Gary said. "You ever see them putting
up those developments? First they dig a hole about six inches deep, then
they jam a couple of Popsicle sticks into the holes, nail a sheet of plywood
to the Popsicle sticks, put on the siding, and they're open for business.
The doors don't hang right, the windows aren't tight, the walls are about
as thick as a saltine cracker."

"I'm sure it's like anything else," Johanna said. "Some developers are
good, some are bad. And a new place, it's true that it wouldn't be so big
—but that means there wouldn't be as much to clean. Say we got an
eleven-room house. Neither of us would be too happy about dusting and
washing and waxing and vacuuming after we got home from work."

"The way I see it," Gary said, "even if a new house is really well built,
the basic price already includes just about all the appreciation it's ever
going to have. Maybe the price will go up a little bit, because of inflation.
But whatever we paid, we'd get it back and maybe a little bit more. If
we get a house that's a fixer-upper, and especially if we can guess right
and pick a neighborhood that's going to get trendy before it does, we
can earn a really good return on our investment. We can start off with
a small house, just for us, or maybe a two- or three-family and pick up
some rental income."

"Oh, no," Johanna said. "You know what we call the landlord every time the rent bill comes in, or when we get a new lease and they jab us for some more money, or when the toilet stops up and we can't fix it and the super doesn't speak any known human language. I'm not going to have them call *us* those things. And, no offense, those bookshelves you made lean at about ten degrees off plumb. Who's going to be the handyman for our tenants?"

"I won't be macho about it. You can do it."

"Hey, only when it's a life-threatening emergency will I do it. Otherwise, they're on their own."

"Fine, okay, even without rental income," Gary continued. "We start out with a fixer-upper, put a little sweat equity and some second-mortgage money into fixing it up, and sell it for a nice profit. Then we buy a house that's maybe in a better neighborhood or doesn't need quite so much work. Then we sell that, and so on. After about ten years, we could really have a good financial picture."

"Yeah, but I don't think it's right for the kids to have to move three or four times. They need some stability. And I'm not going to bring them up in a neighborhood where, instead of Little League, they have tournaments for mugging little old ladies. And it's okay for you, you drive around to different appointments. But I have to be at work right after rush hour. And if Dr. Schechter does have me come along on his routine deliveries, I might have to go out and come back at some pretty strange hours."

"Let's try to narrow down what we want in a house," Gary said. "And let's be realistic. No pipe dreams."

"Well, okay, I want a really nice place, but nothing fancy. Kind of —uh, you know. The kind of house that somebody would live in in an Andy Hardy movie. And a garden. Not like a whole big farm where we'd have to get a tractor just to keep it mowed, but enough to grow some roses, and have a swing set, maybe grow some vegetables."

"And I want a garage," Gary said. "The cars are important enough that I want them kept locked up away from our light-fingered neighbors, and kept warm and pampered in the winter."

"And no picture windows," Johanna said. "Picture windows are tacky."

Gary was about to say that he had grown up in a house with a picture window, and his family had very good taste, but thought better of it. "And if we get a brick house instead of a frame house, we should get one that's never been painted. Because once somebody paints a brick house, you just have to keep doing it every couple, five years, and that's really expensive."

"And it should be energy efficient," Johanna said. "Preferably a new furnace, but anyway a good one in good shape. And hot water is better than steam. And the windows should face the right way, so we can get a breeze, and so we won't roast all summer, and so we won't have to wake up at dawn every day."

"The schools should be good," Gary said. "Because neither of our kids is exactly Albert Einstein, and if they don't have to work hard to keep up, they'll never try, and they'll never get into a decent college."

"And we have to watch out for the local taxes, and the water and sewer. Remember that long story Lou regaled us with?"

"About the reassessment. Yeah. And we probably can't afford a ranch house big enough, but I'd rather have it on two stories instead of three, so we won't have to be climbing stairs all the time."

By the end of the evening, they had a "wish list" that was really fairly practical. And by the next weekend they were chatting with real estate agents, inspecting multiple-listing books, and poring over classified real estate ads over brunch. They firmly resisted all suggestions that they "just take a look" at houses that were completely wrong, or much too expensive. They turned their backs on houses—however charming— that needed major repairs or architectural alterations. They consulted maps to check commuting routes, and behaved just as any really sensible house-hunter would—which put them in a distinct minority, because how many really sensible house-hunters are there?

The Mikulskis' experience illustrates that a house, per se, means different things to different people. He was thinking investment when she was thinking nest-building. When they finally focused on how a house becomes a home, they were able to draw up a shopping list that helped to guide their decision-making.

# 15

## Advanced Investment Techniques: Tips for Aspiring High-Rollers

Maybe you think that it's a good time to invest in stocks, and the best way to do it is to select a high-performance equity mutual fund. But maybe you want more individual control; maybe you think that, by and large, it's a *bad* time to invest in stocks, but you've located a few issues that you have reason to believe will outperform the market.

Perhaps you want steady income, and you want to buy and hold a portfolio of bonds (which should do a little better than bond funds, as long as you choose well). On the other hand, you might want to trade actively in bonds, and fret impatiently at the restraints imposed on bond fund managers. You're prepared to absorb the transaction costs and the risk of loss.

Maybe you don't feel comfortable with stocks, bonds, and similar intangibles—you want something you can see and touch. Then perhaps part or all of your investment portfolio should be in tangible investments: real estate; gold and silver; antiques and collectibles. But, remember, most of these tangible assets do not produce income; the exception is rental real estate. In fact, you'll probably have to pay to have them safeguarded. And you'll probably buy at retail and sell at wholesale—there'll have to be plenty of appreciation in value, or plenty of inflation, for you to come out ahead on the deal.

### Are You a Gambler at Heart?

Then again, you could be a spiritual descendant of the Mississippi riverboat gamblers. You want the chance to score a coup that will free you from the need to work for the rest of your life. The fact that you could go broke, or score that big coup and lose it all by trying to double your fortune, is a risk you can accept. Then maybe you should trade commodities, although 80 percent of those who do lose their shirts.

If you have some of that gambling spirit, but are not quite as reckless— or if you own some stock and would like to add a little income by selling calls, or if you think you know how the market will move but don't have the capital to buy the underlying stocks—then maybe you should invest in stock options, stock index options, or stock index futures.

### The Risks of Greater Rewards

In this chapter, we'll give you a very basic introduction to stocks, bonds, tangible investments, options, and commodities. Just enough to whet your appetite. You'll need to do more research before you invest. Remember that the basic investments we discussed in chapter 4 are risk free or low risk. The investments discussed here have more risk (some of them, much more risk). Frequently, they have higher transaction costs. The incentive, of course, is the possibility of greater rewards, the big brass rings everyone dreams about.

### Corporate Stock and How It's Traded

The stock market exists for several reasons: first, so that corporations needing capital can raise it by selling their stock to the public. (Nearly all corporations in the United States are private—they have not gone through the incredibly difficult and expensive regulatory procedure required before a company's stock can be sold to the public.) The stock market also exists so that those who have bought stock will be able to sell it whenever they want.

Thousands of stocks of major corporations are traded on exchanges such as the American Stock Exchange and the New York Stock Exchange (the "big board," as opposed to the Big Bird, who is on Sesame, not Wall, Street). These stocks are so important to the economy that most newspapers carry their quotes every day.

Then there are many public companies whose stock is not traded on an exchange. These are called "over-the-counter" stocks (probably what the novice investor meant when asking for a "nice under-the-counter stock"). An OTC (over-the-counter) stock is typically issued by a newer or smaller company. Almost five thousand OTC stocks are listed on the NASDAQ, or National Association of Securities Dealers Automated Quotation System, so you can get current price information, and your broker can trade stocks by computer. Price quotes for NASDAQ stocks may also appear in your newspaper. If you want to buy an OTC stock that is not part of NASDAQ, you can get price information from "pink sheets" published by financial publishers. Your broker can make the deal over the telephone.

### From Blue Chips to Pennies

A "blue chip" stock is the high-priced stock of a well established, profitable major corporation. The "Generals"—Motors, Mills, Electric—are examples of blue chips. We say "blue chip," as in the highest denomination of poker chip.

At the other end of the price scale are the penny stocks, which are defined, these days, as stocks selling for $5 or less per share. As you can imagine, they're OTC stocks, and specialized penny-stock brokers, as well as other brokers, deal in them.

Blue chip stocks often sell for well over $50 a share; to buy a round lot (one hundred shares—the basic unit of stock trading; commissions for *odd lots* of less than one hundred shares are larger than for round lots) would cost you well over $5,000, plus commissions.

Why buy blue chips? Because they're considered safe and usually pay generous dividends. But blue chips are usually the wrong investment if you're looking for quick appreciation in price. After all, if you buy a stock at $137 a share, where's it going to go? To $142?

If you buy a riskier penny stock, you can, we hope, afford the potential losses. But if you guessed right, you can earn a high return. Say you buy a stock at $4, and sell it at $14 a share—a very nice profit. If you bought a round lot, and the stock becomes absolutely worthless, you're out $400 plus commissions. No fun, but it probably won't ruin you.

### Stockholders' Rights

A share of stock is literally a share of the corporation: you own 10 percent, 1 percent, or 1/1,000 of 1 percent of the corporation's stock. If you own *common stock,* you are entitled to vote for the directors of the corporation, and on certain important matters of corporate policy. If you own *preferred stock,* you don't get a vote, but you do get first crack at the dividends—owners of common stock come later. Preferred stock has a specified dividend rate. As long as the corporation has any distributable surplus, it will be used first to pay the required dividend on the preferred stock. (If the stock is *cumulative preferred* and the corporation misses any dividends, it must make up for the missed dividends before it pays any dividends on the common stock.)

Theoretically, dividends on the common stock can be skipped if the corporation's directors feel that money is tight. However, investors are very interested in dividends; so, as a practical matter, corporate boards make every effort not only to declare a dividend on the common stock every quarter, but to see that the dividend keeps rising.

*Convertible preferred stock* can be converted to common stock under specified conditions—very handy if the price of the common stock rises, or if the common stock dividends surpass the fixed dividends on the preferred stock. *Tax tip:* If you do convert preferred to common stock, no capital gain or loss will be recognized, no matter what the prices of the common and preferred shares are.

Dividends are usually paid in cash, but can be paid in the form of *stock dividends*—literally dividends of stock: e.g., for every one hundred shares you own, the corporation sends you two new shares as a dividend. If there's a *stock split,* and, for example, it's a two-for-one split, the corporation takes back your one hundred shares and gives you two hundred new ones, each worth half as much. The point of the game is that each cheaper share, like a penny stock, has more potential for price appreciation.

### Who Gets the Dividend?

The person who is registered on the corporation's books as the owner on the *ex-dividend* (without the dividend) date. If you buy before the ex-dividend date, you get the dividend; otherwise, the seller gets it. So take this factor into account when buying stock. And if you're following a stock's price movement, don't be surprised if it hits a peak each quarter—the sellers charge a bit extra for the privilege of receiving the dividend.

If a corporation makes a *rights offering,* it gives its current shareholders the right to buy a limited amount of additional stock, at what might be called an "insider's price," for a limited time such as one month. *Warrants* are similar, but give the stockholder the right to buy additional stock at a stated price at some time in the future. Don't just toss out rights and warrants if you don't want more stock, or can't afford to exercise them—they can be sold to someone else, who *does* want the stock.

## The Rise and Fall of Stock Prices

Investors buy stocks for some combination of two main reasons. First of all, they want to own the stock because they think the stock will provide a steady stream of dividend income. Second, they expect to make a profit (or sustain a tax loss at a time when this is a part of their tax planning) by selling the stock to someone else—at any time from a few hours after the purchase (for a hot IPO—initial public offering) to thirty or forty years after the purchase.

Stock prices can rise as a simple response to inflation—if a dollar is only worth eighty-five cents, you'll be willing to give more dollars to buy the same asset. Stock prices can also rise because the company whose stock it is does well—perhaps an innovative and profitable new product is introduced, or the company gets a lucrative defense contract—because the company belongs to a sector that pundits expect to do well; because the company's financial picture indicates that the stock is a good buy; because there is a rumor of something favorable to the company about to happen; because the stock's chart (we'll get to that in a minute) indicates a coming price rise; and, finally, because plenty of buyers hop on the bandwagon.

Stock prices can fall for the converse of any or all of these reasons. The stock market is particularly fascinating as a study in mass psychology and self-fulfilling prophecies. After all, if everybody thinks Stock X's price will rise, everyone who can get the money together is likely to buy Stock X. When they compete for a limited number of salable shares, the price of Stock X will, of course, rise as they bid against each other. Then more and more investors want to buy Stock X . . . until at some point they realize that they're bidding against each other to drive the price up. Then the price falls, regardless of whether Company X was earning record profits or skirting bankruptcy. Lots of laughs.

If you're interested in a particular stock, you don't want to congratulate the company's management for something that they had no hand in, such as an improved economy or lower interest rates. Nor do you want to blame them for something that wasn't their fault, such as a sharp rise in oil prices, unless, of course, it's an oil company. What you really want to do is to see how the stock performed compared to the stock market as a whole, or compared to other companies that are economically similar.

Therefore, stock market indexes are an important tool. They let you see if the market as a whole is rising or falling; how actively shares are being traded (is everyone trying to buy shares, or, on the whole, would they rather be in Philadelphia?). The two most popular indexes are the *Dow* (actually the Dow-Jones family of indexes) and the *S&P 500*, five hundred stocks selected and monitored by Standard & Poor's.

The DJIA is the Dow Jones Industrial Average of thirty major corporations; the Transportation Average follows twenty stocks; and the Utility Average follows fifteen electric, gas, and telephone utility stocks. The composite aggregates all three averages. The S&P 500 consists of four hundred industrials, forty utility, twenty transportation, and forty financial stocks.

### Approaches to the Stock Market: Technicians Versus Fundamentalists Versus Contrarians

There are all kinds of systems for choosing stocks in which to invest, ranging from the frankly loony to those supported by substantial economic evidence. The sensible systems tend to fall into two camps: technicians and fundamentalists.

A third, rather existentialist group, the random walkers, believe that stock prices are simply unpredictable, so you might as well choose stocks at random. In fact, every year *Forbes* magazine selects a portfolio by throwing darts at the financial pages; the "Dart-Board Fund" usually manages a performance at least as respectable as that of many mutual funds run along more conventional lines.

*Contrarians* are the cynics: they believe in buying whatever everyone else is trying to dump, because they believe that market trends will always reverse. So, when everyone is trying to get into equities, the contrarians buy up the bonds they think have become bargains, and vice versa. When everyone else is fleeing out of aerospace stocks, the contrarians are there, trying to buy at the bottom of the market.

Technicians believe that analysis of a stock's past price history reveals trends showing where future prices will go. To the pure technician (also called a *chartist*, because price charts are an essential tool of technical analysis), it's important to analyze a stock's high, low, and closing price over a number of days of trading. A bar chart shows each day's high and low price as a vertical line, with the closing price for the day shown as a horizontal line crossing the vertical lines. A line chart connects one or more of these points. Charts can also be created for a group of stocks, or a stock index such as the Standard & Poor's 500.

Technicians have identified a number of chart formations that they believe indicate movements in stock prices: "head and shoulders," "M formations," and the like. They use the charts to see how the stock's price has moved in the past, and make predictions for future price movements.

Fundamentalists believe in studying the "fundamentals"—the financial health of the corporation selling the stock. So they read annual reports, statements submitted to the SEC, and other sources of information about the corporation's gross income, expenses, borrowing, and profits.

### Choosing a Broker

Once upon a time, all brokers charged the same (rather high) commissions, because there was a mandatory commission schedule they had to follow when dealing with individual investors.

All that changed in 1975, when brokers were allowed to offer "negotiated commissions." Large-scale investors immediately used this power to negotiate "volume discounts." (And even if you're dealing with a full-service, full-commission broker, you may be able to negotiate rates downward—it's worth a try, anyhow.)

### Diooount Versus Full-Commission Brokers

More important for many investors, the "discount brokerage" was created. Discount brokers started out by offering no-frills service—just execution of orders; no investment advice, no calls from brokers eager to sell a few more shares (or to unload some stock that was Dog of the Week), no analysis or copies of reports on hot new issues.

Today, the lines have blurred (just as the distinctions between load and no-load funds have blurred). Now, there are discount brokers who do nothing but execute orders; others provide some financial advice and analysis; and full-service brokers specialize in availability to clients and willingness to volunteer potentially useful information.

What makes it even more confusing is that a discount broker is not always cheaper than a full-commission broker, because the discount firms charge minimum fees for small transactions that may exceed the full-commission firm's commission schedule. Some discount brokers set their charges based on the number of shares traded, others on the value of the shares—so of course you prefer the former, if you're buying expensive stock.

Not all discount brokerage houses sell municipal bonds, tax shelter programs, or mutual funds—so make sure the brokerage house sells the products you want to buy.

Both discount and full-commission brokers sell OTC stocks at a "markup" over the price charged to brokers. You may have to ask around a lot to find the best price. See if you can find a broker who "makes a market" in the OTC stock you want—the broker makes sure that sellers can find a customer, if necessary by buying the stock for the brokerage house. Also, see if the broker will sell you the stock at their "insider's" price.

In short, you have to shop around and find the broker that fits your needs. Do you want advice? Would you listen if you got it? What's the broker's track record on past recommendations? The broker must also accommodate your trading pattern. Do you buy large blocks of stock and hold them, or are you a "day trader," who continually switches in and out of stocks? Do you buy blue chips or penny stocks?

You might want to open accounts with several brokers—perhaps a full-commission broker for the advice and reports you need; a discount broker for trading when you know what you want to do; and maybe even a penny-stock broker if you want to deal in these exciting, though hyper-risky, stocks.

If you lose money because you picked the wrong stocks, tough luck. Nobody will do anything for you except sympathize. However, a federal agency called the SIPC (Securities Investors Protection Corporation) insures your account for up to $500,000, in any combination of cash and securities, against your broker's bankruptcy, or against your stock being stolen or your account otherwise being manipulated.

### Can You Trust Your Broker?

If you *really* trust your broker, well, then, bully for you! You can give him or her a *discretionary order.* He or she can then buy and sell stocks for your account, at prices and on schedules s/he chooses. Most people, however, don't have that degree of faith in a broker, and they insist on picking their own stocks, and setting limits on prices and timing.

### Orders for Your Broker

A *market order* will be executed at the market price prevailing when the order is processed. Say you want to buy Thingtronics stock, and it's trading at 59 ½ ($59.50 a share). You become the proud owner of a certain number of shares at $59.50 each. If it goes down to $55 a share later on in the day, you're out of luck—you can't change your mind (because you already own the stock), and you get it at the market price at the time of the trade, not the day's lowest price.

A *limit order* has a specific price on it. The broker takes it to the specialist who regulates the market in the particular stock. The specialist holds on to the order until the price is reached. Let's say you want to sell your Thingtronics later on, when the price has run up—perhaps you want to sell Thingtronics at 64. If no one offers $64 or makes a better offer for the stock, you don't sell it. Similarly, you might place a limit order for one hundred shares of Glittering Goldmines at 14—you'll get the stock if it trades at 14, or on terms more favorable to you.

A *stop* or *stop-loss* order also specifies prices; it turns into a market order once the price is reached. Stop-loss orders are also useful for investors who don't want to see a stock's value tumble. They may instruct their brokers to sell a stock if it hits, let's say, $32 a share. That way, they may be able to lock in a profit; or they may lose money, but at least not lose *too* much. Of course, if they put in a stop-loss order at 32, and the stock goes down to 32, the stock will be sold—too bad if it later bounces back to 40.

A *stop limit* order is a hybrid. Let's say you want to sell your Glittering Goldmines, but only within a certain range of prices. If you place an order at 25 stop, limit 24½, your stock will be sold if anyone offers $25 a share or over, but not unless someone offers at least $24.50 a share.

Orders can also specify timing. An *open* order stays good until it's executed, or until you cancel it. So you'd better not forget that you have open orders—or you can find yourself with some stock you don't really want, and an obligation to pay for it that you *really* don't want. A *day order* lasts, reasonably enough, for one day only; market orders are day orders. A *fill-or-kill* order is limited in both time and price: if it can't be filled right away, at the price you specify, the order expires. So you'd better be in touch with your broker to find out if your orders were filled or not.

## Buy and Hold, or Cut and Run?

One of the most common mistakes investors make is to "fall in love" with their stock, or at least to feel an obligation to it. Or maybe they just hate to admit a mistake. So they hang on to stock that pays little or no dividend, that keeps going down and down in price, and has little or no hope of bouncing back.

Although getting into (or out of) an investment is a highly personal choice, these are some criteria you should keep in mind:

- A stock is worth holding if it produces excellent dividend income, and/or you think it will continue to rise steadily, or will be worth much more at a specific time (for instance, you plan to liquidate part of your portfolio when you retire).
- A stock is worth holding if you think it's a bargain—currently underpriced, but with a chance to appreciate later on. In fact, some investors follow a "dollar-cost-averaging" policy for a stock they think has long-term growth potential. They decide to buy a certain number of shares, or a certain dollar value of shares of the stock, every month. Of course, the price will fluctuate, but they don't give up on the stock if the price drops; in fact, they look at it as a way to buy more of their favorite stock at a bargain price (see table 2).

## When Is It Time to Bail Out?

This is the question that keeps people tossing and turning all night. A few hints:

- A stock is worth selling if you need cash and it's the worst performer in your portfolio.
- A stock is worth selling if you think it's reached the highest price it'll ever trade for and has nowhere to go but down. (The Wall Street euphemism for this is "profit taking"—the owners of the stock are bailing out, because they think nobody would be dumb enough to pay anything above current prices for the stock.)
- This is the tough one. A stock is worth selling if its price is declining, and

**Table 2    How Dollar Cost Averaging Works**

| Period | Purchase Amount | Security Price | Shares Purchased |
|--------|-----------------|----------------|------------------|
| 1 | $1,000 | $10 | 100.000 |
| 2 | 1,000 | 20 | 50.000 |
| 3 | 1,000 | 15 | 66.666 |
| 4 | 1,000 | 21 | 47.619 |
| 5 | 1,000 | 12 | 83.333 |
| 6 | 1,000 | 22 | 45.454 |
| 7 | 1,000 | 17 | 58.823 |
| 8 | 1,000 | 23 | 43.478 |
|   | $8,000 |  | 495.373 |

Average *cost* per share: $16.14 ($8,000 spent divided by 495.373 shares purchased).
Average *price* you paid per share: $17.50 (sum of the price at each purchasing point—$140—divided by the number of purchases—8).

you don't think it'll bounce back, at least not before you lose patience with it. (Some investors set numerical goals: if a stock falls more than a certain percentage from the price they bought it at, they sell it and don't look back.)

• A stock is worth selling if it now trades for less than you bought it for, you don't think the price will rise much, and you need a tax loss to offset a gain on the sale of another stock.

Another strategy: a stock has appreciated nicely since you bought it, but you're not sure what'll happen in the future. You could sell enough stock to get back your initial investment, and hang on to the rest of the stock. That way, you can't lose in the long run—you recouped your initial investment (and may gain even more if stock prices continue to rise). And, remember, you don't *lose* money by buying a stock at 11 and selling it at 17—even if you *could* have made more money by hanging on to the stock longer, or selling it earlier.

### Market Mantras, or What to Do When You Make a Lousy Decision

Let's face it—if you do buy and sell stocks, sooner or later you're going to make a bad decision, or at least an unlucky one; and unless you're a very atypical investor, you're *going* to lose some money sooner or later. Herewith: mantras to chant, so you can feel a little better about the losses.

First, if you lost a couple of hundred dollars, imagine that your least-favorite cousin—the creepy one, with the stinky (though expensive) cigar and the loud suits—has a daughter who's getting married. Of course you're invited to the wedding. You have to rent a tuxedo, and your spouse has to buy an expensive new dress she'll hardly ever wear again (or your spouse has to rent a tuxedo, and you have to buy an expensive new dress, depending). Then you have to come up with a sizable gift. Your car breaks down on the way to the wedding, but you finally get there. Everyone patronizes you because they make more money than you do. The flower girl goes around finishing glasses of leftover champagne and throws up on your shoes. The band is lousy. The prime ribs are cold and greasy. What a relief to come back to reality and discover that you haven't been to that horrible wedding at all—you just lost a corresponding amount in the market. Just repeat over and over: "Reality is better, reality is better."

A couple of thousand dollars lost? Well, that would just about pay for a two-week vacation for two at the Caribbean island of Petit-Plagueux-sur-Mer, where the local inhabitants divide their time between studying Marxist anticolonialist texts and working in the hotels and restaurants; where most of the food has to be flown in; where the hurricane season arrives early, just in time for your vacation. You get food poisoning. Your spouse steps on a jellyfish. The swimming pool, in a display either of native craftsmanship or anti-Americanism, has been plumbed into the sewer system. What a relief to get home, with nothing but your brokerage statement to worry about! Just repeat over and over: "Forget paradise, forget paradise."

### Making Sense of the Stock Pages and Annual Reports

Now, a little light reading. Most newspapers print page after page of stock tables. You can skip over them on the way to the sports page, or study them as part of a real or even a paper portfolio.

For stocks listed on major exchanges, the tables have eleven columns of very small type. The first two columns give the highest and lowest price the stock has traded at during the fifty-two weeks before the day in question. These figures help you keep today's price in perspective. They also give you a clue to the stock's *beta,* or volatility—the degree to which the stock's price moves faster or slower than the price of the S&P 500. Most "safe" stocks have betas in the range of .80 to 1.20, that is, they move 80 percent as fast, or up to 120 percent as fast, as the S&P 500. If a stock is even more volatile, you may find yourself buying at the high point and find that the price has plummeted when you want to sell. Note: a few stocks have a negative beta—that is, they tend to go *up* when the S&P 500 goes *down.* You can find the beta of your favorite stock listed in the *Value Line Investment Survey,* available at many local libraries.

The third column in the stock table gives the (abbreviated) name of the stock. The fourth column gives the current annual dividend per share—*not* the most recent quarterly dividend, so don't get your hopes up too high.

The fifth column tells you the yield—the percentage that the current dividend represents of the current stock price. The yield lets you know if the stock is a good investment if your objective is high income. For instance, if the stock sells for $100 a share, and the dividend is $4 a year, your yield is 4 percent—not much of an annual income, but possibly very satisfactory if you have reason to believe you can sell the stock for $125 a share down the road.

The sixth column is a very important figure: the P/E, or *price-earnings* ratio. Price is the stock's current price; earnings are the company's earnings for the past twelve months divided by the number of shares outstanding. If the P/E is low, the stock is, at least comparatively, a bargain. If the P/E is very high, the stock is often speculative. Some start-up businesses have very high, or even infinite, price-earnings ratios, because the stock is issued before there are any positive earnings.

The trend of the P/E is also important. In general, you hope that the P/E keeps rising, because you hope the stock market will place an ever higher value on the earnings of your company.

The next column gives the number of shares sold in that trading day. Usually two zeros are dropped, 750 means sales of 75,000 shares. If there's a z before the figure, it means that no zeros are dropped, that's all that was traded. Blue chip stocks normally trade heavily. After all, they have lots of shares outstanding. When a smaller stock trades heavily, there could be a lot of impact on the price, as frantic buyers drive the price up, or frantic sellers drive it down.

The eighth through eleventh columns relate to that day's trading: the highest price for the day, the lowest price for the day, and the closing price (the information you'll need to make a bar or line chart). The eleventh, final column gives the change between that day's closing price and the closing price on the preceding business day.

OTC stock tables are less elaborate: they give the abbreviation of the stock's name, volume of sales (with two zeros omitted), bid price (the price buyers offered to pay), asked price (the price sellers offered to sell at), and the change in bid prices since the preceding trading day.

*Note:* If you have trouble finding your favorite stock listed in an unfamiliar newspaper, you're not losing your mind. Different newspapers use different abbreviations.

Next, we come to annual reports. If you already own stock in a company, you'll get a copy of the annual report each year. Most stockholders take a quick look at these masterpieces of glossy design, take a puzzled look at the financial statements, then toss the whole thing.

However, if you're willing to take some time—and develop some sleuthing skills—you can learn a lot about a corporation's current financial status and prospects from the annual report. You can decide whether to hold on or sell; and if you're thinking about investing in a company, you'd be well advised to check the most recent annual report. The company will send you one if you ask; your broker may have a copy on file; and a large public library, especially a business library, may have a copy.

Experts suggest that the best place to start is the management's letter to the shareholders. It has a summary of the year's events and goals for the future, but discount them a lot for hype.

Speaking of annual report hype, remember when Time, Inc. had to dump its plans for publishing *TV-Cable Week* in 1983? The company spoke glowingly of the project in its 1982 annual report—as the plan was unraveling—and scarcely mentioned the blunder in its 1983 report to shareholders, despite the fact that the publishing giant took a $47 million bath. We thought we'd mention that just to keep you on your toes.

You'll also want to review management's discussion and analysis of operating results, that is, what happened in the company's actual lines of business —not its investments or acquisition activity. This is a more detailed discussion, and summarizes events for the past two fiscal years. It can be instructive to get some annual reports for past years and compare those forecasts to what actually happened.

After all those words, you should be warmed up for the financial statements—which tell you the real story. Start with the balance sheet, which usually includes current numbers and those for the preceding year, for comparison. Get out your calculator and figure out some ratios. For example, how do the corporation's current assets—cash, marketable securities, accounts receivable, inventory—compare to current liabilities—those that must be paid within a year, minus accounts payable and accrued expenses? You're looking for at least twice as many assets as debts, and a ratio that increases over time as the company gets more prosperous. There should also be at least twice as many assets as long-term debt.

Then take a look at the sales, net income, and earnings per share—there should be a convenient five-year summary provided. This is where the detective work comes in. Sometimes net income goes up, but sales don't—and in that case, where is the money coming from? The corporation may be selling off assets to "massage" the numbers. On the other hand, if sales are way up but income and earnings haven't improved much, the company may be spending too much to get its sales. The cause could be bad management, or the company could be in a mature market where all the easy sales have already been made. Neither possibility should cheer up investors much.

The *really* interesting stuff tends to turn up in the footnotes to the balance sheet and income statement. The explanations for puzzling figures may lie there. For instance, the company might have closed down a perpetually losing division—perhaps earning a generous, but unrepeatable, sum for selling the land under the plant.

Move along and check the auditor's opinion—an independent accounting firm must check the figures provided by the corporation. What you're looking for is a *short* auditor's opinion. Two paragraphs is standard; after that, they're hemming and hawing. A qualified auditor's opinion probably doesn't mean that the corporation is lying, but it does mean that their figures may have to be adjusted. For example, a corporation could be embroiled in a major lawsuit. The corporation may estimate that, at worst, it'll have to fork over $3 million —but, as we all know from reading the paper, multimillion-dollar or even multibillion-dollar verdicts are not uncommon.

Want to see the bottom line? That's not on the balance sheet; it's on the income statement. The balance sheet has often been compared to a "snapshot," showing the corporation's assets and liabilities on the day the books were closed for the year (or quarter, or whatever). The income statement (also called the P&L, for profit and loss statement) shows the operating results for the year. By law, the income statement and the balance sheet must show three years' figures for comparison; companies with a lot to boast about may include five to ten years' worth of figures in a summary, for comparison.

Within the income statement, start with the company's net sales *(total revenues)*—that's the money earned making buggy whips, operating an advertising agency, or whatever. The *operating income* is the total revenues minus the cost of running the shop. You subtract taxes and extraordinary items (e.g., adjustments that must be made because the company's accounting system has changed) to get the fabled bottom line, the *net income,* which is expressed both in dollars and in earnings per share.

With these figures in hand, you can see how the business did this year; how this year compares both to the projections and the past years; and how this company compares to others in more or less the same position. There are many more things you can learn by analyzing annual reports. You can predict the future, to a certain extent. Is the company spending enough for research and development? If not, they could be left behind by more innovative companies. Are they replacing their plant and machinery fast enough, or will they be plagued later on as obsolete equipment hinders productivity, or falls apart outright? If the company has a lot of debt, will it founder if interest rates rise? If a company has a huge and ever-increasing inventory, does that mean that it has poor marketing, or that its product line is not what buyers want?

In short, the seemingly forbidding or sterile figures can be made both comprehensible and fascinating.

In addition to the annual report companies must render to their stockholders, the SEC collects a huge volume of information each year. The SEC filings are public records. If you're a stockholder, you are entitled to request free copies of the 10-K (annual filing with the SEC), quarterly 10-Q (you're welcome!) and the 8-K reports required when extraordinary events occur, such as mergers, bankruptcy, or change of auditing firm—which may conceal funny business.

The annual 10-K contains information that is not found in the annual report: for example, information on corporate stock held by top management and more detailed financial statements. The "selected financial data" section of the 10-K gives five-year trends, so you can see how the company's management has performed over time. By the way, it always pays to get a company's annual report before you get the 10-K, because it's both perfectly legal and common practice for a company to refer to the annual report in the 10-K instead of repeating the information. The 10-K has to be audited by an independent firm, so there's some check on management imaginativeness.

The quarterly 10-Q reports (actually there are only three of them a year; the 10-K includes the fourth quarter) don't have to be audited, so take them with a grain of salt. Still, they give you a more current look at the company's finances. The real news updates come in the 8-Ks, filed within fifteen days of the significant event in the life of a corporation whose stock is listed on an exchange. (OTC companies are obliged to file similar reports called 10-Cs.)

A summary on stocks: in the end, probably neither strict fundamentalism nor strict technical analysis holds all the answers. A company's dividends are affected by its management policies as well as its profits—one management may believe in heavy investing in plant and research, to fuel further growth, while another management tries to buy stockholder loyalty (and higher stock prices) by keeping dividends high.

Stock prices are affected by many facts (and more rumors) other than the company's assets and expenses. A pending, contemplated, or even rumored merger or acquisition can affect stock prices. Also remember that a company may adopt policies and accounting conventions that make earnings look anemic, in order to lower the company's tax burden, or that may show earnings better than they actually are.

Just imagine how difficult your life would be if you were compelled to act rich one day (because you want to show off for your out-of-town relatives, or impress a potential employer) and poor the next (because your ex-spouse hints that a modification of child support is in order).

Corporations are in much the same bind: they want to look good for the stockholders and potential buyers of stock, but they want to demonstrate that the cupboards are bare when it's time to file the tax return. That's one reason why the tax treatment of depreciation is so crucial to corporations.

Obviously, plant and equipment wear out, and must be replaced. But how long can a particular asset be kept in service? How much will the asset cost to replace? How much should be set aside each year to be ready for the replacement? (Of course, corporations don't have to pay cash for new assets —they can borrow; but the corporation's books should reflect the need to replace plant and equipment.) So don't get too frightened if you see a large item labeled "depreciation" in financial statements—it doesn't mean that the corporation is on the verge of poverty, or that the corporation had to disgorge that much cash in the year in question.

There's no doubt about it: investing in stocks can be risky. You can get caught up in a "story" stock, and buy it just at the peak of the market—when the stock price has nowhere to go but the basement. You can buy the stock of a company with healthy operating profits and, yes, sickening litigation losses. You can buy at the crest of a bull market, and decide to pick up a little spare cash by selling your stock—only to discover that the bears have taken over.

So why do people bother to invest in stocks at all? For one thing, because stocks give you the chance to beat inflation. For another, buying growth stock lets you defer taxes: you're not taxed on "paper gains" (the difference between the stock's current price and what you paid for it) until you sell the stock. Don't go overboard on this—you can't *spend* paper gains, either.

### Performance Is Relative

For another thing, stocks simply offer superior performance. The Standard & Poor's 500 has had an annual return of 9.5 percent for the period 1926–84. This is not to say that everything was smooth sailing: in the worst year, the S&P 500's return was a *minus* 43 percent; in the best year, it was up 54 percent. The average return on corporate bonds was only 4.4 percent, but the worst years were less disastrous (−8.1 percent), the best years correspondingly less favorable (43.7 percent).

Treasury bills averaged only 3.3 percent over this time period (from no gain at all, but no loss, in the worst year, to 14.2 percent in the best). So, historically, stocks have outperformed corporate or government bonds, but at more risk.

Plenty of people don't have the instincts, the time, or the desire to research individual stocks and decide whether to hold their purchases or trade them. They're better off staying out of this risky game, and sticking with mutual funds. But for those who have some money they can afford to lose, some time to spend on this absorbing pursuit, and a good nose for a good stock, it's a great way to turn a little money into, if not a fortune, at least an inflation hedge.

### The Name Is Bonds . . .

James Bonds are about the only kind you won't find on the market. Corporations issue bonds; cities and states issue bonds in a variety of maturities, denominations, and interest rates, for a variety of purposes. The United States Treasury issues short-term Treasury bills (T-bills) and longer-term T-bonds.

At one time, bonds were the ultimate safe and boring investment, suitable for little old ladies, widows, and orphans. Today, with interest rates so volatile, bonds can be almost *too* exciting.

There are two major ways to invest in bonds: to buy them and hold them to maturity, collecting interest as you go. The risk here is that you could be locked into an interest rate that is far less than the rates that develop over time. Of course, if you buy when rates are at a peak, you can lock in rates that are far *above* prevailing market rates. The interest is taxed in the year you receive it.

The other way is to trade bonds: to buy them at a discount, and sell them at a premium. Your objective is to earn capital gains. The risk here is that you can misread interest rate trends and find that you must pay a premium to acquire any high-rated bonds, or that bond prices have dived since your purchase.

### Bonds: How They're Traded

A bond is really an IOU: a contract saying that if you buy a bond with a certain face value, the issuer will pay you a set amount of interest every quarter or every year—and will pay you back the face value on the maturity date. Because you could have paid more or less than the face value for the bond, you have the opportunity to earn a capital gain, or suffer a capital loss for tax purposes.

Some bonds are *callable*—the issuer has the right to retire the bonds by paying the owner the face value. The issuer is likely to do this if interest rates have dropped in the interim, because it can get the capital it needs at rates cheaper than the bond provides. Of course, that's precisely when the investor most values the bond. If you do buy a callable bond (you can tell because it's identified as something like "2001–2006," which means the bond matures in

2006 but can be called in 2001 or later), be aware that your excellent investment may be snatched away.

The usual minimum denomination for most kinds of bonds is $1,000, and you can't buy part of a bond—you must buy individual bonds. (If you want to invest smaller, or odd, amounts of money in bonds, your best bet is a bond fund or unit trust.)

However, bonds are quoted based on a "par" of 100. That is, a bond with a $1,000 face value and selling for exactly $1,000 is quoted as 100. If you could buy the bond for only $960 (perhaps because the bond's interest rate is below normal market rates), it would be quoted at 96; if you had to pay extra (perhaps because of a generous interest rate), it would be quoted at 104½ if you had to pay $1,045 for a bond paying $1,000 at maturity, and so forth.

When you're comparing bonds, a bond's *yield* is simply the annual interest divided by its price. However, *return,* which factors in price changes, is a truer measure of a bond's value as an investment.

Originally, there was a distinction between *registered* and *bearer* bonds. Registered bonds were, indeed, registered with the issuer, and interest checks were sent directly to the registered owners, who were the only people entitled to redeem or trade the bond. Bearer bonds had interest coupons; whoever had the coupons could present them to the issuer for payment, and whoever had the bond itself could redeem or trade it. That made bearer bonds awfully convenient for various kinds of shady deals—everything from stealing bonds or coupons to using them as payment for drug deals.

Therefore, TEFRA, the 1982 tax bill, required that all bonds issued after TEFRA's effective date be issued in registered form. However, if for one reason or another you want a bearer bond, older issues are still available.

### Corporate Bonds

When corporations need money, they can issue some more stock (if their charters permit, and if they think the stock will sell and the existing stockholders won't be too dismayed at the dilution of their voting power). They can borrow from banks, even as you and I. But they also have another option not available to us: they can borrow from investors by issuing bonds. (By the way, a bond with a term of ten years or less is sometimes called a *note.*)

How can you tell a good corporate bond from a bad one? Well, it's very unlikely that the corporation will out-and-out default, but interest payments may be delayed if the corporate issuer hits some hard times. (On the other hand, the less stable corporations offer higher, sometimes much higher, returns on their bonds than the real blue chip companies.)

There are two major rating systems for corporate bonds. Standard & Poor's rates bonds from AAA through AA, A, down to D. Moody's Investor's Service uses Aaa, Aa, and so forth. Experts suggest that you should look for bonds rated at least BBB by S&P; the corresponding Moody's rating is Baa. (Buy sheep, sell deer?)

Low-rated, *"junk"* bonds offer the possibility of high interest rates. If you're intrigued, you might do better with a junk bond fund; at least the fund's managers have more time and expertise in telling good junk from bad.

Corporate bonds also include such exotica as *floating-rate* bonds, whose interest rates can be adjusted to contemporary levels, and *put* bonds, which can be sold back to the issuer before maturity, at a price determined by a set schedule. Obviously, you hope that the price will be higher than the bond's market price, so the put feature will be worthwhile. Floating-rate and put bonds yield something less than plain vanilla corporate bonds.

*Convertible* bonds can be exchanged for a certain number of shares of the corporation's common stock (conversion rate) at any time during the life of the bond. The conversion value (conversion rate multiplied by the current price of the common stock) starts out as less than the face value of the bond; sometimes it rises above the face value, over time. Experts suggest that you not pay a conversion premium above 20 percent (that is, that you back away from bonds whose face value is more than 20 percent above the conversion value). An attractive feature of convertible bonds: they may sell for commissions lower than the underlying stock, and you won't have to pay a commission if you convert the bond to stock. (Conversion instructions should be on the back of the bond itself; if not, ask your broker or the company's investor relations division.) Convertible bonds may be an especially good choice in the early years of the new tax environment. They provide income to income-oriented investors—with an easy way to switch over to stock if the investor is ready to get back into equities.

### Treasury Securities

If you want real safety, think about Treasury obligations. After all, if the U.S. government goes under, the safety of your investments is the least of your problems.

T-bills are short-term securities, no longer than a year; most are for three months or six months. T-bills don't pay interest in the conventional sense;

they're sold at a discount, and redeemed when the maturity date comes around, at face value.

T-bills are literally auctioned off each week, but don't expect any bargains. The minimum denomination is $10,000. If you find this amount off-putting, you can become an indirect investor in T-bills by buying shares in a money market mutual fund, because T-bills are a money fund favorite.

T-bonds (sometimes called T-notes) are longer-term securities. The minimum purchase is $5,000 for terms up to four years, $1,000 for longer terms. These bonds aren't callable—except for thirty-year bonds, which can be called after twenty-five years. The T-bond auctions take place only once a month, and the bonds pay interest like conventional bonds. The interest is exempt from state and local taxes, but not, alas, federal income tax.

### Savings Bonds

You can probably do better with a little effort in selecting investments, but you can also do worse: Series EE savings bonds come in denominations anywhere from $50 to $10,000, and have a ten-year maturity. You can buy them, without commission, from banks and S&Ls. They don't pay interest, but you pay only half the face value.

Current rules say that if you hold them for at least five years, you get a guaranteed minimum return of 6 percent or 85 percent of the average yield on Treasury securities during the five-year period—whichever is higher. But if you bail out before the five years have expired, your return is less. We stress "current rules," because every once in a while the Treasury responds to the market conditions that make savings bonds a good deal by cutting the rates.

### Fannie and the Gang

They're not exactly government obligations, and they're not exactly bonds, but Fannie Maes, Ginnie Maes, Freddie Macs, and the like might fit into your investment portfolio.

These instruments are packages of mortgage-based securities. That is, the federal agencies involved (the Government National Mortgage Association, or Ginnie Mae; Federal National Mortgage Association, or Fannie Mae; the Federal Home Loan Mortgage Corporation, or Freddie Mac) guarantee mortgages. Then they assemble a package of mortgages with similar durations (e.g., between five and seven years) and sell the packages on the open market.

If you buy one of these packages, you receive a monthly check. The tricky part: you may think that these checks constitute interest. That's partly true—but part of each check represents repayment of principal. Once the term of the pool of mortgages is up, you're out of the game—you don't get back the face value, as you would with a bond. Remember, most people don't live in the same house long enough to pay out the mortgage. They're apt to sell the house and prepay the mortgage at closing. If interest rates go down, they're likely to refinance, and prepay the mortgage that way. So you may find that your mortgage-backed security is "called" just when you're starting to enjoy it. And if you decide to sell your Ginnie Mae or related instrument, you may find that you get less than you paid for it if interest rates have risen in the interim and your rate of return is not competitive.

The various agencies guarantee the safety of your principal against default by the mortgagors—not all that generous on their part, because very few people ever do default on their mortgages. However, there are no guarantees that you won't lose money because of changes in interest rates, or that you won't be stampeded by a rush of mortgagors racing to prepay their mortgages.

The tax treatment of the checks you receive can be complex, so be sure to check with your tax adviser before you invest, and make sure that you report the return on these obligations correctly on your tax return.

### Municipal Bonds

What does a city do if it wants to build a new sewer system or put up a sports stadium, or if the tax receipts won't be in for six weeks and the workers want to get paid today? Why, it floats a bond issue.

For years, municipal bonds were scorned as the most tedious of wimpy investments, appropriate for the hyper-cautious who would cravenly put up with pathetic piggy-bank returns in exchange for safety. But now, with many cities going to the credit market at the same time, municipal bonds are paying startlingly high rates: for many investors, low-risk municipal bonds offer a return that looks lots better after taxes than fully taxable corporate bonds. Another good thing about municipal bonds (like all other bonds): when interest rates drop, you can sell your bonds at a hefty profit. In short, munis made a sudden transition from neglected journeyman player to star attraction.

One thing you could count on for those boring old municipal bonds: the interest would be free of federal tax. Bonds issued by your own jurisdiction would be free of state and local tax as well. However, those certainties started to erode in 1984, when senior citizens were required to include some municipal bond interest in the calculations that determined whether tax was due on their Social Security benefits. The real shocker came with TC '86, when a strange hybrid creature emerged from the depths of the sea: the taxable municipal bond. The interest on most municipal bonds continues to be tax-free, but interest on "private activity" bonds is now taxable. The rules are complex, and you don't really have to know them; the short version is that a private activity bond is one whose proceeds are 10 percent or more used in a nongovernmental business activity.

However, even some bonds that seem like private activity bonds still manage to be tax-exempt—for example, bonds issued to help local citizens get mortgages or student loans. We can give you the simple advice to check before you buy a municipal bond, to find out if it really is tax-exempt.

With the hot new muni market, some investors get burned. Just like other investments, munis are available in various permutations of risk and return. Whether tax-exempt or taxable, municipal bonds fall into two major classes: *general obligation bonds,* backed by the municipality's full faith and credit (that is, they say that, whatever happens, they'll get you your money somehow); and *revenue-backed bonds,* backed by revenue from a particular source (e.g., a toll road, convention complex, or airport; taxes to be collected; another bond issue to be floated). Only about 1 percent of all municipal bonds issued since the Depression have defaulted—but more than three-quarters of all the defaults were in revenue-backed bonds.

Two agencies, the Municipal Bond Insurance Association and the American Municipal Bond Assurance Corporation, insure municipal bonds; as you would imagine, the yield on insured bonds is somewhat lower, because the risk is somewhat less. Standard & Poor's and Moody's rate municipal bonds, and while S&P gives *all* insured bonds an AAA rating, Moody's bases its ratings on the soundness of the underlying issue.

If municipal bonds confuse you, or you want to make a small investment, or you're not sure how tax rates and your own tax bracket may change, you may prefer investing in a tax-exempt bond *fund* rather than buying individual bonds.

### Zero-Coupon Bonds

Strange beasts indeed. That is, instead of paying interest every quarter or every year, the zeros are sold at a very deep discount. If you hold them to maturity, you get the face value; or you can sell them in the interim—with absolutely no guarantee that the bonds will not have declined sharply in market price.

Zeros can be tricky. You don't get a regular interest check, but you do have to pay taxes on the "interest" you would receive if the bond were an ordinary bond rather than one sold at a deep discount. So you inherit a tax obligation without the cash to satisfy it. However, if you're in the 15 percent bracket, or if your children own the zeros (and they manage to escape taxation at your highest rate—see chapter 13), this isn't too much of a problem. Nor is it a problem in an IRA or Keogh account, where the appreciation won't be taxed until retirement.

But zeros are really designed for investors who will buy and hold. Investors who buy at the bottom of an interest cycle and later try to sell their zeros can find that prices have changed sharply and that their zero-coupon bonds look awfully unattractive compared to other bonds available. The result: a severe loss of capital. If the zeros were part of your retirement portfolio, your retirement security could be compromised.

Parents looking around for some surviving device for accumulating college funds, and the poor unfortunates who already have trusts for their children that have turned into tax time bombs, may find zero-coupon municipals seductive. As long as the bond is one of the tax-exempt variety, there's no taxable "phantom interest" to worry about. Trustees of existing trusts will probably rush to get rid of the trust's taxable investments in order to load up on tax-exempt issues; zeros give "more bang for the buck" for those who are absolutely sure they're investing for the long term.

Remember, however, that just because you buy a zero for your IRA, there's absolutely no guarantee that you'll be able to see any tax-deferred capital appreciation if you sell before maturity. If you're holding a zero in your IRA, and interest rates go up before you trade out, you'll probably experience a loss in capital. Not a good idea if you're trying to nurture your retirement nest egg. *Tip:* Never buy any bond at the bottom of an interest rate cycle.

You can buy federal, municipal, or corporate zeros, often with cute feline names. (Well, would *you* buy something called Debt Obligations Growth System, and nicknamed DOGS?) TIGRs are Treasury Investment Growth Receipts; CATS are Certificates of Accrual on Treasury Securities; STRIPS are Separate Trading of Registered Interest and Principal of Securities. More often than not, they're all dogs!

If you do decide to buy zeros, shop around: some brokers calculate the markup on the face value of the bonds; since you buy at a deep discount, you're paying an awfully large commission.

Add it up: if you want reliable income, even reliable tax-exempt income, you can get government or municipal bonds or high-rated corporate bonds.

If you're willing to take some risk, you can get high income from junk bonds. If you can predict interest rate trends, you can make high profits by trading bonds. (For that matter, you could also be designated as the first person to land on Mars.)

You can also use T-bills at the end of the year to defer income to the next tax year. The trick: put some money into T-bills that will come due in the following year. The next year, you pocket your profits, and pay the tax then, not this year, the way you would if you put your money into conventional bonds. Convertible bonds give you a chance to participate both in a corporation's income (when they pay interest) and the appreciation of its stock (if you exercise the conversion privilege).

### Annuities

Another formerly boring investment. In essence, an annuity is a kind of reverse life insurance policy. When you buy life insurance, you give the insurance company a little money periodically; eventually, they give a chunk of money to your survivors. When you buy an annuity, you give the insurance company a chunk of money; eventually, they give you and/or your survivors a little money periodically. (Not all annuities are purchased with a single premium —some are purchased with annual premiums.)

Annuities present the buyer with the usual investment dilemma. You can buy either fixed annuities (which lock in a particular rate of return) or variable annuities (whose return fluctuates based on market forces). Which should you choose? Well, do you know what interest rate trends will be between now and your retirement? If you responded "Yes" to that question, do you sometimes think your name is Napoleon?

Usually people buy annuities to provide retirement funds. Like an IRA, an annuity permits build-up of value with tax on the appreciation deferred until payments begin. Once annuity owners start collecting annuity funds, only part of each payment is taxable income: the rest is tax-free, because it's considered a return of the owner's investment in the annuity contract. (Similarly, lenders have taxable income when they get interest on loans . . . but not when part or all of the principal of the loan is repaid.)

However, annuity owners do have taxable income when they borrow against the annuity or when they take funds out of the annuity before the payment date scheduled by the contract. Another similarity to IRAs: withdrawals made before the annuity owner reaches fifty-nine and a half (unless the owner becomes disabled or s/he dies and the survivors make the withdrawals) are subject to a 10 percent penalty tax. The penalty is not charged if the withdrawals are made in a series of substantially equal payments.

TC '86 also tries to plug possible tax-shelter leaks by putting restrictions on annuities purchased by corporations (thus making it tougher for corporations to provide top executives with fringe-benefit goodies that are not available to other workers) and on changes in the methods of payout selected by annuity owners.

Although annuities share some of the disadvantages of IRAs, they're starting to look awfully good to middle-income people who want to retire in financial comfort and who are losing all or part of the IRA deduction. For one thing, you can put as much money as you want into annuities—there's no $2,000 limit (and no tax deduction, either, whatever your income).

Annuity salesmen are gearing up to take full advantage of this new high profile. A favorite gimmick is a "package" of IRA plus annuity—but don't buy one of these packages until you find out whether it meets your needs as well as the salesperson's. Also be wary of transaction costs (this is a practical consideration, not one of taxes). Annuities may have a hefty sales charge (ask about this before you buy, and compare the offered contract with comparable annuities from other issuers). Also watch out for "back-end load," which is what happens if you switch annuities too soon (usually before five years have elapsed), not what happens when you eat too many potato chips and skip too many aerobics classes.

### Tangible Investments

Still, there's something kind of cold about a stock certificate or a handful of bond coupons. Some people would rather invest in something they can—if not exactly sink their teeth into—reach out and touch. So they put part or all of their investments into real estate, collectibles, or precious metals.

### Real Estate, REITs, and REMICs

Real estate is a special kind of investment because, as Will Rogers said, "they're not making it anymore." The supply is fixed, and the population keeps growing.

So why isn't everyone investing in real estate? Well, to a certain extent, everyone is, and many of the best buys have already been bought up, and competition intensifies the bidding. Real estate isn't a very liquid investment —you can't count on finding a buyer when you want to sell, and arranging the deal and handling all the financial and legal steps can take weeks or months even after you find a buyer.

There's also the fact that real estate profits are far from automatic. If you buy unimproved raw land, you won't get any income from it. Worse, you may have made the wrong decision about the area's development potential.

If you invest in developed property—rental apartments; shopping centers; office buildings; industrial parks—you're not out of the woods yet. You may have trouble finding tenants. Moreover, tenants may depart suddenly, with the rent unpaid, or may have to be evicted. The buildings may be stuffed with illegal asbestos, or located over toxic waste dumps. Roofs can fall in; burglars can drop by; furnaces break; rent control laws get enacted. Either you have to spend a lot of time managing the property, or you have to pay someone else to do it.

But just because real estate isn't an automatic passport to fortune doesn't mean that real estate doesn't belong in your portfolio. Real estate has some unbeatable tax advantages—especially if you own your own home. If you already own your home, you might want to get into real estate investment fairly easily by trading up to a more expensive home with one or more rental units. Then you can take advantage of the tax breaks available to landlords, and you'll have rental income every month (well, almost every month—you may be in between tenants, or the tenants may be less than reliable about paying up).

Or, if you're happy with your present home and don't want to take on the myriad hassles of landlord-dom, you can become a real estate investor without having to go it alone.

REITs—real estate investment trusts—are almost like mutual funds invested in real estate rather than stocks and/or bonds. (Real estate mutual funds are something else—they invest in REITs and the stock of companies that own a great deal of real estate or are involved in real estate development.)

One of the major advantages of REITs is liquidity. Many are traded on one of the major stock exchanges, and you're likely to find a buyer whenever you want to leave, though you may lose money if the real estate market has turned down, or if enthusiasm for real estate investment has withered.

Equity REITs buy property, mortgage REITs lend to builders and developers, and hybrid REITs do both.

Another way to invest in real estate is the syndication. Real estate syndications are limited partnerships. The general partners manage the property, and are responsible for the partnership's debts. The limited partners can lose their entire investment, but no more—they can't be tapped by the partnership's creditors if deals turn sour. If you're thinking about investing in a real estate limited partnership, you have to assess the credentials of the general partners. Check whether they have the skill and experience to choose property wisely and manage the development well. Is the deal too favorable to the general partners, with minimal rewards for the limited partners? You must also be aware that the terms of many syndications require you to keep your money invested for a long time—perhaps several years. Even if there are no such restrictions, it can be hard to find a buyer for your interest.

There are no hard-and-fast rules, but syndications are more likely to get involved in quick, in-and-out development deals. REITs are more likely to hold property over the long run.

TC '86 adds a brand-new form of real estate investment, the Real Estate Mortgage Investment Conduit, or REMIC. This creation is too new for us to be sure, but we suspect that the REMIC is designed to operate as a kind of private-market Ginnie Mae. That is, the REMIC buys mortgages on the secondary market and immediately resells shares to investors. This infusion of mortgage money should make life easier for potential home buyers (especially if the real estate provisions of the new tax law make real estate less attractive to investors, and thereby drive prices down).

REMICs themselves don't pay taxes; they pass along all their income (and deductions) to investors. There are two classes of REMIC investors: those holding "regular interests," who are treated more or less like owners of corporate bonds, and holders of "residual interests," who are credited (for tax purposes) with all the income of the REMIC that hasn't been assigned to holders of regular interests.

In short, real estate investment can be chancy, especially if you need to get your money out in a hurry. Many great fortunes have been built on real estate, but you need the gambling temperament to make real estate your *only* investment. Nonetheless, real estate has an important place in a balanced portfolio.

Real estate investment has always been a source of tax shelter. For one thing, property values usually increase . . . so investors get to deduct depreciation (for tax purposes) on property that's actually become more, not less, valuable over time. For another, investors can actually claim deductions based on investments purchased with borrowed money—money they can't legally be forced to repay (the real estate exception to the "at risk" rules). That made real estate the ideal investment for the high-bracket person who wanted to invest a little money, "borrow" a lot more, and get big deductions to offset other taxable income. Perhaps the project would even become profitable, someday or somewhere over the rainbow.

However, the rules have gotten progressively tougher. Under TC '86, depreciation schedules have been lengthened. The at-risk rules have had their teeth filed to points (but the real estate exception, though limited, has not been eliminated). Furthermore, "passive" real estate investors are not allowed to use tax losses from real estate to shelter nonpassive income. *Tip:* If you're already stuck in a real estate tax shelter, maybe your best bet is more real estate investment (profitable, this time)—your real estate tax shelter losses can be applied against your real estate profits. If you invest in stocks, bonds, or anything else instead, the real estate losses won't be deductible.

However, "active" real estate investors (broadly speaking, those who own at least 10 percent of the real estate involved and who participate actively in its management) can use up to $25,000 of real estate losses to shelter other income. (This deduction phases out for taxpayers whose adjusted gross income is between $100,000 and $150,000.)

In short, investors (of any income level) who can find profitable real estate investments can rejoice at the (at least nominally) lower tax rates provided by TC '86. Investors whose projects yield a bountiful crop of losses will be less happy, because the tax shelter effect of the losses will be limited or eliminated.

### Art and Collectibles

How would you like to live amid an ever-changing array of beautiful objects? How would you like to turn an absorbing hobby into a money machine? There are dozens of success stories about art and collectibles: the dusty old painting in the attic that turned out to be a Constable; the collection of Depression glass ("You're buying that junk? My *grandmother* used to have that stuff, and I threw it all out") that sells at auction for thousands of dollars.

Of course, no one tells you the failure stories: the Oriental rugs purchased at the height of the market in the seventies, and now moth-eaten both in condition and in price; the object purchased for $700 (plus commission) and sold for $1,000 (minus commission, shipping charges, insurance, and catalog listing).

The key to making money with collectibles is sort of Zen: you have to stop caring. You must surround yourself with wonderful things that you love (but not too much to part with them), and sell them if the omens are right, but not depend on them as a source of income. You must study the field, so you can recognize the genuine from the fake and the pristine from the repaired. Experts say you should try for a small collection of the best objects in your field, not a larger collection of less valuable examples. The best objects hold their value the best.

One problem with collectibles (apart from the fact that, not only don't they produce income but you have to insure them, clean them, and otherwise take care of them) is that you generally buy from a dealer or auction house that charges you full retail prices. When you want to sell, unless you can arrange a private sale to another collector (who will probably want a cut in price for the inconvenience), you have to go back to the seller or the auction house. In effect, you're forced to sell at wholesale.

Remember, you can't use these types of collectibles to fund an IRA or Keogh.

### Jewelry and Precious Metals

How paranoid are you? If you think that the United States is about to succumb to internal revolution or foreign invasion; if you think that nuclear winter starts next Thursday, you'll definitely want some portable, valuable materials like unset diamonds or pure gold ingots.

Even if you're perfectly sane, you may want to own some gold as a hedge against very high inflation. Not only does gold have a historical role as a guaranteed store of value, stable no matter what lunacy governments get up to; gold is also used in many industrial and medical processes, so it has value on that level. However, in one of those little ironies that Providence is so fond of, much of the world's gold is located within the borders of two of the most repressive governments on earth: the Soviet Union and South Africa. Do you really want to do business with them?

Jewelry and unset stones are extremely portable—a great value when you're fleeing for the border, a real problem when you're concerned about the security of your possessions. Think about keeping them in a safe-deposit box or a wall safe. And, like collectibles, you have the problem of buying retail, selling wholesale. This is not to say that you can't make money, if prices rise as dizzily as diamond, gold, and silver prices have done recently. Of course, they eventually fell.

If you think the value of gold will rise, there's a way to profit without actually buying ingots or gold coins: investing in gold mutual funds, which buy gold-mining stocks rather than gold itself.

### Options—Not for the Fainthearted

From the most tangible to the most intangible of investments, if you want to keep your options open, you may in fact want to add some stock options to your portfolio. Options can be used in many ways, from the conservative (writing covered calls) to the wildly risky (writing naked calls).

In simplest terms, an option is simply a right to buy or sell one hundred shares of a particular stock. You might buy options either because you want the stock or want to unload it, and can get more favorable terms on the options market than through conventional stock trading. Or you might be interested in the price movements of the stock but quite uninterested in the stock itself —you may think the stock price will rise or fall sharply, but you don't give a hoot whether the underlying company makes buttons or nuclear power plants, whether they've had a banner year or are just this side of bankruptcy. You might also want to speculate on price movements of blue chip stocks that you couldn't possibly afford to buy outright—it's a lot cheaper to buy options than to buy stock.

### Call Options

A call option gives you the right to buy one hundred shares of a specified stock, at any time within a specified time frame, at a specified *exercise* or *striking* price. At any given time, three different dates are available, three months apart (e.g , December, March, June).

A call is *at the money* when the striking price equals the market price; *in the money* if the striking price is below market price; and you can imagine what an *out of the money* call is. Options are not free: you have to pay a *premium* to buy them, in addition to the commission. The seller (also called the *writer*) of the call gets the premium; the broker gets the commission. *Parity* is the condition at which the striking price plus the premium equal the market price.

The buyer of the call can demand the shares at any time up to the expiration date. If the price of the stock has gone up, but the call buyer doesn't really want the stock, s/he can also sell the call, at a profit, to someone who really does want the stock. If you sell a call at a profit, you have a capital gain —probably short-term, given the nature of options. If, on the other hand, you go through with it and buy the stock, there's no taxable event (until you sell the stock). Your cost basis for the stock is increased by the premium, and your holding period starts on the exercise date.

The price of a call goes up as the difference between the striking and the market price increases—because there's more opportunity for profit. Longer options tend to be more expensive than shorter ones, because there's more chance for the stock price to rise. But option premiums go down as the expiration date nears—once the expiration date is reached, the call is value-less, because it can no longer be used, and the buyer has lost his or her premium and the commissions. Call premiums also increase near a stock's ex-dividend date, because everyone wants to collect those dividends.

You might buy a call if you expect a stock's price to increase enough to leave you a profit post-premium and commissions. You might sell, or write, a call for two reasons: you think the stock price is going to decrease, or go strictly nowhere; or you want to earn a nice little income on stock you already own.

A covered call is a call written on stock you own. That is, someone pays you for the right to demand your stock at a certain price. The risk, then, is that the stock price may zoom up. Instead of holding the stock and chortling, or selling it using normal channels, you have to let the call buyer buy the stock at the striking price. But if you're right and stock prices stagnate or decrease, you can have your cake and eat it too—you still have the stock, plus the premium on the call option.

A naked call is a call written on stock you *don't* own. The risk is that you may have to rush out and buy a stock whose price has soared, and collect only the lower striking price. The risk is infinite; there's no limit to the amount you may be forced to spend over and above the call premium and exercise price you collect.

### Put Options

Put options are a specialty of the publishing business: you get to stick it to the writer. That is, if you buy a put option, you have the right to *sell* one hundred shares of a given stock to the writer of the put. You do this because you expect the stock price to go down. If you expect a price drop, you could also write a call.

You can also buy put or call options on an entire stock market index, if you expect the S&P 500 as a whole to rise or fall. In effect, you're following the ancient practice of betting on the point spread—but in the stock market, not the Superbowl.

### How Options Are Traded

There are four exchanges (Chicago, American, Philadelphia, Pacific) on which options are traded; about four hundred stocks have "listed" options on these exchanges. Commissions on options are higher than commissions on stocks (and you usually encounter commissions at both ends of the trip), so the brokers are happy to tell you about the wonderful world of options. However, the commissions decrease for large transactions—it's always worth asking about discounts.

For real punters, it's possible to buy a *straddle*—a put and call on the same stock, with the same striking price and expiration date; you win if there's a huge price movement in either direction, lose if the stock price stays put. A *spread* involves buying and selling a put (or a call) on the same stock, with the same exercise date and different prices, or the same price and different exercise dates. Some people have made lots of money with these tactics—but most of them are brokers, not investors.

## How to Read an Options Table

The tables give the last closing price for the underlying stock—so you'll have some idea about realistic striking prices—and the premiums for puts and calls from each of three expiration dates three months apart, and for a variety of striking prices. If you see an *r* on the table, it means that no options were traded at that particular combination of expiration date and striking price; an *s* on the table means that no such option exists.

In short, if you have some money that you can afford to lose (this is definitely not the investment medium if you're short of money and must preserve your capital), and if you think the stock market will move dramatically and you don't want to bother with the underlying stocks, think about trading options—either on particular stocks or on an index.

But be aware that you'll put part of your gains into transaction costs, and that brokerage fees will increase your losses. And remember that you can't be passive about options—you must monitor your positions carefully, and must either sell your options to another investor or exercise your call privileges. You gain nothing by letting your options expire worthless.

## Commodities

Last, and certainly least for nearly all investors, we'll discuss commodities trading. Frankly, we don't think you should be trading commodities; it's too risky, transaction costs are too high, and you are very likely to see your entire capital wiped out. If you like to gamble, why not go to Las Vegas? At least you get to see the floor show; and, if you lose enough money the first time, they'll "comp" you (treat you as the guest of the house) when you come back eager to lose some more.

Commodities trading involves "futures"—contracts to buy a certain commodity (wheat, gold, frozen orange juice, and so on) at a defined time in the future. (If you're curious, the renowned pork bellies are what you make bacon out of.) One commodities exchange has the slogan: "We will sell no wine before its time."

The futures markets arose out of the prosaic needs of producers to plan ahead—how much could they sell their products for? If prices would be low, how much should they plant and harvest, or mine? If prices would be high, how could they boost production?

Processors and manufacturers had a complementary need to insure reliable supplies at predictable prices. So the first users of commodities exchanges were people who actually *had* grain, meat, or metals, making deals with people who actually *wanted* the stuff.

Later on, it dawned on people that whenever the price of anything fluctuates, money can be made by speculating on the price variations. Today, you can buy or sell futures contracts on a variety of commodities. To avoid the dreaded cocoa-on-the-front-lawn syndrome, you close out your position by buying an equal but opposite contract: that is, if you agreed to buy three thousand pounds of frozen orange juice in July, you simply agree to sell the same 3,000 pounds in July—hoping, of course, that the price has increased enough to make it worthwhile after the commissions are taken into account. You can also buy stock index futures, based on the New York Stock Exchange Composite, the Value Line Index, or the S&P 500. The futures contracts are based on $500 worth of the underlying index, so a one-point change in the index makes the contract $500 more or less valuable—quite a lot of leverage, and thus quite a lot of risk. Commissions on stock index futures are very high —around 5 to 10 percent of the value of the contract.

Some full-service and discount brokers handle commodities as well as stocks and bonds. There are also specialized commodities brokerage houses. If you trade heavily in commodities, you have to track your cash position every day. You might have placed a "limit order"—to be filled at a certain price, or better—that couldn't be filled because your price was unavailable. Your broker might have had to buy or sell a contract to close out a position just in time to prevent delivery—at a price that depletes your account.

A unique little fillip in commodities trading is the "daily limit," which is the maximum amount a commodity's price is permitted to move in one day from the previous business day's settlement price. Once a commodity reaches the limit, further trades will be permitted at the limit price—but not at higher or lower prices. The limit is adjusted if the commodity trades at the limit for two days in a row: the daily limit is upped until the first nonlimit day, when it goes back to the original limit. The effect is that you can get trapped when you need to buy a contract to offset one that is about to be delivered. You may be willing to pay almost any price—but the commodities exchange won't let you.

In short, commodities trading gives you an almost infinite opportunity to lose money—far more than your original investment. You get a confusing mass of paperwork to deal with: initial statements of account; monthly update statements; a trade confirmation for the entry and exit price of each completed trade; and records of purchases, sales, and open trades (those that have not been closed out by offsetting contracts). If you haven't figured it out by now, we *don't* recommend that you add commodities trading to your portfolio.

### Tips to Remember

- You need to review your insurance coverage, so that emergencies will be easier to deal with if they occur.
- Before you invest, study hard—more advanced books on investment; magazines and newsletters; daily stock, bond, and option tables. You may want to join an investment club—clubs offer access to information, knowledgeable speakers, and someone to cry with if you lose money.
- Make sure you understand your own risk tolerance. And if your risk tolerance is high, make sure you're investing only discretionary income, not the money you need for current expenses and future needs such as retirement and your kids' education.
- If you insist on working with a broker, pick one who fits your trading pattern.
- Diversify—don't just have *one* stock or *one* bond. (This is especially true of your employer's stock, perhaps purchased as part of an employee stock ownership plan. Your employer's stock fluctuates just like anyone else's—no matter what management wants you to believe.)
- Remember, even if you're right about computer stocks, airline stocks, health care stocks, or whatever sector you've decided is headed skyward, you run the risk of investing in the worst stock in the bunch. Examine each potential buy carefully.

- Be able to distinguish between potential growth stocks (usually paying low dividends, because the money is reinvested in research and marketing) and income-oriented stocks; tailor your stocks to your long-range goals.
- Think in the long run—don't sell stocks because of a minor, and possibly temporary, gain or loss.
- Choose bonds to complement your desire for income, or for resale if you think interest rates will go down.
- Remember, bond prices drop as interest rates rise; bond prices rise as interest rates fall. Stock prices also rise when interest rates fall.
- If you invest actively long enough (for some, all it takes is one trade), you're going to lose some money sooner or later. Be prepared for it, and think of it as a cost of education. If you really enjoy investing, think of it as a cost of entertainment. And if you really hate investing, go back and reread chapter 4. You can earn comfortable returns by choosing mutual funds and "leaving the driving to them."

## CASE HISTORY
### Advanced Investment Techniques

"Oh, I always get the mutton chops," Roger McGarry said. "There are so few places that serve them."

As far as Robin Sinclair was concerned, there was a good reason for that; but McGarry was a good client, so he said, "Excellent idea, sir. I'll have the mutton myself." Life was hard enough carrying around the name Robin, the constant aspersions on his masculinity, and the recent spate of mail addressed to Ms. Sinclair and the invitations to join the Financial Women's Round Table and the like. Being named Robin wasn't quite as bad as being named Sue, but it would suffice. There was no point in insulting clients by implying that they couldn't tell well-aged mutton from barbecued galoshes.

"Sir, I think that we can agree that the bull market is no fluke. Stock prices are high, and rising. So I think that we should shift part of your portfolio out of corporate bonds and strengthen your position in equities. Furthermore, because interest rates, while showing some fluctuation, are on a downward trend, you should earn some very satisfying profits on the bond sales."

"Have you discussed your plans with Leverett?" (Leverett was the McGarrys' tax accountant.)

"I had a quick conversation last Sunday; his foursome was teeing off just before mine, at the club. He agrees with me that it's a tax-wise as well as investment-wise move. And then, Mr. McGarry, I'm not recommending that you divest any portion of your tax-exempt bond portfolio. The tax-exempts we've chosen are continuing to perform strongly, and they yield quite a bit of tax-free income."

Roger McGarry finished his consommé, and set down the broad, shell-patterned silver spoon. He poured a glass of claret to give himself a moment for reflection. "Very well, I see your point. Now, which stocks do you recommend?"

"I've rather revised my original list of recommendations since the balanced budget bill was passed. At first, I wanted you to move further into defense contractors, because I felt that they had the greatest potential for expansion. However, since there will be dramatic cuts in the defense budget, I've revised my recommendation in favor of greater investment in a number of blue chip firms that combine defense contracting with sales of producer and consumer goods. I expect their stocks to continue to trend upwards, and they also have a history of strong dividend performance. Please review the charts back at my office." (The club did not permit the undignified display of business papers at the tables.)

"Although most of my recommendations are well within the definition of blue chips, our research department has found some small companies trading over the counter that I think should join your portfolio. Two of them are engaged in laser research, and I think they'll do very well if the Star Wars system continues to be funded. Even if it isn't, they can apply their work to medical uses. Then we've uncovered an initial public offering of a company that has patented a brake shoe that's a substantial improvement over the designs currently used on railways and subways. There's a well-defined market, and I think they can reach it even though their marketing expertise definitely lags behind their inventive genius.

"Now, for something more speculative, we have good reports on a small cosmetic company that has a new collagen product that is patentable—though they haven't yet gotten through the patent process—and that is especially successful in eliminating facial lines in men. That's a new angle—most collagen products are sold for women. They have to get through the FDA, of course, so it'll take awhile before the product is on the market. And I—and they—may be wrong about the market for a product like this for men. But, first of all, it could be a winner; and, since we're making a market in the stock, it's available at a very favorable price." (He didn't mention that the brokers got a special bonus for succeeding in convincing clients to buy some of it.)

The trifle arrived for dessert. If possible, Robin hated trifle even more than mutton chops. Still, after a couple of glasses of claret, the sherry in the trifle, and a snifter of Armagnac, he felt pleasantly muddled enough to ignore the horribleness of the lunch in favor of its potential profitability.

"I'm not at all sure that this rally can last," Roger McGarry puffed out with expensive cigar fumes. "Odd-lotters. Unstable types make an unstable market."

"Ah, yes, as they say on the Bourse, a *foule* and its money are soon parted," Robin ventured. His client stared at him narrowly, suspecting him of having said something clever, then continued.

"However, I think your recommendations are basically sound, especially since you're concentrating on income-oriented stocks. I don't mind shifting out of those bonds, either; perhaps you're right, and they've achieved all they're going to achieve."

They were helped into their Chesterfields and hats. Robin sometimes thought about getting a homburg, but that verged on parody. Sometimes he wondered if he was solemn enough to be a really successful stockbroker.

Roger McGarry spent the afternoon reviewing the charts, prospectuses, and annual reports presented for his inspection. He was ushered to a computer terminal, given a demitasse, and turned loose to play the wealthy adult's version of Space Invaders. The upshot was that he authorized all of Sinclair's recommendations, except for the OTC brakeshoe company (which had been thrown in more or less as a makeweight; Robin had long observed that, while customers of full-service brokers like to get recommendations, they also like to disagree occasionally).

Both men were satisfied with the afternoon: McGarry found it interesting and enjoyable, with some immediate profit and prospect of more to come; Sinclair, because it had yielded a gratifying sum in commissions, and confirmed his own good opinion of himself as a securities analyst.

Not everyone has the financial wherewithal of Roger McGarry—if his investments went sour, he would feel a very painful pinch, but he would not be wiped out. The lesson here is that you should tailor your investment program to fit your ability to tolerate loss, your willingness to study the markets, and your capacity for healthy and rational skepticism toward surefire deals.

# 16

## Family Taxes

The love-hate relationship between taxpayers and the IRS took a new turn in the fall of 1986, when a new tax code was enacted. Theoretically, the new system was supposed to provide tax simplification (hah!) and greater fairness. For most taxpayers, the upshot was a small cut in federal taxes—though some people face an uncomfortable 1987, because most of the tax deductions eliminated by the new code disappeared on January 1, 1987, while the new (lower) rates don't take effect until July 1, 1987.

The essence of the new tax system is that the existing system, with fifteen tax brackets and lots of elaborate and confusing deductions and credits, is replaced by a system with five brackets in 1987 and three brackets in later years. Many of the old familiar deductions you've grown to know and love (and that you've incorporated into your tax planning) have been limited or eliminated.

We won't deal with them here, but you should also know that the new tax code makes extensive changes in corporate taxes. You don't have to know all the rules, but you *should* care about the way corporations are taxed. Corporations now face higher tax rates; they can no longer use the investment tax credit to reduce taxable income; and they are subject to a stiff minimum tax. All these factors will affect corporate profits (and probably the prices the corporations charge for their products and services). Changes in corporate profits mean changes in stock dividends. If you're a "fundamentalist" investor, you'll be very interested in the impact that new taxes have on corporate balance sheets and income statements.

### Tax Revolution?

First, there was President Reagan's own plan for tax simplification and reform. Next, the House of Representatives passed a bill that didn't have a lot in common with the President's plan. The Senate weighed in with its own bill, which was different from the two earlier tax proposals. Then they locked a bunch of Congressional tax writers in a little room and didn't let them out until they had devised a Conference Committee agreement, which was duly passed by both houses of Congress and signed into law. It would take a historian ruthlessly devoted to trivia to run down all the differences among the four plans and to explain why certain provisions appeared in some plans and not in others. All we'll say is that politics played an important part (no elected official likes to have to tell a constituent that he or she voted to *increase* the voter's tax liability) and that there will be big winners and big losers under the plan.

If you are heavily involved in tax shelters, you'll lose big under the new bill. If you have an elaborate structure of trusts to shift income to other family members, gee, we're sorry. (Even if you can't get rid of the trust, one step you can take is to instruct the trustee to shift from taxable to tax-free investments —that'll lessen some of the pain.) And if you once qualified for lots of itemized deductions, you'll enjoy April even less than you used to. Depending on the state you live in and the state's response, you may score a state-tax bonanza, or get stuck with a bigger bill for state taxes.

On the other hand, if you're just scraping by, you may find that the new system doesn't make you pay any income taxes at all. And you may be delighted to find that your tax rate is cut and that the decrease in the number of deductions allows you to focus on the economic value of your investments, not their tax status.

But this new tax system certainly isn't the equivalent of a cushy, comfy, down-filled armchair. Don't sink into it with a blissful sigh and settle down with the Sunday paper. The Senate amendments to the House bill included a five-year moratorium on changes in the new tax code—a provision that Congress pointedly chose *not* to include in the final bill. So just when you get used to the new tax system, there's a very good chance that it will be changed *again.*

Watch out for legislation with the innocuous title of "Technical Corrections Act": some major tax changes can be sneaked in under the heading of fixing minor confusions and snarls.

## Keeping Up with the IRS

Our tax system has many objectives and, naturally, some of them are contradictory. For example, the tax system is used to assemble enough money to run the country and buy expensive screwdrivers for the Department of Defense. It's also used to soak the rich and help out the poor (or at least those who fit into certain categories). The tax system is also used to encourage people to do certain things (e.g., own their own homes) and discourage them from doing others (e.g., invest in tax shelters that the IRS finds "abusive").

Tax law starts with the Internal Revenue Code, which is legislation passed by, and frequently and lavishly amended by, Congress. There have been four versions of the Internal Revenue Code: one in 1918, one in 1939, one in 1954, and the present Code of 1986. Every few years, there's a major Tax Reform Bill. During the in-between years, there are less drastic bills or Technical Corrections Acts to clean up the bloopers that no one noticed when the tax bill was being written.

The IRS is responsible for enforcing whatever version of the Code happens to be the law at a given time. The IRS writes up volumes and volumes of administrative rulings, called the Internal Revenue Regulations and universally known as the Regs. The IRS also publishes hundreds of decisions each year, which aim to interpret fine points. The decisions known as Treasury Decisions, Revenue Rulings, and Announcements are binding on the IRS—if one of these decisions applies to your situation, you can quote it to the IRS and expect the IRS to back down. To avoid losing, the IRS may claim that your situation is really different from the seemingly identical one you mention.

Some taxpayers with particular kinds of tax problems can write to the IRS for "advance rulings" (much as preteen girls ask their moms if they can wear lipstick to school; as you can imagine, the IRS, like many moms, tends to say no). Then there are "private letter rulings." These rulings are not binding on the IRS, but tax professionals want to keep abreast of rulings, which, after all, indicate the direction of IRS thinking.

Sometimes tax cases end up in court. As we'll explain below, if the IRS audits a tax return and claims that the taxpayer didn't pay enough, the taxpayer may want to take the IRS to court to prove that s/he doesn't owe any taxes, much less any penalties. So the tax professional also has to understand court cases with a bearing on his or her clients' tax situations.

In other words, for a thorough understanding of federal income taxes, you have to know (1) what Congress has said so far (and what it's likely to say and do in the future); (2) what the IRS says (usually, that a debatable item *is* taxable income and *isn't* deductible); and (3) what the courts say. No wonder good tax advice is hard to find, and expensive when you find it.

### The Two Stages of Tax Advice

If all you want is tax advice, most of your relatives or any cabdriver will be happy to oblige. But if you want *valid* tax advice—the kind that will have you cashing refund checks instead of singing "How Are Things in Dannemora"—you'll need to go to a pro. Before we discuss tax experts and the kinds of services they provide, it is important to have a clear view of tax advice and how it can affect the way you live.

From the one-income couple with a straight salary and a little bit of interest income to a multinational corporation, tax advice has two phases:

- Tax compliance—which forms do you have to file, on what schedule, when do you have to pay, and how much is the bill?
- Tax planning—how can transactions be arranged in the future so that their tax impact will be cushioned?

Let us assume that you have a fairly straightforward financial life: one or more salaries in the family, perhaps some self-employment income, bank account and/or bond interest, dividends or profits on investments, maybe some rental income from real estate investments. We also assume that you qualify for some or all of the common deductions such as medical expenses, casualty losses, charitable contributions, and travel and entertainment expenses.

For you, tax compliance will also be fairly straightforward. Income and Social Security taxes will be withheld from your salary at work; you may have to pay estimated taxes four times a year if you're self-employed, or if you have extensive nonsalary income and you don't have withholding increased to compensate. (In most states, state income tax will also be withheld, but we're concentrating on the federal tax in this chapter.)

Once a year, the annual tax follies that culminate on April 15 will be enacted; you'll have to file a tax return explaining your tax situation for the year, paying any tax that is still due, or claiming any refund you're entitled to.

If you're like most people, once April 15 has come and gone, you resolve to set up a proactive tax plan that, you hope, will help stave off the IRS in the coming tax year. Be honest with yourself; year after year those heady plans for astute tax planning fall by the wayside. Now, however, let's assume that you'll never again drag your heels.

### Tax Planning Gets Tougher

The classic rules of tax planning called for income deferral and income shifting. "Deferral" means postponing the payment of income in the hopes of enjoying lower tax rates later—say, after retirement, after a general cut in tax rates, or in a year when lots of tax losses cushion income. But with lower rates and fewer tax brackets, many taxpayers will be in the same tax bracket before and after retirement. For them, the incentive to take the money now, when it can be spent or invested, may be compelling. Furthermore, tax losses have been curtailed dramatically.

As for income shifting, the theory is to shift income from high-bracket earner to low-bracket family member (say, from top-executive Dad and internist Mom to preteen kids). Trusts used to be highly useful for this purpose. But now much trust income is taxed to the person who set up the trust anyway, and there are strict rules about the taxes children under the age of fourteen must pay on their investment income. So substantial income shifting is impossible for most families.

### The Exception Experts Versus the Tax Preparers

As we'll see throughout this chapter, with limited exceptions, you can't have your cake and eat it too—you have to give up something to get tax advantages. What you want to do, then, is be sure to take advantage of the limited exceptions. "How?" you ask. The better question is: "Who's going to teach me about these limited exceptions?"

Finding top-flight advice at an affordable price has never been easy. The dramatic changes in tax law make it harder than ever in 1987 and 1988. Make sure that your advice-giver really understands the new law. Did he or she attend professional seminars and study intensively, or did the information come from the back of a cereal box?

- Tax lawyers—people with law degrees who have decided to learn the ins and outs of the tax code. An LL.M. (master's degree) in taxation is a plus, but expect to pay even higher fees. Tax lawyers can be expected to tell you the best way to arrange a transaction for tax purposes. If you hire a lawyer for another matter (for instance, a divorce or business start-up), you'll need tax advice. And if your lawyer doesn't have this knowledge, you may need help from a tax specialist. Of course, you won't need to know this, *but* if you're in trouble with the IRS or plan to do something outright crooked or seriously dubious, you're better off with a lawyer than with an accountant, because the general rule is that accountants can be made to testify against you, while lawyers can't. Your accountant, however, should know when to call in a tax lawyer.

- Tax accountants—"numbers runners" who approach the tax code from the point of view of balance sheets, debits, and credits. If your tax problem involves interpretation of disputed points of law, you're probably better off with a lawyer. However, if the real question is one of setting up proper records or reconstructing the financial effect of a transaction, you're probably better off with an accountant.

- Tax preparers—the most famous is H & R Block, but every winter, several storefront services spring up. The preparers have a limited amount of training, but can probably handle a straightforward or semi-straightforward return if it's too much for you to handle, or if you just don't want to bother. However, tax preparers, unlike lawyers and accountants, are only interested in the tax compliance end—they won't help you plan your tax future. Also note that commercial preparers may give you a guarantee that they will pay any penalties and interest. This is not always helpful; it tends to make them more conservative.

- Books and magazines—lots of books (like this one) and magazine and newspaper articles will give you general principles and information. However, to apply those principles to your family's unique situation, you'll need individual advice from a lawyer, accountant, or tax preparer.

- The IRS itself—the IRS maintains special telephone lines and personnel to counsel "walk-in" questioners. The IRS also issues an extensive library of free publications explaining (well, talking about) literally hundreds of tax issues.

In fact, some fairly expensive books sold in bookstores are just reprints of these free IRS publications, so don't pay for a tax book until you check to see if you could get it free from the friendly folks at the IRS. But be wary of IRS advice: the IRS is *not* bound by the advice its staffers offer. So, if the IRS-ite you talk to makes a mistake, or interprets a difficult provision differently from the one who eventually audits your return, it's no defense to say you just did what you were told. What's more, the IRS's free publications will not tell you about court decisions that the IRS does not agree with.

Of course, the question of where you can get tax advice implies that you *need* tax advice. You may be able to handle all your tax problems and planning yourself, by keeping good records and following the instructions on the IRS forms.

## Tax Return Forms

Virtually everyone who has a significant amount of income (and everyone who's entitled to a tax refund—say, a student who works part-time and doesn't have to pay tax, but who has tax deducted from his or her paycheck) must file a tax return at least once a year. The vast majority of individual (nonbusiness) filers are *calendar-year* taxpayers; that is, for tax purposes, their year runs from January 1 to December 31. There are many good reasons for a business to have a *fiscal year* (a tax year different from the calendar year) but virtually no reasons acceptable to the IRS for an individual to have a fiscal year, so we'll ignore that possibility in this book.

For calendar-year taxpayers, the return is due on April 15 of every year. The exception to this rule involves an extension.

There are three kinds of tax return:

- The 1040EZ "short form" for single taxpayers
- The 1040A "short form," which can be used either by single or by married taxpayers
- The 1040 "long form," which can be used by any taxpayer

The advantage of the short forms is that they're easier to fill out; the disadvantage is that not all taxpayers are allowed to use them, and the taxpayers who *do* use them are not entitled to claim most deductions or credits. However, 1040A filers are entitled to use the earned income credit, which benefits low-income heads of household.

If you do use the long Form 1040 (e.g., you have investment income or profits to report or you choose to take, say, a medical expense deduction), you'll need several forms in addition to the basic Form 1040. The forms and schedules you may need include:

- Schedule A (itemized deductions)
- Schedule B (interest or dividend income over $400)
- Schedule C (self-employment income)

- Schedule D (capital gains/losses)
- Schedule E (rent, royalty, partnership income)
- Schedule F (farm income)
- Schedule G (income averaging)
- Schedule R (credit for the elderly or disabled)
- Schedule SE (Social Security self-employment tax)

As a general rule, things called forms explain and document a deduction or credit that you take. Frequently used forms include:

- 2106 (employee business expenses)
- 2119 (tax consequences of selling your house)
- 2210 (underpaid estimated tax—explaining, if possible, why you shouldn't have to pay an underpayment penalty)
- 2441 (child-care credit)
- 3468 (investment tax credit)
- 3903 (deductible moving expenses)
- 4562 (depreciation and amortization)
- 4684 (casualty and theft losses)
- 4868 (automatic extension of time to file a tax return)

### Where to Get Forms

For one thing, whether you like it or not, the IRS will probably mail you a package of forms each year, based on the forms you filed the year before. If you filed quarterly estimated tax vouchers, you'll get another package; if you filed Form 1040A, you'll get another 1040A, and so forth.

However, if you moved or got married, the IRS may have lost track of you, and you won't get the forms; or you may get a set of forms appropriate for last year's tax needs but inappropriate for this year's situation. Or you may be a 1040 filer who needs a form or schedule that is not included in the standard package. In that case, you have several choices.

Local banks and post offices should have a supply of the more common tax forms, starting about February and running through April. Your public library may have a looseleaf book containing all the official IRS forms; you can photocopy the ones you need, and file those. If you go to a tax preparer, the preparer should have the forms. If you need a very unusual form, maybe you need more tax sophistication. A tax lawyer or accountant should have all the forms, or should be able to photocopy them.

If you live near a good-size city, there should be an IRS office in the central business district. There'll be a special area set up to distribute forms and publications. Be prepared, however, for marathon lines, especially at lunchtime and especially as April 15 approaches. *Tip:* Be sure to get at least three copies of the forms you need—one to file with the IRS and a couple of scratch copies so you won't have to rush back to the office if you louse up a calculation. Don't be piggy and take ten copies of each (the maximum you're permitted at each visit)—nobody likes to find that the supply has run out.

If you give yourself plenty of time, you can order the forms by mail from the IRS itself. The country is divided into eight regions, with a distribution center in each. The forms are free (you only get two copies of each), but you can also get a free copy of a number of IRS publications. Some of the publications you may find helpful in preparing a return and for ordinary tax planning include:

- No. 17—*Your Federal Income Tax*—a long, well-written summary of basic tax planning and practice. (Make sure you don't buy an expensive commercial publication that simply reprints this copyright-free treasure.)
- No. 334—*Tax Guide for Small Business.*
- No. 502—*Medical and Dental Expenses.*
- No. 503—*Child and Dependent Care Credit*—also summarizes your responsibility for withholding and paying taxes if you employ a housekeeper or child-care worker.
- No. 504—*Tax Information for Divorced or Separated Individuals.*
- No. 505—*Tax Withholding and Estimated Tax.*
- No. 506—*Income Averaging.*
- No. 508—*Educational Expenses.*
- No. 521—*Moving Expenses.*
- No. 523—*Tax Information on Selling Your Home*—don't leave home without it.
- No. 530—*Tax Information for Owners of Homes, Condominiums, and Cooperative Apartments.*
- No. 533—*Self-Employment Tax.*
- No. 547—*Nonbusiness Disasters, Casualties, and Thefts.*
- No. 554—*Tax Benefits for Older Americans.*
- No. 575—*Pension and Annuity Income.*
- No. 587—*Business Use of Your Home*—the "home office" deduction changes frequently; be sure you're following the current rules.
- No. 915—*Tax Information on Social Security Benefits*—as we explain

in chapter 17, part of your Social Security benefits *could* be taxable income, depending on the level and nature of your other income.

### What's Your Filing Status?

Once you've decided whether to file the long form or a short form, one of your first tax-paying decisions is to decide which filing status you're entitled to. As far as the IRS is concerned, you can be:

- Married, filing a joint return. This option provides the lowest tax rates. Note: Some widows and widowers are entitled to use this filing status for tax relief.
- Single, head of household.
- Single.
- Married, filing a separate return. This option provides the highest tax rates, and married couples normally avoid it like the plague. However, there are several situations in which filing separate returns makes sense: (1) The spouses are separated (but not yet divorced) and one spouse holds out and refuses to sign the joint return. (2) One spouse suspects that the other is a tax cheat, and protects himself or herself by refusing to sign a joint return. As we'll discuss below, the IRS can collect *all* the tax due on a joint return from *either* spouse; it doesn't matter which spouse earned most or all of the income, or which is in a better financial position to pay the tax. (3) The situation may be the converse: one spouse expects major tax trouble, or already has a tax bill he or she can't pay, and wants to protect the spouse. The IRS can seize the couple's joint property to pay a delinquent tax bill. If the couple signs a joint return, the IRS can also seize the separate property of *either* spouse. But if each spouse files separately, the IRS can't collect tax due on one spouse's return from the separately owned property of the other spouse.

**Who's Married?**     As far as the IRS is concerned, a couple is "married" if they are legally married in the state in which they live. A few states do recognize common-law marriage; but, in general, couples living together (and same-sex couples) are not entitled to file joint returns. What counts is your legal status on December 31 of the tax year. Separated couples who do not come under a court's decree of separate maintenance can (and often do) file joint returns.

A widow or widower is usually entitled to file a joint return for the year of the spouse's death. For the two years following the year of death, the widow or widower may be able to figure her or his tax bill using the joint rates. That can be beneficial. It can be complicated, however, so check IRS instructions, or get professional advice, for more details.

As explained above, it's usually worthwhile for a couple to file jointly if possible. What's more, the child-care credit is limited unless a joint return is filed; and various other tax provisions are more favorable to joint returns. By the way, if a married couple files separate returns, either both of them must itemize deductions, or neither of them may.

Some separated married persons get a tax break: they can file either as single or as heads of household, avoiding the higher rates on married people filing separately. To qualify for this break, you must have been separated from your spouse for the entire year; you must have paid more than half the cost of maintaining your home for the year; and for at least half the year, you must have been providing a home for a child or stepchild who is your dependent for tax purposes. You can file as a "single" taxpayer if you meet all these tests. If your home was also the *principal* home for your child or stepchild for the whole year, you qualify for preferential head of household rates.

**Who's a Head of Household?**    You are a head of household if you're unmarried; separated under a decree of legal separation; or separated and meeting the tests above—*and* if you pay more than half the cost of maintaining a home for specified groups of relatives. There are fairly complex rules, which we'll leave to your tax adviser to explain; but think about this status if a child, parent, sibling, or other relative lives with you.

### Tax Rates

Before TC '86 there were fifteen tax brackets, ranging from 11 percent to 50 percent. TC '86 has been ballyhooed as reducing the number of brackets to two and cutting the rates to 15 percent and 28 percent. However, as we'll show you, that's not quite accurate.

Remember, taxable income is computed by an elaborate series of calculations. Not all of a taxpayer's income is included. Adjusted Gross Income (AGI) is a very important tax number. AGI equals gross income reduced by certain expenses, such as the alimony you pay and deductible IRA contributions. Many itemized deductions are allowed only if they exceed a certain percentage of AGI. Last but not least, taxpayers are entitled to claim personal exemptions for themselves and their spouses and dependents.

TC '86 brings significant increases in the standard deduction and personal exemptions—so significant that many taxpayers will be removed from the tax rolls, because the standard deduction and personal exemptions wipe out their entire tax liability.

However, middle-class and wealthy taxpayers must pay rates higher than the much-vaunted 15 percent and 28 percent on some of their income, because the personal exemption and the benefit of the 15 percent rate are phased out at higher income levels. There's a special, five-bracket system for 1987, with a top rate of 38.5 percent. After 1987, there will, in effect, be three brackets. The first "step" of taxable income is taxed at 15 percent, the next "step" at 28 percent, the third at 33 percent (as the personal exemption is phased out); any remaining taxable income is taxed at 28 percent again, once all of the personal exemption and the benefit of the 15 percent rate have been phased out.

### Keeping Tax Records

Sometimes, as the saying goes, you can't win for losing. If you do your own tax returns, you need accurate records, and if you hire a preparer, accountant, or attorney to do it, you have to give him or her accurate records, or pay for endless hours as s/he tries to make sense of the junk in the shoebox.

You'll need at least these basic records to prepare a tax return, or have it prepared:

- W-2 forms (if any) showing your salary.
- W-2P forms (if any) showing pension payments from your ex-employer.
- Records of any self-employment income—when the income arrived, from whom, in what amount, and in return for what services.
- Records of the cost of doing business.
- 1099 forms showing miscellaneous income received—e.g., bank interest or return on money market fund accounts.
- Investment records—how many shares purchased, when, at what price; dividends received; date and price of sale.
- Household records—if you own a home, keep track of anything affecting the basis (tax value) of your home, such as repairs, improvements, casualty losses.

- Documentation of deductions—how much tuition did you pay for that continuing professional education course? How much did you pay the dentist for the kids' braces?

Keeping records should not spark anxiety attacks. It's good family financial planning to enter all checks in the check register immediately, and to balance the checkbook once a month. You may find it helpful to put a check mark in the check register, or highlight the check number with a felt-tipped pen, if the check amount is tax deductible.

It can also be helpful to file all canceled checks, with the bank statements, in an easily accessible place. Be sure to keep these files for several years— three is an absolute minimum, seven is better.

To make your tax tasks easier, try keeping a simple notebook with a page for each class of deduction you take (e.g., charitable or medical). Make an entry with date, amount, and explanation whenever a deductible expense arises. Another alternative: get a set of manila envelopes. Keep a running record of transactions on the outside of the envelope; keep receipts and other documentation inside.

## Common Deductions

Although tax returns are not *quite* as individual as fingerprints, there are plenty of variations on the theme. We can't hope to cover every tax problem you could ever encounter in this short chapter. However, we'll try to alert you to the rules about some of the most common tax deductions.

You might deduct (or at least try to deduct):

- Medical expenses.
- Casualty and theft losses.
- Moving expenses.
- Expenses of maintaining a home office.
- Business expenses—whether you're an employee or a business owner.
- Educational expenses.
- Some of the interest you paid to others. TC '86 phases out the deduction for consumer interest (e.g., credit cards and personal loans used to buy consumer goods) over a five year period ending in 1991. (We discussed the rules on investment interest and home-equity loans in chapter 7.)
- Charitable contributions.
- Alimony (see chapter 12).
- Professional fees.

The basic rule is that your personal expenses of living and supporting your family are *not* deductible. (That's one reason why child support is not deductible.) To qualify as a deduction, an expense must either be "gain seeking" (aimed at making a profit—which the IRS will, of course, try to tax) or must fall into a category specifically favored by Congress (e.g., medical expenses).

### Medical Expenses

Let's hope your health problems aren't so bad that you'll qualify for this deduction. To get *any* medical expense deduction, you must have medical bills that are not paid by insurance, reimbursed by your employer, or otherwise satisfied; and that exceed 7.5 percent of your adjusted gross income (AGI). (AGI equals your gross income—all the potentially taxable money you receive —minus certain deductions such as alimony and money contributed to your IRA.) There's no ceiling on the amount you can deduct; but if your unreimbursed medical expenses equal 7.4999 percent of your AGI, you get no deduction at all.

You only get to deduct medical expenses in the year you pay them, no matter when they were accrued. Let's say you take the kids to the dentist in December; pay the bill; and file an insurance reimbursement claim. The claim isn't processed until after the New Year hangovers subside, so you have to wait until February for a check. The key point here is that if you pay an expense in one year, and get reimbursed in the following year, you can forget about the whole thing *if* you didn't take a medical expense deduction, or if the deduction didn't reduce your tax. Otherwise, you must include the reimbursement in your taxable income—but only to the extent that the reimbursement would have reduced your medical expense deduction if you had received it in the year the bills were paid.

For tax purposes, "medical expenses" include:

- Health insurance premiums, including Medicare Part B.
- Prescription drugs and insulin—but not "over the counter" drugs like cold pills.
- Psychological or psychiatric therapy, as long as it's aimed at curing a mental condition (therapy that's part of training as a therapist doesn't count).
- Transportation to and from the doctor's office, hospital, etc. You *may* be able to deduct meals and lodging if you must leave your home for treatment, or if you're accompanying another patient. You may even be

able to deduct the cost of trips to a warm climate, a drier climate, or whatever your doctor recommends—but get tax advice first, because these are controversial areas of tax law.

Naturally, you can deduct your own medical expenses, but if it's a joint return, you can deduct both spouses' expenses on the return. Moreover, if you report any dependents on your tax return, you can deduct their medical expenses too.

What if you and your brothers and sisters have a "multiple support" agreement, under which you share the cost of supporting an elderly parent? In that case, the agreement must designate one person who is allowed to deduct the parent's medical expenses.

### Nursing Homes and Taxes

By the way, if you pay the nursing home bills of a parent (or other aged relative), you're entitled to some tax relief. First of all, no matter how much you pay, you will never have to pay gift tax, as long as you pay the medical bills directly. You *will* have to pay gift tax if you give money for medical costs directly to your relative, and if the amount given exceeds $10,000 per year per recipient ($20,000 per year per recipient if your spouse joins in the gift) and you have exhausted the so-called "unified gift and estate tax credit." It's a good idea to consult with your tax adviser on these matters. As we discuss in chapter 17, when we're talking about Medicaid, it's a better idea *not* to give money to aged relatives—they'll suffer fewer adverse consequences if you pay their bills than if you give them cash.

You may also qualify for an income tax medical-expense deduction for the amount of medical expenses (including nursing home expenses you pay for an aged relative who is dependent) that exceed the "floor" of 7.5 percent of your AGI. To claim the entire nursing-home expense as a medical deduction, you must be able to show that your relative is in a nursing home principally for medical care. If you can show this, the entire payment ranks as a potentially deductible medical expense, even though part of it represents the equivalent of ordinary living costs. But if your relative is primarily in the nursing home for other reasons (e.g., he or she can't live independently, and no family member is available to provide help with self-care), the costs of medical care and nursing are deductible, but the costs of food and lodging are not. So before your relative enters the nursing home, try to get documentation from the home that your relative needs round-the-clock nursing attention, which *does* count as a medical need.

### Home Improvements the Doctor Orders

Sometimes people have to alter their homes to make them accessible to people in wheelchairs or with mobility problems; sometimes they add elevators for heart patients, or swimming pools for patients who need to swim for exercise or to maintain mobility. These improvements are only deductible if you own the property (not if you install them in a rental apartment, or put the pool in your parents' house for convenience). Furthermore, the amount you can deduct is limited to the cost of the improvement minus the value it adds to the property. You can also deduct maintenance and operating costs.

### Charitable Deductions

Either out of the goodness of their hearts, or out of a desire to do *anything* with money other than give it to the IRS, Americans make substantial charitable contributions every year. There are limits on maximum charitable contributions, but they're so high they don't concern the average taxpayer. As long as you itemize your deductions, there's no minimum; you can deduct all contributions of money or property made to organizations on the IRS's list of legitimate charities. (Be careful: there are organizations that are tax exempt in the sense that *they* don't have to pay income taxes, but contributions to them are not deductible by the contributors.)

You can deduct sums of actual money contributed, or the value of property contributed. Get a receipt for the clothes and old paperbacks you give to the church rummage sales; and get a professional appraisal if you claim that you've donated an item (or group of related items) with a value over $5,000. You can also deduct the cost of using your automobile for charitable purposes (e.g., driving blood donors back to the office)—but you *can't* deduct the value of services contributed, whether you spend an hour blowing up balloons at the May Festival or forty-five hours giving high-level business advice.

If you donate a work of art created by somebody else, and if the charitable organization uses it (let's say, you give your Andy Warhol lithograph to a museum), you get to deduct the full value of the artwork. If the charity plans to resell it, your deduction is limited to what you paid for it plus 60 percent of the appreciation in value.

However, if you donate a work of art *you* created, your deduction is limited, usually to what it cost you to create the work. So you can deduct the canvas and paint, or the typing paper, but not the value of the work itself. You can understand the possibilities of abuse if the rule were otherwise, but you can also get pretty teed off if you feel your services or your creativity is more valuable than your kids' outgrown clothes or your old magazines.

In the common situation where a sum is partly a charitable contribution, partly a purchase—say, you attended a theater party where the tickets are extra-high-priced for the benefit of the charity—you can deduct the extra, but not the cost of your ticket, the banquet, the dance, or whatever. Naturally, everyone deducts the full amount, but we just thought we'd let you know the facts.

### Donating Securities

Sometimes it's a smart tax move to give your favorite charities stocks or other investments that have appreciated in value. If you held the investments for over six months, they're long-term assets, and you get to deduct the full value at the time of the donation. So you get a nice healthy deduction—and you never have to pay capital gains tax on the appreciation.

What if you donate short-term assets? Well, then, your deduction is limited to your *basis.* Basis means "tax value"; usually, your basis for something is what you paid for it. If you inherited it or were given it, other rules must be applied.

And if you have an investment that's an utter dog, and you're in a charitable mood, your best bet is to sell the investment, take your loss, and donate the proceeds to charity. You can't claim a loss deduction if you give the losing investment to charity directly.

Finally, if you donate inventory from your business—perhaps those blouses are moving so slowly you'd rather give them to Goodwill than have them cluttering up the store—you can deduct your basis, but nothing more.

### Business-Related Deductions

It's not appropriate here to delve into a full discussion of business deductions for the self-employed. However, we do want to mention that the general rule is that the "ordinary and necessary" costs of doing business can be deducted from a corporation's income, or on the Schedule C of a sole proprietor.

Of more interest to most of our readers is the fact that employees are entitled to deduct certain expenses related to employment, as long as the employer doesn't reimburse them for the expenses, of course. Employee business expenses are deductible only to the extent that, in addition to the taxpayer's other "miscellaneous itemized deductions," they exceed 2 percent of AGI. Furthermore, the deduction for business meals is limited to 80 percent of the cost of the meal, and a deduction is denied for expenses that are "lavish or extravagant" under the circumstances. (The IRS hasn't come up with Regulations explaining what is "lavish or extravagant," but we hear they've subcontracted the job to an austere, enclosed religious order.)

An employee can deduct away-from-home travel expenses that are related to his or her service as an employee. These expenses include the cost of transporting yourself, baggage, and samples; hotel expenses; and expenses of maintaining a business automobile.

## The Home Office

It's possible—though difficult—for an employee to deduct the cost of maintaining a home office. Get tax advice before you do this. It's one of the most volatile areas of tax law. In general, to win, you'll have to show that the office was really maintained for the convenience of your employer, and/or that you habitually saw clients there—it's not enough that you frequently took work home, and used the "home office" to deal with the unruly contents of your briefcase. A wise precaution: get your employer to give you a letter explaining that the home office is essential—and get it in the year you set up the office; don't wait until the IRS casts suspicious glances at your tax return. If you qualify for home office treatment, you don't have to be a homeowner—you can, at least theoretically, deduct the portion of your rent, utility bills, etc., attributable to the room or areas used as your home office. A strategy worth considering: you can have your employer rent part of your home from you for use as an office. Make sure that the rent is not higher than the fair market value of the space. Report the rent as income; deduct the cost of maintaining the home office as expenses for the production of rental income.

It will also be necessary to show that the home office was used exclusively for business; it's no use trying to deduct the family room, where you maintain a desk, your spouse handles the family finances, the kids watch the VCR and set up their model railroads, and you keep your suitcases and out-of-season clothes.

The "exclusively for business" test also applies to self-employed persons. There are five types of home offices that can qualify for deductions:

- The principal place of business for the taxpayer—if it's your *only* office, you have a pretty good chance of getting the deduction, if the other requirements are met.
- A place of business used to meet clients or customers in the normal course of business.
- A structure separate from the rest of the home (e.g., a garage, barn, shed) used in connection with a trade or business.
- A home office used to store inventory.
- A day-care center that is legal under local law.

The home office deduction is not infinite—it's limited to your net business income. Net business income is the business's gross income minus allowable business deductions. In short, if the business isn't profitable, you'll get no home office deduction. If it makes you feel any better, home office expenses that you aren't allowed to deduct in the year in which you incur them can be carried over to later tax years.

Note, however, that the home office deduction can backfire if you decide to sell your house. Among other complications, the IRS will want to recapture office depreciation you claimed in previous years. By all means, talk to your accountant about this.

### Education Expenses

In general, education expenses are nondeductible personal expenses. However, you do get a deduction for job-related education costs that are not reimbursed by your employer. Once again, a letter from your employer stating that you *had* to take the courses can help you out at audit time.

You don't get a tax deduction for education that qualifies you for the minimum requirements of your profession (e.g., a college degree for a third-grade teacher), nor for education that qualifies you for a new trade or business (e.g., a third-grade teacher who gets graduate degrees qualifying her as a chemist or economist).

Compulsory continuing professional education courses are deductible. For some reason, the IRS has taken a particular hostility to law school studies—it's damn near impossible for anyone to deduct the cost of getting a law degree. The IRS's position is that, even if you never intend to practice, the law degree qualifies you for a new trade or business, so there.

The maximum amount of educational assistance from your employer that you can exclude from income is $5,250 a year. The education-expense provision was scheduled to expire at the end of 1985; however, TC '86 extends it for the 1986 and 1987 tax years. But there's bad news for some learned taxpayers: the costs of educational travel (e.g., a sociology professor's sojourn in Tahiti, a Spanish teacher's trip to Caracas) are no longer deductible.

Give my regards to Cohan! There's a tax principle called the "Cohan rule" (yes, it's named after George M.) that allows taxpayers with inadequate records to estimate business deductions other than travel and entertainment expenses. So, if the IRS questions any other kinds of business expense, you can reconstruct the expense and get a deduction for a reasonable estimate. Of course, if you spent *more* than the minimum reasonable amount, you'll lose part of the deduction—another argument for keeping complete and accurate records.

### Interest Deductions

This is another victim of zealous tax reformers. Under previous law, taxpayers could deduct virtually all business and consumer interest. Under the new law:

- Mortgage interest on your first or second home is deductible under the rules about "qualified residence interest" we discussed in chapter 7.
- Investment interest (that is, interest on money you borrowed to make investments) is deductible, but only up to your net investment income. "Leftover" interest can be carried forward to later tax years, but only if you have net investment income in those years. If you're a passive investor, you (or, more likely, your accountant) will have to do some fancy footwork to deal with both the passive investment rules and the investment interest rules.

    These new rules are phased in over a five-year period. If you have investment interest expenses that would have been deductible under the old law but are not under the new law, you may be able to deduct some of them until the new rules take full effect in 1991.
- From 1991 on, personal interest (including interest tardy taxpayers must pay the IRS on tax deficiencies) will be completely nondeductible. Between 1987 and 1991, the deduction for personal interest is phased out. If personal interest was deductible under the old law, 65 percent of the interest will be deductible in 1987, 40 percent deductible in 1988, 20 percent in 1989, 10 percent in 1990, and zilch from then on (unless, of course, bank lobbyists and angry borrowers manage to get the law changed).

However, even under the old law, certain transactions did not involve deductible interest:

- Borrowing to buy tax-exempt investments, such as municipal bonds.
- Borrowing to buy a single-premium life insurance, endowment, or annuity contract.
- Borrowing under a plan for buying life insurance—unless at least four out of the first seven years' premiums are paid without borrowed funds.

Sometimes a buyer and seller will adjust the purchase price under a transaction to call sums that are really part of the purchase price "interest." The IRS can (and will) characterize part of the alleged "interest" as part of the purchase price, if this conforms to the economic reality of the transaction.

As chapter 7 explains, interest is only one of the costs of borrowing money. Charges that represent fees for services are *not* deductible as interest. On the other hand, if your bank puts a one-time charge on cash advances or overdraft checks (say, 1 to 2 percent of the face amount, with a $1 minimum), you can deduct these amounts as interest, provided that they are not charges for services in connection with your account. Save those slips—the pesky little charges do add up.

If you're a home buyer, the points you pay out of your own funds to get a mortgage (e.g., loan origination fee, loan processing fee) *are* deductible as interest as long as they're charged for "use or forbearance of money," not for services. A 1980 private IRS ruling says that this rule applies even if the amounts at issue are subtracted from the mortgage proceeds—at least if the buyer was prepared to pay the amounts in cash. These rules apply to financing when the home is purchased—points on refinancing and re-hab loans must be spread out over the life of the loan.

If you're a home seller, the points *you* pay—such as a loan placement fee you have to give the lender for arranging financing for the buyer—are not deductible as interest. However, they *are* deductible as selling expenses, so they reduce the potentially taxable profits you get on the sale of your house.

It may not make you feel any better, but if you're stuck with a prepayment penalty on your mortgage, you get to deduct it as interest.

## Deductible Taxes

This may not make you feel any better either, but under current law you can deduct certain state and local taxes: income taxes, real estate taxes, school taxes, and the like. You can deduct your state income taxes from your federal income tax return, but not vice versa. And Social Security tax, alas, is not deductible on your federal return.

## Taxes and Investments

Before TC '86, there were elaborate rules providing preferential tax treatment for long-term capital gains (gains earned on investments held longer than six months). In effect, those rules have been swept away: long-term capital gains are now treated just about the same as ordinary income. (For 1987, there's sort of a break: long-term capital gains won't be taxed at rates higher than 28 percent—the former maximum was 20 percent—even though the top tax rate for 1987 is 38.5 percent.)

However, the term "capital gain" hasn't been abolished from the tax code. There are two reasons for this. First, although you can be taxed on any amount of capital gains you earn, up to and including the national debt, the maximum capital loss you can deduct is $3,000. (Capital losses you can't use in the year you suffer them can be carried forward to later tax years.) The second reason is a sneaky one: Congress just might see its way clear to changing the new tax code, either to put back preferential rates for capital gains or to raise rates across the board to help cope with the deficit. Congress doesn't want to have to go to the trouble of rewriting all those capital gains provisions.

By the way, you used to be able to exclude $100 in dividend income (or $200 for a married couple filing jointly) from your taxable income: no more. TC '86 eliminates the exclusion.

## Paper Losses

The rules above apply to *realized* gains and losses only. That is, you won't be taxed on a "paper gain"—the appreciation in value of something you bought at, let's say, $3.13 a share that is now worth $11.75 a share. Similarly, paper losses won't reduce your taxable income.

There are several good reasons to sell an investment:

- You need the cash, and you can get it quickly by realizing the investment.
- You think the investment has reached its peak, and has nowhere to go but into the basement.
- You were primarily interested in receiving income from the investment, less interested in capital appreciation, and it isn't performing. You think

you can get better performance (even after all the transaction costs) by selling the investment and reinvesting somewhere else.

- The investment offends your conscience—you've just found out that "they" do business with South Africa or the Soviet Union; or you've found out that they're a major polluter.
- The company is doing okay now, but you're afraid that the major litigation they're involved in will push the stock values straight down the tube.
- You own stock, and think you should be in bonds (or: you own bonds, and think you should be in stocks).
- Your investment is already less valuable than it was when you bought it—you want to cut your losses before it becomes completely valueless.
- Last but not least (and perhaps foremost in complexity), you need a short-term gain or loss, or a long-term gain or loss, for your tax picture.

Finally, be sure to ask your tax adviser if you're subject to the alternative minimum tax (AMT). The AMT exists in the tax code to make sure that fat-cat corporations and individuals don't escape all taxation by exploiting loopholes. Taxpayers must pay whichever is *higher*: either the regular tax or the alternative minimum tax (for individuals, 21 percent of taxable income, figured under special rules that "add back" tax shelter amounts otherwise excluded from income).

"Whatever happened to the 15 percent bracket?" you may be asking. Well, taxpayers can reduce their taxable income for AMT purposes by $30,000 (single taxpayers) or $40,000 (married couples filing jointly). That solves most taxpayers' AMT problems.

### Gimme Shelter

The sixties and seventies were the golden years for tax shelter promoters, for a number of reasons:

- Federal income tax rates could be as high as 70 percent; with state tax rates taken into account, taxpayers would do almost anything for a write-off.
- During some years, investment income was taxed more heavily than salary income, so there was a need for extra protection for this "unearned" income.
- Tax shelters were fashionable.
- The IRS hadn't caught on to some of the rampant tax shelter tomfoolery.

- Tax shelter investors could claim that they had invested huge amounts of money (and take corresponding loss deductions) when they had put in a small amount of actual money, and signed a sheaf of meaningless "nonrecourse" notes to borrow the rest. A "nonrecourse" note meant that they couldn't be sued if they didn't pay their share of the tax shelter operation's expenses—as everyone knew they wouldn't.

### Tax Shelters: Honest in Theory, at Least

The way an honest tax shelter works, theoretically, is that it takes a while for most businesses to turn a profit. The investors put in some money; deduct their share of the early losses; and are rewarded right away with smaller tax bills. Then, when the business springs gloriously to life, they'll be rewarded with fat, juicy profits. Sometimes the profits never materialize. (Of course, in a dishonest tax shelter, the promoter simply vanishes with the money.)

### Death Knell for Tax Shelters

The eighties are rotten years for tax shelters. The IRS moved against them vigorously in the mid-eighties, and TC '86 has made most shelters positively repulsive.

- Tax rates have gone down. With a maximum rate of 33 percent, the incentive to shelter has less appeal.
- Although interest rates have moved down, they could bounce right up again.
- Whatever shelters escape TC '86 fall afoul of the "at risk" rules of the earlier tax code—that is, investors (except real estate investors) can't claim tax losses based on "nonrecourse" notes. You can't claim a tax loss unless you are genuinely at risk for the money—that is, unless there's an authentic creditor who can authentically repossess your BMW.

The IRS devotes a lot of attention and resources to cracking down on what it calls "abusive tax shelters." What's abusive? Don't worry, you'll know. The IRS publicizes the shelters it thinks are abusive. If you go ahead anyway and invest in one, they'll run you ragged with audits and other legal forms of hassling.

Of course, if you insist on being chic, you can still dump some money into exotic cattle-feeding or Polish Arabian shelters (that isn't an ethnic joke—it's a kind of horse). If you'd rather be sensible, you can make use of the limited number of shelters available for ordinary middle-class people:

- You can have an IRA, and maybe your contributions will be partly or fully deductible. If you own a business (or even start a business just for this purpose), you can maintain a Keogh plan.
- You can buy tax-exempt securities *if* they're safe; if they fit into your investment plans; and if their aftertax return is comparable to the aftertax return of equally safe taxable investments.
- You can buy a home.
- Maybe—if your professional advisers agree—you can participate in real estate deals such as buying occupied apartments or investing in real estate limited partnerships. Real estate still gets favorable tax treatment.

One way to lower your tax burden, apart from obviously unacceptable alternatives like having less money, is to invest in a tax-deferred retirement savings plan. (See chapter 8.)

## All in the Family: Intrafamily Transactions

**Intrafamily Loans**    In many families, a child (or, for that matter, a sibling or parent) needs a large sum of money—for college; to buy a house; to start a business; to clear up debts. Either the other family members want to help out, but can't afford an outright gift, or the recipients simply prefer to pay back what they borrow. In some families, the psychological complexities of gifts are even more atrocious than those of loans.

The traditional solution was the no-interest demand loan, a hang-loose kind of financial transaction in which the family member with the money transferred it to the family member who needed the money. The recipient repaid it without interest whenever he could. At least theoretically, the family lender could demand the money back at any time.

However, Congress cracked down on intrafamily loans, setting up elaborate rules under which many (though not all) intrafamily loans would generate "interest" income for the lender (equal to the amount he would have received if interest had been charged at a fair-market rate), with compensating "interest" deductions for the borrower—even though no money changed hands. (Under similar rules for small corporations, an executive or stockholder who got a bargain-rate or no-interest loan could be taxed as if he had received a raise, or dividends on his stock.)

It's unclear how these rules will be applied after TC '86, given the changes in the way interest is taxed. About all we can say is get professional advice once TC '86 is old enough for interpretive rules to have been issued.

**Kiddie Condos and Retirement Roosts**    In many areas, real estate is a great investment; and real estate investment gets favorable tax treatment. Put these two facts together, and you may come up with a strategy that calls for buying a house, co-op, or condo for your college-age kids or elderly parents to live in.

Let's say junior wants to go to Snowplow State University, but you live in another state. You'd save tuition if he were a resident of Snowplow State. What to do? Perhaps you can get a house near campus for a decent price and a manageable down payment. If so, you buy the house; junior moves in; and you rent out the other rooms. To top it off, he gets the job of property manager. The result? He's a state resident—at least if he moves in early enough to satisfy the residency requirement. You own a property that you hope will appreciate in value. You have cash flow every month from the rentals—with any luck at all, they'll more than cover your mortgage and utility payments on the place. But watch out if you're not actively managing the property—you won't be able to deduct any tax losses involved on the deal if you run afoul of the IRS rules on passive investment.

As a property owner, you get to deduct your interest and real estate taxes. In fact, because you own the property for investment—it's neither your principal residence nor a vacation home for you—you get to deduct all the costs of producing rental income, and you get to claim depreciation on the building.

Once junior graduates, he may have a younger sibling ready to step into his ski bindings. If not, you can hire another manager, and keep the house as an investment property; or you can sell it.

This is not a strategy for everybody (but, then, what is?), and it's not without risks. First of all, you have to have enough money to buy the place; you may have to spend a lot of money for repairs; your student-tenants may move out in the middle of the night, taking the dishwasher with them. The basement may be used as anything from a house of ill repute to a bomb factory to a marijuana-baling facility. On a less dramatic note, the tenants may simply fail to pay their rent, or house prices could depreciate by the time you want to sell the property.

At the other end of the age scale, your retired parents may own a house that they don't want to take care of, or that has become a financial burden on them. Or they may live in an apartment, and be afraid of constant rent increases. They *should* be concerned about protection from health care costs and income for the so-called "community spouse" (a healthy spouse living in the community, not in a nursing home).

There are lots of strategies that can work here; we'll run through them briefly, and stress that you need professional help to choose and implement the strategy that conforms to the laws of your state, and fits your personal financial picture. Here are a few ideas:

- Maybe the best thing would be for your parents to transfer the house to you—perhaps as a gift; perhaps as a sale, especially if the proceeds can be sheltered from Medicaid. Then, they continue to live in the house, paying you a rent at a fair-market, but not exorbitant, rate. Once you become a landlord, you qualify for depreciation deductions and other tax breaks.
- If your parents don't own a home, maybe you should buy one for them, once again charging a fair rent that covers your carrying costs. Your parents don't have to worry about rent increases, or about being evicted if the building goes co-op. As well, they know they can rely on the "landlord" to maintain the property, and you add an asset to your portfolio while making sure your parents' housing needs will be met.
- As we explained earlier in this chapter, if you pay nursing home bills for your parents, you may be entitled to a medical-expense deduction on your own tax return.
- If your parents live with you, there's a pretty good chance that they will be your dependents, so you can claim each of them on your tax return, and take a dependency exemption for each. You'll also qualify for head of household rates if you're single or divorced and maintain a home for a parent.

### "ET Phone Home"—Coping with Estimated Taxes

If all your income derives from salary, the IRS can sleep easily at night. Your employer simply withholds an amount that's at least large enough to pay your tax bill for the year. (In fact, most people are severely overwithheld. See chapter 10 for strategies to deal with this.)

If part of your income derives from interest or dividends, the IRS knows how much you get—no point in cheating by "forgetting" to report some of this income—but tax has not been withheld on these amounts. If you sell your home, your art collection, or your vintage Bentley, the IRS won't even know about the transaction until you report it; and, of course, no tax will have been withheld.

The IRS *could* wait patiently for April 15 for you to report (and pay) all your taxes. However, perhaps inspired by a knowledge of human nature (very few people would have any money left over by April 15), the IRS insists that if you have a substantial amount of income that is not subject to withholding, you must pay taxes four times a year, not one.

You must make quarterly payments of estimated tax (ET) if you will owe income tax, Social Security self-employment tax, or the alternative minimum tax. The four payments are due on April 15, June 15, September 15, and January 15 (or a day or two later if one of these dates falls on a Saturday or Sunday). Then, every year when you file your Form 1040, you have to pay any tax for the preceding year that was not paid either through withholding or through estimated tax.

You have several things to consider about each April 15 if you're an ET filer:

- Whether you'll have enough money to pay your tax bill for the preceding year.
- Whether you're stuck with a (nondeductible) penalty for underpaying your estimated tax.
- How much to send in as estimated tax for the first quarter of the new tax year.

For most taxpayers, estimated tax is a crapshoot: they haven't got the foggiest idea of what their income will be for the current tax year, or what their deductions and credits will be. After all, how can you tell in April whether the roof will need replacing in November, or whether your spouse will be confined to the hospital with a gallbladder attack, or, on the more positive side, whether you won't get an enormous contract in August that sends your income spinning dizzily upwards?

The penalty is imposed on each of your quarterly tax payments that is less than the required amount. The required amount of each payment is either 22¼ percent of your tax for the year or 25 percent of the *previous* year's bill, whichever is less. In other words, if your 1985 tax bill (including self-employment tax) was $8,000, and you sent the IRS $2,000 in each of the four quarters of 1986, you did not have to pay the penalty. Of course, if your tax for 1986 turned out to be $11,000, you had the pleasure of reducing the federal deficit by the $3,000 you had to pay the IRS in April 1987.

So, the strategy for hardball players is to assume that your income will go up each year; to pay exactly 25 percent of the previous year's tax bill in each quarterly installment; and take the money that you know you'll owe the IRS in April and keep it in a high-yielding account in the interim. For God's sake don't invest it in some high-flying "sure thing" and lose it all—the IRS is no more sympathetic on this score than your employer is to someone embezzling the contents of the petty cash box.

The so-called sinister penalty isn't really that bad. The penalty is measured by the market interest rates (the 1985 rates range from 10 to 13 percent), from the time an installment was due, until the time the deficiency was removed. So if you find out that you dramatically underpaid one installment, you can minimize the damage by paying lots more in the next installment.

You can also be excused from paying a penalty on your fourth and final installment for the year (normally due around January 15) if you file your Form 1040 for the year—including payment of all the tax due—by January 31. This can be tough to do, because it's hard to get financial records and even some of the more obscure tax forms in time. But it can be worth a little extra effort if you'd otherwise face a large (and nondeductible) penalty.

*Tip:* If you are stuck at home without plans on New Year's Eve, and you *really* want to wallow in self-pity, do your taxes for the year. That way, you'll have an accurate fix on the size of your fourth-quarter estimated tax payment, and you'll know if it's worth filing by January 31 to avoid the penalty on the fourth quarter.

### Exceptions to the Penalty

The IRS *can't* assess a penalty for underpayment of estimated tax in any year where the prior year's tax liability was zero. That is, if it's the first year where estimated tax would be due, and you didn't have to pay income tax for the previous year, you escape the penalty. In effect, you paid 25 percent of the previous year's $0 tax bill with each "installment" of estimated tax.

The IRS is almost certain to forget about the penalty for the year of your retirement (if you were over sixty-two or disabled when you retire); or if the underpayment is caused by unusual circumstances. Perhaps all your tax records were destroyed by a tidal wave.

Most estimated tax filers are free-lancers of some sort, and they can't count on a steady stream of income. What happens if they have a rotten first quarter, pay a small amount as their first installment, then finish up the year with lots of money? Theoretically, they might face an underpayment penalty, because the first installment might be less than 20 percent of the eventual tax bill.

The IRS has an ungodly complex set of "annualization" rules permitting the penalty to be abated if each quarterly installment is appropriate based on the assumption that the rest of the year's income had followed the same pattern.

So, if an actor waits on tables in January through March, earning a total of $5,000, then gets a tire commercial in April (a $10,000 check) and a part in a TV show in August, with a hefty residual check in November, he won't be penalized for making a first-quarter payment based on the assumption that the whole year would be spent at tableside rather than at poolside on Rodeo Drive. Of course, if he spends the residual check on a T-Bird—or even some T-bills—instead of paying the IRS, the IRS will show no mercy. If you think that you fit the bill for annualization, you should read the IRS publication on estimated tax (No. 505) from cover to cover, or check with your accountant or tax lawyer.

There's a special rule for the confusing tax year of 1986. Individual taxpayers have until April 15, 1987, to catch up on their 1986 tax liability without penalty; no penalties will be charged for underpayments that can be blamed on the chaos arising out of the new law.

### Estimated Tax Strategy: Avoid Choking the Goat

As we mentioned before, you're absolutely safe if your income rises each year, and you pay 25 percent of the *previous* year's tax bill in each installment. The downside of this strategy is that every April you get a tax bill that would choke a goat.

Of course you could be really boring and try to pay exactly 25 percent of this year's tax bill in each installment. If you underpay by a little, make it up in your January installment, or with your Form 1040; if you overpay, the overpayment can either be mailed to you by the IRS, or used as part of the first installment for the following year. If you're a hardball player, you can try to pay 22¼ percent of the tax bill in each installment—the minimum to avoid the penalty. You can even sail nearer to the wind and hope that your investment return will make up for any penalty you encounter.

If you have both a salaried job and self-employment income, or if your spouse has a salaried job, you can adjust withholding so that the withholding satisfies at least 90 percent of your current tax bill, or represents at least 100 percent of the previous year's tax bill.

If all else fails, you can try to salvage the situation by deferring some income from the end of one year to the beginning of the next—the people you do business with would probably be delighted to pay you two or three months later. You can also beef up your deductions—perhaps you can prepay your real estate taxes or go wild and repaint all your rental properties. Maybe this is the time to sell that stock that has been barking loudly.

### Playing for Time: Extensions

Not everyone realizes that you can get a four-month extension of time to file your 1040, automatically. All you have to do is file a Form 4868 on or before April 15, and you will still be on time if you finally manage to file on or before August 15.

However, the IRS is once again giving away ice in the wintertime. Extension of time to *file* is not equivalent to extension of time to *pay,* and if you do owe tax and get an extension, you should fork over 100 percent of your estimated tax bill. If you pay less than the final tax you owe, you are excused from penalties for failure to file an income tax return, but will still be charged interest for the length of time the amount of the underpayment remains unpaid. If the tax paid on April 15 is less than 90 percent of the amount actually due, you also may be subject to a late payment penalty of 0.5 percent per month, up to a maximum of 25 percent.

In addition to the automatic extension, you can get an additional extension, which is discretionary on the part of the IRS. They can turn you down, and will, unless you have a damn good reason for the extension (perhaps you just got out of a coma; the earthquake destroyed not only your tax records but your accountant's office, your bank, and all your employer's records). The form for the discretionary extension is 2688. You have to explain why you need the extension; how much time you need (if you've already received an automatic extension); whether you've paid any required estimated tax on time; and whether your tax returns for the preceding three years were filed on time —if not, why not. Technically, you can apply for the discretionary extension without having received an automatic extension first, but there doesn't seem to be any reason why anybody would bother to do this.

In short, in the first situation for getting an extension that comes to mind —the stark fact that you haven't got the money to pay your taxes—an extension won't do you much good. You'll avoid the penalty for nonfiling, but that may be the least of your worries.

If you have trouble getting your records together, or waited so long that all the accountants you know are busy, or if your chronically disorganized employer or bank never manages to get out its information returns on time, you have several choices. You can get the extension, making estimated tax payments if necessary, and trying to be sure that your tax is at least fully paid. It may be a good strategic move in this situation to overpay and get a refund. Or, you can file the return on time, on a "quick and dirty" basis, estimating the figures you don't have. Later on, you can file a Form 1040X (amended return) with the actual figures.

If the bottleneck is your own fault, let it be a lesson to you—improve your record keeping, and start looking around for an accountant around August for the following April.

Surprisingly enough, the IRS is *less* likely to audit returns with extensions than returns filed on time—probably because, by the time your return comes in, the friendly folks at the Service are so busy with the deluge of returns from April 15 that all they can do is note that your return *did* show up, and cash the check. So, if you're afraid of what an audit might turn up, it could be good strategy to get the extension and either make sure all the tax is paid on or before the extended due date, or accept some interest as a cost of doing business.

And if you're being audited for a past year's return around about April, it can pay to get an extension for the current year's return. The IRS rule is that auditors can ask to see books and records for completed tax periods, but not for years that are still "up in the air." The extension can keep the IRS from inquiring into your current financial affairs.

### Unwise Tax Tricks

Far be it for us to encourage anyone to cheat on his or her taxes, a moral fault which has about as much class as stealing pennies from a blind beggar. (In either case, the risk of detection is rather small.) But even the court system recognizes the difference between tax *evasion* and legitimate tax *avoidance*— arranging transactions in a way that minimizes tax consequences. The tax code is so complex that there are certain areas in which there is legitimate controversy, and one can certainly be excused for giving him or herself the benefit of the doubt in a situation where some courts favor the taxpayer.

On the other hand, there are some things that are not merely reprehensible but obvious tax fraud, and, if detected, are almost certain to result in underpayment penalties; are likely to result in negligence penalties; and may lead to penalties for civil fraud, or even a criminal fraud prosecution. Stunts to avoid:

- Failure to file a return at all, when a return is due.
- Claiming nonexistent dependents, or claiming persons as dependents who have become economically independent (or, for that matter, have gone to the Big Tax Shelter in the Sky).
- Claiming charitable deductions for donations you allegedly put into the collection plate at religious services you didn't even attend.
- "Tax divorce"—an end-year divorce (so you can file as single persons), followed by immediate remarriage. Not only is it ludicrous that you can save enough in taxes to make up for the costs of a divorce (even on a do-it-yourself basis), but the IRS figured out this tactic a long time ago, and it receives no sympathy from the courts.
- Clumsy fabrication of records, either to "substantiate" nonexistent deductions, or to create a sort of docudrama if you really did encounter deductible expenses but don't have the necessary records. If the deductions exist only in your fertile imagination, either repent, or make sure you don't do something stupid like entering the 1985 "expenses" in a 1987 diary, or alternating regularly among blue, black, and green ink for entries supposedly made months apart. If the deductions are legitimate but the proof is defective, you can use the Cohan rule. If the problem is defective records for travel and entertainment deductions, too bad; your deduction will be disallowed if you can't produce the adequate records. So make sure the records for subsequent years meet IRS standards of documentation.
- "Forgetting" to report income. Outside of the real underground economy, almost all transactions are reported to the IRS somehow. And even if you work "off the books," if the person who paid you gets audited, and the payment to you was deducted, the IRS is likely to call you in for a chat. Even in the underground economy, remember that the mere fact that an activity is grossly illegal does not render its proceeds tax exempt. (Remember, what finally got Al Capone—"Snorky" to his friends—was tax evasion.) There are groups of people who put "marijuana farmer" or "drug dealer" on the "occupation" line of each year's tax return; the IRS's unofficial policy is that it's in the tax-collecting business, not the morality business, and they'll take tainted money at least as cheerfully as clean money.

### IRS Audits—The Long Arm of the Law

Greetings! Now that draft notices are no longer sent out, an audit notice from the IRS competes with a phone call from "60 Minutes" or a letter from the local VD clinic for the title of "most unwelcome communication." The typical response to an audit notice is some combination of indignation (that one's probity would be doubted), fear (Allenwood, here I come), and guilt (I knew I should have reported that barter deal).

Tax audits will certainly never replace video cassettes as family entertainment. But there's no need to panic. There are several reasons the IRS chooses a return for audit:

- There's something funny about the way the return looks. This is by no means the same as a statement that there's something wrong with the return. It's unusual for a couple to have eleven dependent children, and the computer may mark the return for audit; but if they really do have the eleven kids, the exemptions are legitimate, and the audit can be concluded quickly, with a score of Taxpayers 1, IRS 0.

    Similarly, a return may have unusually high—but quite legitimate—deductions or creditors. One IRS agent was sent to audit a return filed from a decidedly affluent area, showing gross income of a mere couple of thousand dollars. His suspicions burgeoned as he arrived at the mansion. It turned out that the return was perfectly legitimate. The taxpayer had inherited a couple of million dollars from his father (back when a couple of million bucks meant something), invested it all in tax-exempt bonds, and lived on the interest. The income he reported came from occasional sales of poems and essays to literary magazines.
- The return includes an IRS target. Right now, the crackdown is on abusive tax shelters. Some experts feel that returns claiming home office deductions are also targeted for audit attention.
- The IRS doesn't like the taxpayer. There *is* a protective procedure to prevent repeat audits of the same issue if the taxpayer wins each time; but it's perfectly legitimate for the IRS to keep checking up on someone with a history of taking unsustainable tax positions. There's also some evidence that the IRS can be used as a way to hassle people on political "enemies lists."
- The return has high "audit potential"—there's a high probability of error (the taxpayer used complex tax provisions) *and* the taxpayer has enough

income and enough potentially controversial deductions to make the audit cost-effective for the IRS.

- On the contrary, the taxpayer may be an average Joe, and the return is selected for audit precisely so the IRS can release news stories about some run-of-the-mill taxpayer who got caught chiseling, and who got socked with penalties or even got sent to jail. The Service particularly likes doing this just before tax returns are due each year, much as Napoleon had one of his field marshals shot "to encourage the others."
- Last but not least, there may be absolutely nothing wrong with the return, and it may quite literally have been selected at random. The IRS does a number of hair-splittingly literal TCMP audits (Taxpayer Compliance Measurement Program) each year. The point of the game is to find out the reasonable range of deductions for taxpayers with certain levels of income. We hope for your sake you don't get tagged for a TCMP audit —if you do, you have to prove *everything,* from the existence and birth dates of your children to the exact reason for the cab ride you deducted on February 4.

Most of the audit selections are done by computer, based on mathematical factors, but the returns are also examined by genuine human beings; so it may be helpful to attach a little explanatory note about unusual items.

Whether your return is honest or crooked, whether you were conservative or took daring positions, whether you figured out all the tax rules correctly or applied them wrong, the odds are that you won't be audited—less than 5 percent of all Form 1040s are audited. Fewer short forms are audited, because the audit potential is slim.

As a general rule, if the IRS hasn't selected your return for audit within two years of the time it's filed, they probably won't audit it. The general legal rule is that most returns can't be audited more than three years after they are filed; but the statute of limitations is longer in criminal cases, and if you neglect to file a required return, the IRS can get you for it at *any* time.

In short, you can be audited even if you haven't done anything wrong, and even if the IRS doesn't even think you've done anything wrong. It's a likely consequence that you will emerge from the audit with a tax deficiency (an amount that the IRS thinks you should pay). But, as we'll explain below, you have ways to challenge the IRS, and you may well win. Some people emerge from an audit with unchanged tax liability; in fact, you may even find out that you're entitled to a refund.

## Types of Audits

There are three basic types of audit:

- *Correspondence audit*—you're asked to mail in proof of some easily verified point (e.g., a canceled check showing that you paid $278.69 for a work-related plane ticket; invoices from a business supplier; your Blue Cross bill).
- *Office audit*—you (or your designated representative) go to the IRS office, bringing the materials they ask for. Usually, an office audit will be restricted to whatever issues you were asked about in your audit notice. If new issues are mentioned, you can demand a conference with the group manager—a threat that may cause instant capitulation by the IRS-ite. If the notice calls for an office audit, but all the issues involved are relatively simple to document, you may be able to stave off the office audit by sending copies (*not* the originals) of the documentation to the IRS and requesting that they handle it as a correspondence audit. They may agree since they get Brownie points for closing cases quickly.
- *Field audit*—the IRS sends one or more staffers to your home or place of business. You can ask for a field audit, if you can't go to the IRS; but, in general, field audits are much harder on the taxpayer, because the IRS is in contact with more records, and it's much easier for the examiner to raise new issues.

No matter what kind of audit is involved, you can make your life (and your tax bill) much easier by following some basic rules of conduct. *Never* ignore any communication from the IRS. It only infuriates them, and they have far more things they can do to you than vice versa. It's not always necessary to pony up any sum of money demanded, but at least you have to answer.

## Be Nice to the IRS

It's truly stupid to do anything that could be interpreted as the offer of a bribe; however, it's almost as stupid to create an atmosphere of hostility by insulting the IRS person. If the person handling the audit thinks you're a fairly decent individual, he or she is likely to be inclined to restrict the audit to the original issues, and to accept reasonably plausible explanations. On the other hand, if you've managed to antagonize the auditor, s/he may look for new issues to hassle you about, and may demand that everything be checked, proved, and double-checked and double-proved.

On the other hand, don't *volunteer* anything. One advantage of a friendly smile is that it keeps your mouth shut. If the IRS person asks for a particular record, either turn over that record, or explain courteously why it is unavailable. Don't just hand him a shoebox and invite him to dig in. Who knows what evil lurks in your canceled checks?

### The Cast of IRS Characters

The IRS has eight service regions, each with a central Service Center where data processing is done and returns are selected for audit. Each state also has at least one District Office. The districts have four divisions: Examination, Collections, Taxpayer Service, and Criminal Investigations.

The Examination Division does the audits. Tax auditors do the office audits, revenue agents do the field audits. As a general rule, revenue agents have more training and more sophistication about taxes than tax auditors, who may have received some training on a few narrow points, but who may feel insecure outside those small areas of tax practice.

As you would expect, the Collection Division collects money that the IRS has determined it's entitled to. Revenue representatives handle the small accounts, and revenue officers deal with the big accounts, so the title of the person you deal with is a rough index of the size of your problem.

You're in *real* trouble if you're introduced to Special Agent Such-and-such (fraud investigations are handled by special agents), or if an IRS person gives you a Miranda warning ("You have the right to remain silent, etc., etc."). In either case, you would be well advised to terminate the interview and get another appointment to come back with your lawyer.

By the way, the IRS rules provide that no one can be prosecuted for failure to file a tax return if the revenue officer handling the case has told the taxpayer to file the missing returns. So you can breathe a little easier if you *are* instructed to file (though of course you're going to have to get the money from somewhere), and can get correspondingly frightened if the revenue officer omits this little detail.

Although a commercial preparer can go with you, you can be represented before the IRS only by a lawyer, a CPA, or an enrolled agent, who is a person who is neither a lawyer nor an accountant, but who has passed a rigorous exam. (This is a fairly popular career choice for ex-IRS personnel who switch to the private sector.) If you file a joint return, either spouse or both can appear for an office audit. You can also bring witnesses with you; bring your representative; or send your representative instead (in which case you must file IRS Form 2848 or 2848-D, depending on whether you give your representative full or limited authority to deal with the IRS on your behalf).

Well, *should* you be represented, just because you have a right to be? One theory is that you should send your lawyer, accountant, or enrolled agent in your place, because s/he won't panic, will be able to cite obscure provisions of the tax code and the IRM (the *Internal Revenue Manual*—the IRS's own Bible of tax interpretations and practice), and won't be inclined to shoot off his or her mouth to the friendly tax auditor. The disadvantage is that the representative gets paid for all the time spent waiting around in the IRS office for your case to be reached. Common sense should prevail—it doesn't make sense to spend $1,000 for professional representation when the IRS is asserting a deficiency of $139.29.

A compromise position (and, as we'll show you, there's a surprising amount of leeway for compromise with the IRS): invest in a couple of hours' professional advice about documenting the disputed items, then go to the IRS by yourself.

### See You in Court?

The usual outcome of an audit is that the IRS staffer conducting the audit will present the taxpayer with a list of "proposed adjustments" to the audited tax return. In the nature of things, these are generally increases in tax liability.

The taxpayer's (or representative's) first step is to go over the list carefully, ask how the numbers were derived, and try to negotiate. For instance, the taxpayer may have filed a return based on the premise that an automobile was used 85 percent for business. The upshot of the audit may be that it was used less than 85 percent for business—but the taxpayer may stoutly hold out for 75 percent business use, where the proposed adjustment specifies 50 percent business use. Maybe the auditor will settle for an agreement that the car was 60 percent devoted to commerce. This is also a good time for the taxpayer to throw in evidence of any deductions or creditors that could have been claimed on the return, but were not.

At this stage of the game, both the taxpayer and the auditor may be relieved to dispose of the case without too much time or trouble (or too much of the taxpayer's money). But don't be too quick to agree to paying a negligence penalty. Under the tax code, "negligence" means more than pure ignorance. A taxpayer is negligent if s/he refuses to keep proper records after several admonitions—but not necessarily if s/he misunderstood or misapplied a tax provision.

There are many steps a taxpayer can take if s/he disagrees with the IRS's preliminary verdict on audit. At this stage, professional advice is useful, so the taxpayer can decide which alternatives should be taken, and which strategies should be followed. For instance, some alternatives are final, and no appeal is permitted. On the practical level, some alternatives require the taxpayer to pay the disputed amount, and then try to get it back; others allow the taxpayer to wait until there's been a final determination before ponying up. Some alternatives prevent the IRS from assessing interest or penalties, or limit the time during which these unpleasant actions can be taken; others create the possibility of heavy interest and penalties.

### Beyond the Audit

After the audit, you will be given two choices. You can sign a form agreeing to the proposed "deficiency assessment." Once you agree, you're finished with the matter: you *can't* appeal. You will be sent a "ten-day letter" giving you ten days to either pay or work out some sort of payment arrangement with the IRS. If you don't sign, you get the "thirty-day letter" telling you that you have thirty days to appeal to the IRS; after the appeal, unless you prevail completely, the IRS will send you a Notice of Deficiency, known as the "ninety-day letter." You have ninety days to petition the Tax Court to hear your case; if you don't, you'll get a final tax bill after the ninety days have expired.

Let's say (as is not uncommon) you think the agent handling your audit was wrong. You can go to the IRS Appeals Division. The personnel of the Appeals Division are more sophisticated and better trained than the tax auditors and revenue agents, so complex legal arguments, or arguments based on sophisticated use of accounting, stand a better chance.

If you had a correspondence examination or an office audit, or if you had a field audit and the disputed amount is under $2,500, you can apply for a hearing by the Appeals Division merely by sending a short, informal note of request to the district director within thirty days of the time the IRS mailed you the agent's report of the audit. Otherwise, you have to file a formal written protest.

Going to the Appeals Division is not without risks—the Appeals Division is not restricted to the issues taken up at the audit; anything about your tax return (including the points the auditor missed) can be taken up.

If you don't choose to go to the Appeals Division, or if you've been there but don't think much of their decision either, and if you've gotten your ninety-day letter, a probable next step is to litigate the case in the United States Tax Court, a special-purpose court that hears nothing *but* tax cases. The Tax Court frequently sides with taxpayers and against the IRS, a fact that may incline the IRS attorneys to settle with you if you propose to go to the Tax Court.

The good news is that the Tax Court has a rather informal procedure for handling "small tax cases"—those involving alleged deficiencies of $10,000 or less in any tax year. You don't even need an attorney. You can use this procedure by writing to the United States Tax Court in Washington, D.C., for copies of the Petition (Form 2) and Request for Place of Trial (Form 4); you must file the petition with the Washington Tax Court within ninety days of the date of mailing of the "ninety-day letter." The bad news is that you can't appeal the Tax Court's decision if you use the small case procedure.

The Tax Court is not the only federal court that hears tax cases—you may also be able to go to the District Court or the Court of Claims. However, you can litigate in the Tax Court *without* paying the disputed taxes first; you can't use the other courts unless you pay the deficiency, then try to get it back.

In fact, if you pay the deficiency before you go to the Tax Court, you're considered to have agreed to the assessment, so the Tax Court will toss out your petition. But if you go to the Tax Court and lose, you're stuck for interest on the tax deficiency for the whole time between the notice of deficiency and the time you pay. There *is* a way out of this Catch-22: you can pay the deficiency, but tell the IRS that the money is not a payment but a "cash bond." That way, your obligation to pay interest to the IRS will not accrue, and you can still go to the Tax Court.

Another strategy: *don't* litigate the case. Pay the deficiency, then file a Form 1040X (amended return) asking for a refund of the disputed amount, just before the last date on which you can legally file a refund claim for the year in question. You may luck out: the IRS may simply process the refund, or may try to audit the return, but find out that it's too late to challenge the return for the year in question. This is for hardball players only, and it pays to check with a professional tax adviser first.

You have to realize that there are several aspects to the IRS collection effort. First of all, there may be taxes that everyone agrees the taxpayer owes; or, the taxpayer may still be disgruntled, but unwilling to litigate any further. Then, the problem is deciding if any interest and/or penalties are required—and the taxpayer has the problem of finding the money. It's a little-known fact, but the IRS doesn't want to waste time trying to wring blood out of a turnip; you may be able to get the IRS to agree to accept less than 100 cents on the dollar of your tax liability. Bankruptcy won't help much—it doesn't eliminate your tax liability, but it does remove your assets from your control, making it less likely that the IRS can seize them.

Yes, the IRS does take away people's houses and cars; padlock their businesses; dip into their bank accounts; and garnish their salaries. If the IRS has reason to believe that the taxpayer is a scofflaw, it can even take these actions without a court order. At all costs, you want to avoid becoming the subject of IRS enforcement actions. Once again, *never* ignore a letter from the IRS, much less one that demands something. If you respond, you may be able to negotiate some kind of compromise, and you can almost certainly avoid having your property seized or your salary checks mailed to Uncle Sugar.

## Interest and Penalties

Let's face it, if for any reason you've underpaid your taxes (including reasonable errors and creative tax interpretations that were eventually decided in the IRS's favor), the effect is that you borrowed money from the IRS. If you had known all along that you owed the taxes, you would have had to pay them; you've had the use of what is really the IRS's money for a certain amount of time. That's why the IRS charges interest on tax deficiencies. This is true of underpayments of estimated tax as well as deficiencies found when a return is audited.

If you do get audited, and throw in the towel at that stage by agreeing to the proposed deficiency assessment, interest will be suspended for at least thirty days; otherwise, the general rule is that the IRS will charge interest (at market rates; the IRS sets its interest rates twice a year) as long as a tax deficiency remains unpaid.

The Tax Code also allows the IRS to impose both civil and criminal monetary penalties *without* going to court. There's a penalty for late filing (unless you have an extension, of course): 5 percent of the tax due for each month or fraction of a month that you miss the filing date, up to a maximum of 25 percent of the tax. If you're sixty days or more late, there's a *minimum* penalty for late filing—either $100 or the tax owed, whichever is less.

If the underpayment was due to negligence or intentional disregard of IRS rules (not an honest mistake about what the rules are or how they're applied), there's a negligence penalty, in the amount of 5 percent of the underpayment detected by the audit, plus 50 percent of the interest attributable to negligence or disregard of the rules.

One step worse: the underpayment may have been due to outright fraud.

If the IRS finds fraud but doesn't want to institute a criminal prosecution, it can impose a civil fraud penalty of 50 percent of the underpayment detected by the audit, plus 50 percent of the interest attributable to the fraud. If it's any consolation, the same action can't give rise to both a negligence penalty and a civil fraud penalty; it's one or the other.

If you are socked with a penalty, and you think you had a reasonable cause for your action, or you feel the penalty is unjust, write to the IRS Service Center immediately. They may agree with you, and take away the penalty; if not, ask to have the case sent on to the regional director of appeals so you can explain why you should be relieved of the obligation to pay the penalty. Remember, interest is deductible (except interest on underpayments of estimated tax)—penalties, including penalties computed as a percentage of the interest you owe, are not.

You can "offer in compromise" about penalties, even if you don't compromise the underlying tax. That is, if the IRS demands $250 in penalties, you can offer to pay $100, and the IRS may accept, especially if you can show financial hardship. But you can't try to compromise a penalty once you've already paid it.

### Let's Make a Deal

Strange as it seems, you may be able to make a deal with the IRS to pay your tax deficiency on the installment plan, or even to pay less than the amount you owe. The key is IRS Form 433, the Statement of Financial Condition. You must disclose all your assets, and either state a plan for selling them and getting cash you can give the IRS, or explain why they can't be liquidated. Your objective is either to show that you can pay your current taxes and satisfy your past tax liability within a year to a year and a half—or prove to the IRS that it has no reasonable chance of collecting your full liability, so it might as well be sensible and settle for less than the full amount and let you get on with your life. Another possibility: the tax deficiency may involve a genuine legal dispute, and the IRS may be willing to forgo some of the money to avoid litigating a case it may lose.

Offers of compromise are submitted on the IRS Form 656. Use your noggin—make it clear that you're offering a compromise to the IRS, not a retirement-plan contribution to the agent to forget the whole thing. To be acceptable, the offer must represent your "maximum ability to pay," by using all your assets—including any assets that are protected from seizure by the IRS. (We won't go into detail about IRS seizure and levy provisions—if you're in *that* much trouble, you need advice from your own lawyer.) You'll probably have to sign an agreement using your assets as collateral, and you'll probably have to agree to turn over a percentage of your income to the IRS.

## Summary

Maybe your tax strategy is simplicity itself: collect your W-2 every year; file a short form, or have your long form prepared by a tax preparer. Maybe you have a bevy of tax experts on tap, and read the daily tax advance sheets with your morning coffee. Anywhere in between, you must have accurate tax records (but that won't take much time or give you much trouble). You probably shouldn't be involved in complex, risky, and potentially illegal tax shelters—but you probably *can* save taxes by deferring or shifting income, accelerating deductions, having an IRA or Keogh plan, and may be able to use real estate investments and intrafamily transactions profitably.

You can save a world of trouble by filing all required tax forms on time (or getting extensions). If you do, God forbid, get audited, you can use your records to limit or eliminate your tax deficiency; if you pay promptly, you can limit your interest risks.

The IRS doesn't always have the final say—you can appeal unfavorable decisions within the IRS or take the IRS to court (and maybe even win). The worst-case scenario is that the IRS will seize your house and bank account, but this income-tax Armageddon can come about *only* if you refuse to deal with the IRS. If you have a tax bill you can't pay, you may very well be able to convince the IRS to accept payments over time, or to take less than the full amount.

Some Pollyannas say that a hefty tax bill is a positive sign of prosperity. You probably won't agree—but you should be able to arrange tax compliance and planning without suffering outright trauma.

## CASE HISTORY
### *Family Taxes*

"At least, this year you beat Social Security," Neil Milner told his client.

"How does that work again?" she asked. "All this tax stuff really throws me."

Thanksgiving had come and gone; there was a light coating of snow on the streets and you couldn't walk five feet without a whisker-bristling

Santa brandishing a bell in your face. Helen Donato was at her accountant's office, trying to get a handle on the latest version of her tax bill.

"There's a maximum amount of salary on which you have to pay Social Security taxes," Milner told her. "Once your salary gets higher, you pay the maximum amount, but in effect your FICA tax rate goes down because you're paying the maximum amount, but on more income."

"Oh, sure, now I get it," Helen said. "Delta-t goes down." (She was a chemical engineer, and graphs and logarithms held no terrors for her.)

"I hope you listened to me and opened that IRA?"

"You should be proud of me. I was very good. I saw you this time last year, and I opened the IRA right after my birthday [which was February 4] and I put in the maximum. I put it all into an aggressive growth fund, because I have quite a few more years until retirement. So far it seems to be doing pretty well, and I'm going to do the same thing this year."

"Does your employer have a pension plan, and if so, are you a participant in it?"

"Get outta town!" Helen exclaimed. "Those scrooges? No pension plan."

"Great! Well, not so great in the long run, but at least you get to deduct your entire IRA contribution. Did you earn any money apart from your job, so you can have a Keogh plan on top of your IRA?"

"A little—I gave a speech to the Northeast chapter of the Chemical Manufacturers' Association, and I had a couple of articles published, but it only came to about two thousand dollars altogether."

"Then it probably wouldn't be worthwhile setting up a Keogh plan, because the transaction costs would be higher than the amount you could put away. But keep reassessing it; if you ever have a substantial outside income—and, knowing you, if you don't spend the money right away as if it was going to burn a hole in your pocket—then a Keogh plan would be a very good idea. Okay, let's have a look at those deductions."

Donato reached into the battered leather briefcase she had been carrying since she was a computer nerd in high school, and produced a volume of printouts.

"Charities, okay, okay, okay . . . I've never heard of half these organizations. I'm going to have to look them up to see if they're on the IRS approved list. Real estate taxes . . . yeah, here it is. Boy, they really hit your condo complex hard, didn't they? Did they assess you based on having a gold mine in the common areas?"

"Well, it used to be a bank building," Helen said. "So I guess in a way there was a gold mine there."

"Yeah, and look at these interest deductions. Jeez, you must have gotten the last mortgage before the mortgage rates dropped. At least it's deductible—it's your personal residence. What are all these other interest numbers? You know, more than one-third of that amount won't be deductible this year . . . and the deduction will be phased out completely."

"I went to Antigua last March. I took a cash advance for that. And I have some bills on my MasterCard and some department-store cards."

"I don't want to sound like your mother or anything, but maybe you should get a handle on that. Sure, you get a deduction, but to run up interest like that, your bills must be enough to gag a camel."

"Not anymore," Helen said. "The money from the speech and the articles, I used it to pay the bills. Well, some of the bills. And I really cut back on new spending. And the other thing is, I sold some stock."

"Let's take a look at that." Neil flipped through the pages of the printout. "Okay, you sold four stocks . . . you took a loss on the Debenham Industries, and you'd only held it for four months. Why'd you do that?"

"I found out that they were really heavy in South Africa, and I didn't want to give them the satisfaction. And Blade Runner Associates was a little OTC stock I picked up at three and a quarter, and frankly I don't think it's ever going to get much above eleven, which is what I sold it at. Vansittart Limited, well, that's been up and down and up and down, so I said the hell with it and sold it, I was tired of worrying about it, and I made a little money. Not too much. Glamour Air? Every time I open the paper, there's another hassle about airlines, fare wars, I just don't want to be in that sector."

Neil punched his pocket calculator. "Overall, that's forty-two hundred dollars in gain. Well, this year there's a limit; you'll only have to pay twenty-eight percent. Of course, if you'd had a forty-two-hundred-dollar gain before the tax bill, you would have been paying about half that rate, but hey, who's counting. Not a bad year in the stock market. Did you sell any bonds?"

"Held 'em. Rates went up, so the prices went down. I'd rather hang on to the bonds and collect the money than take the hit by selling them and losing money."

Neil looked through the records, all so tidily kept that his heart warmed. "I think you're a little light on your estimated taxes . . . yeah. Either you're going to have to send them . . . let's see . . . an extra two hundred dollars in the January 16 installment or you may have a penalty to worry about. It wouldn't be a really big penalty, but it's not deductible, so you wouldn't enjoy it. And I think you should step up your estimated tax next year . . . that or have your company increase your withholding."

"I'm only taking two exemptions now," Helen said, "and that includes my IRA. But if the penalty isn't that bad, shouldn't I try to tough it out, hang on to the money instead of giving it to the IRS early in the year?"

"That might have been very viable strategy a couple of years back, when you could get fourteen or fifteen percent in your money market fund, but I don't think you can make any sizable amount of money that way anymore. I don't recommend it. Now, let's take a look at your end-year options. If you're really dying for a deduction, you could prepay some of your real estate taxes for next year. Hmmm . . . your medical expenses are nowhere near seven and a half percent of your adjusted gross income—the deductible level; otherwise I'd ask you to check if you can get some bridgework done or something before the end of the year. Don't forget to increase the estimated taxes. And give me a call before you sell any more stock. Let's see how the sale works out under the new tax rates. You might be able to do a lot better if you use some options, or hang on to the stock until after the first of the year. By the way, I'm not Sherlock Holmes or anything, but am I right that there will be a major change in your tax situation soon?"

(He had made this brilliant—ahem—deduction from the fact that she was wearing a largish marquise diamond on the fourth finger of her left hand.)

"We're getting married next May," Helen said. "His name is Edward McGarry. He's an investment banker."

"Uh-oh," Neil said. "Bad choice. Couldn't you fall in love with an unemployed actor or someone who'll give you a little tax shelter? Once you marry this character, your tax rates will be strictly maximum bracket every year, and there isn't even any more deduction for two-earner couples. Forget the actor. Why don't you just live with the fella? You can cut your expenses, have him pay half the bills, and you won't get stomped over by the tax code."

"Yeah, definitely," Helen said. "My brother Tommaso is performing the ceremony. He's a priest. My sister Clara is a Sister of Charity. Sure, there's nothing my family would rather hear. It's bad enough that Teddy isn't Italian."

"Does it have to be May?" Neil pleaded desperately, not because he was in love with his client but because he was in love with reducing her tax liability. "You know, if you're married on December 31, you're married for the whole year, in the eyes of the IRS though not necessarily those of God. Can't you wait until the *following* January?"

"I'll do a lot to save taxes," Helen said. "But there's a limit."

"Does he own a house, a co-op, condo?"

"No, he rents an apartment. It sure is expensive, and it's not all that nice. We figured that we'd live in my place—either that or sell my condo and buy a house, maybe out in the suburbs."

"Well, talk to me first," Neil said. "We'll go over the effect of the local real estate taxes on your tax picture, and see if maybe we can find you a nice place outside the city. That way, you can pay local taxes at the lower nonresident rate."

"There are some nice places about forty miles out of town," Helen said. "I could make a fortune selling the condo—I got in at the insider's price, and now the prices are just nuts—and probably get a really good house, maybe some land, out in the country. Not really out in the country; commuting distance. And for a lot less than I'd get for the condo."

"Ah, a profit," Neil said, without conspicuous enthusiasm. "Don't forget, unless you get a more expensive house and roll over the profits, you'll have lots of profit to pay taxes on. No special capital gains rates; no income averaging—a horrible thought. Anyway, my best wishes. I hope you'll be very happy . . . and that I'll see you next year so we can work on your joint return. Listen, since both of you have significant income and assets, maybe you should have a premarital agreement. And have you made an appointment to revise your wills? Do you have enough insurance?"

"It sure was a lot simpler in the old days," Helen said. "I almost wish that all I had to do was go for fittings on my bridal gown and go to kitchen showers."

Helen and Teddy got married on schedule. They invited Neil to the wedding; he looked elegant in his tuxedo with custom business-card pocket; gave out seventeen cards, got two new clients, and fell in love, which lasted almost until the December day when Helen and Teddy came into the office to discuss year-end planning and have their very first joint return drawn up.

Few of us relish the thought of managing our tax plans. To ignore your taxes as you encounter lifetime transitions, however, can amount to throwing money away. There are a number of legal tax-saving strategies you shouldn't ignore. Moreover, good tax planning habits, such as record keeping, can help you keep things to a manageable level.

# 17

# Preparing for Retirement and Staying Retired

Retirement is a fairly new phenomenon in human life. Today, people have the opportunity of remaining vigorous and active into extreme old age. They have a choice: either to continue working as long as they can or to retire, not because they are too infirm to carry on but because they want to enjoy relaxation, a change of scene, or even a change of career from the business world to artistic creation or public service.

Some retirees are healthy, gregarious globe-trotters, enjoying comforts and pleasures they didn't have time for during their working lives or while raising families. Others are stricken both by illness and poverty, eking out miserable lives of hunger and isolation in cold, solitary apartments. Much of the difference between the two groups is simply a matter of luck: being born into a wealthy family can hardly be counted as a personal accomplishment. But a lot of the difference comes from intelligent financial planning. If you take advantage of the retirement tax breaks Uncle Sam offers during your working life; if you have a sound investment strategy, and the financial self-discipline to put it into practice, then your chance of a comfortable retirement is good.

## Retire or Not?

The first choice is whether you want to retire at all. Some people find that the activity, challenges, and status provided by working are very important to them, and they stagnate in retirement, even if their retirement income is perfectly sufficient for their needs.

Other people are more interested in leisure activities than in business activities; they look forward to having enough time for golf, fishing, sailing, oil painting, detective story reading, or whatever their particular passions are. For these people, a financial goal (and a goal in career choice) is the possibility of early retirement—at sixty-two, perhaps even at fifty-five, under some pension plans. Civil service jobs often provide the option of retirement after twenty or thirty years' employment.

Another option is a second career: to hold down a particular job long enough to qualify for a retirement pension, then move on to another (paid or unpaid) job: a retired policeman could become a security guard; a retired teacher could open an antique shop; a retired steelworker could become a choir director, a computer programmer, a tour guide . . . whatever.

A federal law, the Age Discrimination in Employment Act, protects most workers against involuntary retirement before they reach seventy. An important exception: senior policy-making executives can be required to retire at sixty-five. A worker who is no longer capable of doing his or her job can be fired for good cause, but no one between the ages of forty and seventy (except a highly paid executive) can be fired merely for reasons of age, unless it can be proved that being younger than a certain age is a legitimate qualification for the job. Very few jobs have been found to have such qualifications.

### Retirement, but When?

Okay, let's say that, like most people, you do want to retire at some point, preferably while you're still young and healthy enough to enjoy leisure. A report made to Congress in July 1985 shows that half the workers who retired on private pensions retired before sixty-two, half retired later, and almost 60 percent have retired before the "normal" retirement age of sixty-five. (Some of those who retired early did so because of poor health, not by choice.)

Apart from the personal considerations, there are financial consequences involved in the decision on retirement timing. (By the way, don't forget that many men are married to women younger than they are; a man who retires at sixty-four may have a fifty-eight-year-old wife who continues working for ten or fifteen more years.)

- If you retire at an age between sixty-two and sixty-five, your Social Security benefits will be lower than if you retired at sixty-five. (The minimum age for receiving Social Security benefits, and the normal retirement age, are being increased very gradually over the next few decades.) This is done because you'll be receiving benefits over a longer period of time. The lower benefits also affect your spouse and your survivors' benefits.

- If you retire after sixty-five, your benefits will be slightly higher to compensate, once you *do* retire. On the other hand, your wages will continue to be subject to Social Security tax when you continue working.
- Depending on your income, up to half your Social Security benefits may be taxable income.
- If you get another job, start a business, or work as a consultant after you retire and start collecting Social Security benefits, your benefits will be reduced by an amount that depends on your age, the amount of your income, and when it was earned.
- If you retire early and start drawing a private pension or funds from your IRA and/or Keogh plan, you face two problems. If the payout of benefits is based on a certain number of years (say, twenty years), you may live longer, and face years of greatly reduced income. On the other hand, if you call for a payout spaced over your life or your life and your spouse's life, and you have a long expected life postretirement, the monthly benefits may be uncomfortably small.

### Calculating Postretirement Needs

After you retire, many of your financial needs will be exactly the same. If you haven't paid off the mortgage, or if you rent your home, the monthly payments continue. Even after you make the last mortgage payment and hold the traditional mortgage-burning party (or the New Wave mortgage-banker-burning party), you'll have to keep paying real estate taxes, water and sewer bills, fuel and other utility costs, and homeowner's insurance.

Some costs will decrease: you don't have to worry about a stylish business wardrobe, a commuter ticket, or those unreimbursed three-martini lunches anymore.

Other costs will increase. Unfortunately, people can count on spending more on doctors, dentists, podiatrists, and other health-care providers as they grow older.

If your health is good, you'll probably spend more on entertainment. This is the time to take a long cruise, or that trip to see the grandchildren, the Louvre, or whatever strikes you as a promising destination.

People over sixty-five get certain tax breaks. They are entitled to compute their taxes based on standard deductions $600–$750 greater than non-elderly individuals and may be entitled to a federal income tax Credit for the Elderly. (See the IRS's free publications, No. 524, *Credit for the Elderly and the Permanently and Totally Disabled,* and No. 554, *Tax Benefits for Older Americans,* for the lowdown.) Your state income tax may have similar provisions, and there's an excellent chance that you'll be entitled to property tax rebates, or to relief from increases in property tax.

### Calculating Postretirement Income

Your monthly postretirement income will consist of:

- Your retirement pension from your employer. If you take a lump-sum payout, your monthly income depends on your success in investing the lump sum.
- Your Social Security benefits.
- Income from your investments.
- Income from your IRA and/or Keogh plan. Again, if you've taken a lump-sum distribution, what counts is your investment return.

If your strategy up until now has been to concentrate on long-term, growth investments, retirement might be a good time to switch: to realize those gains that have been building up, pay the tax on the profits and use the money to pay off your mortgage, buy a retirement home, or enter a retirement community. Another possibility: switch from growth investments to income investments—say, a bond fund or Ginnie Mae fund that provides income each month. These strategies are not for everybody; it depends on your life expectancy, your estate plan, and your tax bracket, as well as more subjective considerations like your investment preferences and your beliefs about trends in the economy.

### Social Security

For those who are currently retired, Social Security is an important source of income. For those now in the work force, Social Security is a guaranteed source of eye-popping deductions from their paychecks and a very uncertain source of future income. So if you're at or near retirement age, Social Security is likely to be an important element in your retirement financial plan. If you have a number of years before retirement, well, we're not so sure. . . .

The thing to remember is that Social Security is basically a Ponzi scheme. Ponzi schemes are named after Charles Ponzi, an innovative swindler who invented the pyramid club. He promised vast investment returns to his investors—returns that he was able to provide the first round of suckers from the money invested by subsequent suckers. After the scheme had been going for a while, the supply of suckers dried up, with negative consequences for those who had not yet received any money.

Similarly, when you pay Social Security taxes, the federal government doesn't put the money safely away in an account with your name on it—they use the money to pay benefits to people who are now retired. As a result of demographic trends and medical advances, there are more people retired and about to be retired than the original planners of Social Security could have forecast; and the balance between older people and young workers is out of whack. Hence the parade of newspaper stories about the Social Security crisis, and the never-ending increase in Social Security taxes and the Social Security wage base. (Many people now pay more Social Security tax than income tax.)

Like the first few rounds of Mr. Ponzi's acquaintances, the first round of retirees who benefited by Social Security got a lot more than they put into it. Today's employees may find themselves in the position of the *last* round of Ponzi victims.

The Social Security system is also outrageously sexist. Social Security taxes are assessed quite impartially: they'll take anybody's money. But when it's time to collect benefits, a woman can collect *either* a benefit as a retired worker, or as her husband's spouse—not both. (It's just as true for men, but men usually retire before their wives, because they're usually older.) If she earned a low salary, she'll be better off collecting dependent's benefits. Therefore, all the Social Security taxes she paid were wasted. On the other hand, if she earned a high salary, she'd probably be better off with a benefit based on her own earnings—but, if her husband earned a good salary, she won't be able to collect a full benefit because there's a maximum benefit per family.

### How Benefits Are Computed

The basic concept of the Social Security system is in the retired worker's "PIA." This doesn't stand for "pissed-off in aging"—it stands for "primary insurance amount." A person who is "fully insured" (to oversimplify a little, someone who has worked for at least ten years at a job covered by Social Security) can retire at sixty-five and collect his or her primary insurance amount. Benefits for his/her spouse, widow or widower, or ex-spouse are based on the worker's PIA. Those who retire between sixty-two and sixty-five get a lower benefit, reduced to deal with the longer period of benefit payments; those who retire between sixty-six and seventy get a higher benefit, although, before 1985, this "delayed retirement credit" was not sufficient to offset the shorter payment period. For years after 1985, the credit will be increased.

Right now, the normal retirement age is sixty-five. Starting in the year 2000, the normal retirement age will increase by two months a year until it reaches sixty-seven in 2022.

We're not going to tell you how to compute your PIA—it's a complex process, involving multiplying your birthdate by the winning number in the Illinois lottery, then consulting the entrails of a chicken . . . (well, actually it involves your wages for every year you've been employed, up to a maximum amount that, of course, changes each year). You can get the forms from the Social Security Administration, and it's probably a good idea to work through the transaction every couple of years to get an idea of the kind of retirement benefits you can expect.

Just as a ballpark figure, the maximum benefit for an insured worker in 1986 is $739 a month. But this amount is based on earning the maximum amount covered by Social Security in each year of employment. The average benefit is quite a bit lower: $478 a month for a retired worker.

The spouse's benefit, payable to the spouse of a retired worker, is half of the spouse's primary insurance amount. The spouse can begin to collect half the worker's PIA when s/he is sixty-five (or a smaller benefit when s/he is sixty-two).

Once a person retires and begins to collect Social Security benefits, his or her surviving spouse is entitled to collect an amount equal to the deceased worker's PIA. However, if the deceased worker retired early (and therefore got reduced benefits), the widow's or widower's benefit is also reduced, to equal the benefit the deceased worker was receiving, or 82.5% of the worker's PIA —whichever is *greater*. A surviving spouse is eligible for widow's or widower's benefits at age sixty (or at an earlier age, if the surviving spouse is disabled or caring for a minor child of the deceased worker). In order to qualify for the widow's or widower's benefit, the surviving spouse must have been married to the deceased worker for at least nine months.

Benefits are also available for ex-spouses of retired workers (and divorced "widows"). As long as the marriage lasted at least ten years, the divorce occurred at least two years before the application for benefits and as long as the ex-spouse is at least sixty-two when s/he applies for benefits, s/he is entitled to collect half the worker's PIA. In fact, the worker doesn't even have to be retired; s/he could be eligible for Social Security but continuing to work —so divorced spouses have an advantage over current spouses. If the worker retires early, his or her reduced benefit will reduce the amount payable to his or her spouse or surviving spouse—but not to his or her ex-spouse.

Remember, a person is entitled to collect a benefit as a retired worker, or as the spouse, ex-spouse, or surviving spouse of a retired worker—not both.

### Postretirement Employment

See, there were these two novices at a retreat. The one who was going to become a Dominican went up to the priest in charge of the retreat, and said, "Father, may I smoke while I pray?" The retreat master, infuriated, said, "Of course not. Don't they teach you anything at that seminary of yours? Don't you understand that prayer is the most important part of life, and can't be debased by worldly diversions?"

A Jesuit-in-training overheard, and five minutes later went over to the retreat master. "Father, may I pray while I smoke?" "Certainly, my son," beamed the older priest. "Surely you must realize that even the simplest of daily activities can be ennobled by prayer." So it's all in how you word the question.

You can't collect Social Security benefits as a retired worker unless you retire. But what if you retire from one job, but occasionally serve as a consultant for your ex-employer? What if you started the business, and want to turn it over to your successors, but want to make sure that they do a good job? What if you get bored with fishing and shuffleboard, and want another, perhaps less strenuous or time-consuming job to replace the one you retired from? What if you start a business?

Your Social Security benefits won't be terminated, but they will be reduced, if you earn any money between the time you retire and the time you reach seventy. (There's no reduction for post-seventy earnings.) The reduced amount also affects your spouse's benefit, but not your ex-spouse's benefit. Now (and until 1990), each dollar you earn over the permitted amount will reduce your Social Security benefits by fifty cents. (As of 1990, the reduction will only be $1 of benefits lost for every $3 earned over the limit.) In 1986, the limit for people who retired at sixty-five is $7,800; for those who retired early, it's $5,760 a year.

Naturally, your earnings after "retirement" are subject to federal and state income tax, and of course to Social Security tax, so you don't get to keep much unless your Social Security check was a trivial part of your monthly income.

The year in which you retire is a "grace year." Your monthly earnings, as well as your earnings for the year, are considered in deciding whether you're entitled to a Social Security check for that month. You can collect for any month of the grace year in which your earnings are less than $610 ($450 for retirees who are sixty-two to sixty-five)—even if your income for the year as a whole is way above the limits. This is especially important if you retire toward the end of the year, after earning a substantial amount. If the first year weren't treated as a "grace year," you couldn't get any Social Security checks at all that year if your "excess" earnings wiped out your eligibility or any amount you would otherwise receive because of the reduction.

### Taxation of Social Security Benefits

If you have a lot of earned income postretirement, you'll lose some Social Security benefits. If you have a high overall income (regardless of the source of the income), part of your Social Security benefits will be taxable income. (How will you know? Don't worry, the Social Security Administration sends all Social Security recipients—and the IRS—an information return every year, giving the lowdown.)

The National Commission on Social Security Reform estimates that only 8 to 10 percent of Social Security recipients will have to pay tax on these benefits. Still, we'll give you the drill, because we hope you'll fall into this affluent group.

If you fit the bill, you'll have to pay taxes either on half your Social Security benefits, or on an amount we'll call A—whichever is smaller. You compute A by adding your modified adjusted gross income (we'll explain in a moment) to half your Social Security benefits, then subtracting the base amount. Your modified adjusted gross income is the adjusted gross income computed on your tax return, plus certain tax advantages. Most of them are terribly obscure, but the one you may have to worry about is tax-exempt income, such as that provided by most municipal bonds. The base amount is $32,000 for a married couple filing a joint return; $25,000 for a single person or a separated married person, and $0 for a married person who files a separate return but is not separated from his or her spouse. So be very careful about using a separate return as a tax-saving device—it can backfire. By the way, Medicare Part B premiums are counted as part of your Social Security check, even though you never get to see this money.

### Private Pensions

Where there's a law, there's a loophole. One very powerful incentive for businesses to establish pension plans is the belief that the owners and the top executives will stay with the company until retirement, but the run-of-the-mill workers will come and go. The top management, of course, earn higher salaries than the average Joes and average Janes. Given these two facts, there's a temptation to set up a pension plan, contribute lots of money for each worker, knowing that most of the workers will leave long before they're entitled to collect any pension money.

The game was made more difficult in 1974, by a federal law called ERISA (Employee Retirement Income Security Act). ERISA sets minimum standards that plans have to meet to be "qualified." In practical terms, an employer wants to have a qualified plan, because the money it contributes to a qualified plan is tax deductible. More to the point, if the IRS decides that a plan *wasn't* qualified in a particular year (because it failed to meet ERISA requirements), it can present the company with a hefty tax bill for the taxes that would have been payable without the deduction.

The game was made more difficult, but not impossible, and pension plans are *still* tilted toward top executives. In acknowledgment of that, the 1982 tax bill added special rules for "top-heavy" plans (plans providing 60 percent or more of their benefits to owners and/or highly paid employees). To be a qualified plan, a top-heavy plan must make it easier for an ordinary employee to have a right to some or all of the money the employer contributed to the pension plan for the employee. (This entitlement is called *vesting*.)

If the employer contributes 3 percent of everyone's salary to the pension plan, and your salary is $20,000, the employer will contribute $600 for you. If the president of the company earns $100,000, the employer will contribute $3,000 for her. As you can imagine, her retirement is likely to be a bit more comfortable than yours, even though the contributions are "equal."

The problem is even more severe for rank-and-file employees in an "integrated" plan. In this context, "integrated" means integrated with Social Security, and it's probably bad news for you. Let's say that, when you retire, your years of service (the terminology is a bit feudal, but that's what it's called) and your salary history entitle you to a pension of $532 a month. The same facts entitle you to Social Security benefits of $500 a month. If the plan is integrated, the employer considers $532 your total pension entitlement—and Social Security pays $500, so the employer only has to pay the remaining $32.

(If the annual employer contributions are based on your final pension rather than a percentage of your salary, the employer treats its share of your Social Security tax as a contribution to an integrated pension plan.)

## Why Bother?

To explain why pension plans are so important, we'll break for another corny joke.

Once upon a time, there was a court jester who did something or other to infuriate his royal master. The king ordered the jester's immediate execution. However, the king was inordinately proud of his favorite steed. (Perhaps the jester was flirting with the horse?) "Spare me, sire, for only one year," the victim-to-be pleaded, "and I will teach your favorite horse to talk." Intrigued, the king granted this boon.

The next day, one of the jester's friends spotted him at the royal stables, desperately playing Charades. "Nice try," he said. "But what are you going to do?"

"I figure it this way," the jester said. "A year is a long time. In a year, the king could die. I could die. The *horse* could die. Who knows? Maybe the horse will talk."

This philosophy has had a profound impact on tax planning. If your employer gives you a big raise, the good part is that you can spend the money, or save it, or invest it; the bad news is that you get taxed on it. Now, if the employer *doesn't* give you a raise, but instead contributes the money to the qualified pension plan, you can't spend or save or invest the money now, but you're not taxed on it either. Later on, when you collect the money, you'll be taxed on it. But by then, you could be in a lower tax bracket (because you're retired and have a lower income); or you could be in a *higher* tax bracket (because you have lots of investment income), but tax rates could have gone down (as, in fact, they have, and may again).

If you agree to (or pressure your boss for) a high proportion of deferred compensation in your overall pay package, or if you take advantage of a plan to defer payment of bonuses and other incentive compensation until post-retirement, you're hoping either that the tax will be lower when you eventually collect the money, or that there will be the IRS equivalent of a talking horse.

In addition, watch out for magical thinking about Keogh and company pension plans. Some people really think, in some primitive corner of the brain, that these sums will *never* be taxed. In fact, what happens is that the money accumulates tax free until retirement; then, unless you qualify for capital gains treatment (that is, if you participated in a plan before 1974) or income averaging, whatever amount you take out each year is ordinary income, taxed at your regular tax rates.

Aha, you counter, so the obvious strategy is to avoid taxation by leaving the money in the IRA or Keogh account forever, hoping that my estate will qualify for either the unified credit or the marital deduction. Or, if I really need the money, I'll take out tiny amounts and leave the rest in the account.

Heh, heh, heh, sneers the IRS, twirling its waxed moustache. Thought you could fool me, eh, me proud beauty? Unless you begin to withdraw from the account by the time you reach seventy and a half, there'll be tax penalties. The general rule is that distributions have to begin at seventy and a half whether the senior citizen is retired or not. But TC '86 includes a special rule for those who reach the age of seventy and a half before January 1, 1988: they can defer distributions until their actual retirement date without tax penalty. You can withdraw all the money in a lump sum, or arrange payments in the form of an annuity; you can stretch out the payments by having them extend over your lifetime, or the lifetime of yourself and another person (perhaps a much younger person). If you're a sturdy sort and likely to live longer than the average life expectancy for your age group, you can recalculate your life expectancy each year (and thus get smaller payments per year, for a longer number of years) without tax penalties. But you'll have to pay the piper sooner or later.

Okay, I'll be careful, you now say. But can't I put one over on the IRS by using my IRA or Keogh account as a private bank, taking out funds that I need when I'm in my thirties or forties, assuming that I'll have replaced them by the time I actually retire?

What a lousy class of proud beauties we get these days, sighs the IRS. There's a 10 percent penalty tax on withdrawals from an IRA, Keogh, or 401(k) plan made before fifty-nine and a half, unless the withdrawal is made by your estate, is made while you are disabled, or is made to meet medical costs. (By contrast, employees are allowed to borrow against their employer-provided pension accounts, and many employer-paid plans permit early retirement at fifty-five, although the pension payments will be lower than if retirement had occurred at the "normal" age. TC '86 requires the "normal" retirement age for this purpose to increase slowly but steadily, keeping pace with the "normal" age for receiving Social Security benefits.)

There is one circumstance in which you can use the IRA or Keogh funds before retirement: you're allowed a limited number of "rollovers" (shifting of funds from a qualified plan or a Keogh to an IRA, or vice versa; shifts from one IRA to another). You have sixty days to make the rollover and shelter the funds in an IRA, safe from taxation until you begin withdrawals. Theoretically, you could use the money in the interim and replace it, but this is risky unless you really know what you're doing and are sure you can replace the money.

## Pension Funds from Your Employer

Let's start with the simplest case: you've spent your whole working life employed by a single company, which has a qualified pension plan. The plan itself contains either a formula for deciding how much your retirement benefits will be (this is a defined benefit plan; the retirement benefit will probably be defined as a percentage of your average salary for your highest-paid three or five years, multiplied by the number of years you worked for the employer), or a formula for deciding how much the employer should contribute to your pension account each year. If the plan is of this latter, defined contribution type, your retirement benefit will depend on the plan's investment success.

Some plans give employees a choice between taking their retirement funds in a lump sum when they retire, or receiving periodic (usually monthly) payments from the plan. Defined benefit plans may insist on your receiving your benefit in annuity form; or the plan may call for a joint and survivor annuity for married employees, a lump sum for single employees, unless they elect another payment method.

The choice, like most financial choices, has both practical and tax consequences. If you need a lump sum for personal reasons, and can cope with the tax results, take the lump sum. A lump-sum payment is also a good idea if you think you can beat the pension plan's investment results. If you prefer monthly payments, the tax results are better. What's more, if you don't think you can manage the money very well, take the periodic payments.

If you're one of the unusual people who really doesn't need the money, you can also roll over the lump sum received from the pension plan into an IRA, and leave it there without tax penalty until you reach seventy and a half. You can take money out of the IRA without penalty once you reach fifty-nine and a half (even if you're not retired), but you must include the amount you withdraw in your income for tax purposes. However, most people will either need the lump sum as soon as they retire, or will need the monthly income.

Most pension plans are written so that the amount of lump-sum or periodic retirement benefits you're entitled to depend on several factors. *Vesting* is an important factor. Vesting determines the percentage of the money in your pension account you're entitled to. Depending on the way the plan is written and on whether it's top-heavy, you can be fully vested in anywhere from your first day on the job to after seven years of employment. Before you're fully vested, you're entitled to a percentage of the money in the account (say, 45 percent), not all of it.

The *break in service rules* also affect your pension. If you have a break in service—stop working for the employer, then return—the employer may be able to disregard the years you worked before the break in service, when computing your pension. However, a 1984 federal law called the Retirement Equity Act helps out workers who take time off from work to raise a family; most maternity- and paternity-related time out will no longer be considered a break in service.

What if you work for Employer A, quit or get fired, and get a new job with Employer B? What happens to the pension contributions Employer A made for you? That's a tougher question. If you're a unionized employee in certain trades, either your union or a group of employers may have a pension plan covering the employees of several employers. All employers' contributions to the plan are treated as interchangeable. Otherwise, you can always get back any contributions *you* made to the plan; and you may be able to roll over the vested portion of contributions made for you to another employer's qualified plan, or to your own IRA. Ask the employee benefits or employee relations coordinator at your first job, or ask a lawyer for advice.

## Taxes and Pension Payouts

The IRA rules are the easiest to understand, so we'll start there. Once you reach fifty-nine and a half (retired or not), you can take out as much as you want in any year. The money you withdraw is taxable income for the year you withdraw it. TC '86 has eliminated income averaging, so you won't be able to use that device to "smooth out" variations in your income. Nor can you use the five-year forward averaging available to employees who take their benefits from employer-sponsored plans.

After fifty-nine and a half, you can withdraw any amount (up to all) of the IRA funds, for any purpose, and without limits on the way you invest the funds. (If tax avoidance is your priority, you can put the whole amount into tax-free municipal bonds or a tax-exempt mutual fund.) You can start taking money out of your IRA at fifty-nine and a half even if you're not retired.

You *must* start making withdrawals by April 1 of the year following the year in which you reach seventy and a half. After that time, there's a 50 percent penalty tax on the difference between the minimum required withdrawal and the amount you actually did withdraw. The minimum required withdrawal depends on your age and your life expectancy. That is, each year you must divide the amount remaining in your IRA account by your life expectancy at seventy and a half, minus the difference between your age and seventy and a half. If you're seventy (male) or seventy-five (female), you divide the amount in your account by 12.1; at seventy-five (for men) and eighty (for women), the figure is 9.6.

To see how it works, let's say that a seventy-five-year-old man has $96,000 in his IRA account. His required withdrawal for the year is $10,000. If he withdraws only $5,000, he must pay a penalty of $2,500—half of the difference between the minimum required withdrawal and the $5,000 he actually withdrew.

These figures assume that the IRA owner chooses to withdraw the IRA funds over his or her own life. You can also choose withdrawals over two lives —yours and your spouse's, or yours and a child or grandchild's. In that case, the calculations will be based on both life expectancies, and withdrawals can be smaller without encountering a penalty tax. If withdrawals are calculated based on your life and your spouse's life, you can recalculate your life expectancy each year. You don't get the benefit of this calculation if the joint life is anyone other than your spouse.

### Withdrawals from Employer Plans and Keoghs

If the plan sponsored by your employer permits it, you can choose to take all your pension funds in a lump sum. If you do this before you reach seventy and a half—but tax deferral is more important to you than immediate use of the money—you can roll the funds into an IRA and, for the time being, escape tax by keeping the lump sum intact until you reach seventy and a half.

The usual rule is that all withdrawals from a pension plan are taxed in the year they're taken. That could create a very uncomfortable situation if your lump-sum pension is in six figures.

Tax relief is available: you can use five-year forward averaging. If you choose to use five-year forward averaging, the entire lump sum is taxed in the year you withdraw it—but it's taxed as if you withdrew it for five years, one-fifth at a time.

Plan participants who were at least fifty on January 1, 1986, have extra options. First of all, they can use ten-year forward averaging, paying taxes in the year of the distribution as if the money had been received over a ten-year period. The trade-off is that five-year forward averaging applies the lower TC

'86 rates, while ten-year averaging applies the older, higher rates. The second break: the part of a lump sum that can be traced to contributions for work before 1974 may qualify for taxation as a capital gain, at 20 percent. You don't have to claim capital gain treatment for qualifying amounts if averaging yields better results. When you make your retirement plans, assess the tax consequences of all possibilities.

Another thing to think about: apart from the income tax issues, TC '86 contains a special 15 percent penalty excise tax on oversized distributions. If you get more than $112,500 a year from an employer-sponsored plan or IRA, or a lump sum over $562,500, the penalty applies in addition to any income tax you must pay. (*Money* magazine suggests an easy way out of this dilemma: roll a lump sum from an employer plan into an IRA; keep IRA withdrawals below $112,500 a year.)

**Periodic Payouts**    Your pension plan may not be drafted to permit lump-sum payouts, or you may prefer regular income (most plans call for monthly payments) to a single lump sum with a corresponding need to make investment choices.

Regular payments from a pension plan are annuities, and therefore any part of the annuity that comes from your own contributions that were not tax-deductible will not be taxed. (You paid the tax already.) The Internal Revenue Code contains quite technical rules for analyzing each annuity payment to determine how much of it comes from the employer, how much comes from income on the employer's contributions, and how much stems from the employee. The most an employee can exclude from income over the course of receiving annuity payments equals the total amount he or she contributed to the plan. But if benefits stop before all of the employee's contributions have been recovered, he or she gets a deduction for the unrecovered contributions in the last taxable year.

How long do annuity payments continue? Nontax pension law requires employers to give employees several choices:

- An annuity for a certain number of years (the longest period you can choose is your life expectancy plus the life expectancy of the beneficiary you choose).
- Annuity payments extending over your life.
- Annuity payments extending over your life plus the life of your spouse. (The plan may let you choose another beneficiary, but there's no legal requirement that this choice be made available.)

For married employees, the joint and survivor annuity is the normal one —the other options must be requested specifically, and the spouse's written consent is needed to pass up the joint and survivor annuity.

**Keogh Plans**    Self-employed people who have Keogh plans must pay a 10 percent penalty for withdrawals from the Keogh before they reach fifty-nine and a half (unless they're disabled). After fifty-nine and a half, withdrawals can be made without paying the 10 percent penalty; however, if the plan is a defined benefit Keogh, set up to provide a certain annual benefit, then the benefit must be adjusted downward to conform to the tax rules if the Keogh owner retires before reaching age sixty-five.

Self-employed people can take money out of their Keogh plans before retirement—in fact, if they don't begin withdrawals by April 1 of the year following the year they reach seventy and a half, the IRS can claim that the plan was never a legitimate retirement plan, open up past income tax returns, and assess higher taxes because the deduction for Keogh contributions is disallowed.

TC '86 doesn't include any provisions about Keogh plans, so it's probably still true that taxation of Keogh benefits is similar to taxation of benefits from plans provided by an employer. Keogh funds can be withdrawn in a lump sum (our interpretation is that five-year or ten-year averaging will be available on the same terms for Keoghs as for employer-provided plans); 50 percent or more of the amount in the Keogh plan can be rolled over into an IRA (as long as the self-employed person is under seventy and a half at the time of the rollover); or you can arrange for periodic payments. (Self-employed people don't have to offer themselves a choice between joint and survivor and single-life annuities and don't need spousal consent to choose a Keogh payout option.) The entire amount of annuity payments from a Keogh plan is taxable income—in effect, the whole annuity comes from the self-employed person in his or her role as "employer," none from the role of "employee."

The choice of a payment method depends on your financial plans but also on plain luck. The simple rule is that the longer payments can be expected to last, the smaller each payment will be. On the one hand, you risk cutting your retirement income to the point that you'll be short of money each month; on the other hand, you risk outliving your income. If you have plenty of income from nonpension investments, you have nothing to worry about, right? Not quite.

Just to make things a little more complex, you must consider the effect of your choice on your potential Medicaid eligibility. If you ever have to enter a nursing home or need expensive care that is not covered by Medicare, or if your spouse is in either of these situations, a lump sum that you took from your pension fund and invested will probably be considered an "available asset"—that is, it may make you "too rich" for Medicaid. (See the next section for advice.) If you're entitled to a monthly pension check, the check will be considered in determining if your monthly income is "too high" for the Medicaid limits.

One thing you *don't* have to worry about is having your Social Security benefits cut because of the size of your pension. (Nor can employers use increases in Social Security benefits to reduce the amounts they pay retirees.) However, if your income exceeds limits set by law, part of your Social Security benefits will be taxable income.

## Retirement and Health Care

We've said it before (in the insurance chapter and the estate planning chapter), and we'll say it again: planning for the cost of long-term health care is one of the most important financial tasks you can undertake.

While you're in the labor force, you'll probably have some kind of health insurance provided by your employer (let's hope that it meets most or all of the health care needs for you and your family; if not, adding extra insurance is another very smart financial move). Many employers do keep health insurance in force for retirees: 91 percent of large corporations keep health insurance in force for early retirees until they reach sixty-five, and 86 percent keep it going for retirees over sixty-five. However, about half the employers coordinate the coverage for over-sixty-five retirees with Medicare: that is, the health plan doesn't pay for items that Medicare would pay for. About half the plans require the retirees to pay something for the coverage.

Few large employers, however, provide health insurance for retirees' dental expenses, or costs of vision or hearing care. (These costs are also excluded from Medicare.) As you can imagine, these bills can be heavy for people over sixty-five.

Smaller corporations are much less likely to continue health benefits after retirement (if, in fact, they have a health insurance plan at all). So, if you work for a small company, or a large company that does not provide postretirement health plans, you'll have to look to Medicare, Medicaid, and private insurance to cover the health costs you can't or don't want to pay out of pocket.

### The Ins and Outs of Medicare

Remember, Medicare is designed to cover the expenses of acute illnesses of people over sixty-five. It doesn't cover preventive medicine, routine checkups, or chronic illnesses. A limited amount of coverage is available for home care, but not enough for the needs of a person who needs full-time nursing and/or housekeeping care to continue living independently. And if s/he can't live independently and can't get care from family members or live-in help, and must go to a nursing home, Medicare won't pay for the nursing home. (Medicare will pay for a certain amount of nursing home care if a person is convalescing from an operation or hospitalization for illness—but not for nursing home care that is required by a person who can't live independently.)

Medicare also limits the amounts it will pay for visits to physicians; many Medicare recipients find that they have to pay quite a bit of money to their doctors in addition to the amount Medicare will repay. As a result of new cost-cutting policies, Medicare patients may find themselves discharged from a hospital before they feel really well enough to leave.

As we discussed in the insurance chapter, you can buy private insurance to fill in some of the gaps in Medicare. However, it's close to impossible to buy private insurance that will pay for nursing home care. And, since a decent nursing home will probably cost more than $30,000 a year (and even a very bad one is almost certain to cost more than $20,000 a year), very few families can meet this burden comfortably. The end result is that many older couples find that the resources of a lifetime are spent on custodial care for one or both of the spouses.

### Who Qualifies for Medicaid?

The federal government and the states jointly operate the Medicaid program. The Medicaid program is not specifically a program for the elderly; instead, it pays the medical bills of the indigent. In effect, it's a welfare program, and some people refuse to accept Medicaid benefits they're entitled to because of the stigma of welfare.

Medicaid will pay nursing home bills. However, to qualify, an applicant must have *available assets* and income below a certain level. (The level depends on the state. Some states restrict Medicaid to people who fit a stringent definition of poverty; other states will allow a person to get Medicaid benefits if s/he is "medically indigent"—able to meet normal costs of living but not stratospheric medical bills.) Not all assets are considered "available" for Medicaid purposes. The family home is considered an exempt asset—not considered "available" to pay nursing home bills—as long as the applicant's spouse and/or minor or disabled child continue to live there.

If you think you or your spouse might ever need long-term custodial care (if one of you develops Alzheimer's disease, or a crippling illness, or heart or respiratory problems so severe you need constant nursing care), you should make long-range plans. If you can find an affordable policy, private insurance covering nursing home care is a good choice. If you have substantial assets, consult a lawyer. You may have to transfer assets, create a durable power of attorney, or set up one or more trusts. The sooner you act, the better— Medicaid authorities can disregard transfers made within two years of an application for benefits, but there's nothing they can do about earlier transfers.

### Will You Outlive Your Income?

Especially during times of high inflation, people on fixed incomes must be concerned. If your retirement income is entirely derived from Social Security and a fixed annuity or defined benefit plan payout, you'll have a very good idea of how much income you'll have each month—and a very legitimate concern that you won't be able to increase your income (except for Social Security COLAs) but your expenses are very likely to increase.

One solution is to make *sure* you have investments in addition to your Social Security and employer-paid pension. Then you can manage your investments, and make sure you have at least some variable-rate investments that will provide you with some shelter against inflation. Another solution is to structure your pension in the form of a variable annuity. (Of course, if rates go way down, you'll be a big loser.)

It's also a good idea to diversify in terms of time of payout. For example, your pension from your employer could be paid as an annuity for a certain number of years (in which event you could certainly outlive the income) or for your lifetime or joint lifetimes. A pension based on someone's lifetime can't be outlived. As we explained earlier, you can structure an IRA payout to continue throughout your life expectancy; if you die sooner than expected, some funds will be available for your heirs. But if you confound the IRS tables and live longer, you could exhaust the funds in your IRA. The solution? Maintain some investments like income-oriented mutual funds that continue to pay periodic income indefinitely.

In short, if you build up a balanced portfolio of investments—taking advantage of the marvelous tax savings allowed for do-it-yourself retirement plans like IRAs and Keoghs—and protect your assets against the costs of medical care; if you balance investments between inflation-sheltered (but risky) variable investments and stable fixed-rate investments; if you balance investments that continue to pay income indefinitely against investments over your lifetime (or your lifetime and your spouse's) and investments that provide income for a certain number of years, your retirement years should be prosperous indeed.

## CASE HISTORY
### Preparing for Retirement and Staying Retired

"Those tarpon have been waiting all their lives for me," Nick Donato said. "They will give up their lives with pleasure, because it's such an honor to be caught by me. I will immediately transport them to fish heaven. All through Florida, little tarpon will be telling their friends that someday they're going to be mounted on plaques in our living room."

"Maybe *one* tarpon mounted on a plaque," Pauline Donato told her husband. "Our town house isn't very big, and I'd rather look at pictures of our kids  our *live* kids and the grandchildren—than a bunch of dead fish."

"Women have no sense of priorities," Nick said, pretending to be hurt. "Can't you remember what our kids look like, without staring at their photos all the time?"

"Can't you remember what a dead fish looks like?"

"Of course. But what I want are trophies, demonstrating my great prowess as a fisherman. Did I complain, that forty years at the Hacberlin Silicon and Glass Works kept me from trout pools, from party boats, from spearfishing through glorious coral reefs?"

"Only for about forty years. But I'm not going to miss these cold winters. It would drive me nuts to stop working, but if there's one thing I can count on, there'll be plenty of work for nurses in Florida." (She was fifty-eight to Nick's sixty-three, and still had the luxury of fondness and sympathy for the "old folks," feeling that she wouldn't be joining their ranks for many years to come.)

"And I can keep up the business . . . there should be lots to buy, and if I can't sell locally, I can do mail order business." The "business" was a profitable little sideline Nick had: it started out with some funny old records his uncle Pietro had given him—funny old Caruso records, and

Galli-Curci records. And some old wax cylinders in the attic of the house his best friend had inherited from an elderly, widowed great-aunt. Goodness knows where *she* had gotten them. But there were people willing to pay plenty of money for old opera records; for ten years or so, Nick had searched for the old records at flea markets, bought them for a nickel or so apiece at church rummage sales, gone straight from the graveyard shift at Haeberlin's to country auctions where old records might or might not turn up. The hobby had never been absorbing (or profitable) enough to get him to quit his job; but the extra few thousand dollars a year had been gratifying, especially after his son Joey the financial planner explained to him about Keogh plans.

The Donatos were basically conservative people, and had hung onto the two-story frame house in the "old neighborhood." Where else could they get mozzarella and sausage an hour after they were made but at Lazzaro's? Where else could they get crusty bread freshly baked, and racing tips freshly half-baked, but at Boccherini's Bakery? So they had hung on, through years when they were afraid to leave the house at night, when they had kept a gun (prudently unloaded) in the night table, in case a prowler was impolite enough to enter, and polite enough to stand still while they groped for bullets and loaded the gun. And now a peculiar group of people called "Yuppies" had rampaged into the area, bearing bulging checkbooks and American Express cards as weapons of conquest. And a pair of them had offered to pay—imagine!—$120,000 for the old house. The 4.5 percent, thirty-year mortgage had been paid off for years.

True, the adorable doll's house of a town house in Florida cost even more than that; but they could use part of the $120,000 for closing costs and moving expenses, and put the rest toward the town house. It hadn't been easy to get a bank to give a mortgage to a retired couple, but then retirees are hardly a novelty in Florida. They got a small mortgage, at a rate far above the 4.5 percent they had once found so shocking, and were careful to get mortgage insurance. Their daughter Patricia (the lawyer) was dubious about this at first, but she checked with their insurance agent, and found that term insurance would have been unavailable (given Nick's age, high blood pressure, and diabetes) and adding to their cash-value life insurance would have been costlier than the mortgage insurance.

Nick's pension (they took the joint-and-survivor annuity option) from Haeberlin's wasn't much, and neither was his Social Security. But Nick took his Keogh funds in a lump sum, took advantage of ten-year forward averaging, and invested the aftertax amount in a tax-exempt bond fund that had a good year and sent a gratifying check every month.

Pauline found a job as nursing supervisor at a nursing home about forty miles from their town house. The salary was not what she was used to, but the job carried an important benefit: a comprehensive health insurance policy covering Pauline and her husband. Although the nursing home had a defined benefit pension plan, it couldn't keep her from participating, because its normal retirement age was sixty-five, and she was fifty-eight—not within five years of normal retirement age. However, after three years, she found the job (and the commute) too strenuous, and quit—before she had any vested benefits. But she had vested benefits from an earlier nursing job, and was able to start collecting a pension once she reached sixty-five. And, in the meantime, she worked part-time as a private duty nurse.

The Donatos didn't live in luxury in Florida (but, then, they hadn't lived in luxury in Kansas City). They had a small monthly payment on the town house; an electricity bill that could be hefty during the summer months; a phone bill (reduced by canny shopping for long-distance phone service) inflated by calls to the kids and grandchildren; and a steady expenditure for fishing tackle and Nick's share of boat rentals. He did manage to catch quite a few tarpon, but only three of them made it to the living room wall. After all, you can't stay married for forty years without making a few compromises.

Retirement can be enjoyable, but with it comes a need for careful financial planning. There are many new financial choices to consider once you retire—don't hesitate to learn what you need to know to brighten your golden years.

# 18

## Estate-Planning Basics

> The key here, I think, is to not think of death as
> an end, but to think of it as a very effective way to cut
> down on your expenses.
>
> —WOODY ALLEN

The two most desirable estate plans—taking it with you and not going—are, unfortunately, unavailable to most people. The average person should, therefore, think about estate planning.

### State Law: De Facto Estate Planning

True, if you never bother to take any practical steps, you do already have an estate plan by default. Every state has laws of "intestate succession" that govern the disposition of property of people who die intestate (without wills). Although the laws vary from state to state, they usually provide that a married person's spouse (or a married person's spouse and children) will inherit the deceased person's estate. A single person's siblings and/or parents will divide the estate; or, if there are no legal heirs to be found, the estate will "escheat" —be forfeited to the state.

What if these rules—what you might call intestate commerce—don't fit your plans? You'll notice that no provision is made for friends (including live-in lovers); no provision for giving to charity, or for cutting out relatives whom you can't stand, but who have a statutory right to some or all of your property.

### A Will Is a Must

Unless the state rules fit your plans, you must have a will (and must review your plans frequently, to make sure your will and the rest of your estate plan continue to suit your family and financial situation). In fact, even if the state law is precisely your cup of tea—and gives your teacups to the person you want to have them—it's still a good idea to have a will. Why? That way, there's no uncertainty about whether you have a will somewhere; no need to search for the hypothetical (but really nonexistent) will. It simply saves everybody a lot of trouble.

Furthermore, if you have a will, you can name your own executor or executors (people or institutions administering your estate). In most cases, you can control the cost of estate administration. If you die intestate, the probate court (the court responsible for dealing with wills, trust administration, and related matters) will appoint an administrator—generally a lawyer who has distinguished him- or herself more in the political clubhouse than in the halls of justice. The administrator is entitled to fees, which can be sizable—and which reduce the estate available to your heirs. After spending lots of energy accumulating and preserving wealth, do you really want to see it fatten the wallet of a total stranger?

### Components of an Estate Plan

You'll be hearing a lot more about wills in this chapter. But right now, what we want to convince you is that there's a lot more to an estate plan than a will.

This whole book explains to you how to create, if not a family fortune, at least a comfortable amount of money to satisfy family needs. Leaving money to your children may not be a priority for you; you may feel that you and your spouse should use the money you've spent a lifetime earning, for your own needs.

On the other hand, many people do want to leave money to their children. Almost everyone wants to be sure that his or her spouse will be financially secure in case of widowhood. *Hint:* Many people make inflexible estate plans based on the assumption that the husband will die first, or that the younger spouse will survive the older. Not always true—so either build flexibility into your estate plan, or be prepared to change it.

Although the will is a cornerstone of estate planning, a full-scale estate plan can include many other devices:

- Trusts—arrangements under which a person, law firm, bank, etc., takes care of money or other property; distributes income from the trust; and distributes the trust assets at a prearranged time.
- Life insurance—an absolute must if you have limited assets and major family responsibilities. Later on in this chapter, we'll give you some guidelines for deciding the best beneficiary for your life insurance policy or policies.
- Retirement funds—sometimes pension payouts or payments from your IRA or Keogh plan stop with your death; frequently, however, they continue for your spouse's life; or your spouse is entitled to a lump sum after your death.
- Jointly owned property—also called the "poor man's will." If property is owned by two or more people as "joint tenants," and one of the joint tenants dies, the other joint tenants automatically inherit his or her share of the property. The transfer of ownership doesn't require a will or court approval.
- Lifetime gifts. These can have very positive tax-saving consequences. Anyway, isn't it nice to see how grateful your friends and relatives are?

## The Perfect Estate Plan; the Perfect Martini

An estate plan is the expression of individual taste and circumstances. Remember James Bond?—007 ordered his favorite drink "shaken, not stirred." The will takes the place of gin or vodka. Some estate plans include only the merest whiff of "vermouth" (will substitutes). Others bring the proportion nearer to half-and-half. And who's the bartender? Usually, lawyers have overall responsibility for the estate plan, and their services will be necessary for drawing up wills and trust instruments. Not every lawyer is financially sophisticated, so you may want input from accountants and/or financial planners as well.

## The Taxable Estate

Two important concepts for you to understand: the taxable estate (which is the amount that the IRS could, conceivably, collect taxes on) and the probate estate (which is stuff that a probate court has jurisdiction over). Some property is in the taxable estate, but not in the probate estate; some in the probate estate, but not the taxable estate.

In general, property will be in the taxable estate if you had control over it when you died. Unless it comes into a category exempted by the tax laws, property will be in your probate estate if it can be transferred by your will instead of by a will substitute.

Most people don't have to worry about estate taxes, because you have to have an awfully large estate, and to forgo the use of the various exemptions. But if you have to pay estate tax at all, it will be hefty—about one-third to one-half of the taxable part of the estate.

Even if there won't be any federal estate tax on your estate, the state in which you die may have an estate tax (charged against the estate, for the privilege of passing the stuff on), inheritance taxes (charged against the heirs for the privilege of inheriting the stuff), or both. The taxes may be set up like the federal tax, or may have idiosyncratic rules. Ask your lawyer.

### The Probate Estate

Every estate plan should include both probate and nonprobate assets. Probate, do we hear you say? Wasn't there a book about that?

Some years back, a nonlawyer named Harry Dacey sparked a great deal of controversy—and improved his personal financial condition quite a bit—by writing a best seller called *How to Avoid Probate*. Mr. Dacey had several charges to make against the probate system:

- Probate takes too long—your survivors could be left without funds at a crucial time.
- Probate is too expensive—too many lawyers stick their noses into the process, and the estate pays through the nose.
- Once a will is probated, it's a public document, and anyone can look at it and see how you left your money—including the bequests to your fourteen illegitimate children, all with different mothers or fathers.

In brief, the solution Mr. Dacey suggests is the revocable *inter vivos* trust used as a will substitute. (Don't know what a revocable *inter vivos* trust is? Don't panic, we'll discuss it under "trusts.") The revocable *inter vivos* trust really is a useful device, but it's not for everyone. (After all, not everyone even likes martinis.) The main problem with the revocable *inter vivos* trust is that all the money in the trust is part of your taxable estate even though it isn't part of your *probate* estate.

No sweat, if there isn't any taxable estate; a big problem, if it leads to a big tax bill. As for Mr. Dacey's other objections, they're not insuperable as long as you have a balanced estate plan, one that provides some liquid assets for the period until your will is probated. (This is one of the major functions of life insurance.)

As for the cost of probate, you can get this way down if your spouse or a family friend is willing to act as executor without charging the estate a commission. With so many lawyers wandering around, you should be able to find one who can provide legal advice on the probate process, reasonably inexpensively. (Not a bad idea to shop around while you're still aboveground; leaving instructions for your survivors gives them one fewer thing to worry about.)

And as for publicity, he's right, but so what? Very few people go around reading old moldy wills for jollies. If that's what worries you, you can phrase your will very discreetly. Name the fourteen as worthy infants who deserve a break, not as the products of your heedless youth. And if you do want to disinherit someone, be tactful—just say that you're not leaving anything to Roderick or Natasha "for personal reasons known to him/her" and leave it at that.

### Will Basics

To be valid, a will must be written, signed by the testator, and signed by witnesses. That's it. Many states also permit less formal "holographic" wills in the testator's handwriting, but we're talking here about formal wills. We strongly urge you to have a formal will if you have a will at all—and you *know* that we think you should have a will.

There's no legal requirement that a formal will be prepared by a lawyer, but it's a good idea. Acting by yourself, you could probably come up with a document that would be legal and could be probated—but you probably wouldn't take all the important factors into account, and you probably wouldn't know about the variety of legal devices that could streamline the transfer of your property.

A few states (for example, California and Maine) have "statutory wills"—basic forms that have been codified as part of state law. To use a statutory will, you fill in the blanks, sign the form and have it witnessed according to state requirements; then you have a valid will. Where they're available, statutory wills are great for people with simple estate-planning needs who can't afford a lawyer. Residents of other states, and those with more complex planning needs, should consult a lawyer for a personalized plan that's less cut-and-dried than the simple categories of the statutory will.

By the way, many lawyers in general practice use wills as a "loss leader" —they charge a low price to attract clients, who they hope will come back for more expensive services later. To save money, many lawyers use question-naires and forms very much like the statutory will. That's a good place to *start,* but don't let yourself be fobbed off with a "canned will" instead of a complete estate plan that fully reflects your needs, your financial circumstances, and your plans for your property.

A perfectly legal will can be written on a paper bag, the side of an elephant (though you're taking a substantial risk that your executor will have to drag a dead elephant into the probate court), a wastebasket—but not on a floppy disk. A will must be written or printed and physically signed.

A valid will also requires witnesses—either two or three, depending on state law. It's always better to have three, in case one is unavailable when needed to testify. Again, state laws vary. Sometimes the witnesses have to actually see you sign the will, sometimes it's okay to sign the will privately, then tell them that that's your signature. Sometimes you must "publish"—tell the witnesses that the document is your will; other states don't require this. Some laws require all the witnesses to sign at the same time, some don't.

Most state laws provide that an "interested witness"—one who inherits something under the will—can't inherit under the will unless there are at least two disinterested witnesses. (But the will itself does not become invalid be-cause a witness is interested.) Some states hold that a person is an interested witness if his or her spouse inherits under the will. So, to be on the safe side, pick two or three strangers—employees in law offices are accustomed to this task.

Ask your lawyer if "self-proving affidavits" are allowed in your state. This efficient device allows the witnesses to sign a statement about the circum-stances under which the will was signed; a valid self-proving affidavit saves a lot of time and trouble, because it makes it unnecessary for the witnesses to testify before the probate court.

### Tips for Writing a Will

The purpose of a will is to give away exactly 100 percent of your property that could pass by will. This is trickier than it seems at first glance.

Remember, as we've explained above, joint property passes automatically, not by will. If you live in a community property state, you can dispose of your separate property by will, but only half of the community property. You can't dispose of life insurance proceeds by will unless your estate is the beneficiary.

Then again, you may have more property than you thought when you wrote the will, and you may not have provided for the disposition of all the property. You may have *less* property than you thought; you may have disposed of $300,000 cash when the estate has only $150,000 cash.

You can't guarantee that the people you love will live forever, or even as long as you do. You might leave something to a person who predeceases you. So every time you leave something to a person, you should provide for a *gift over*—a disposition to someone else in case the original beneficiary dies before you do, or dies within a certain number of days or months of your death.

Most of the states have adopted some form of the Uniform Simultaneous Death Act, which provides a set of rules when it's impossible to tell which of two people has survived a common disaster (say, when spouses die in a plane crash, and it has to be determined how the estate of each spouse should pass). Check with your lawyer—if the state rules don't fit into your estate plan (say, if they have negative tax consequences), it's perfectly legal to write your own simultaneous death provision in your will. You may also want to have a special arrangement if your spouse dies within a short time after your death, to save the trouble and expense of having the same property administered as part of two different estates.

### The Typical Will

Here's a "map" of a typical will:

- An *introduction* explaining whose will it is; the testator's address; if s/he is now married or ever has been married; if s/he has or ever had children. (In these days in which divorce and remarriage are common, it's important to note whether references to "children," "brothers," or "sisters" include adopted children, stepchildren, half-brothers and half-sisters, etc.)
- *Specific dispositions* of property—say, $5,000 to my sister Elizabeth Conover; my 1932 Duesenberg to the Classic Car Club. It's a very good idea to indicate what you want done if the estate isn't large enough to pay out all the money, and what to do if specifically mentioned objects aren't included in your estate when you die. (The general rule is that a person who is supposed to inherit an object that isn't part of the estate

is simply out of luck—s/he doesn't get a substitute item unless the will provides one.)

- *Formula dispositions* of property—say, 10 percent of my gross estate to each of my children. Naturally, you have to be concerned about whether the formula will add up to more than 100 percent!

- A *residuary* clause disposing of property that hasn't been disposed of any other way. Many wills are set up so that the residuary clause is the main part of the will. There may be a few minor, preliminary bequests; the main action is disposing of the residue.

- An *antilapse* clause providing gifts over if the intended heir dies before the testator.

- A *simultaneous death* provision.

- If the testator has young children, a *guardianship* provision. If the testator is survived by a spouse, the spouse is the natural guardian of the children. But if both spouses die together, or if the surviving spouse later dies without naming a guardian, the designation of the guardian saves a lot of trouble and lets the testator decide who should be the children's guardian(s). The testator can name a person (or a married couple) as guardians; or s/he can name a person (or people) as guardian of the child's person—responsible for physically taking care of the kids—and can name a bank, law firm, lawyer, or accountant as guardian of the child's property—responsible for financial management. It may be a good idea to name young friends or relatives, rather than grandparents or great-uncles and aunts, as guardians (so the children's lives won't be further disrupted by another death). Some testators like to name a married couple as guardians, and specify that if they divorce, guardianship will shift to another couple. Again, the purpose is to prevent disruption and instability in the children's lives.

- Naming one or more *executors;* explaining their powers (if they will have any powers in addition to those provided by state law); explaining how they will be compensated.

- A will can create a *testamentary trust,* to take effect after the testator's death; or, if the testator is also the grantor of an *inter vivos* trust, assets can be *poured over* into the trust. That is, estate funds (or property other than money) can be put into the trust, and administered like the other trust property.

- The testator's signature; the witnesses' signatures; maybe a self-proving affidavit.

A will can be a brief note on a single sheet of paper, or roughly the size of *Gone with the Wind;* it depends on the amount of the estate, and the complexity of the provisions for distributing it.

### Problems with Personal Property

Some of the most vicious disputes involve some of the least valuable property —grown-ups can spend years and thousands of dollars hassling over who's going to get Grandma's souvenir plate collection or Wilbur's baseball cards and barbed wire collection. If you dispose of specific items in your will, you face the problem of leaving someone an item that is no longer in the estate at your death, or of leaving your daughter Alice your silver candlesticks (which she's always hated), creating lasting resentment in Alice (who wanted the portrait of Grandfather Simpkins) and in Marie, who coveted the candlesticks.

Well, you could throw up your hands and have your executor sell every-thing and distribute the cash. Or you could give the executor the discretion to divide up your personal property into a number of shares, and give one share to Alice, one to Marie, one to Robert. . . . Better provide that your executor's discretion is final and absolute, to prevent nuclear war. You could make a list of people, and let each one of them select a certain number of items from your estate (perhaps after specific, very valuable items like jewelry have been disposed of). You could have the executor divide your personal property into groups of items of approximately equal value, and let the people on the list choose one group of items, or take turns choosing, with the value of the various items balanced.

Be very careful when you leave someone the "contents" of your house, or of a desk or a safe-deposit box. Think carefully about whether you want particularly valuable items to be handled separately, not as part of the con-tents. For example, if you leave your spouse the contents of your desk, do you want the stock certificates in the desk to be considered part of the contents, or part of your stock portfolio?

Many states allow you to draft your will to refer to a separate letter that disposes of items of personal property. This is a good solution, because you can change the letter as often as you want, without going through the formali-ties of making a new will or a codicil (amendment to a will). You can change the letter as frequently as your collection of property changes; and if you're the sort of person who enjoys disinheriting your friends and relatives on minor provocation, this is the easiest way to do it.

### Nothing for Harry

Within limits, you can do anything you want with your property. However, if your will provides less for your spouse than the amount required by law—unless you have an antenuptial agreement surrendering the right to this *elective share*—your spouse has the right of election. That is, s/he can go to court and demand the statutory share, and your estate will be readjusted to provide him or her with this minimum amount.

Most states let you disinherit your children, if you want to. However, most states have "pretermitted heir" statutes saying that if you don't mention your spouse or children in your will, it's assumed that you forgot them—so your estate will be redistributed to include these "forgotten men."

To escape a pretermitted heir statute, all you have to do is mention the person you want to disinherit, and say that you don't want to leave him or her anything. It isn't necessary to cut him or her off with a shilling. Just the mention is enough. And, if your idea of a really good time is cutting people out of your will, the personal property letter described in the preceding section is the ideal tool. Just rip up the existing letter, and redraft a new one.

Some testators who want to keep being bossy after death use an *in terrorem* clause that says that anyone who challenges the will is automatically disinherited. Most states will enforce a clause like that, but some states say that a will challenge brought for good cause (say, the testator was mentally ill or subject to undue influence) will not trigger the *in terrorem* clause.

### Choosing an Executor

Depending on the size and complexity of your estate, being executor could be a simple procedure indeed, or a full-time job for six people for a year.

For a small, simple estate, your spouse or a close relative or friend is an ideal choice (provided that s/he is good at handling money, and can cope with the psychological burden of administering an estate that wouldn't exist if you hadn't died). Why? Because s/he will probably serve without a fee, and executor's commissions reduce the estate.

You can also leave an executor something in your will, instead of (or in addition to) the executor's commissions provided by state statutes. By the way, if you leave something to the executor, to be paid as soon as s/he qualifies as executor, the legacy is considered a gift; if it's paid after s/he finished acting as executor and the affairs of the estate are wound up, it's considered compensation for being executor, so the executor has to pay income tax on it. See if you can guess which way executors prefer.

If your estate is complex, or if there's no relative or friend financially and emotionally qualified to act as executor, your attorney or accountant, or a bank trust department, could be a good choice as executor. (Check their availability, fees, and minimum size of estate they'll act for.) Or, you could name a friend or family member as one executor, a lawyer, institution, etc., as a second executor. (Be sure your will provides a process for deciding who wins when the executors are in conflict.)

### Taking Care of Your Will

Once your will is prepared, take good care of it! Your will can't be probated unless all the signed copies are produced (so don't sign multiple copies unless there's a darned good legal reason) or unless the special procedure for probating a lost will is followed.

Naturally, your spouse and/or executor will have to be told where the will is kept. Your safe-deposit box is not a good choice—your state may require a court order to open a dead person's safe-deposit box, creating delay when the administration process should be expedited.

One solution is to keep the will at home, in a fireproof filing cabinet. Another is to have your lawyer keep it—provided that s/he has a safe, fireproof filing system. But, if you later change lawyers, getting the will can be awkward.

Twenty-three states (including Colorado, Massachusetts, Ohio, Texas, and Virginia) will allow you to deposit your will with the probate court during your lifetime; after your death, the will is retrieved from probate court files. In fact, four states (Arkansas, Indiana, North Dakota, and Ohio) will even allow you to have your will probated during your lifetime—you can petition the court to check over your will and see if it's valid.

### Beyond the Will

Probably the most important will substitute—and one you may very well acquire long before you have a will—is life insurance. The simplest (though not necessarily the best) way to handle life insurance proceeds is to buy one or more life insurance policies, continue to own them, and name at least one beneficiary and one alternate beneficiary for each policy. The alternate beneficiary is required in case the original beneficiary dies before you do. Naturally, you could have several policies, each with a different beneficiary, suiting the size of the policy to the provisions you want to make for each beneficiary.

Why is that not necessarily the best choice? For one thing, if you have "incidents of ownership" in a life insurance policy, the proceeds of the policy are included in your taxable estate. Incidents of ownership are more or less equivalent to control over the policy—for example, the right to change the beneficiary of the policy, or to convert the policy to paid-up insurance. Don't even worry about it if your estate is far too small to incur federal estate tax; give the question some serious thought if it will or could be taxable.

You can handle the problem simply by giving the policy away. You can let your spouse, or someone else you choose, have the incidents of ownership (it's okay if you keep on paying the premiums). If you want to set up a program of lifetime gifts, insurance is one way to give a very valuable gift with a small outlay.

Usually, life insurance is payable to a "named beneficiary": a person chosen by the insured person. However, it's quite possible to have the proceeds made payable to your estate. The disadvantage of this choice is that the insurance proceeds will be part of your taxable estate. The advantage is that, once the proceeds become part of your estate, they can be divided any way your will provides, so you gain flexibility.

Imagine what the insurance company would say if you ordered the insurance proceeds paid to seven people and three charitable organizations, using several complex formulas. But your executor could handle that easily if you make the insurance proceeds part of your residuary estate, or if you have the insurance proceeds distributed to a trust created by your will (or to a *living trust* created during your lifetime).

Insurance proceeds paid to a named beneficiary can be paid out in several ways. The most familiar is a lump sum: say, a $100,000 death benefit. (That's what the insurance company calls it, though the insured person is unlikely to consider his or her death a benefit.) The beneficiary (or the executor, if the money is paid to the estate) must decide whether to take the money in a lump sum or use a *settlement option.*

Settlement options are ways of paying out benefits periodically. The insurance company may agree to pay a monthly sum to the beneficiary for a certain number of years, or over his/her lifetime; the insurer may also agree that at least a certain amount of money will be paid out. Are settlement options a good idea? It depends on whether the beneficiary needs a lump sum (for example, to buy a retirement home, start a business, or enter a life-care community); on the beneficiary's own investment skill or ability to hire the right advisers; and on the investment return the insurer provides on settlement options, as compared to market rates of return.

### Lifetime Gifts

Ostensibly, rich people are philanthropists because they're warm, generous, noble folks. The real reason is to beat the tax collector. As we've seen, there's no estate tax at all if you can get your taxable estate below the exempt amount ($500,000 if you die in 1986; $600,000 if you die in 1987 or later). One way to do this is to use the marital deduction (next section); another way is to leave heaps of money and property to charity in your will (charitable bequests are excluded from the taxable estate); still another way is to reduce the taxable estate by making gifts during your lifetime. In some cases, there's a substantial tax saving if you give money to your friends and relatives instead of leaving it to them.

Theoretically, there's a gift tax on large gifts made during your lifetime. However, there's never any gift tax on a gift of any size made to your spouse at any time. (Do you own property jointly with your spouse? If you put the property solely in his or her name, you've given him or her half the value of the property—but there's no gift tax.)

Nor is there ever any gift tax if you pay someone's medical or educational bills, no matter how much money is involved. In the legal sense, you are making a gift to your mother if you pay her nursing home bills, and you're making a gift to your nephew (or, really, his parents) if you pay his college tuition. But a benevolent Congress has decided to free you from the burden of gift tax in this situation. To qualify for this exclusion, you have to pay the bill directly; you can't give the money to your mother, or your nephew, or your brother and sister-in-law and tell them to pay the bill. Furthermore, if you meet someone else's support obligations—pay a bill that someone else has an obligation to pay—s/he has to pay income tax on the amount of the gift used to meet support obligations.

Last, but by no means least, you're entitled to an annual *gift tax exemption* of up to $10,000 per recipient. That is, you can give any number of people up to $10,000 a year each without having to pay gift tax. If your spouse agrees to join in the gift, together you can give up to $20,000 a year per recipient without gift tax. Somehow we doubt if you'll ever have to pay gift tax. However, if you're that rich and that generous, Bill would like a Rolls and Dana would like a laser printer. Send them care of the publisher.

If your estate is close to the taxable level, sensible use of lifetime gifts can get it below the tax threshold, or can lower the taxable amount if estate tax is due. Talk to your financial planner, lawyer, and accountant about the right way to apportion gifts among your family and the charities you want to benefit.

### The Marital Deduction

Another way to avoid estate taxes is to use the unlimited marital deduction. That is, you can leave any amount of money to your spouse without estate tax. If your estate is $15 million and you leave all of it to your spouse, there's no estate tax on your estate.

Why doesn't everyone do this? For one thing, if you have $15 million, you have a lot of friends, and you may well feel that your children and various other people should inherit something from you rather than waiting for your spouse to die. For another thing, unless your spouse remarries, s/he won't be able to use the marital deduction, so everything in the estate when s/he dies, minus the $500,000 or $600,000 exclusion, will be taxable. That's why a lot of lawyers believe that the best estate plan for a married couple "equalizes" the estates, so that each spouse will have an estate of about the same size—preferably both below the estate-tax limit.

To equalize, your lawyer may recommend changes in your life insurance plans; transfers of title from one spouse to the other, or from joint property to separate property (or vice versa); changes in your investment portfolio, bank accounts, or a mixture of all of these. *Warning*: Don't take action with an estate-planning motive until you think through the way it could affect a possible future divorce.

The general rule is that to qualify for the marital deduction, you must leave something to your spouse outright, with no restrictions. However, recent tax law does permit the use of *QTIPs*—qualified terminable interest property. If your will is drafted correctly, you can get the estate tax marital deduction even if your spouse has only a life estate (the right to use property during his or her lifetime; then it goes to the person you named) or other interests less substantial than outright legal ownership. You can also leave property to your spouse in trust, so that s/he gets only the income but not the property itself, and still qualify for the estate tax marital deduction. But these are abstruse matters, to be settled by a sophisticated lawyer or estate-planning team.

## Trusts: Not for Millionaires Only

In general terms, a trust is a simple arrangement under which one person (the *grantor, creator,* or *settlor*) transfers property to a *trustee* (an individual or institution such as law firm or bank). The trustee takes care of the property; invests it, if it's money or investable property; collects the income, if it's income-producing. Usually, the trustee pays the income (generally once a year or once a quarter) to the *income beneficiary* or *beneficiaries* chosen by the grantor. Depending on the way the trust is written, the trustee may also have the option of *accumulating* the income—adding it back into the trust *principal,* which is also called *corpus.*

The *trust instrument* or *indenture,* the legal document setting up the trust, specifies the length of time the trust will last. When the trust ends (either after a certain number of years, or when an event—such as a particular person's death—happens), the trustee distributes the trust principal, plus any accumulated income, to the *remainderman* or *remaindermen* chosen by the grantor. Note: it's a unisex term. Again, depending on the way the trust is set up, the remainderman could be the grantor him- or herself; the grantor's spouse; one of his or her children; a friend; or a charity.

Sometimes a trust is written to allow the trustee to *invade* the principal —that is, to take some of the principal and give it to the income beneficiaries. This might be done if the income beneficiary is the grantor's spouse and s/he is short of money; or if the income beneficiary needs more money for education, medical bills, or to buy a house.

Some trusts are set up by a contract between living people; these are called *inter vivos* trusts, or trusts "between the living." Other trusts, called *testamentary* trusts, are set up by a person's will, to take effect after his or her death. An *inter vivos* trust can be either *revocable* or *irrevocable.* If the trust is revocable, the grantor has the right to change its terms, or cancel it entirely and take back the property. If it's irrevocable, the grantor can't do this. Given the high degree of control, a revocable living trust will be part of the estate of the person who created it.

In one sense, testamentary trusts are always revocable, since you can change your will as long as you're alive and legally competent. In another sense, you'd have to be a real optimist to think you could amend a trust after it takes effect as a direct result of your own death. So, for all intents and purposes, testamentary trusts are legally irrevocable once they become effective.

You can set up a trust and *fund* it immediately by transferring money or other property (say, stocks and bonds, income-producing real estate, art works). Or you can set up an *inter vivos* trust with little or no funding and provide for a *pour-over*—a transfer of part of your estate to the trust after your death. You can also have life insurance proceeds payable to a testamentary trust or poured over to an *inter vivos* trust, or you can use life insurance policies as some or all of the funding of a trust.

On this simple foundation, many kinds of trusts can be built. Originally trusts were used to serve practical purposes, such as to transfer property to minors or disabled people who couldn't manage it themselves or to provide continuing professional management. Then, for many years, trusts provided tax advantages for the rich and the upper middle class. A high-bracket donor could set up a trust in such a way that the trust's income would be taxed either to the trust or to the beneficiaries—at tax rates far lower than the donor's.

Yes, all that is in the past tense. Income from trusts whose grantors retained a lot of power was always taxed to the grantor, at the grantor's rates. Income from trusts that met a person's obligations to support his dependents (say, a doting grandpa) is now taxed at pretty much the same rate as the grantor pays. The first $5,000 of a trust's income is subject to a tax rate of 15 percent; the rest is taxed at 28 percent or 33 percent.

What can you do if you've already set up a trust? If the trust is revocable, it may pay to revoke it, unless the practical advantages the trust provides outweigh both the transaction costs of operating the trust and the tax consequences. If the trust is irrevocable, you have a real problem—attempts to revoke it could lead to the IRS or a court hearing the case to decide that the trust was *always* invalid, landing you with an obligation to pay back tax advantages derived from the trust. At least the trustees can change the way the trust assets are invested, even if the trust has to remain in force. A change to tax-exempt investments will help. (As Sam said in *Casablanca* as he, Rick, and Ilsa prepared to drink up the last of the champagne from Rick's restaurant in Paris, "This should take some of the sting out of being occupied.")

Will TC '86 make estate planners throw away that old trust? Not necessarily. Trusts still provide the practical advantages of uniting an entire estate or group of assets under a single, presumably skilled, management and making it possible to distribute trust income among a group of people. Trusts still provide housekeeping services for the assets of people who lack the mental capacity, or simply the investment skills, to handle them.

On the practical level, you have to decide whether a trust is the easiest way to get what you want, and what the transaction costs will be (a bank trust department may refuse to deal with a trust below a certain amount, and may charge dramatic fees every year; it takes time for a lawyer to research tax alternatives and draft a complex trust).

On the tax level, you have to ask your lawyer what the income tax, gift tax, and estate tax consequences of a particular trust would be. Usually, either the beneficiary or the trust itself pays the income tax on the trust's income each year.

However, if a trust satisfies someone's support obligations (say, by buying a kid's clothes), then the person whose support obligation is satisfied has to pay the income tax. If the grantor maintains too much control over the trust, s/he will have to pay the income tax. Trusts can be used to qualify for the estate tax marital deduction, and to shift assets out of a taxable estate. As for gift tax, there's a strong possibility that you'll have to pay gift tax when you set up a trust, unless you follow a complex set of rules.

### Powers of Attorney

On the simplest level, asking someone to pick up a quart of milk for you is a power of attorney. You, as the principal, are appointing an agent to act for you in this very limited area.

On a more sophisticated level, a power of attorney is a very important part of an estate plan. You can—and should—designate your spouse or other appropriate person as your agent in case you ever become temporarily incapacitated (e.g., undergo surgery) or permanently incapacitated (suffer an irreversible brain disease).

All the states allow you to sign what is called a *durable power of attorney,* naming the agent; the designation will continue good even if you become mentally disabled. Some states will even allow you to use what is called a *springing power of attorney*—one that doesn't take effect *until* you become mentally incapacitated.

Because your agent can have very broad powers, you'll have to choose carefully—you don't want someone who will steal your money! Also be sure to select an alternate if your agent dies or becomes incapacitated. It may be a good idea to give your agent extra powers—say, the power to make gifts or the power to disclaim bequests under other people's wills—for estate-planning and Medicaid purposes.

### Putting It All Together

It may take an entire team and a full-court press to set up the best estate plan for you and your family. You'll have to review the amount of insurance coverage you have, and decide whether the policies should be given away, put in trust, and whether the beneficiaries should be changed.

You'll almost certainly need a will, though it's an individual question about how complex it should be. Maybe you'll need one or more trusts.

So think about what you own now, and what your financial plans can be expected to yield; think about what you want for your spouse and your children; and be prepared to review your plans regularly as your assets and needs change, and as tax laws change.

### CASE HISTORY
### *Estate-Planning Basics*

"And who referred you?" Cathy Tomlinson asked. She was Marsha Blumbaum's legal secretary, computer operator, telephone wizard (and ace liar when Marsha was supposed to be in more than two places at once).

"My son and his fiancée," said Roger Stewart McGarry. "His wife, now. Ms. Blumbaum did their wills and an estate plan just before they got married. I was just ventilating a little steam about the attorney who handles our corporate work, and young Edward said that his experience was quite different. That Ms. Blumbaum was most courteous, and the plans seemed eminently sensible and were drawn up quickly. I have a will, of course, but it was drawn up many years ago, before I went on a business trip, when commercial aviation was not what it is today—but, I suppose, before hijacking was what it is today!—and my wife has never had a will at all."

Mrs. McGarry—Charlotte—gave a watery smile, as if to say that she had never had a will of her own in a more cosmic sense. But, then, she had known what she was getting into by marrying a man with a predilection for walrus moustaches and tartan waistcoats.

"I'm going to have to ask you some questions, which you may find rather personal," Cathy said. "You see, I'm compiling this preliminary information form for Ms. Blumbaum's use. As you can see, I'm entering the information in our computer, so it will be readily available, in both its original and updated form. Now, could I please have your dates of birth?"

(He was sixty-four; she was sixty-one.)

"And you are both United States citizens?" They nodded. They gave their addresses—both their elegant sixteen-room house on two acres (inherited from her family) and their little ski lodge. His occupation was president and chief executive officer of the McGarry Machine Tool Company; he gave her occupation as "none," but Cathy tactfully coded in, "Homemaker."

He earned close to $100,000 a year from the tool company, and owned a substantial block of stock—although no one could remember the stock ever having paid a dividend. They also owned quite a bit of other companies' stock, much of which did pay dividends. Some of the stock was in their joint names, bought during their marriage; some of it was in her name, because she had inherited it. They had fine English furniture, she had fur coats and some modest jewelry—which, like the silver, spent most of its time in the safe-deposit vault, emerging only for major holidays in the company of family and others not easily impressed.

Cathy coded in a few more items—referring to the presence of a closely held business in the estate; inherited wealth; and an almost certainly taxable estate. It all added up to "live one." If Marsha could hold on to them as clients for a full-scale estate plan, it would turn a rather disappointing month into a prosperous one indeed. That two-day continuing legal education course she had taken in advanced estate-planning techniques would turn out to have been a very sound investment.

As luck would have it, Cathy completed the brief interview just at eleven, as the coffee cart came through the building. So she was able to settle the McGarrys down with coffee, croissants, and copies of the *Asian Wall Street Journal* and *Town and Country*. Cathy went into Marsha's office, where she was yelling into the phone, "Well, forget it, Dale! If that's what it takes, we'll pay it to the IRS before we'll let that rhymes-with-rich of a client of yours get it. So stop wasting my client's money by wasting my time with this garbage!" Then she swiveled her chair, skimmed over the top page of the questionnaire, and said, "Good work, Cathy. Send 'em in."

After the opening civilities of introductions had been completed, Marsha said, "I hope you don't mind, but after I ask you a few more questions, I'd like to adjourn this meeting. I think you should bring an accountant into this estate-planning process. You're fortunate enough to have quite substantial assets, and I'd like to be sure that I have accurate valuations, and that everything is being handled properly on the financial end. Now, let me clarify—you have two children?"

"That's right," Charlotte McGarry said proudly. "Our sons, Teddy and Kevin. Both very successful young men."

"Both married?"

"My son Teddy is—you remember? He's your client too."

"Of course," Marsha said desperately. The computer terminal to the rescue: she punched a few keys, and the first page of his file appeared on the screen. "Oh, yes. A fairly basic estate plan for a newly married couple. Each of them has a will. They left most of their estates to each other, if they die without children; most of the estates to the children, in equal shares. And I included a simple testamentary trust in case they both die while their children are minors. But that wouldn't be the appropriate estate plan for you. For one thing, although both Teddy and Helen are quite successful financially—for people their age—they don't have anything approaching a taxable estate. However, unless you do some fairly sophisticated estate planning, you *will* face substantial estate tax liability.

"Now, one thing I often do is to have each spouse leave the entire estate to the other. That means that there won't be any estate tax for the first one to die, because there's an unlimited marital deduction. But in a larger estate, such as yours, that would mean that the estate tax is bunched up in the second estate. So we have several options. For one thing, would you like to leave money to your children—and grandchildren, if you have them?"

"I suppose so," Roger McGarry said. "Still, I'd rather see my sons work and make something of themselves, instead of sitting on their bottoms—excuse me, dear—waiting for my money."

"Oh, certainly," Charlotte McGarry countered. "If one is privileged to have nice things, or if one has been fortunate, I think those things should be kept in the family."

"Very good," Marsha said. "Now, would you be interested in making substantial charitable contributions?" The McGarrys answered simultaneously: he said, "A lot of damned superstitious nonsense," and she said, "Yes, the good sisters, and there are some local organizations that do so much good. . . ."

The rest of the interview went that way. The McGarrys agreed to see an accountant about the valuation of the stock in the machine tool company. The stock was covered by an agreement under which the company would buy it back from Mr. McGarry's estate, for its "fair market value" at the time of his death—but no one was too sure what that was. The business was flourishing, but the stock wasn't traded on any stock exchange; it would either be impossible to sell outside the company, or all too easy—if a competitor wanted an easy way to take over the business. It was also necessary to get appraisals of Mrs. McGarry's stock portfolio, and of the houses, the antiques, and the silver.

Marsha attempted, delicately, to point out that Mrs. McGarry could either learn about financial management or could hire competent professional help if she survived her husband and inherited much of his wealth. But she never put political correctness ahead of keeping a rich client happy, so she yielded to Roger McGarry's desire that trusts be established for the benefit of his widow.

Marsha followed traditional estate-planning principles, and took steps to try to equalize the two estates. After all, it would be impossible to predict which would die first (especially since Mrs. McGarry had had a mastectomy). Mr. McGarry made large outright gifts to his wife—again, there was no gift tax, and the effect was to get the amounts out of his potentially taxable estate (at the risk of ending up in hers). Both houses were in his name; he left them to her, but only for life. After her death, the family home would go to Teddy, and the ski house would go to Kevin.

Other traditional estate-planning techniques were used. For one thing, the McGarrys set up a program of gift giving during their lifetime. They could give up to $20,000 a year to any number of happy beneficiaries (each could give up to $10,000 a year per donee); they did make regular gifts to Teddy and Helen, and to Kevin. Charlotte McGarry began to make regular lifetime charitable contributions, but Roger McGarry could only be persuaded to do so in his will.

The final result was an eleven-page will for each of them (Teddy's and Helen's wills had been three pages each), with a complicated structure of trusts. Each of them signed a durable power of attorney. Charlotte designated Roger as her agent, with Marsha Blumbaum as an alternate if Roger died before she did or became incapacitated while he was acting as her agent. Roger couldn't be talked out of his belief that his wife fell inalterably into the classification "airhead," so he named his banker, Martin Carmody, as his agent.

Roger's will provided substantial bequests for his two children and any grandchildren who had come along by the time of his death; small bequests for his favorite nieces and nephews; and medium-sized charitable bequests (to his alma mater and the town public library and historical society). He also set up trusts that ensured that Charlotte would have more than adequate income throughout her life, although she would not have control over the investment or disposition of the money. The trusts provided that if Charlotte survived him, the trust funds would be distributed among their children and grandchildren after her death.

Charlotte's will provided that all her assets would go to Roger if he survived her; because this was considered unlikely, the will went into much greater detail about the possibility that she would survive him. Charlotte left large charitable bequests (to her local church, to the Sisters of Charity, to the American Cancer Society, and the Sierra Club). The charitable bequests were designed to be large enough to reduce her estate so that no estate tax would be payable. The rest of her estate was to be divided among her children, grandchildren, nieces, and nephews.

Helen and Teddy continued to visit their lawyer regularly, for updates on the will. (They changed lawyers a couple of times, once after an argument with Marsha, and once when they moved to Seattle.) Eventually, they had a daughter (Kevin got married and had two sons and a daughter), and duly worried about her education costs—but they never did have to worry about estate tax, because they never accumulated a large-enough estate.

Astute estate planning invariably calls for professional assistance. Keeping up with laws in flux is beyond the ken of most of us who do not hold law degrees. But legal jargon is not the only thing that keeps many people from dealing with estate-planning issues—the idea of discussing death is very uncomfortable for many. Think of it this way: to ignore estate planning may cause unnecessary distress for heirs and would-be heirs. Charlotte and Roger McGarry took the proper steps when they set their estate-planning strategies. You can too.

# 19

## Create Financial Success

Your success in life does not altogether depend on ability and training; it also depends on your determination to seize opportunities that are presented to you. It's one thing to read up on the principles of personal financial planning. But putting those principles to work is another matter. The question is: Can you be a winner in the lifetime race for financial success? Or are you content to be a mere champion of wishful thinking? So many people go through life developing lists of good intentions. The winners, meanwhile, are busy putting their plans in motion.

Veterans of the stock market will tell you that for every winner there's a loser. For every smart play, there's a gambit gone sour. The same polarity applies to financial security. You have a choice: you can either take charge of all the money in your life—and become a winner!—or you can let opportunities slip through your fingers.

### Become a Winner!

What does it mean to become a winner? For one thing, a winner does not waste time and energy fretting over financial decisions. A winner approaches money decisions with confidence. A winner studies all the options, considers the short- and long-term effects of different scenarios, then acts. A winner does not get blind-sided.

What's more, a winner does not know the meaning of the word "lazy." There was an interesting study done last year of America's self-made millionaires. The one thing they all had in common was an incredible energy level. Each and every one reported working upwards of sixty hours per week building their fortunes. Whether a chocolate chip cookie bakery, a dry cleaning business, or a personal computer manufacturer, the owner literally built the thing with true grit. The study also showed that most of these financial heroes still worked night and day, even after they had hit the jackpot.

That ability to create a financial empire is rare—not everyone is prepared to make the personal sacrifices required to become a self-made millionaire. But the quintessential American drama, the rags-to-riches story, is inspiring. It says that you *can* wrap your family in a blanket of financial security, if you put your mind to it.

### Your Ability to Win

This chapter began with the idea that there is more to financial success than ability and training. Let's now return to the subject of money management skills; for most assuredly, the ability to make smart money decisions comes after you have learned to use the right tools and techniques.

Throughout this book, we have introduced you to the principles of sound money management. We urged you to get your ducks in order, so to speak, by setting realistic financial goals. We talked about creating a family budget and why you should stick by it. Different kinds of savings goals were explored, as was the sudden impact of life's financial transitions. We taught you how to manage credit, invest wisely, handle family taxes, and plan for retirement. In essence, we tried to demystify the subject of smart money management. We gave it to you in plain English, so you'd know how to make clever financial moves at different times of your life. In a word, we gave you perspective. "Don't Take Any Wooden Nickels!" could have been the subtitle of this book.

What you need now is the confidence to pull the right levers, the nerve to seize opportunities for creating financial success. But financial confidence comes gradually. If you are just getting your feet wet in the world of investing, for example, we do not expect that you will be playing the options market next week. In fact, we want you to go at your own pace. Get a good feel for what you are doing, and be prepared to make a few mistakes. When it comes to aggressive investing, one surefire way to gain a healthy respect for the risks involved is to experience the pain of a poor decision. Once you've taken a bath or two in the stock market, you'll know why we advised you to seek long-term capital appreciation through mutual funds.

### One Step at a Time

You should begin taking charge of the money in your life one step at a time. It makes sense to first study your sources of income. How much money do you need today to live the way you want to? What steps must you take to bring your life-style in line with your ability to generate income? Next, how much money will you need over the course of a lifetime? Are your goals realistic? Or should you begin to prioritize your expenditures now so that you won't be broke when your children go off to college or when you are retired? Do you have a financial contingency plan? Put another way, are you living too close to the edge? If your spouse gets sick and cannot work, and you find yourself suddenly hurtling toward insolvency, how will you cope?

Building financial security is like building a house. You have to pour the concrete before you can install the picture window. The point is that before you begin practicing some of the more savvy wealth-building techniques described in this book, you must create a solid foundation. It does you no good to start buying rental properties if you cannot survive an acute financial crisis.

Once your financial foundation is under way, you ought to consider how you might simplify the plethora of financial services in your life. For example, you do not need four bank accounts between you and your spouse. Close out the ones you do not really need, and allocate family cash flows so that you achieve what businesspeople affectionately call "economies of scale."

For example, you might have both spouses' paychecks deposited directly into a money market mutual fund. From there, you can easily call the fund, perhaps on a regular monthly basis, and instruct it to move certain amounts into each spouse's IRA. Retirement plan investing is much easier—and you get more bang for your buck!—when you use this self-disciplining technique. You make your IRA contributions in small chunks as the tax year progresses, and, as we discussed in earlier chapters, you can capture more of the power of tax-deferred compounding that IRAs provide.

Your IRAs, of course, reside in mutual funds administered by the same investment company that runs the money fund. The idea is to get your paycheck in an interest-earning vehicle pronto. If, instead, you take your paycheck to the bank each week, deposit it, and pay household bills from that account, it is hard to maintain the balance minimums some banks require to qualify for money market interest rates. Why not pay your larger household bills with checks written on the money fund account? While the mortgage check is in the process of collection, you will be earning competitive rates of return on your cash. And if you need to pay lots of smaller bills with checks, and your money fund requires that its checks be written for at least $500, you can still use a bank checking account. Why not fund your bank account with a money fund check? There's no reason why you should not take advantage of check-clearing float—banks make money from check-clearing float; you should too!

There is more to this notion of economies of scale. Let's say you are an active investor. By using your money fund as a home base, you can attempt to time the financial markets, moving certain amounts out of your money fund and into a stock market mutual fund when you believe the market is about to take off. Similarly, when you feel the stock market has reached a temporary high (you expect stock prices to decline), you can deftly switch certain amounts back into your money fund account. You can be out of harm's way with one simple phone call to the fund family. How do you know when to switch? Take another look at chapter 4 (we explained the Donoghue approach to market timing and how we track the effectiveness of mutual fund switching in our investment newsletters).

Moreover, if you are a very active investor, you may want to consolidate your finances in a central asset account (such as Merrill Lynch's CMA or Fidelity Investments' USA Account). The idea is to have your credit/debit card purchases, margin account loans, direct market investments, mutual funds, and checking account all conveniently located under one umbrella. The most practical benefit you receive from this umbrella account is that every transaction you make is recorded on one comprehensive monthly statement. Why spend your precious leisure time sorting through mountains of paperwork? Get the financial service companies to do some of the grunt work for you.

### Never Stop Simplifying

We think it makes sense to look for economies of scale wherever they may lurk in your financial life. Next time an insurance agent comes calling, be sure you really need more insurance before you sign on the dotted line. Tally how much coverage you and your spouse already have before you add to it. Perhaps you are adequately covered already. Many people forget about the insurance coverage (health care, disability, and life) provided by their employers. Maybe you are better off allocating your resources so that you have more money to invest. Why load up on unnecessary insurance coverage? And why, for goodness' sake, add more complications to your busy schedule? Unnecessary insurance policies also mean more record keeping.

### Search Out and Destroy Hidden Fees

Throughout this book we spent a lot of time discussing the hidden fees that permeate financial services. One of the major challenges you face as you begin your quest for financial security is to slash the costs of buying financial products and services. Once you have poured the concrete for your financial plan, you can search out and destroy unnecessary fees. In this book, we have described alternate routes to the financial markets; for example, we suggested that you invest through no-load or low-load mutual funds instead of paying a stockbroker to sell your securities. We also urged you to consolidate your credit cards so that you are not paying hefty annual maintenance fees to every bank under the sun. Most important, we gave you the tools to begin making financial decisions on your own. In the final analysis, you should not have to pay a financial planner to tell you, for instance, that you need a budget and an IRA.

In our discussion of family taxes, we mentioned common, and quite legal, tax deductions that many people never bother to take. You must realize that paying Uncle Sam more than necessary is, in a sense, getting hit by hidden fees. Why should you pay when you don't have to?

We often read in the newspapers that a certain company has gone on a cost-cutting binge. A hiring freeze, layoffs, and cutbacks in expenditures are the buzz words. (You also hear that the federal government is trying to trim its fat, but, well, we know that is a never-ending story.) When it comes to creating financial success, you must remember, as long as your expenses outpace your income, you are never going to make any progress. With that in mind, we urge you to review all your expenditures carefully, including your purchases of financial services, and, where appropriate, trim the fat. Once you have a firm grip on where your money is going—and the power to stem the tide of unnecessary expenses—you will be able to use effectively the strategies described in this book.

### A Final Word on Financial Transitions

In addition to the principles of sound money management, we considered many of life's financial surprises. For example, we observed the tax consequences of divorce and the burden of medical expenses on the elderly. These scenarios should get you thinking about lifetime finances in a context that is broader than, say, investing or building a credit rating.

There is no easy way, as far as we can tell, to weather the emotional stress of divorce, family illness, or any number of unexpected family crises. But it helps if you do not have to face financial chaos or complexity at such a trying time in your life.

Perhaps the trusted "uncle" of yesteryear's extended family would advise during troubling times: "Life is not a bed of roses." How true. Nonetheless, the ability to make smart money decisions goes a long way—no matter where the winds of fate are blowing.

In that spirit, we urge you to use the financial lessons presented here as reference points. Go back over the appropriate chapters as life's financial transitions head your way. Never relent in your efforts to learn more about the money in your life, and never give up your quest for financial success. We have given you the tools and described the techniques for seizing financial opportunities. Now you must do what it takes to become a winner.

# Appendix A

| Firm | SLYC Funds | Money Market Mutual Funds |
|------|-----------|---------------------------|
| AMA Advisers, Inc.<br>5 Sentry Parkway West<br>Suite 120<br>P.O. Box 1111<br>Blue Bell, PA 19422<br>(800) 523-0864<br>(215) 825-0400 (PA-collect) | AMA Advisers: Medical Technology Fund | AMA M.F./Prime Port.<br>AMA M.F./Treas. Port. |
| Jones & Babson, Inc.<br>2440 Pershing Road G-15<br>Kansas City, MO 64108<br>(800) 821-5591<br>(816) 471-5200 | Babson Growth Fund | Babson M.M.F. Federal Port.<br>Babson M.M.F. Prime Port.<br>Babson Tax-Free Income Fund M.M.P. |
| Boston Company Fund Dist., Inc.<br>31 St. James Avenue<br>Boston, MA 02116<br>(800) 225-5267<br>(617) 956-9740 | Boston Co. Capital Appreciation Fund | Boston Co. Cash Mgt.<br>Boston Co. Gov't M.F.<br>Boston Co. MA Tax-Free Fund<br>Boston Co. Tax-Free M.F. |

| Firm | SLYC Funds | Money Market Mutual Funds |
|------|-----------|---------------------------|
| Bull & Bear Group, Inc.<br>11 Hanover Square<br>New York, NY 10005<br>(800) 847-4200<br>(212) 363-1100 | Bull & Bear Capital<br>Growth Fund | Bull & Bear Dollar Reserves |
| Columbia Management Co.<br>P.O. Box 1350<br>Portland, OR 97207<br>(800) 547-1037<br>(503) 222-3600 (OR-collect) | Columbia Growth Fund | Columbia Daily Income |
| Dreyfus Service Corp. II<br>666 Old Country Road<br>Garden City, NY 11530<br>(800) 645-6561<br>(516) 794-5200<br>(718) 895-1206 (NYC) | Dreyfus Growth<br>Opportunity Fund<br>Dreyfus Third Century<br>Fund | Dreyfus Liquid Assets<br>Dreyfus M.M. Instruments<br>Gov't<br>Dreyfus Tax-Exempt<br>M.M.F. |
| Fidelity Investments Corp.<br>82 Devonshire Street<br>Boston, MA 02109<br>(800) 544-6666<br>(617) 523-1919 (MA-collect) | Fidelity Contrafund<br>Fidelity Discoverer Fund | Fidelity Cash Reserves<br>Fidelity Daily Income<br>Fidelity U.S. Gov't Reserves<br>Fidelity Mass. T-F/M.M.P.<br>Fidelity Tax-Exempt M.M.<br>Trust |
| Financial Programs, Inc.<br>P.O. Box 2040<br>Denver, CO 80201<br>(800) 332-9145 (CO)<br>(800) 525-9831<br>(303) 779-1233 | Financial Dynamics Fund | Financial Daily Income<br>Shares<br>Financial Tax-Free M.F. |
| Founders Mutual<br>Depositor Corp.<br>3033 E. First Avenue<br>Suite 810<br>Denver, CO 80206<br>(800) 525-2440<br>(800) 874-6301 (CO) | Founders Growth Fund<br>Founders Special Fund | Founders Money Market |

| Firm | SLYC Funds | Money Market Mutual Funds |
|------|------------|--------------------------|
| Janus Capital Corp., Inc.<br>100 Fillmore Street<br>Suite 300<br>Denver, CO 80206<br>(800) 525 3713<br>(303) 333-3863 | Janus Fund | Cash Equivalent Fund |
| Lexington Management<br>Corp.<br>P.O. Box 1515<br>Saddle Brook, NJ 07662<br>(800) 526-0057<br>(201) 845 7300 | Lexington Growth Fund<br>Lexington Research Fund | Lexington Gov't Securities<br>M.M.F.<br>Lexington Money Market<br>Lexington Tax-Free<br>M.F., Inc. |
| SAFECO Asset<br>Management Co.<br>P.O. Box 34890<br>Seattle, WA 98124<br>(800) 426-6730<br>(800) 562-6810 (WA)<br>(206) 545-5530 | SAFECO Growth Fund | SAFECO M.M.M.F.<br>SAFECO Tax-Free M.M.F. |
| Scudder Stevens & Clark<br>175 Federal Street<br>Boston, MA 02110<br>(800) 453-3305<br>(617) 482-3990 (MA-collect) | Scudder Capital<br>Growth Fund<br>Scudder Development<br>Fund<br>Scudder International<br>Fund | Scudder Cash<br>Investment Trust<br>Scudder Government M.F.<br>Scudder Tax-Free M.F. |
| Stein Roe & Farnham<br>P.O. Box 1143<br>Chicago, IL 60690<br>(800) 621-0320<br>(312) 368-7826 (IL-collect) | Stein Roe & Farnham<br>Capital Opportunities<br>Fund<br>Stein Roe Special Fund<br>Stein Roe & Farnham<br>Stock Fund<br>Stein Roe Universe Fund | SteinRoe Cash Reserves<br>SteinRoe Gov't Reserves<br>SteinRoe Tax-Exempt M.F. |
| T. Rowe Price<br>Associates, Inc.<br>100 E. Pratt Street<br>Baltimore, MD 21202<br>(800) 638-5660<br>(301) 547-2308 (MD-collect) | T. Rowe Price Growth<br>Stock Fund<br>T. Rowe Price<br>International Fund<br>T. Rowe Price New<br>Era Fund<br>T. Rowe Price New<br>Horizons Fund | T. Rowe Price Prime<br>Reserve<br>T. Rowe Price U.S. Treas.<br>M.F.<br>T. Rowe Price T-E M.F. |

| Firm | SLYC Funds | Money Market Mutual Funds |
|------|-----------|--------------------------|
| USAA Investment Management Co. 9800 Fredricksburg Road San Antonio, TX 78288 (800) 531-8181 (800) 292-8181 (TX) (512) 498-7270 | USAA Mutual Growth Fund USAA Sunbelt Era Fund | USAA Federal Securities M.M.F. USAA Money Market Fund USAA Tax-Exempt M.M.F. |
| Value Line Securities, Inc. 711 Third Avenue New York, NY 10017 (800) 223-0818 (212) 687-3965 | Value Line Fund Value Line Leveraged Growth Investors Value Line Special Situations | Value Line Cash Fund Value Line Tax-Exempt Fund |
| Vanguard Group P.O. Box 2600 Valley Forge, PA 19496 (800) 662-7447 (215) 648-6000 | Vanguard Explorer Fund Vanguard Morgan Growth Fund Vanguard Windsor Fund | Vanguard M.M.T. Federal Vanguard M.M.T. Insured Port. Vanguard M.M.T. Prime Vanguard Muni. Bond M.M. |

# Appendix B

**Compounded Savings Interest Rate Table**

| Nominal Annual Rate | The True Annual Rate If Compounded | | | | |
|---|---|---|---|---|---|
| | Semiannually | Quarterly | Monthly | Weekly | Daily |
| 3.00 | 3.0225 | 3.0339 | 3.0415 | 3.0445 | 3.0453 |
| 3.25 | 3.2764 | 3.2898 | 3.2988 | 3.3023 | 3.3032 |
| 3.50 | 3.5306 | 3.5462 | 3.5566 | 3.5607 | 3.5617 |
| 3.75 | 3.7851 | 3.8030 | 3.8151 | 3.8197 | 3.8209 |
| 4.00 | 4.0400 | 4.0601 | 4.0711 | 4.0701 | 4.0808 |
| 4.25 | 4.2951 | 4.3182 | 4.3337 | 4.3397 | 4.3413 |
| 4.50 | 4.5506 | 4.5765 | 4.5939 | 4.6007 | 4.6024 |
| 4.75 | 4.8064 | 4.8352 | 4.8547 | 4.8623 | 4.8642 |
| 5.00 | 5.0625 | 5.0945 | 5.1161 | 5.1245 | 5.1267 |
| 5.25 | 5.3189 | 5.3542 | 5.3781 | 5.3874 | 5.3898 |
| 5.50 | 5.5756 | 5.6144 | 5.6407 | 5.6509 | 5.6536 |
| 5.75 | 5.8326 | 5.8751 | 5.9039 | 5.9151 | 5.9180 |
| 6.00 | 6.0900 | 6.1363 | 6.1677 | 6.1799 | 6.1831 |
| 6.25 | 6.3476 | 6.3980 | 6.4321 | 6.4454 | 6.4488 |
| 6.50 | 6.6056 | 6.6601 | 6.6971 | 6.7115 | 6.7152 |
| 6.75 | 6.8639 | 6.9227 | 6.9627 | 6.9783 | 6.9823 |
| 7.00 | 7.1225 | 7.1859 | 7.2290 | 7.2457 | 7.2500 |
| 7.25 | 7.3814 | 7.4495 | 7.4958 | 7.5138 | 7.5185 |
| 7.50 | 7.6406 | 7.7135 | 7.7632 | 7.7825 | 7.7875 |
| 7.75 | 7.9001 | 7.9781 | 8.0312 | 8.0519 | 8.0573 |
| 8.00 | 8.1600 | 8.2432 | 8.2999 | 8.3220 | 8.3277 |
| 8.25 | 8.4201 | 8.5087 | 8.5692 | 8.5927 | 8.5988 |

**Compounded Savings Interest Rate Table** *(Continued)*

| Nominal Annual Rate | The True Annual Rate If Compounded | | | | |
|---|---|---|---|---|---|
| | Semiannually | Quarterly | Monthly | Weekly | Daily |
| 8.50 | 8.6806 | 8.7747 | 8.8390 | 8.8641 | 8.8706 |
| 8.75 | 8.9414 | 9.0413 | 9.1095 | 9.1362 | 9.1430 |
| 9.00 | 9.2025 | 9.3083 | 9.3806 | 9.4089 | 9.4162 |
| 9.25 | 9.4639 | 9.5758 | 9.6524 | 9.6823 | 9.6900 |
| 9.50 | 9.7256 | 9.8438 | 9.9247 | 9.9563 | 9.9645 |
| 9.75 | 9.9876 | 10.1123 | 10.1977 | 10.2310 | 10.2397 |
| 10.00 | 10.2500 | 10.3812 | 10.4713 | 10.5064 | 10.5155 |
| 11.00 | 11.3025 | 11.4621 | 11.5718 | 11.6148 | 11.6259 |
| 12.00 | 12.3600 | 12.5508 | 12.6825 | 12.7340 | 12.7474 |
| 13.00 | 13.4225 | 13.6475 | 13.8032 | 13.8643 | 13.8802 |
| 14.00 | 14.4900 | 14.7523 | 14.9342 | 15.0057 | 15.0242 |
| 15.00 | 15.5625 | 15.8650 | 16.0754 | 16.1583 | 16.1798 |

# Glossary

**accrued interest**  The interest due on a bond or other fixed-income security that must be paid by the buyer of the security to the seller.

**annuity**  A contract where the buyer (annuitant) pays a sum of money to receive regular payments for life or a fixed period of time.

**asked price**  The net asset value per share plus sales charge, if any. The asked price of a stock refers to the price at which the seller is willing to sell.

**asset**  Any item of value. Several classifications including: tangible asset—an item that can readily be assigned a dollar value (hard assets fall into this category, but it is usually reserved for gold and silver); current asset—an item that can be turned into cash in a year or less; fixed asset—an item used for business, such as machinery; intangible asset—an item that cannot be readily assigned a dollar value, like the goodwill of a business.

**automatic reinvestment**  A plan that allows shareholders to receive dividend distributions in the form of new shares instead of cash.

**automatic withdrawal**  See check-a-month plan.

**back-end load**  The fee charged when a redemption takes place. See load.

**balance sheet**  A financial statement showing the dollar amounts of a company's or person's assets, liabilities, and owner's equity.

**balanced fund**  A mutual fund that has an investment policy of "balancing" its portfolio, generally by including bonds, preferred stocks, and common stocks.

**bankers' acceptances (BAs)**  Short-term, noninterest-bearing notes sold at a discount and redeemed at maturity for full face value. Primarily used to finance foreign trade. BAs represent a future claim on a U.S. bank that provides lines of credit to U.S. importers. BAs are collateralized by the goods to be sold and are guaranteed by the importer's U.S. bank.

**basis point**   Term used to describe amount of change in yield. One hundred basis points equal 1 percent. An increase from 8 percent to 10 percent would be a change of 200 basis points.

**bear market**   A sustained period of falling stock prices usually preceding or accompanied by a period of poor economic performance known as a recession. The opposite of a bull market.

**beta**   Term used to describe the price volatility of securities. Standard & Poor's Index is set at a beta of one; anything assigned a beta above one is considered to be more volatile than the Index; anything below one has less volatility than the S&P Index.

**bid**   The price at which someone will buy a security.

**blue chip**   The common stock of a major corporation with a long, relatively stable record of earnings and dividend payments.

**bond**   A security representing debt; a loan from the bondholder to the corporation. The bondholder usually receives semiannual interest payments with principal being refunded at maturity.

**bond fund**   A mutual fund whose portfolio consists primarily of bonds. The emphasis is normally on income rather than growth.

**bond maturity**   The time at which an issuer redeems a bond. The investor is paid the full face value plus any accrued interest.

**broker**   A person in the business of effecting securities transactions for others, for a commission. There are two types of brokers: full-service brokers, who give advice, and discount brokers, who do not give advice (the investor must do his own research).

**bull market**   A stock market that is characterized by rising prices over a long period of time. The time span is not precise, but it represents a period of investor optimism, lower interest rates, and economic growth. The opposite of a bear market.

**capital appreciation**   An increase in value, such as in real estate, stock or bond prices.

**capital gain**   A long-term capital gain is a profit from the sale of a capital asset, such as a security, that has been held for over six months. A short-term capital gain is the profit from selling a capital asset in less than six months. Both are subject to federal tax at ordinary income rates.

**capital loss**   A loss from the sale of a capital asset. Up to $3,000 may be deducted in one year, and if the loss is greater than the amount allowed for one year, the excess may be carried over to future years until it is used up.

**cash flow**   The cash flow from an investment is the total of dividends, interest payments, realized profits, and any return of principal you receive.

**cash value**   Certain types of life insurance policies allow a "savings portion" of the premium payment to accumulate to a cash value.

**certificate**   The actual piece of paper that certifies ownership of stock in a corporation.

**certificate of deposit (CD)**   Generally, a short-term debt instrument certificate issued by commercial banks or savings and loan associations. (Euro CDs are issued by foreign branches of U.S. banks; Yankee CDs are issued by U.S. branches of foreign banks.)

**check-a-month plan** An arrangement many open-end companies have that enables investors to receive fixed payments, usually monthly or quarterly. The actual payout is determined by the investor.

**closed-end management company** A company that issues a fixed number of shares that usually must be traded in the securities market. Closed-end investment company shares are usually bought and sold through brokers.

**COLA** Cost-of-living adjustment.

**collectible** A physical object that has value by virtue of its rarity, intrinsic or artistic value.

**commercial paper (CP)** Unsecured promissory notes of corporations, with maturities of up to 270 days. Used as a money market instrument.

**commission** The fee paid to a broker for buying or selling securities as an agent.

**common-law employee** An employee who works for a self-employed person, a partnership, or a corporation but who has no financial interest in the employer's trade, business, or profession.

**common stock** Securities that represent ownership in a corporation.

**compound interest** Interest computed on the interest as well as the principal.

**consumer price index (CPI)** Index that analyzes the change in prices for consumer goods and services over time.

**conversion privilege** See exchange privilege.

**convertible securities** A bond, debenture, or preferred stock that gives its owner the right to exchange that security for common stock or another type of security issued by the same company.

**correction** Used in conjunction with a bull market. It is a sustained period of stock price declining in the midst of long-term rising stock prices. Corrections are usually followed by another period of rising stock prices. A major correction refers to a decline of 10 percent or more in the widely accepted stock market indexes.

**coupon** A promise to pay interest when due, coupons are usually attached to a bond. When the coupon comes due, it is clipped and presented for payment. The term also refers to a bond's stated interest rate.

**custodian** The organization that holds in custody and safekeeping the securities and other assets of a mutual fund or individual.

**DEFRA** Deficit Reduction Act of 1984.

**dealer** A person or firm who regularly buys and sells securities for others from his or her own account of securities. In contrast, a broker acts as an agent for others. Frequently, broker and dealer functions are synonymous.

**debenture** A bond secured by the general credit of the corporation, and usually not secured by any collateral.

**debt instrument** Any instrument that signifies a loan between a borrower and a lender.

**declaration of dividends** Announcement by issuer of bonds or equities of their decision to make a payment to their shareholders. Some companies do this on a regular basis, while others may declare a dividend only when company earnings have reached a certain predetermined level. Many money funds declare dividends daily but pay monthly.

**deep discount bond**  A type of bond that is selling below 80 percent of its par (face) value. The face value of a bond is usually $1,000.

**defined benefit plan**  A retirement plan offered by employers that promises to pay out a predetermined annual amount during retirement years.

**depreciation**  The estimated decline in the value of property due to use, deterioration, or obsolescence over a period of time.

**discount**  The amount by which a preferred stock or bond may sell below its face value.

**discretionary accounts**  An account in which an investment adviser or broker has the full right to buy and sell securities without consultation or authorization of the investor.

**distribution fee**  Under 12b-1 plans, a fund that does not have its own sales force is allowed to take a percentage of the assets as a fee to pay indepedent brokers for selling its funds.

**distributions**  Dividends paid from net investment income and payments made from realized capital gains of a mutual fund.

**distributor**  The principal underwriter—either a person or a company—that purchases open-end investment company shares directly from the issuer for resale to others.

**diversification**  The policy of spreading investments among a number of different securities to reduce the risk inherent in investing. Diversification may be among types of securities, different companies, different industries, or different geographical locations.

**diversified investment company**  To be so classified, the Investment Company Act requires that 75 percent of a fund's assets be allocated so that not more than 5 percent of its total assets are invested in one company. In addition, it can hold no more than 10 percent of the outstanding voting securities of another company.

**dividend**  A payment declared by a corporation's board of directors, and made to shareholders, usually on a quarterly basis.

**dollar cost-averaging**  Method of investing equal amounts of money at regular intervals regardless of whether the stock market is moving upward or downward. The theory is that the investor's average cost will be lower than if he invested larger amounts irregularly over the same amount of time.

**earned income**  Net profits derived from the business, less retirement plan contributions, for a self-employed person. For "common-law" employees of a self-employed or corporate business, earnings are taxable wages received.

**employee stock ownership plan (ESOP)**  A qualified employee benefit plan that invests in securities of the parent company.

**equity**  Represents stock ownership of a company.

**equity fund**  A mutual fund that invests primarily in stocks.

**ERISA**  The Employee Retirement Income Security Act of 1974. It represented the most sweeping overhaul of pension and employee benefit rules in four decades. ERISA requires that if an employer elects to provide employee benefits, the benefits must meet ERISA guidelines under labor and tax law provisions. ERISA rules have since been overhauled by legislation enacted in 1982 and 1984.

**Eurodollars**   U.S. dollars deposited in foreign branches of U.S. banks or foreign banks located outside the U.S.

**exchange privilege**   The right to take all or some of the shares of one fund and put them into another fund within the same family of funds. This is considered a sale and new purchase for tax purposes. (Same as a conversion or switching privilege.)

**ex-dividend date**   The date on which stock is sold without dividend. Under the five-day delivery plan, buyers of the stock on the fourth business day preceding the stockholder of record date will not receive the declared dividend. Most stock exchanges operate on the five-day plan.

**face value**   The value that appears on the face of a bond. This is the amount the issuing company will pay at maturity, but it does not necessarily indicate market price.

**family of funds**   A group of mutual funds managed by the same investment company. One company may manage several different funds, each with different objectives, such as growth, income, or tax-exempt funds.

**FDIC (Federal Deposit Insurance Corporation)**   The federal agency that insures deposits up to $100,000 at member banks. FDIC also makes loans to buy assets from member banks to facilitate mergers or help prevent bank failures.

**fiduciary**   An individual or corporation who is entrusted with certain assets for a specified purpose. Also known as trustee, executor, guardian.

**fixed annuity**   An annuity contract that provides for fixed payments at regular intervals.

**401(k)**   A qualified employee benefit plan where employee contributions are made on a pretax basis. Both employer and employee contributions compound tax free until withdrawn.

**front-end load**   A sales charge for buying into a mutual fund.

**frozen plan**   A qualified retirement plan to which contributions are no longer being made.

**FSLIC (Federal Savings and Loan Insurance Corporation)**   The federal agency established to insure funds on deposit at member S&Ls.

**fully invested**   One hundred percent invested position. All money is considered to be earning dividends, capital gains, interest, or a mixture of any of these, in contrast to only a portion of the invested money having earning capabilities.

**fund assets**   The total dollar amount invested in a fund.

**fund representative**   A federally licensed (registered) person qualified to give investors information about, and sell, a fund.

**government securities**   A general term that includes any instruments of debt issued by the U.S. government.

**gross income**   Income before any deductions or expenses are taken out.

**growth fund**   A mutual fund that has growth of capital as its primary objective, to be obtained principally through investments in common stocks with growth potential. This type of fund will primarily generate long- and short-term capital gains rather than pay dividends.

**growth-income fund**   A mutual fund whose objective is to provide both income and long-term growth.

**guaranteed investment contract (GIC)**  A fixed income investment with a specified interest rate and date of maturity. Offered by insurance companies, it is a common investment vehicle selected for voluntary contribution funds.

**holding company**  A company that owns the majority of stock or securities of, as well as manages, one or more other companies.

**illiquid**  An asset that is difficult to quickly convert into cash.

**immediate annuity**  An annuity contract that starts making payments to the annuitant almost immediately—within one year of the contract's purchase.

**income fund**  A mutual fund that has current income as its primary objective.

**index**  A mathematically derived number used as an indicator of trends in the market.

**Individual Retirement Account (IRA)**  A retirement plan that can be started by anyone who earns employment income. Investment earnings on IRA money is tax-deferred, usually until retirement at age fifty-nine and a half or older. The deductibility of annual IRA contributions is limited to taxpayers who meet income guidelines defined in the Tax Code of 1986.

**inflation**  The economic condition of rising prices for goods and services. It is characterized by an increasing volume of currency in circulation and a decline in the buying power of cash.

**institutions-only funds**  Funds that allow only corporate, depository institution, or pension fund investors to buy shares. Some funds that claim to be institutions-only will allow individuals to invest if they can meet the (usually high) minimum initial investment.

**interest**  Periodic payments made to a lender of money by the borrower for use of the money borrowed.

**investment company**  Generic term including mutual funds, unit investment trusts, and other types of companies that sell their shares to the public and invest the proceeds according to stated investment objectives.

**investment objective**  The specific goal, such as long-term capital growth or current income, that the investor or mutual fund pursues.

**IRA**  See Individual Retirement Account.

**IRA rollover**  The removal of IRA money from one investment and placement of this money into another investment. A rollover involves the individual receiving the money and reinvesting it. Rollovers must be completed within sixty days and are only allowed once a year.

**IRA transfer**  Movement of IRA funds from one investment to another. The IRA investor does not receive the money; it goes directly into the other investment. A transfer is allowed at any time.

**Keogh plan**  A tax-qualified retirement program for self-employed individuals and their employees.

**leverage**  The use of borrowed money with invested funds to increase returns. The effect is to magnify profits or losses and increase the amount of risk.

**liability**  Any debt owed by a company or individual. Usually classified as a current liability (due in one year or less) or a long-term liability (due in over one year).

**liquid**  May be easily converted into cash or exchanged for other assets.

**liquidate**  To convert an asset into cash.

**load**  A portion of the offering price that goes toward selling costs such as sales commissions and distribution. A front-end load is the fee charged when buying into a fund. A back-end load is the fee charged when getting out of a fund.

**long-term investment**   For federal tax purposes, an investment held for over six months.

**lump-sum distribution**   A payment made to an individual of the proceeds of his or her employee benefit plan account.

**management company**   A company that manages the day-to-day operations of a mutual fund (see open-end and closed-end management company). Also called an investment company.

**management fee**   The amount paid to the administrator and/or management company (who may also serve as an investment adviser) for service.

**margin account**   A brokerage account that allows an investor to buy or sell securities on credit. An investor can purchase additional securities against the value of cash and securities in the account.

**margin, buying on**   Buying securities on credit from a broker.

**market order**   An order to buy or sell a stated amount of a security at the best possible price as soon as it can be accomplished.

**market price**   The last reported price at which a security has been sold.

**market rate**   A general term used to describe the current interest rate on a given instrument.

**maturity**   The scheduled date for repayment of the principal amount of a debt instrument.

**money market fund**   Mutual fund that invests in short-term, relatively riskless money market instruments such as bank certificates of deposit, bankers' acceptances, commercial paper, and short-term government securities.

**municipal bond fund**   An open-end company or unit investment trust that invests in diversified holdings of federal tax-exempt securities issued by state, city, and local governments.

**mutual fund**   An open-end or closed-end investment company that pools the money of its shareholders into one professionally managed account; investments are made in a wide variety of securities.

**net asset value per share**   The total market value of an investment company's shares—securities, cash, and any accrued earnings—minus its liabilities, and then divided by the number of shares outstanding.

**net income**   Income less expenses and deductions.

**no-load fund**   A fund that does not charge sales fees. Investors purchase shares directly from the fund, rather than through an investment dealer or broker.

**NOW account**   Negotiable order of withdrawal account. An interest-bearing checking and savings account.

**odd lot**   The usual amount when buying shares of stock is 100 shares (a "round lot"). When you buy less than 100 shares it is called an odd lot; commissions vary with the number of shares bought.

**offering price**   The lowest price at which shares are offered for sale. (Also called asked price.)

**open-end management company**   An investment company that continuously sells and redeems shares.

**option**   The right to buy (call option) or sell (put option) a fixed quantity of a security, at a stated price, within a specific amount of time.

**options fund**   A mutual fund that sells options on its shares to increase its income.

**ordinary income**   Income taxed at the maximum rate schedule, such as employment income or income from a business.

**over-the-counter**   The nationwide network of brokers/dealers who buy and sell securities that, for the most part, are not listed on an exchange.

**owner-employee**   A self-employed person who owns or who has at least a 10 percent interest in a business or partnership.

**penny stock**   Any stock that is very low-priced and often speculative.

**periodic payment plan**   An arrangement that allows an investor to purchase mutual fund shares periodically, usually with provisions for the reinvestment of income dividends and the acceptance of capital gains distributions in additional shares.

**plan administrator**   The individual who maintains records, prepares reports, and generally manages a group's employee benefit plan.

**portfolio**   The total investment holdings owned by an investment company or an individual.

**preferred stock**   A class of stock that has prior claim on dividends before common stockholders. In the event of corporate liquidation, preferred stockholders have a prior claim on assets over common shareholders.

**premium**   The amount by which a bond or preferred stock sells above its face value.

**profit**   The amount earned when the selling price is higher than the cost.

**prospectus**   The official written statement that describes a mutual fund, or any security, and offers it for sale. In the case of a fund, the prospectus contains information required by the Securities and Exchange Commission on: investment objectives and policies, services, investment restrictions, officers and directors, procedure to buy and sell shares, fees, and financial statements.

**proxy**   The written transfer of voting rights to someone who will then vote according to the wishes of the shareholder. Usually done if the shareholder cannot be present at the stockholders' meeting.

**qualified retirement plan**   A private retirement plan that meets the rules and regulations of the Internal Revenue Service. Earnings on contributions made to such plans are tax-deferred, usually until retirement. Most company pension plans are qualified retirement plans.

**redeem**   To buy back shares from the present owner (see redemption price).

**redemption price**   The amount per share a mutual fund shareholder receives when he cashes in his shares (also known as "liquidating price" or "bid price"). The value of the shares depends on the market value of the company's portfolio securities at the time.

**reinvestment privilege**   A service provided by most mutual funds for the automatic purchase of additional shares with the shareholder's dividends and capital gains distributions.

**return on investment**   Percent gain including reinvestment of capital gains and dividends, if any.

**rollover**   Reinvestment of funds into a similar investment. With retirement plans, a rollover occurs when assets from one type of qualified plan are moved to another.

**round lot**    The accepted standard number of shares (100) used to trade stocks. It is also the number of shares to which prevailing broker commission rates apply.

**sales charge**    The amount charged in connection with public distribution of fund shares. It is added to the net asset value per share in computing the offering price and is paid to the dealer and underwriter.

**Securities and Exchange Commission (SEC)**    An independent agency of the U.S. government that administers the various federal securities laws for the protection of the shareholder.

**SEP (simplified employee pension)**    A qualified employee retirement plan in which the employer makes contributions to the employees' IRAs.

**series funds**    A broad range of funds offered by a fund family. Each fund has its own investment philosophy whereby it invests in only certain industries or companies.

**short-term investment**    An investment of less than one year. For tax purposes, short-term is now considered less than six months.

**signature guarantee**    A required signature by a fiduciary representative (banker or broker) to verify the identity of the shareholder.

**Social Security integration**    A method of coordinating employer Social Security and retirement plan contributions.

**special purpose fund**    A fund that has certain requirements that must be met by prospective investors before they may invest.

**specialized mutual fund**    A fund that focuses on a particular segment of the market and has a philosophy or stipulation the fund must follow or meet when investing.

**speculative**    Considered to have a high degree of risk.

**split**    A division of a company's shares into a greater or lesser number. Often a split is designed to lower the cost of a share, making it more attractive. A stock split does not affect a shareholder's proportional interest in the company.

**stock dividend**    A dividend paid in securities rather than cash.

**switch**    See exchange privilege.

**tax avoidance**    Legal actions that may be taken to reduce or eliminate tax liabilities.

**tax-deferred**    Income on which a tax is levied only when it is distributed.

**tax-exempt fund (tax-free fund)**    A mutual fund whose portfolio consists of securities (usually municipal bonds) exempt from federal income tax.

**tax-exempt securities**    Usually refers to municipal bonds that are exempt from federal taxes. Some municipal bonds, known as triple exempt bonds, are also exempt from state and local taxes depending on the state laws where the bond was issued and where the buyer of the bond resides.

**tax shelter**    An investment used for deferring taxes.

**TEFRA**    The Tax Equity and Fiscal Responsibility Act of 1982.

**total return**    Dividend plus change in price on an investment.

**Treasury bill (T-bill)**    Short-term debt issued by the U.S. government at a discount from its face value. Maturities are three months, six months, and one year. Minimum order is $10,000 with subsequent multiples of $5,000.

**Treasury bond**  Debt obligation issued by the U.S. government with a maturity ranging from ten to thirty years and with $1,000 as the lowest denomination.

**Treasury note**  Debt obligation issued by the U.S. government with a maturity between one year and ten years. Lowest denomination issued is $1,000.

**trustee**  The institution that maintains administrative control over another's assets: a commercial bank, savings and loan association, mutual savings bank, trust company or stockbroker.

**truth-in-lending law**  A federal law stating lenders must specify the terms and conditions of the loan to the borrower.

**unit investment trust (UIT)**  A type of mutual fund that buys a fixed number of debt obligations and sells them to investors in units. Most common types of obligations are federal agency obligations, municipal bonds, and utility obligations.

**variable annuity**  An insurance annuity contract under which the dollar payments received are not fixed but fluctuate with the market. Most frequently, investors will have a choice of stock, money, or bond funds.

**vesting**  An employee benefit plan participant's rights of ownership to the employer contributions made on his or her behalf, plus earnings on those contributions.

**wire transfer**  Use of a bank to send money to a fund or vice versa over the Federal Reserve System's payment network.

**withdrawal plan**  A mutual fund plan that allows a specified amount of money to be withdrawn at specified intervals.

**yield**  Income earned from investments, usually expressed as a percentage of market price; also referred to as return.

**zero-coupon bond**  A bond sold at a deep discount on which no periodic interest payments are made prior to maturity. Payment of principal at maturity provides an effective yield on the amount for which it was purchased.

# Index